ROSTENKOWSKI

ALSO BY RICHARD E. COHEN

Congressional Leadership
Washington at Work
Changing Course in Washington

Richard E. Cohen

ROSTENKOWSKI

The Pursuit of Power and the End of the Old Politics

IVAN R. DEE

Chicago 1999

THIRD PRINTING

Library of Congress Cataloging-in-Publication Data:
Cohen, Richard E.
    Rostenkowski : the pursuit of power and the end of the old politics / Richard E. Cohen.
        p.   cm.
    Includes bibliographical references and index.
    ISBN 1-56663-254-4 (alk. paper)
    1. Rostenkowski, Dan.   2. Legislators—United States Biography.   3. United States. Congress. House Biography.   4. United States—Politics and government—1945–1989.   5. United States—Politics and government—1989–   I. Title.
E840.R66C65   1999
328.73'092—dc21
[B]   99-25239

To members of the House

—the Good, the Bad and the Forgotten,

but each representative of America

Contents

ROSTENKOWSKI

Introduction

AN ERA ENDS

AS HE EMERGED from the courthouse at the foot of Capitol Hill into the bright sunlight of a mid-June afternoon in 1994, Rep. Dan Rostenkowski stood defiant. "Talk is cheap, and allegations come easy," he proclaimed. "When all is said and done, I will be vindicated." Surrounded by four-hundred-dollar-an-hour lawyers, the Illinois Democrat was reduced to denying that he had engaged in rampant corruption. It was not a pretty picture for a congressional titan. According to a federal indictment, he had "engaged in a pattern of corrupt activity for more than 20 years." He was said to have used his official accounts to pay for personal expenses that ranged from cleaning his Washington apartment to taking photographs at his daughter's wedding. Worse, prosecutors charged he had converted House of Representatives Post Office stamps into cash, which he used to line his pockets. And he allegedly urged a witness to lie to federal prosecutors. The charges "represent a betrayal of the public trust for personal gain," said U.S. Attorney Eric Holder. To an angry public, the indictment fit the worst stereotypes of Chicago politicians.

Privately Rostenkowski found the U.S. attorney's case a mystery. He claimed—as have so many others in recent years—that few citizens are sufficiently pure to withstand the cost of such an inquiry and the pressure imposed by a prosecutor who has targeted a "trophy" suspect. But he firmly disavowed that he had pocketed any cash from the post office or that he had personally benefited from the transactions. Granted, he acknowledged some of the other allegations as valid. He did not deny that he had placed on his payroll family members of longtime pals; they kept

3

the grass clipped at his Wisconsin lake house much as Rostenkowski's four daughters had sometimes performed make-work tasks on the payroll of other Chicago pols. "Did I put a kid on my payroll because he was my buddy's son?" he said later, with a rhetorical shrug. "Did I expect him to do some work? Yes, but not a lot." Likewise, he had directed his staff to make official purchases such as glass sculpture and wood-backed chairs from the House stationery shop; these he gave as gifts to supporters and dignitaries. In Rostenkowski's mind that was both perfectly legitimate and no big deal for a sultan of Congress. Indeed, he was proud that many years earlier he had helped to expand the legions of staff courtiers and official perks for his colleagues. House officials had officially sanctioned such activities for decades. Former Speaker Tip O'Neill had kept a crony on his payroll to make an occasional inspection of his Cape Cod vacation home in Massachusetts. Everybody did it.

If this was graft, Rostenkowski growled in bewilderment, then even the purest members of Congress were guilty. And if such nickel-and-dime practices were now forbidden, then political morality had taken an odd turn from the accepted rules of the Chicago neighborhoods where his father had taught him the family business. He came from a world that operated with a mass of small favors for constituents and with bit players playing their clearly defined roles within an organization, where authority was unquestioned. "In Chicago we have a very unusual association with the people who work for us," he told a television interviewer two days after his court arraignment. "I mean they're our friends as well." His indictment threatened to erase informal political customs that had become an essential lubricant for getting things done.

And so a career, a way of life, and an era came to a close. Rostenkowski's downfall was more than a personal ruin. Democrats who had held the reins in the House of Representatives for forty years, the longest period of single-party control in the nation's history, were about to lose a landslide election. After four decades in which they were rarely challenged in a chamber that has been aptly termed the "forge of democracy"—but which gives virtually unchecked power to a well-oiled majority—Democrats were running out of time, ideas, and public support. In hindsight, Rostenkowski's attorney Dan Webb was more than a bit wistful when he told reporters on the courthouse steps that June afternoon, "I'm confident that the congressman will be exonerated of all wrongdoing and will be returned to his rightful place as the chairman of the House Ways and Means Committee." It would be several years at least until another Democrat would lead that all-powerful committee, which Rostenkowski had chaired for thirteen years. And Rostenkowski soon would be confined to less grandiose surroundings.

The indictment came at a most inauspicious moment for House Democrats. According to the game plan they had written months earlier, June also was to be the month that would culminate their attempt—under Rostenkowski's steady command—to pass a modified version of the sweeping national health-care plan that President Clinton proposed during his first year in office. For Washington policymakers the proposal was a landmark, and the Ways and Means chairman's active support was essential to its passage. If they succeeded, Clinton and his legislative patron would rightly gain a place in history. In the 1930s President Franklin Roosevelt's New Deal had rescued the nation from the depression and charted a more activist role for the federal government with new economic regulations and then-modest Social Security benefits. In the 1960s Lyndon Johnson won enactment of landmark civil rights and Medicare programs, the keystones of his Great Society. Now, three decades later, Clinton had hoped to close the twentieth century with a health-care plan that Democrats considered the final leg of the social-policy trilogy. "Let us agree on this," he told a joint session of Congress on September 22, 1993. "Whatever else we disagree on, before the Congress finishes its work next year, you will pass, and I will sign, legislation to guarantee . . . security to every citizen." As Republicans glumly sat on their hands, exuberant Democrats cheered confidently.

But as the administration's proposal met withering criticism, that speech became the high-water mark of the health-reform crusade. Even with the mindless complications and regulatory controls of Clinton's plan, a few House members clung to the torch by insisting that Rostenkowski could have made it happen. Had he been chairman, "we would have passed a bill in committee that would have reached out to 218 members," said Rep. Mike Andrews of Texas, a Ways and Means Democrat who had sought support for his centrist alternative. Instead, with Rostenkowski stripped of power, the debate moved so far to the left that the proposal approved by Ways and Means "became an embarrassment," Andrews lamented. "Everyone knew that the bill was a dead duck." Other senior Democrats, such as Energy and Commerce Committee chairman John Dingell of Michigan, took what became a shortsighted view: Democrats should pose the choice to the nation as a referendum in the 1994 election rather than make legislative concessions. To House Democrats, it seemed, there was no reason that their control should not last forever. As it turned out, the health-care plan failed on both fronts—legislative and electoral. With its failure, the gavel came down on six decades of an activist and ever-expanding federal government.

Whether Rostenkowski could have rescued the ill-fated bill is doubtful. But the symbolic crashing of a man, a party, and a plan were linked. House Democrats failed even to bring the health-reform bill to the House floor for a vote before the 103rd Congress—and with it their forty-year era—closed with a whimper that October. A month later the disgusted electorate cast its devastating judgment: Republicans scored the largest partisan gain of House seats in nearly a half-century. In came Speaker Newt Gingrich, who had campaigned on a manifesto to overhaul how Congress did its business and what it produced. The picture was not much different in the Senate. There Democrats had at least brought health-reform to the floor for debate that summer; but they too quickly bogged down and never came close to agreement among themselves. The election verdict on the Democrats, including the loss of their majority, was just as devastating for their august senators.

Today voters evince little enthusiasm for Rostenkowski's old-fashioned politics. The disdain for that era stems either from a sense that it was corrupting, that its time had passed, or that its survival stemmed from voter apathy. Yet even the most passionate conservatives abstractly understood that being a Democrat mattered—at least in the 1930s and 1960s, when they produced action—though it might be difficult to describe their optimistic and positive belief in government. Granted personal reputations have worn less favorably, certainly in the case of Rostenkowski. Brusque and burly, this powerful Chicago politician was a caricature of the wheeler-dealer image of Congress and a formidable figure to those who dealt with him. He retained the guttural tones, the broad shoulders, and the bullying drive that evoked the image of a Chicago Bears linebacker. He was a legislator at a time when public officials were eager to extend government's reach. Back in Chicago, however, he was just "Danny." He kept his identification as Ways and Means chairman out of his campaign literature because the locals were more interested in the money he funneled home to build local highways and sewers. No doubt, as he feared, less-informed citizens will recall him chiefly as the politi-

cian who served most of his career in Congress only to reach an ignominious conclusion in federal prison. News coverage of his indictment pre-
dictably played to the jaundiced image of politicians by emphasizing his
disgrace. But the reality was so much more than that for a man who was
among the half-dozen most influential members of Congress during the
second half of the twentieth century. His gruff style and obsession for
control defined a flesh-and-blood character that has all but disappeared
from increasingly bland American politics. His story, part tragedy as it became at the end of his career, helps to tell the story of a major historical
era.

THE RISE AND FALL of Dan Rostenkowski tracks the rise and fall of
Democrats in the House.* It is a story of power, accomplishments, and,
ultimately, failure and humiliation. As an advocate of old-style deal-making who revered strong leadership, he took command as chairman of
Ways and Means when the rules were changing radically from what he
had learned in his early days, both in Chicago and in Washington. For
lawmakers like Rostenkowski who advanced under the House's old traditions, monumental changes during the forty-year Democratic era eventually laid waste to a chamber in which representatives did their job with
little public attention. He arrived in 1959 in a House that retained many
vestiges of a sleepy, part-time place where television cameras were virtually unknown and most of the work was done by a few indomitable old-
timers. By the time Rostenkowski moved into a position of power,
reformers had diluted the House's power centers and eroded camaraderie.
Instead of the "good old days" in which lawmakers spoke on the House
floor to alert a news reporter about a federal action affecting their district,
he reminisced, now they started the day "hating each other" by exchanging partisan volleys for the House's expanded television audience.

In the end, the Democrats' successive rounds of reform served chiefly
to complicate and hinder their exercise of power. They had succeeded by

---

*Although I have sought to relate incidents that give the flavor of the House's entire forty-
year Democratic era, obviously no book can cover every incident of such a complex institution over such a lengthy period. While not ignoring them, I pay less attention to
important conflicts that received little or no attention from Rostenkowski or the Ways and
Means Committee, such as education, foreign policy, and campaign finances. I expect
most readers will be grateful that even within Ways and Means I have not sought to cover
every detail of every fight during Rostenkowski's tenure.

horsetrading; often, especially in conservative suburbs and in the South, their members survived by conveying a different message at home than they did on Capitol Hill. In retrospect, critics charged, Democrats retained their grip on power chiefly by exploiting corrupt powers of incumbency, both within the House and from special-interest campaign contributions. But many other forces were at work, including an age-old distance from the public eye that gave legislators room to operate. And the Democratic party meant something to a citizenry that believed government could serve the public interest. Both factors would vanish with Rostenkowski's indictment and subsequent imprisonment. Ideology, by contrast, would flourish.

Chapter One

THE BUNGALOW BELT
AND THE MACHINE

MOST OF THE WHITE MEN who dominated American politics until the 1970s came from neighborhoods whose features, such as ethnic composition or historical landmarks, meant something, both locally and to a national assembly. For young Dan Rostenkowski, a community of mostly first- and second-generation Polish immigrants shaped his background and values. He was proud of his heritage, which endured at the end of the twentieth century in the Polish-speaking shops and markets along Chicago's Milwaukee Avenue corridor. But he was even more loyal to his party and to the organization built by his father Joe and fellow Democrats of many nationalities. Eventually local tensions caused a momentous setback for his father. As his career began, though, Dan quickly reaped rewards from the family's decision to move beyond its ancestry and join the American melting pot.

Alderman Joe Rostenkowski, from whom Dan inherited politics as the family business, was a city alderman in Chicago and a Democratic ward boss. That clout proved vital in giving his son an advantage in climbing the political ladder. Like Dan in the early years of his own career, Joe tended to the minutiae of constituent needs and became a cog in the intricate network of service and favors at city hall during three decades as a local Democratic boss. "He is not aggressive, but has the wholesome respect of his colleagues in all council matters," the *Chicago Sun-Times* wrote in endorsing his reelection in 1947.[1] Young Dan learned firsthand how one of the last great urban machines used trusty lieutenants in a tightly structured hierarchy to deliver patronage and entrench itself in power. For the remainder of his public life, he staunchly defended that system and lamented the loss of old-fashioned community values and organization.

The Rostenkowskis served a local community that was more deeply conscious of its immigrant ancestry and religion than its political affiliation or influence. The Poles were "one of the most culturally bonded, ingroup peoples to be found anywhere," according to a study of Chicago's diverse ethnic groups. But their "greater sense of wholeness than most ethnic groups" came at the price of "diminished influence in the wider non-Polish community."[2] Most of the first generations of Poles were poor, and their separate language made it difficult for them to blend into the larger urban population. Consequently, despite their status as the largest ethnic group in the Chicago polyglot, they failed to secure their share of power in the city at large.

Polonia, as the Polish-American community termed its new nation, was first settled in the 1850s. But it did not gain significant size until about 1890, when it counted 40,000 local residents among Chicago's 250,000 total population. These Poles grew to 250,000 by 1903 and to more than 400,000 by the end of the 1920s, when U.S. restrictions slowed the gushing immigration to a trickle.[3] They came to America's heartland to escape German chancellor Otto von Bismarck's threats to exterminate the Poles in Prussia, hostile edicts from Russian tsars, and economic misery following the exploitation of their homeland by powerful rulers who hemmed them in from the west and the east. Just as they settled in other Northern cities on the Great Lakes, such as Buffalo, Cleveland, Detroit, and Milwaukee, Poles were drawn to Chicago by the promise of blue-collar jobs in the stockyards or in steel mills and other booming industries. As a transportation mecca, Chicago had an additional economic advantage in the late nineteenth century as the entry point to the expanding West.

But the change was jarring for Polish immigrants. Most of them had worked the soil as serfs in Poland and had little experience with politics or with property rights. According to a 1911 U.S. government study, 81.5 percent had been farmers or farm workers in Poland; in their new country, the majority were unskilled urban laborers.[4] "The only way they could survive in this strange environment was by trying to recreate the Polish village, with its familiar customs and habits, on this side of the Atlantic," wrote Edward R. Kantowicz, a prolific chronicler of Chicago's Polish community.[5]

For most Chicago Poles, the Roman Catholic church was the chief social forum in the New World. And most prominent in the early years was St. Stanislaus Kostka Parish, which was Chicago's first Polish Catholic church and dates its active organization to 1866. By 1869 the St. Stanislaus Society included sixty members and began to charge dues averaging the then-princely sum of five to ten dollars a year. In the next two years it completed the construction of a modest building for its church and school at the corner of Noble and Bradley streets on the city's near northwest side. Noble Street, which later received a trolley track and became a busy thoroughfare, was already the "principal trading center of the Polish community of Chicago."[6] The site selection, three blocks west of the Chicago River, proved fortuitous in 1871, when everything east and north of the river burned down in the Great Chicago Fire.

The church grew from four hundred families in 1874 to about forty thousand parishioners in 1900, the largest membership of any Catholic church in the United States.[7] Its permanent home on Noble Street, completed in 1877, remains a magnificent Basilica-style edifice, with a seating capacity of fifteen hundred in its main sanctuary and twin steeples that rise two hundred feet. The $20,000 cost of the church and the adjacent three-story rectory was an enormous expense for the predominantly working-class parishioners. But Father Joseph Barzynski, who supervised this growth as leader of St. Stans from 1874 to 1899, felt that it was justified given the church's rapid growth.[8]

On a typical Sunday in 1900 more than 20,000 persons attended Roman Catholic Mass by squeezing into either the main sanctuary or the smaller prayer hall in the basement. The services began at 5 a.m., and groups were quickly shuttled in and out so that everyone could participate.[9] School enrollment at St. Stans was as high as 4,500 children at the start of the 1900s, when Joe Rostenkowski was a student. Because of difficulty in raising needed funds, church members delayed in acquiring several important items until they made useful contacts during the 1893 Columbian Exposition in Chicago. The famous designer Tiffany created eight huge lamps that hang over the main sanctuary; the Johnson Organ Company constructed an organ with 49 pipes. Displaying the customary

Polish frugality, the church members made their costly purchases on a cash basis.

Centered on the church, the Stanislowowo neighborhood grew rapidly in size but remained mostly low income. In the early 1900s "the Poles had the worst jobs in the city and got the worst pay," wrote Andrew Greeley, the Roman Catholic scholar and author. "These were the poorest of the poor; they had little else in life besides their religion. In the first two decades of this century, the population density of the ten square blocks around the old [St. Stans] church on Pulaski Park was three times higher than Tokyo's or Calcutta's. The air was foul, the plumbing inadequate or nonexistent, and even mild rain showers filled the basement apartments with raw sewage, frequently up to knee level."[10] For many homes the toilets were outside, under the vaulted sidewalks. Coal was delivered into bins and stored alongside the street. Some residents kept goats in the backyard for milk. But they built grand edifices like St. Stans in the hope that "the steeples of those cathedrals would bring back the memories of those that dominated the towns from which the immigrants had come," Father Greeley wrote. "They strove to recreate the Polish community because there seemed to be no other way to preserve the faith."[11]

In addition to Stanislowowo, by the start of the twentieth century Chicago had four other large Polish communities; eventually they supported more than three dozen Polish churches. The other communities were on the city's south side. Because of geographical barriers posed by the Chicago River and many railroad tracks, plus poor transportation within the city, St. Stans in its neighborhood northwest of downtown remained independent of the other churches. That generated ill will. "Poles in outlying areas sometimes felt that the leaders in Polish Downtown either ignored them or else put on airs in considering the Stanislowowo the intellectual and spiritual heart of Polonia's capital," Kantowicz notes.[12] When he was a youth, Rostenkowski recalls, he and his pals might travel two miles to the city's commercial center to shop, but "no one had friends outside their community." The lack of cohesion among the Poles also helps to explain why—despite the fact that they long remained the largest ethnic group within Chicago's Roman Catholic diocese, with between one-third and one-half of the local church population—they wielded less influence within the larger church than did the more savvy Irish or Italians, among others. That same pattern applied in the city's politics, then and throughout the twentieth century. "Behind the scenes, the Poles are united," said Father Joe Glab, the recent pastor of St. Stans. "But publicly they fight." A Polish newspaper cartoon of 1922 depicted a hod carrier labeled "Irishman" standing on a sleeping giant termed "300,000 Poles in Chicago," while boasting, "Be gorra, he's sleeping, and I'm de Boss."[13]

Dan Rostenkowski's grandparents, all but one of whom were born in Poland, were well suited to serve as community leaders. Because they were among the few Poles financially equipped to move into the middle class when they arrived in Chicago, they quickly rose to a status akin to the gentry from the old country. Family records are incomplete on when they moved to Chicago. But one of Rostenkowski's frequent tales is that of his maternal grandmother, as a young child, watching the Great Fire of 1871 from an earlier steeple at the St. Stanislaus Church. Dan's mother, Priscilla Dombrowski, had three brothers; one of them, Edward, became superintendent of the Chicago State Hospital and was a prominent researcher of osteomyelitis, a bone disease. Three other siblings died during a diphtheria epidemic.

The most important early influence on young Dan was Peter Rostenkowski, his paternal grandfather, who was born in Poland in 1868 and settled as a child in Stevens Point, a timber center in central Wisconsin. His grandson believes that, when he moved to Chicago at about age eighteen, Peter helped to deliver the lumber needed to rebuild the city after the Great Fire. Peter soon entered the home-loan business, which would have marked him as a local power broker. Because most Poles lacked the assets in those days to obtain credit from downtown banks, the community established many of its own credit unions to finance the widespread desire for home ownership. Peter became influential in Polish fraternal organizations. From 1913 to 1918 he was national president of the Polish Roman Catholic Union of America (PRCU), which remains headquartered in Chicago. "Because he was so considerate in giving loans to the people, he was a tremendous political broker in Chicago," said Ed Dykla, who became the PRCU president in 1986 and was a friend of Dan Rostenkowski when both were young men. During World War I the family patriarch also was a national chief of Americans organizing relief assistance for beleaguered Poland. "One of the most honored places in [the church's] annals justly belong to the late Peter Rostenkowski," says a 1942 St. Stans tribute. Peter married the former Katherine Giersh. Their only child, Joe, was born in Chicago on September 15, 1892; he married Priscilla Dombrowski on June 8, 1918.

Their large three-flat residence at 1372 Evergreen Street, at the corner of Noble Street, was only a few yards across the street from the church. At the start of the twentieth century, Peter Rostenkowski conducted his home-loan business on the ground floor of his residence, and Dan's grandmother Dombrowski ran a bakery shop in the same block. Although the Rostenkowskis were not especially active in St. Stanislaus religious activities, they had a lofty social standing among parish members. Their financial and political influence made their relationship with the church "like that of a personal chapel," says an associate of Dan's. Most of the family's major events, from baptisms to funerals, took place there.

If St. Stanislaus Kostka marked the place where the Poles became a cultural force, their political home was the Democratic party. As in most Northern cities, the Republicans' national dominance at the turn of the century gave immigrant groups little opportunity for advancement among the vested classes. So for Poles, like other nationalities, the Democrats became the focal point for all sorts of favor-seekers looking for jobs and other city services and contracts. In Chicago, home of the preeminent big-city machine, the party fashioned an elaborate hierarchy that paralleled and overlapped the governing structure of city hall. In many of the city's fifty wards throughout the twentieth century, the local alderman and the Democratic committeeman often were the same person; if they were not, the party boss might have been the more important source for someone who wanted results from local government. The Irish moved early into most positions of power. But, unlike the party's rule in some other large cities, such as Tammany Hall in New York, Chicago's Democrats in the early twentieth century did not enforce an ironclad internal discipline. Historians observe that "Chicago's Democracy was a loosely knit Balkan treaty organization of Irish fiefdoms, a patchwork quilt of uncoordinated parts fighting fratricidal inside wars for control and boodle."[14]

In that party, Poles were loyalists from the start, long before the New Deal cemented the nation's majority coalition. Even in the late 1800s they viewed the Democrats as the home for average workers, and they were confident that Democrats would accommodate the religion and customs of new immigrants. In the seemingly mysterious operation of urban American politics, many Poles looked to the party for their personal needs. "The political boss seemed vaguely reminiscent of the feudal lord in the old country," Kantowicz wrote. "Like the lord, the boss was a man of importance who lived well and held the keys to government and business. The boss was someone you went to for a job or a favor. Like the best of the old lords, he frequently helped the people out in times of need, bringing a bucket of coal or a basket of food to a cold and starving immigrant family. But unlike the old lord, the American boss asked relatively little in return for his benevolence. . . . The boss asked only for a vote on election day, a small enough price for the immigrant to pay."[15]

Why did the Poles fail to take more power? The standard answer is provincialism. "Polish politicians organized their bloc voting around in-group concerns, constantly tried to perfect the unity and solidarity of the bloc, and neglected the building of coalitions with other political blocs," Kantowicz wrote. "Polish leaders were misled by the fact of their large numbers into thinking that political power would fall to them like a ripe fruit if only they could perfect the solidarity of their group."[16] The reluctance of many Poles to learn English was another factor that impeded their influence, Dan Rostenkowski says. That failure has been most apparent in the Poles' inability to elect one of their own as mayor of Chicago, despite their status as the city's largest ethnic group. Instead, in the byzantine politics, leaders of two much smaller eastern European nationalities moved to the top of the heap at city hall. Bohemian-born Anton Cermak, who was elected mayor in 1931, united the various Democratic segments into a relatively cohesive coalition. He quickly gained a national reputation and a fateful alliance with Franklin Roosevelt: on a visit to Florida in February 1933 with the President-elect, Cermak was murdered during an assassination attempt on FDR. Later, in 1976, after the death of Richard J. Daley, Michael Bilandic, a Croat, was named interim mayor by the Board of Aldermen and subsequently won election to the remaining two years of Daley's term. With those exceptions, the Irish held the mayor's office from the Democrats' 1931 takeover of city hall until the 1983 election of Harold Washington, an African American.

Still, some Poles attained prominence during the early twentieth century. Stanley Kunz, who served as alderman in the Stanislowowo district for nearly three decades starting in 1891, was the first political boss of Polonia, but he suffered an unsavory reputation. He "was a table-thumper, a yeller, a screamer, and a fighter, who always acted as if he owned the 16th Ward," according to Kantowicz. "The Chicago newspapers dubbed him 'Stanley the Slugger' and the 'terrible Pole.' . . . [But] Most Polish-Americans did not read the American press and the Polish papers generally backed Kunz because he used his influence to gain jobs and favors for Poles."[17] In 1920 Kunz became Chicago's first Polish-American to win election to Congress. (John Kleczka of Milwaukee, a Republican who was elected in 1918, was the first Polish-American to win a House seat; Democratic Rep. Gerald Kleczka of Milwaukee, a distant cousin, more than seventy years later became a spear-carrier on Dan Rostenkowski's Ways and Means Committee.) Kunz served for a dozen years with the exception of a few months in 1931 while the House settled the outcome of a contested election. But he left little mark in the Capitol. In a pattern that would later apply to most Poles from Chicago who were elected to Congress, he focused more on local matters, including precinct politics, than "in attending to dull routine in Washington."[18]

Edmund Jarecki was another successful Pole in Chicago politics; he won election in 1922 as county judge, which gave him supervision of the city's election board. A maverick, Jarecki remained a good-government insurgent who battled the Democratic machine, prompting the party's slate-making committee to reject him in 1938. Although he won reelection anyway, Jarecki's independence "undermined Polonia's organized force for further success and recognition."[19]

As for the Rostenkowskis, grandfather Peter was a prominent Democrat as early as 1912 when he was a delegate to that year's Democratic National Convention in Baltimore. He was chiefly responsible for securing a visit by Woodrow Wilson, the presidential nominee, to Stanislowowo soon after the convention, according to a St. Stans archive. As a young man, his son "Joe Rusty" was a natural choice to enter politics. In addition to taking over his father's home-loan and real-estate insurance business, Joe ran a thriving tavern in the front of the family home. The city prohibited taverns within five hundred feet of the church, but the influential operator somehow won a lucrative exception to that rule. Like many of his neighbors, Joe also produced "bathtub gin" in the basement of his home, at least in the years before Prohibition. That was another family tradition. When grandfather Peter hired salesmen to deliver liquor, "my father said that the horses knew the routes better than the drivers, who often were half-stiff," Dan recalls. Joe also gained a federal government job after World War I as a "rectifier," sampling the liquor.

After successfully challenging the Kunz organization for a state legislative seat in 1930, Joe Rostenkowski a year later became part of the Democrats' new city hall coalition when he was elected alderman from his near northwest ward. In a contest that a contemporary newspaper account described as one in which "personal acquaintances and friendships are said to outweigh politics" among the Polish voters, he defeated a Republican, George Rozczynialski, who held the seat for two years.[20]

During his two dozen years as an alderman, Joe Rostenkowski's prowess was based on personal relationships with his constituents plus his loyalty to the Democratic organization. "Anyone who needed help or generous gestures, Joe never refused them when it was needed," said Ed Dykla. "He was beloved by his people." Joe Rostenkowski fully subscribed to onetime House Speaker Tip O'Neill's adage that "All politics is local." According to a 1937 commemorative volume prepared by members of the Polish community, Joe was "responsible for many improvements in his ward, such as clean streets and alleys."[21] He gained a wide following among local youth by converting vacant property into playgrounds for sports and by sponsoring local teams. Some of the teams played in Pulaski Park across Noble Street from the Rostenkowski home, where Joe sometimes would sit on the stoop and watch a game. "When I was a little kid [in the late 1940s and '50s] we grew up with the Rostenkowski name," said Terry Gabinski, who eventually won Joe's seats as both alderman and Democratic ward committeeman. "Joe's office sponsored basketball and baseball teams and local parks. . . . Rosty was a name we all knew as kids."

During the 1930s, when countless people were out of work and uncertain how they could keep their families and homes together, Rostenkowski's 32nd Ward organization provided many other forms of assistance from the home on Evergreen Street, including seasonal gifts and special programs to commemorate important local events during the year. "During the hard depression years, Rosty's ward organization kept busy distributing coal and food baskets and helping to pay gas and electric bills for constituents," Kantowicz wrote. "He attended carefully to the physical appearance of his ward, giving personal attention to garbage pickup and street cleaning."[22] In return, the local Democratic organization deployed a network of fifty to sixty precinct captains whose only demand was loyalty at election time. In what became a practice followed by his son, Joe also helped many local charitable projects. "If you wanted to make money, you had to see Joe," said Dykla, who grew up in the neighborhood. According to several accounts, Alderman Rostenkowski was loyal to friends and faithful to his word. His son often told the story that when immigrants applying for citizenship were asked who was the President of the United States, they answered with the name of Joseph Rostenkowski.

On legislative matters Joe exercised his influence most directly on businesses with which he was most familiar. For many years he chaired the City Council's licensing committee, whose chief responsibility was to set operating fees and permissible business hours for taverns. He and his fellow aldermen no doubt winked at the conflict of interest with his saloon on Evergreen Street. In focusing on local details, he revealed either a modesty or a lack of self-confidence by refusing to pursue opportunities for office that extended beyond his neighborhood. As would become the case with his son, Joe avoided taking risks that might have ended his career but that could have advanced him up the city's chain of command. A steadfast team player for the Democratic organization, "he just never made it to the Inner Room" at city hall, where the most important decisions were made, said the local political scholar Paul Green. In 1942 he turned down the opportunity to take a seat in Congress that went instead to his son's predecessor. In 1945 he won news clippings as a potential candidate for a Cook County Board; in 1946 it was the city treasurer's office; in 1953, again, he was mentioned as a candidate for the county board.[23] But he never showed the combination of personal ambition and outside support needed to move up in the Democratic hierarchy. "Somewhat limited in intelligence and cunning, blunt, straightforward and emotional, he was as strong as a feudal lord in Polish Downtown but was not the man to appeal to respectable America, any more than the other ward bosses of Polonia's capital were," wrote Kantowicz in his book on Chicago's Polish community.[24] He also was a victim of the Democratic slate-makers' customary deference to Irish contenders for citywide positions.

Still, Joe Rostenkowski was not afraid to play hardball in the city's rough-and-tumble politics. "You didn't mess with him," Dykla said. That lesson was truer than life, according to incidents that are chronicled in musty Chicago newspaper files and have survived in family lore. In 1939 two workers for another candidate filed a police complaint that accused Rostenkowski of threatening them when they were posting election signs. As reported by the *Tribune*, Rostenkowski approached one of the workers, "chased him nearly a mile through alleys to his home, and then told his wife he, the alderman, would 'get even.'"[25] A more serious incident a year earlier was never resolved. Shortly after six o'clock one morning, two of Rostenkowski's precinct workers were sitting in a parked car in front of the alderman's house when another car pulled alongside. The passenger stepped out and fired four bullets that killed the two other men; then he and his driver sped away. "I haven't the faintest idea of what happened or why," Joe Rostenkowski claimed at the time. "Both men worked for me but I don't know of any enemies they might have had and I haven't any myself who might have wanted to get them."[26] Newspaper reports later implied that the victims were targets of crime bosses who were punishing them for attempting to bring stolen slot machines into neighborhood bars without the "mob's" permission. Shortly after they were stolen, the machines, "carrying marks identifying them as property of the gambling syndicate operating in the territory, began to appear in saloons in the 32nd ward."[27] Although there were no reports linking Rostenkowski to the mischief, the newspaper report added that the two murder victims had been "using the alderman's name in pushing the [slot] machines."

Joe Rostenkowski was unabashedly devoted, above all, to the party organization. The Polish Democratic regulars were Democrats first and Poles second. The most revealing proof of this attitude was Joe's single setback, which came in 1955 and was a defining moment in the city's ethnic politics. In advance of a three-way Democratic primary, the party had voted to deny endorsement for reelection to two-term mayor Martin Kennelly. Following his 1947 victory on a pledge to clean up local corruption, the bosses eventually grew weary of "his stubborn insistence upon dismantling the patronage machinery on which the Chicago Democrats depended."[28] They complained that Kennelly's public works projects were directed to improving transportation to the suburbs more than to fixing local problems. In a preelection letter to Polish-American Democrats, the regulars wrote, "Look at our transportation, why it's a joke, look at those sewers, look at those basements that are flooded everytime it rains, there is absolutely no excuse."[29] Joining in the Democratic machine's endorsement of Cook County Clerk Richard J. Daley to replace Kennelly were most of its leading Polish-Americans, including Joe Rostenkowski.

What was most significant about the Polish leaders' choice was not their abandonment of the incumbent mayor but their opposition to the third candidate, Benjamin Adamowski. He was a maverick Pole who had sparred frequently with his party's top brass. Under prevailing customs, Joe Rostenkowski's decision to stick with the party rather than back his ethnic brother was hardly surprising. At a preelection meeting of the Polish-American Democratic Organization, Joe advised its members to "ask Adamowski where he was all these years and why he has never helped to support any Polish-American candidates."[30] Rostenkowski was one of six to sign "an open letter to the Poles of Chicago," which cited the Democrats' extensive support of their community. "Supporting any party is a two-way street," they wrote. "For years, our group has been working toward a definite political goal. It has been our constant endeavor to place Americans of Polish descent on the Democratic ticket, as well as in other places of prestige and influence." After listing numerous Poles who had been elected with the party's endorsement, they asked, "Is there any doubt in your mind of the sincerity of the Democratic Party's intentions?"[31] But, given the Polish community's proud insularity, the regulars' plea fell on deaf ears. Even after World War II, Polonia remained a close-knit community in which blood ran deeper than politics. Its population gave Chicago the second-largest Polish community in the world, behind only Warsaw. The cloistered domain of modest homes and old-fashioned urban shopping areas remained more insular than other Chicago ethnic villages. Rostenkowski and the Democratic loyalists could not counter Adamowski's strong support from those voters. Although he finished a distant third in citywide balloting with 15 percent of the vote, Adamowski handily won the four predominantly Polish wards, including Rostenkowski's.

As a "regular Democrat," Joe felt he had no choice other than to back Daley and the organization. "Joe knew exactly what he was doing, but he thought he could survive it," said Terry Gabinski, the protégé of Dan Rostenkowski. "It was a very difficult decision because the neighborhood was so Polish. But an organization can't function as an organization if you pick and choose who to support." Later Mayor Daley would repay his gratitude for Joe's loyalty to the organization. "It was a gutsy thing for a Polish alderman to go against Adamowski," said William Daley, the son and brother of the Mayors Daley and a prominent Democrat in his own right, who served as secretary of commerce under President Clinton. "It's hard to understand now. But that was the way people succeeded then, by staying together in politics. There was strength in numbers. . . . Joe Rostenkowski made the ultimate sacrifice in some ways. There was a lot of loyalty by my dad to Danny because of Joe's support for my father."

That decision to support Daley had devastating consequences for the alderman. Former state representative Bernard Prusinski, who ran

Adamowski's campaign in the 32nd Ward, had challenged Rostenkowski's bid for a seventh term as alderman in another Democratic
contest held the same day—February 22, 1955. A lifelong engineer for the
city and the Cook County highway department, Bernard Prusinski did not
style himself as a politician, said his son Joseph. True enough, after two
terms, Prusinski's legislative career ended abruptly in 1954 when Joe
Rostenkowski engineered his reelection defeat as part of a maneuver intended to move his son to the state Senate. "The organization wanted
someone else," Joseph Prusinski recalled. A year later, Prusinski unexpectedly exacted his revenge in the Democratic primary for the alderman's seat. In the initial balloting in February, Joe Rostenkowski led the
vote count, 6,380 to 4,796.[32] But the failure of either candidate to receive
a majority of the vote in the five-candidate contest forced a runoff on
April 5, the date on which Daley comfortably won the general election for
mayor. In abandoning its earlier support for the incumbent and endorsing
Prusinski, the *Sun-Times* editorialized that the challenger had "consistently espoused the kind of progressive measures that Chicago must have
to combat crime and corruption" and that he was a "refreshing contrast to
the incumbent, Ald. Joseph P. Rostenkowski, an undeviating member of
the plunderbund which now controls the council." Prusinski also benefited from the support of Robert Merriam, the Republican nominee for
mayor.

When the votes were counted, Joe Rostenkowski was stripped of the
seat he had held for twenty-four years—9,709 to 7,830. "I represented my
people for a long time," he told a reporter the next day. "And they were
satisfied. But when Adamowski came along, they thought I should drop
the organization cold and support him."[33] Ever the loyalist, Rostenkowski
said he had an obligation to "a lot of men" who had been stalwarts in his
organization. "I couldn't just say, 'Boys, you're on your own.' I owed it to
them as a leader to stick by them and I did." In a scenario reminiscent of
the tumult that doomed his son four decades later, Joe Rostenkowski also
suffered because his gruff style offended many voters; even though he
had done much to help them, they wanted a fresh face. The outcome
showed the limits of machine politics, even in 1955.

Still, the battle was not over. In Chicago's tangled politics, Joe Rostenkowski remained boss of the 32nd Democratic Ward organization despite losing the aldermanic seat. And he began immediately to plot
revenge. The showdown came in April 1956 when Prusinski opposed

Rostenkowski in another election, this time for the party job of ward committeeman. To "regular" Chicago Democrats there was no mistaking the importance of this battle within the Polish community. "While this primary may not be very important to some," Rep. Lillian Piotrowski said at a preelection organization meeting, "every worker in the 32nd Ward was told to go into every home and that for us Poles every election is important."[34] The contest was bitter, with charges and countercharges of intimidation and vandalism of campaign offices. "Beer bottles were hurled through two windows of Prusinski's office," the *Tribune* reported. Rostenkowski responded that "tires and seats of four automobiles bearing his campaign stickers were slashed."[35] This time Joe Rostenkowski won by 826 votes. Prusinski soon left the Democratic party and supported Adamowski that November in his successful campaign as a Republican for Cook County state's attorney (in that office Adamowski became a Daley nemesis). "I find that I cannot sacrifice my principles of government in favor of blind party devotion," Prusinski told a reporter. "I am not alone in recognizing the gross injustices because of which several high-minded Democrats have left the party."[36] In 1959 the tables turned again. By a nearly two-to-one margin, Robert Sulski stomped Prusinski—who ran that year as a Republican—and regained the aldermanic seat for the Rostenkowski organization. With his political career over, Prusinski won Daley's blessing to return to his job as a highway engineer, where he remained until his retirement in the early 1970s.

Joe Rostenkowski's city hall friends, meanwhile, did not forget him. In 1958, at age sixty-four, he was placed on the city payroll as superintendent of sewer repairs, with a monthly salary of the then-ample sum of $763 per month. When Republican Alderman Elnar Johnson charged two weeks before the election that year that Rostenkowski was doing no work in his patronage slot, the plea fell mainly on deaf ears. "He's superintendent of all" the thirty-four bricklayer crews repairing the sewers, responded Thomas Garry, deputy commissioner in charge of the sewer department. "He checks the foremen and he checks the gangs. We'll prove it by his requests."[37] But, according to the news report, Garry submitted no written report in response to Alderman Johnson's charges.

FOR YOUNG DAN ROSTENKOWSKI, who was born January 2, 1928, politics quickly became a natural calling. One of his earliest photographs shows the boy, roughly eight years old, at his father's headquarters, packing clothes for the poor during the depression. Joe had more ambitious plans for the young lad. But the busy father, who wanted to give his son the best opportunities, lacked the time and ability to teach him worldly skills. After Dan attended St. Stans school for eight years, Joe sent his son to St. John's Military Academy, a preparatory school in the Milwaukee suburb of Delafield. In those four years, during the heart of World War II, the rebellious neighborhood kid became disciplined and more refined. In a 1964 interview he said the education was "one of the greatest things my father ever did for me." He was no longer merely "the alderman's son"; going away to school "taught me responsibility and how to make my way on my own."[38] He played second base on the baseball team. He was 6 feet, 2 inches and 180 pounds of muscle. "His grades were average but his status was superstar," according to a profile. "In his senior year, he was voted best athlete, most popular cadet, and runner-up as most conceited."[39]

On one pledge to his father, young Dan changed his mind. When he entered St. John's in 1942 his father urged him to pursue a military education. "He said the war would go on a long time, so why shouldn't I be a lieutenant?" Rostenkowski recounted. But with the war over when he graduated in the spring of 1946, Rostenkowski, like most young men of that period, wanted to complete his military service quickly. He joined the army. "It was for eighteen months and I wanted to get it over," he said. His 32nd Infantry unit was shipped to Korea near the 38th parallel, which soon became the dividing line between North and South Korea. During the fifteen months he was based overseas in 1947–1948, his assignment was to hire local Koreans to staff the officers' quarters. With the Korean War more than two years away, he had plenty of time to practice baseball. When he returned to the United States, professional teams expressed interest in him. But he turned them down. His mother, who died of cancer in 1949, had hoped he would become a doctor. Instead he followed his father in the family business. He enrolled part-time at Loyola College in downtown Chicago, and gained a patronage slot as an investigator reviewing personal injury cases for the city corporation counsel's office.

In 1952, while still attending night school, the twenty-four-year-old Rostenkowski entered a race to fill a vacant seat in the state House of Representatives. In those days each state Senate district in Illinois also had three House seats. With two incumbents, both Democrats, seeking reelection to the House from the near northwest district, a contest would have been likely if an outsider had applied for the third seat. But that wasn't the case when the candidate was the local boss's son. "My dad encouraged me to run," said Rostenkowski. "Every bank president wants his son to be a teller and then to become the president of the bank." The party organization endorsed the newcomer plus the two holdovers; the primary outcome was tantamount to election in November. With the help of his father's name recognition, young Dan was elected with 14,271 votes, a few hundred more than each of the incumbents. Established in office, Rostenkowski worked closely with his father in the local Democratic apparatus. "Public service then was constituent service," he said. "I would go to the precinct captains to see what were the problems. . . . I would see that the lights were fixed, the street curbs were fixed, and so on. I felt I was the lawyer for the community." He never completed his degree requirements at Loyola.

After two years in the House, he won election to the more exclusive state Senate in 1954. In endorsing Rostenkowski for the Senate seat, the Democratic county committee unseated the incumbent, Stanley Mondala. Rostenkowski was getting a fast start on a career track that had been pursued by many young Chicago pols, not the least of whom was Richard J. Daley. "Daley believed in a very important principle: 'As West Point is to the United States Army officer corps, so Springfield and the legislature are to the city of Chicago,' " according to a study of Illinois politics. "The perception of the state legislature as training ground went hand in hand with another idea, that Chicago (not Springfield or Washington) constituted the most desirable locus of political life."[40]

As Dan Rostenkowski learned at an early age and readily accepted, serving as one of Daley's young lieutenants in the 1950s required obedience to certain principles. But Rostenkowski's loyalty, once reciprocated, offered abundant opportunities. After Daley took office he moved quickly to consolidate forces in city hall and strengthened his rule of the Cook County Democratic organization, which he already chaired. "Chicago's mayor could use the power of the party chairmanship to discipline unwieldy Democrats," wrote a Daley biographer. "And the party leader's control of the city council majority allowed for swifter and easier decision making."[41] Under the Daley reign, his proposals usually received speedy approval, and the Council rarely functioned as a deliberative body. Despite some cutbacks in patronage jobs, local government still operated with a mass of small favors for constituents and with bit players filling their clearly defined roles in an organization where authority was unquestioned.

During his six years in the legislature, Rostenkowski was a dutiful backbencher and a reliable soldier who watched and learned how things worked. "In those days you got recognition by your presence, not your voice," he said. He voted with other Chicago Democrats for the most part, and did his best to bring home a little bacon. Some of the bills on which he played an active role reflected the public's focus at the time, including polio vaccinations for schoolchildren. Another of his favorite legislative causes was a package of benefits for Korean War veterans, but voters defeated the $75 million proposal in a November 1958 statewide referendum. In the Senate he gained the stature—and displayed sufficient loyalty—to earn a seat on the Budget Committee, which handled most spending issues. Although the usual conflicts were never far away, he also gained useful lessons about crossing partisan lines. Legislative coalitions and deal-making often were based less on party affiliation than on regional interests. "We didn't have as many Republican-Democratic divisions as those between counties," Rostenkowski said. In the battle for funds and other forms of influence, Chicago and other parts of Cook County usually opposed the rest of the state, much of which remained rural at the time. "Illinois is a state of unusual diversity," according to a 1962 study. "The regional differences and animosities that grow out of such diversity contribute importantly to the politics of the state."[42] In the 1950s, and decades later, the Democratic mayor of the state's largest city often struggled with the Republican governor to divide influence and run the state. In those battles the mayor typically relied on his troops for advice and support; for most of them, loyalty was never in doubt.

As a state lawmaker, Rostenkowski worked on the planning and financing of a major federal highway from downtown to the new O'Hare airport in northwest Chicago, which became a centerpiece of the city's economic growth during the Daley years. (Rostenkowski had additional reasons to encourage the use of automobiles. After he entered the legislature, he also became president of Chicago's Automobile Salesmen Association so that he could earn additional income to support his young family. That job, which he held for about two years, later led to some incorrect references to Rostenkowski as a former used-car salesman.) The original design for the roadway to O'Hare included a direct route that would have cut through both St. Stanislaus Church and Rostenkowski's home. During the initial planning, federal officials enticed property own-ers to sell their homes with the standard offer of payment to relocate to a new site in the suburbs. Most church members heatedly objected to relo-cating their grand edifice. Rostenkowski faced a difficult dilemma. "Some people wanted to take the church down," he said. "It might have been a good idea, given that we now have fewer parishioners and smaller collections." What emerged was a solution that is now part of the daily routine for hundreds of thousands of persons who travel on what has be-come ten lanes on the highway renamed as the Kennedy Expressway as it twists around the church—the sharpest curve along the entire route. The design left the rectory at St. Stans's far eastern end virtually on top of the highway, separated only by a tall fence; conveniently, planners placed an exit at Division Street, just two blocks to the south.

Ironically, a church member who played an important role in creating the compromise was Bernard Prusinski, the state representative and civil engineer. According to his obituary, "he was credited with saving" St. Stans from destruction by designing the plan that rescued most of the church by moving the busy Chicago, North Western Railway lines and what were then large coal fields several dozen feet to the east to make way for the expressway.[43] By sparing the church's demolition and moving the highway into more open territory, the compromise also saved the fed-eral government $3 million, according to Father Joe Glab. Still, unavoid-ably, "more than five hundred families in the church were uprooted" by the federal and state actions, he said, and much of what remained of the old Polish community was destroyed.

In Springfield, as in most state capitals in those days, much of the leg-islative business was transacted in restaurants and hotel rooms where law-makers met with lobbyists at night. It was often not a pretty picture. Chicago journalist Mike Royko colorfully described Springfield in the late 1930s and early 1940s when Richard J. Daley served in the legisla-ture: "Money was there for those who wanted it, and many did. Lobbyists expected to pay for votes. Their generosity was matched by the lobbyists' greed. . . . Every night was like New Year's Eve, the hotel bars echoing with laughter and song, the chomping of steaks, the happy giggles of the young typists, and the sound of the cash registers ringing up the lobbyists' money. There was little effort at pretense. Everybody knew the next man's appetites and his price."[44] Corruption comes in many different forms, of course. But Daley kept close tabs on his loyalists and rising stars, and he made clear that he did not wish to be embarrassed by them. Ed Derwinski, a Republican who served two years in Springfield with Rostenkowski before they were both elected as freshmen to Congress in 1958, recalled that Rostenkowski was "loyal" and "knew his place" in the legislature.

As much as anything, Springfield was a social experience for Rostenkowski, Derwinski added. "He was not considered a thinker. . . . He had not completely sown his wild oats." In the tradition of that time and later, suspicions of extracurricular social life did not surface publicly, as other political figures and reporters treated with discretion whatever dealings he might have had. As was the case throughout Rostenkowski's career, his wife LaVerne—whom he married May 12, 1951—remained at their home in Chicago and rarely appeared with her husband at public events. They both strived to permit her to lead a separate life, which included work in the insurance business. Although she could be tough on him in private, Rostenkowski was very "old school" with her, said those familiar with the relationship: in compartmentalizing his life, he protected her from the painful aspects of his professional life.

Later, Rostenkowski was tainted by problems in Springfield that generated serious allegations of wrongdoing. In a 1964 article that received national attention, Illinois state Sen. Paul Simon—who later would serve ten years in the U.S. House and twelve years in the Senate—called the legislature, where he was still serving, "polluted almost beyond belief." At least one-third of its members accepted payoffs, he wrote. "A few legislators go so far as to introduce some bills that are deliberately designed to shake down groups which oppose them and which will pay to have them withdrawn. . . . Nor are there any real safeguards against conflicts between the public's and the legislators' private interests."[45] Simon, a lifelong reformer whom Rostenkowski viewed with barely concealed disdain throughout their careers, selected for special criticism a group of "influential legislators" who held stock in Illinois racetracks, which typically received favored treatment from state officials. For tidy investments at highly favorable terms, these legislators often made sizable profits. In exchange, Simon wrote, the state's racing interests enjoyed a "privileged position" in the state House.[46]

Years later it became clear that Rostenkowski was among this favored group of lawmakers, at least peripherally. In 1971 Chicago reporters uncovered his ownership of 2,500 shares in the Egyptian Trotting Association, which operated harness racing at Washington Park in Chicago's southern suburbs. After initially claiming that he had sold the stock perhaps a decade earlier, Rostenkowski soon conceded that he still owned it. He had purchased it in 1957 for $500 and had received a huge return in dividends. The news reports set off alarms at city hall. "Mayor Daley was angered and disappointed to learn that Rostenkowski secretly had bought $500 worth of racing stock at 'insider' bargain prices in 1957 and had made about $40,000 in dividends on the stock since that time," wrote Charles Nicodemus, the *Chicago Daily News* political editor. "More important, Daley was infuriated that his political protégé was caught lying to the press about the stock deal."[47] Another newspaper reported that Daley "gave a long-distance telephone tongue lashing" to Rostenkowski over the incident.[48] Although no charges were filed against him, the timing was particularly bad for local Democrats because the allegations were tied to a more sweeping scandal that former Democratic Gov. Otto Kerner had failed to disclose his own racetrack stock transactions. Kerner, who had become a federal judge in 1968 after seven years as governor, was tried and convicted in February 1973 on charges that he had granted favors to racing interests.

Reviewing the racetrack investment years later, Rostenkowski said he had no regrets. But, he added, the newspapers had not told the entire story. "John Stelle, an ex-lieutenant governor, was opening a track," he recounted. "There was an offering and we [legislators] bought stock. I bought $2,500 worth. It was a bust. Then they wanted more and I gave another $2,500. That didn't do any good either." (As a legislator, his annual salary was $5,000.) Years later, when Rostenkowski was in Congress, a new racetrack operator gained ownership of Washington Park. "He asked me for another $2,000," Rostenkowski said. "I went to my father for some money. He said, 'Go to hell.' So I borrowed $2,000 on my car and they started to make some money. I made seven or eight thousand dollars on it. People told me I should get rid of it. But I got stubborn." He retained the stock in Washington Park, which became valueless in 1978 when the track was destroyed by fire.

For Rostenkowski, the incident revealed his weakness for making a quick buck, even in questionable projects where he might be over his head financially. He "learned a system of politics where he could get away with abuses," said Tom Gradel. As a campaign aide to former alderman Dick Simpson, who challenged Rostenkowski in 1992 and 1994 Democratic primaries, Gradel documented these shady practices with bulging files of records and news clips. Gradel blames major news organizations for not doing more to spotlight these problems and to crusade for change.

ROSTENKOWSKI'S ELECTION to Congress came the old-fashioned way, as a quiet reward rather than an expensive, noisy public showdown. Thomas Gordon, his predecessor and a loyal ally to Joe Rostenkowski's machine, had served since 1942. Like most Chicago Democrats who served in the House, he gained little national attention—even in 1957 when he became chairman of the House Foreign Affairs Committee. "He was a very quiet, proper, dignified man," said Ed Derwinski. "He was very unlike most of the machine pols of those days." But at age sixty-five Gordon decided in 1958 to retire. (Perhaps he had a premonition. On January 22, 1959, only days after Rostenkowski was sworn in, Gordon died while shoveling snow outside his home in Chicago.)

With the seat unexpectedly vacant, Dan Rostenkowski had no serious competition. His father made sure that the path was greased. Gordon made a futile attempt to secure the party's endorsement for his son Thomas Jr., a lawyer for the Metropolitan Sanitary District, and contended that he was better qualified than young Rostenkowski, who was then on the city payroll as a part-time assistant director of public information for the Park District. Mayor Daley, grateful for Joe's support in the 1955 mayor's race, backed the Rostenkowskis. "Loyalty was the heart of my dad's support for Danny," said Bill Daley. "This was a nice guy and he was Joe's kid. . . . And there was a big chit." As the Democratic organization's nominee, he won 74 percent of the vote to defeat William Schmidt, a political unknown. More than three decades would pass before Rostenkowski would have to work to win an election.

Like his father, Dan was a Democrat first and a Pole second. This became especially clear when he was elected to Congress with two other Poles from Chicago: Derwinski, a Republican, and Roman Pucinski, a Democrat. "Danny stayed away from ethnic politics," Derwinski recalled. "Pooch [as his friends called Pucinski] was more of a professional Pole," participating in Polish-American organizations and speaking the language. "Danny was proud to be an American of Polish descent," said Ed Dykla, the president of the Polish Roman Catholic Union. "But he was not excessive in promoting the Polish. . . . Some in the community thought he was not active enough as a Pole." With occasional exceptions such as White House events that spotlighted Polish-Americans or historical events for Poland, he had disdain for Polish-American groups and made a point "not to hang out with them," according to Democrats who watched Rostenkowski closely in Washington. By contrast, Pucinski—whose mother Lydia owned a Polish radio station in Chicago—"catered to the Polish community" because, Dykla said, "he had no choice."

In addition to their other differences, Roman Pucinski was a more flamboyant personality than Rostenkowski. Having been a *Sun-Times* reporter for nearly two decades, "he was very effective in getting press coverage" on Capitol Hill, Derwinski said. "He was eager, ambitious, and he loved to pontificate. He hit Washington like a whirlwind and was popping off on every subject." In his first term Pucinski pushed proposals to provide federal funds for construction of private schools, subsidize housing for the elderly, and curtail the Labor Department's monitoring of the Teamsters union; in each case he was defeated. Rostenkowski kept his head down and focused on constituent service and the local Democratic organization. Eventually Rostenkowski's approach served him better. When population losses on Chicago's northwest side took away a congressional seat during the 1972 redistricting, Pucinski became the odd man out when political insiders drew the new maps. (He later served more than a decade as an alderman. In a sign of the city's shifting politics, Pucinski's daughter Aurelia—a longtime local officeholder—switched to the Republican party in 1998 and lost a spirited campaign for Cook County Board chairman against the incumbent, an African American.)

Derwinski's focus on foreign policy issues highlighted other shifts in the Polish-American community. After World War II many Poles abandoned their strong identification as Democrats because they were outraged that Presidents Roosevelt and Truman had agreed to divide Europe in a way that placed Poland under the iron fist of Joseph Stalin's Soviet Union. "I came back from World War II in the Pacific to find that my dad had become anti-Roosevelt because of the perceived sellout of Poland at Yalta," Derwinski said. The postwar settlement in the Chicago area of more than 100,000 displaced persons from Poland accentuated this sentiment. As earlier generations of Poles moved to the suburbs, the new emigrés became more influential among the city's Poles. "Many of them were anti-Communist and they wanted to piss on Franklin Roosevelt for turning over so much of Europe to Stalin," said Mitchell Kobelinski, who became a top Republican among Chicago's Poles. For the most part, Rostenkowski sought to steer clear of this conflict.

Notwithstanding his election to Congress, Dan Rostenkowski held to his concern with local interests as he took control of the 32nd Ward organization. Even while his father retained the title of boss, the youngster hired Wally Nega, a graduate of DePaul and a decorated World War II veteran, to serve as the new lieutenant. "They were a team," said Terry Gabinski. "They rebuilt the organization. . . . Wally Nega was everything. He could pass, punt and kick. He was totally loyal and dedicated." With Nega performing the grunt work of running the organization on a daily basis, Dan Rostenkowski served as the "outside" man to city hall and beyond. Rostenkowski typically joined Nega at the 32nd Ward office on Monday nights, when two or three dozen constituents showed up for private meetings to present problems or request favors.

Rostenkowski and his aides called it "one-stop shopping." A constituent on the northwest side visiting his headquarters at 2148 North Damen Avenue could go to one desk to receive assistance for a federal problem, to another desk for help on a local matter, or to a third desk for a political deal. The business ran the gamut from federal legislation to local parking violations. Indeed, the *Chicago Daily News* reported in 1963 that Rostenkowski's organization "spends $1,000 to $1,400 a year for traffic tickets brought in by residents of the area." Although Rostenkowski acknowledged that his ward committee paid the fines for parking violations and sometimes sought to lower the penalties, he cautioned, "We don't touch speeding cases." Rostenkowski told the reporter that he worried about the ramifications of the news story. "If word gets out that we are paying some persons' fines, everyone is going to get after us."[49] Changing customs soon forced Rostenkowski to abandon the practice. Later, in the 1970s, Nega created his own organization after he won a state Senate seat; by that time Gabinski—a former high school chemistry teacher—had become alderman and a more prominent figure on the Rostenkowski team. After redistricting changes forced Nega from the legislature in 1982 and he took a state government job, he resumed working for Rostenkowski and his local machine until he died of heart failure in 1986.

Even with the organization's decline, serving as a local boss remained serious business in Chicago. Facilitating the government's role in their communities was more important to these politicians than was the sweep of events elsewhere in the city, let alone across the nation or the world. As one of fifty Democratic ward committeemen, Rostenkowski maintained a busy schedule on his party's board of directors. Even with his enhanced influence in Washington, tending to neighborhood business remained his foremost assignment, at least to many people in Chicago. He also took special interest in the party's selection of campaign slates. "He lunched and dined with corporate giants in Chicago," said David Axelrod, a leading Democratic consultant in that city. "But politically he was a powerful ward committeeman."

Within his family, Dan's election to the House gave him the opportunity to secure for his father a final appointment—and a choice plum it was. Soon after he took office in 1961, President Kennedy selected Joe Rostenkowski as collector of customs for the Port of Chicago, with an $18,000 annual salary; as congressman, Dan was then drawing a $22,500 salary. The appointment had some amusing twists. Federal civil service laws required that Joe step down from his political post, an unusual action in an organization where most members were carried out in an election box or a funeral box—usually the latter. "My dad was a stubborn man, and he didn't want to give up anything," his son said. "When I told him that he'd have to give up as ward committeeman, he was not happy. He said I was scheming with the guys in Massachusetts." The day he succeeded his father as Democratic ward committeeman was, Rostenkowski said, "the saddest day" for his father. Joe also resented the Treasury Department's extensive inquiry into his personal finances. As federal agents combed Joe's financial records and discovered unreported income for which they required him to pay several thousand dollars in back taxes, his son later said, "My dad called to say that they want me to pay for this job. He said, 'To hell with the job' and 'You criticize us for taking money under the table.' He was livid. I was hysterical."

For the next eight years Joe mostly performed his job and stayed out of the news. But an incident in the middle of his tenure revealed the experience and wisdom of the "organization" man. In March 1965 President Johnson announced that he was abolishing fifty-three customs jobs across the nation that were not filled by civil service procedures; included was Rostenkowski's. Ever the loyalist, Joe said publicly that he would go quietly: "I'm a Democrat and I abide by the wishes of the President," he told a reporter. "I like the job and would like to stay on. But politics is a funny thing. To be a good fellow, a good organization man, you have to abide by the wishes of the organization."[50] As it turned out, his son came to Joe's rescue. "I went to the White House and Lyndon Johnson agreed that those in the job could stay until their retirement," Rostenkowski said decades later. Joe retained his position until 1969, when Johnson left office. He died a year later, at age seventy-seven.

When he entered the House, Rostenkowski was in an unusual position for a Chicago Democrat. He was barely thirty-one years old, about half the age of many local pols who gained a House seat as a retirement gift. He was eager to play the Washington game. And, unlike Pucinski, he had a safe seat. Few of the locals were very interested in the details of what he did there. The major exception was Daley, to whom Rostenkowski reported regularly on the latest news from Washington, especially party politics. Typically they met in the mayor's office on Friday morning, often after Rostenkowski had driven much of the night from Washington with an aide or other House colleagues from Illinois. When the mayor was in Washington, Rostenkowski served as his loyal confidant and liaison. "When dad flew to Washington, Danny was always there," Bill Daley said. "He did everything. From the logistics to telling him who was who, Danny was at his side all the time. From the beginning of his service in the House, he was viewed as the head of the delegation." Soon enough, however, he would exercise his growing influence on behalf of committee chairmen, House speakers, and presidents.

Chapter Two

DEMOCRATS AND A GOVERNMENT ON THE MOVE

ONCE THEY ARE ELECTED, members of Congress move in myriad directions. The classic distinction is between the "workhorses" who get their jobs done without much grandstanding and the "showhorses" who place a higher priority on gaining headlines than results. But there are other options. In a chamber where the rules give virtually unlimited control to any group of 218 among the 435 members, those in the majority party generally wield far more influence than do their minority counterparts. Likewise, even following a decline in the power of seniority, veteran lawmakers who know the ropes or chair a subcommittee have obvious legislative advantages over novices. Another variable results from committee assignments: some members are content to toil on largely parochial issues such as agricultural or urban concerns; others seek the national stage on which causes such as taxes or foreign policy often play. And still others focus mostly on constituent business, content to be viewed on Capitol Hill as members of the "Anonymous Caucus." Still, each member casts one vote when the bells ring for a House roll call.

Dan Rostenkowski was content as a workhorse from day one. He was a product of a disciplined big-city organization, voted the party line, and lacked the training or inclination for self-promotion. But his advancement in the House was not a foregone conclusion; there were choices to be made. He had to determine his friends, his legislative interests, and his career path to power. As a member of the House's "Tuesday-to-Thursday club," he also needed to connect his work in Washington to his life in Chicago, where he returned each weekend. Without much reflection, he made those decisions early; they would have a great impact on his ultimate clout. He pursued Joe Rostenkowski's course of proving himself worthy to the dominant members at the top of the ladder. In a Capitol of growing influence and reach, he quietly sought to insert himself into the center of the action—on the big issues and in the struggles for power. And he quickly struck friendships with the power brokers.

When he arrived in Washington, the thirty-one-year-old "kid" put himself in the hands of the crusty eighty-year-old "Sheriff Tom" O'Brien, the chief of Chicago's Democratic delegation and a former Cook County sheriff. O'Brien was a loyalist who usually left the legislative details to others; he had neither the skill nor the inclination to deal with policy minutiae. His influence stemmed chiefly from his ability to deliver the Chicago-area Democrats to party leaders on most House votes. In return he showered benefits on the most loyal members of his team. Since young Rostenkowski was elected with Mayor Daley's blessing, O'Brien was ready to call in a favor from other senior Democrats.

When the Washington neophyte walked into the office of O'Brien, who had served twenty-two years in Congress and whose career had begun in Springfield more than a half-century earlier, Rostenkowski found him wearing a white straw hat, sitting with his long, skinny legs propped up on his desk. "Blind Tom" (so named because "he couldn't see much evil" when he was county sheriff, Rostenkowski said with more than a trace of amusement) told his visitor that he assumed Rostenkowski would want to follow his predecessor's footsteps to the Foreign Affairs Committee, where Thomas Gordon had been chairman. It was a throwaway comment. Given the new member's lack of interest or experience in world affairs, both knew that was unlikely. "I said no," Rostenkowski remembers. "I'll go on any committee you want me to go on." O'Brien then told Rostenkowski he could join the Interstate and Foreign Commerce Committee, an influential panel which legendary Speaker Sam Rayburn had once chaired. The deal had been cut elsewhere, and the grateful Rostenkowski quickly accepted his spoils. "I didn't choose Commerce," he explains. "Tom O'Brien was a close personal friend of Sam Rayburn."

Sheriff O'Brien was selective in doling out favors: the two other first-term Democrats from Chicago were assigned to less influential committees.

Rostenkowski also courted Eugene Keogh, fifty-one, a fastidious dresser and savvy Brooklyn lawyer who was the key power broker in the New York City delegation. Like many members at the time, he retained a law practice back home, which benefited financially from his work in Congress. He also controlled the reins in Washington for New York City's Democratic machine, which was still referred to as Tammany Hall. First elected in 1936, Keogh—like O'Brien—was a senior member of the Ways and Means Committee. He gained his legislative mark as the father of a major pension benefit to which he gave his name; not coincidentally, it especially benefited self-employed workers such as himself. Rostenkowski wasn't yet ready to serve on Ways and Means, but he found a way to hang out with those who did and to learn how power was exercised in the Capitol. Keogh typically held court with other big-city Democrats at fancy Washington restaurants during the two or three nights a week they spent in the Capitol. Rostenkowski was invited because the others saw him as a "comer"; and he was willing to pay homage to the elders. During the "bonding" sessions, large amounts of food and beverages accompanied devious plots and improbable tales. James Healey, Jr., who was Rostenkowski's top political aide on Capitol Hill during the 1970s and later became a high-powered lobbyist, often attended those dinners starting in the early 1960s, when he was a Georgetown University undergraduate and his father, James Healey, was a New York City congressman. "I learned more about this business [of politics] at those dinners than I did in the classroom," said the junior Healey. "But you needed a thick skin. In a jovial way, they were very insulting." Chuck Daly, a White House aide who was a liaison to the House during the Kennedy years, had similar memories. On one occasion, Daly recalled, Keogh asked an influential Chicago alderman what he did. The visiting pol boasted "a congressman carries my bags," Daly said. "That set Keogh on his heels."

The dinners were an important part of Rostenkowski's education. These other leaders "controlled a lot of votes," said Rep. Jake Pickle, a Texas Democrat who was close to Lyndon Johnson. "Danny learned a lot of power politics from them." In one such tale from the "Tuesday night club," Rostenkowski recalls that one evening in 1965 the usual big-city Democrats were seated around a table at Paul Young's, a popular meat-

and-potatoes restaurant four blocks north of the White House on Connecticut Avenue. After several drinks and dinner, the waiter brought a telephone to the table for Keogh. As he respectfully responded, "Yes, sir. . . . Yes, sir" to the caller, the others at the table boisterously poked fun at him. But when Keogh finished, he passed the phone to Rostenkowski, who quickly began a "Yes, sir" retort of his own. As it turned out, Lyndon Johnson had located the lawmakers and was trying to persuade them to sign a discharge petition to circumvent a committee that had stymied legislation to grant limited home rule to District of Columbia residents. LBJ's lobbying proved successful at the dinner table and in the House. (As Rostenkowski later lamented, it was the only time he succumbed to pressure to circumvent the House's regular order and sign a discharge petition.) Years later Rostenkowski would invite junior members to similar dinners to badger them and to pass on his often exaggerated stories. As he had learned from his mentors, he used these get-togethers to encourage independent and often fractious colleagues to become better acquainted. Although the nation's politics changed, some of the old customs remained handy.

Rostenkowski also hitched his star to Hale Boggs of Louisiana, another powerful House Democrat who served on Ways and Means. When Rostenkowski entered the House, Boggs was only forty-four. But he was first elected in 1940 and quickly gained influence as a young disciple of Sam Rayburn. Boggs commanded attention as a smooth orator with robust self-confidence, whose relatively progressive views on civil rights stood out among the Southern Democrats' mossbacks. After Rayburn died in 1961, House Democratic leaders tapped Boggs to move into the party's top ranks as majority whip, a position that gave him access to White House meetings to plot Democratic strategy. Rostenkowski was one of many junior members who sought guidance from Boggs. That connection proved useful in 1967 when Speaker John McCormack of Massachusetts bestowed on Rostenkowski the retiring Keogh's position as Democratic Caucus chairman. With encouragement from Boggs, Rostenkowski moved to inject youth and a fresher outlook into top Democratic ranks. It was Rostenkowski's idea to convene a group of House Democrats every Thursday morning to discuss the latest House and party business and to alert the leaders to problems in their ranks. "Hale liked the idea," said Gary Hymel, a top Boggs aide. So Boggs's wife Lindy (who later served in the House for eighteen years following her husband's 1972 death) awoke early each Thursday to bake two coffee cakes for the meetings. "About ten members showed up, and they would shoot the shit and talk about the schedule and things," Hymel said. Gradually Rostenkowski was catching the insiders' attention.

Fitting in comfortably, Rostenkowski joined a House where the majority party was controlled mostly by conservatives. Even though Franklin Roosevelt after 1932 greatly expanded the federal government's scope and brought new voters to the Democratic party, and Harry Truman later moved to desegregate the military after he became president, congressional Democrats in the 1950s were not yet the party of civil rights. (In a 1938 speech, FDR had disparaged Democratic opponents of the New Deal as "copperheads," a historical reference to Northern foes of the Civil War.[1]) Among blacks permitted to vote—especially in Northern cities—many remained comfortable with the Republicans, who continued to posture themselves as the party of Lincoln; for blacks in the South, voting and other civil rights were largely illusory in the 1950s. Even though the Democrats' big national gains in the 1958 election left them with a nearly two-thirds majority, mostly conservative Democrats continued for the next few years to dictate business as usual on most House committees. Many were defiant or oblivious to their national party's growing advocacy for civil rights and enhanced federal programs. Absent more dramatic change in Washington, the young Democrats ambitious for change were left to do little more than draw up an agenda for the nation and gradually to reshape their own party that was balkanized into three wings— Southerners, Northern urban machinists, and liberals. Each of those blocs was fractured by further divisions, based on factors such as age, region, and personal style. Melding these diverse interests into a coherent majority would take time, savvy, and a new political climate.

For the young Rostenkowski, the "machine" Democrats were the group with whom he felt most comfortable. Typically they were white, Roman Catholic, and centrist in their views, though a handful were African American or Jewish. They were mostly older and cautious lawmakers, like O'Brien of Chicago and Keogh of Brooklyn. Many would publicly cheer Kennedy's election as the first Catholic president but privately view the "lace-curtain" Irishman as an upstart dilettante whose Harvard advisers had dangerous notions about expanding the federal government. Most were loyal, above all, to the urban party organization that had been responsible for their election. When Rostenkowski first took office in 1959, Chicago had ten House members who could be termed "machine Democrats," Philadelphia had six, Detroit had five, and New York City had seventeen. (By the time he departed, there was only a handful.) For these and others—some called themselves "organization Democrats"—local constituency service had a higher priority than national lawmaking. Even when they attained sufficient House seniority to acquire an influential committee chairmanship, they spent little of their time in Washington. They thought of home, not the House, and they accepted the slow-motion workings of the system in Washington. For Rostenkowski, these kinds of bosses became his Washington role models.

A prime example was Charles Buckley of New York, who served thirty years in the House, including twelve years as chairman of the pork-barrel-dispensing Public Works Committee. For most of those years Buckley also was the "boss" of the Bronx Democratic party organization, which gave him far greater celebrity and influence among local pols and a larger payroll of staff to supervise. Among most voters, both in New York and around the nation, he was unknown and liked it that way. "Keep your mug out of the newspaper," he advised Tammany Hall boss Carmine DeSapio.[2] Buckley conducted much of his business from his Bronx office, even when Congress was actively at work. He typically devoted at least as much attention to accumulating his share of patronage jobs at city hall as he did to crafting billions of dollars in federal spending, such as the new interstate highway program. In the House, Buckley's committee aides had great power to conduct legislative business in his name as long as they followed his directions and protected his interests.

The machine Democrats were important in 1958, but they were less numerous or potent in the House than the Southern Democrats. Today the suburbanization of Southern politics and changing racial influence have shifted power to Republicans in that region. But when Rostenkowski entered Congress, the South was still mostly rural and Democratic, and its members had disproportionate influence nationally. Of the House's 20 committee chairmen in 1959, 13 were Southerners; of the region's 124 House members when Rostenkowski entered, only 8 were Republicans. The lack of a credible Republican party throughout most of the South, plus the iron grip of the seniority system on Capitol Hill, meant that control inexorably fell into Southern Democrats' hands. Occasionally these Southerners were populists who welcomed the New Deal expansion of the federal role. Some, like Rayburn of Texas and Carl Albert of Oklahoma, became party leaders. But a larger share had already become political fossils who were far more conservative in their views than the newcomers. They opposed any new federal expenditure except when it benefited their districts, such as flood-control projects, farm subsidies, or military installations. That posed problems for Northern Democrats who sought to expand federal aid to their cities. "I said to Dick Daley, the South has won the Civil War because they have the chairmen," Rostenkowski said pragmatically. "We'll win the Civil War, I told him, when we don't send members to the House as a springboard but to move into positions of authority."

Among senior Democrats—both rural Southerners and big-city Northerners—there was little interest in waging partisan warfare. Most influential Democrats were comfortable with Eisenhower, and they worked well with the Republican administration. "I think the minimum of partisanship existed during those eight years," concluded Rep. John McCormack of Massachusetts, who was the No. 2 Democrat during the 1950s. "We felt that a party not in control of the White House owed a responsibility to the people to act constructively."[3] The powerful Rayburn, who usually refrained from involvement in details, gave Democratic chairmen considerable leeway to operate by a consensus among themselves. "Rayburn at times was criticized for not exercising more control," said Frank Eleazar, who covered the House for the Associated Press during most of Rayburn's speakership. "From time to time he laid down the law with the chairmen, but not as often as his critics wanted." The price of peace was built-in consensus. Liberals were frustrated because conservatives dominated Democratic ranks on the key committees; in coalition with House Republicans they wielded an effective majority, making it hard for the most important liberal proposals even to reach the House floor. "Indeed, the true test of the conservative coalition's voting strength in the Eisenhower years was that medicare never came out of the [Ways and Means] committee," wrote a congressional scholar, "and, if it had been reported, it would have been rejected in the House by a wide margin."[4] Even the Education and Labor Committee, which would soon become the rallying point for the Democrats' progressive agenda, spent much of 1959 debating a proposal that was anathema to the liberals: enactment of the Landrum-Griffin bill, which was designed to expose and eliminate corruption in labor unions.

Many newly elected Democrats of Rostenkowski's class faced conflicting pressures in deciding how to position themselves and to exercise their new power. At a January 1959 Capitol breakfast for the freshmen, sponsored by Rayburn, former President Harry Truman was the guest of honor. "Truman said to me that his advice to a freshman was always vote with the leadership," John Brademas of Indiana later said. "But to the television cameras a moment later, he said his advice was always vote in the public interest." By the 1970s new members would feel few restraints about asserting their independence among Democrats and defying the power structure. But in 1959, even for stalwart liberals such as Brademas who represented "swing" districts that rejected lockstep partisanship, there were plenty of risks for members who challenged the House's established order. A party regular like Rostenkowski did not face that kind of dilemma. Serving in a solidly Democratic district, he was among the relatively few first-term Democrats who had little reason to worry about reelection two years later. He could do what came naturally for a junior Chicago politician: make friends and learn the ropes from the insiders. "Rostenkowski got few notices in the hometown press about his work in Congress," according to a newspaper account of his first term.[5] Instead he knew his place as a foot soldier and a party loyalist. And he faithfully supported the Democrats' national agenda: a minimum-wage increase from $1.00 to $1.25 hourly, more federal assistance for education, and medical care for the elderly.

A major difference between the thirty-one-year-old Rostenkowski and the typical Chicago machine Democrat was his age. He was the youngest House member. Of the nine other Democrats who represented at least some part of the city in 1959, their average age was sixty-one; for them Washington was a sinecure at the end of their careers. Still, Rostenkowski was only a bit player. His most significant accomplishment on the Commerce Committee, he recalled, was helping to draft the 1962 legislation granting modest federal aid to the nation's embryonic educational television stations. "I don't have much memory of Danny" from the early days, said Brademas, "except that he was a solid Democrat, a champion of Mayor Daley, and he had no particular orientation on issues." Alice Rivlin, a young Johnson administration expert on health and welfare issues who later was appointed by President Clinton as Office of Management and Budget director and a Federal Reserve Board member, recalled Rostenkowski as "a blustery Chicago politician" during the 1960s. The simple fact of his committee assignment was all that mattered. "To a guy like [Rules Committee chairman] Howard Smith or [Appropriations chairman] Clarence Cannon, it was a signal that there is the next apparent leader" of the Chicago delegation, Rostenkowski now says. Given O'Brien's advancing age, the youngster would not have to wait long to take the next step up the ladder and claim his benefactor's Ways and Means seat.

Despite a modest legislative record during his first years in the House, Rostenkowski gained vital lessons about the institution that would play an important part in his own career. Although Rayburn was reaching the end of an illustrious House tenure that made him the most revered and influential lawmaker of the twentieth century, he remained the House's dominant leader until a few months before his death (he died in November 1961, at age seventy-nine, having been speaker for seventeen of the twenty-one preceding years). Rostenkowski recalls that Rayburn sometimes seemed "gruff," a characterization that should amuse many who dealt over the years with the blunt and sometimes intimidating Chicago congressman.

One of Rayburn's most effective tools for information-gathering and parliamentary mastery was the "Board of Education," an informal group that he convened in the late afternoon nearly every day the House was in session. About a half-dozen confidants, and occasionally some invited guests, met informally in a small room on the first floor of the Capitol to swig liquor and discuss the latest legislative news and political gossip. Participants who joined Rayburn in the late 1950s usually included Majority Leader McCormack, Majority Whip Albert, and Hale Boggs. Others included Bill Arbogast, the Associated Press's chief House reporter. (Even though changing ethical standards would have made such fraternizing unthinkable years later, press colleagues noted that Arbogast used the information he gleaned from these sessions with great discretion and with the informal understanding that Rayburn would not "remember" what he had said.) For participants, the social gatherings were mutually beneficial. Rayburn could count on his guests to give him a good sense of the House's mood and the prospects for coming votes—especially, in some cases, after they had been loosened up with bourbon; in return, he used the sessions to convey his sentiments. Rostenkowski would later adapt Rayburn's "Board of Education" model—in addition to separate Tuesday night dinners—to respond to complaints that members had too little opportunity to talk with one another.

John Kennedy's 1960 election stands as a historical turning point, the beginning of an upsurge of liberalism that crested in the Great Society programs of the mid-1960s. "The torch has been passed to a new generation," he proclaimed in his January 1961 inaugural address. But to those who were watching closely, the congressional Class of 1958 had already begun the major shift from Eisenhower-era complacency. Its members enhanced the Democrats' third force: the liberals, mostly from the North but scattered among the farm states' prairie populism, the universities and other intellectual bastions, and the suburbs that were emerging as centers of wealth and energy in postwar America. The commanding generals personified by Dwight Eisenhower were giving way to the dashing lieutenants like JFK and GI grunts like Rostenkowski. After six years in which the unflappable Ike worked with a bipartisan conservative coalition in Congress, the nation's voters in 1958 demanded aggressive government action. An emboldened Democratic majority in Congress began to take shape.

Speaking for a generation that had sacrificed mightily during the gruesome world war of the preceding decade, these Democratic freshmen said it was time to reap the peacetime benefits. They spoke forcefully for former soldiers who used federal educational and housing benefits to settle into growing neighborhoods with their young families and now were seeking to harness the booming economy and to prove the strength of democratic values. No longer required to focus on saving the world from the Nazi scourge or to stem the gut-wrenching depression, Congress directed resurgent federal spending to education, technology, and other avenues for domestic growth. "The Soviets' launching of the world's first man-made satellite, Sputnik I, on October 4, 1957, not only sparked the beginning of a race in space but set in motion political forces that were to alter profoundly the relationship of the federal government to the nation's schools, colleges and universities," John Brademas wrote in a retrospective three decades later.[6] Seizing the moment, the new Democrats set the framework for Kennedy's New Frontier with initiatives on urban development, civil rights, health care, and aid to the poor. Although it would take them several years to convert their ideas into laws, the mandate was clear. Sputnik and a damaging recession in 1958 gave Democrats a gain of 49 House seats and 15 Senate seats (bolstered by the new states of

Alaska and Hawaii)—their biggest election triumph in the half-century following World War II. Their 283 House seats were their most since the New Deal in the 1930s and would come close to setting the high-water mark for the 40 years of the Democrats' reign. Their gains were striking because House control had fallen within a narrow range during the 1950s, when neither party held more than 234 House seats.

Rostenkowski later emerged as the most influential member of that 1959 freshman class. But he was not in the early vanguard. New senators such as Philip Hart of Michigan and Edmund Muskie of Maine boldly redefined issues ranging from civil rights and consumer protection to the environment; Eugene McCarthy of Minnesota, a former House member who initially stayed in the Senate background, would later seize on growing opposition to the Vietnam War to launch a presidential campaign challenge that spurred Lyndon Johnson's 1968 retirement decision. In the House the 63 new Democrats included several future party leaders and committee chairmen: Brademas of Indiana served as majority whip during the 1970s; Robert Giaimo of Connecticut chaired the House Budget Committee during the Carter administration; Robert Kastenmeier of Wisconsin became prominent at the Judiciary Committee, notably during its impeachment inquiry of President Nixon. Compared with Washington's old-guard Democrats, these fresh faces were predominantly young, Northern, and liberal.

An important innovation that emerged with Rayburn's tacit blessing in September 1959 was the Democratic Study Group, which a small band of freshmen and other activist House Democrats launched to coordinate efforts in confronting the well-oiled conservative domination. It was designed to respond to "a certain slackness in the organization and methods of liberal forces [that] caused them, through ignorance or negligence, to miss opportunities to pass legislation they wanted," wrote Rep. Richard Bolling, a Rayburn protégé, in one of his two controversial books in the 1960s that harshly critiqued the House Democrats' lack of direction. The DSG's purpose, he added, was to emulate the conservatives' skill in preparing "a common strategic plan so that each supporting Member had an assigned role" in a legislative battle.[7] By 1960, according to a brief history of the DSG prepared by Frank Thompson of New Jersey, "For the first time, liberals were working together on a sustained basis toward a set of mutually agreed upon legislative objectives."[8] In later years the group became an important legislative adjunct for Democratic leaders and a

bane of some committee chairmen. DSG members made Ways and Means
a prime target because it too often disregarded the views of most House
Democrats and instead tended to special-interest lobbyists. Not surprisingly, Rostenkowski had few dealings with the DSG and even fewer good
things to say about its activities, even in its early days. He contemptuously dismissed its leaders, especially Bolling, as "the so-called intel-
lects." By playing his cards with the machine men and their Southern
allies, he comfortably fit in with the "all politics is local" crowd. For lawmakers in those groups wielding power at the time, DSG members, more
than the Republicans, were the enemy. Insiders viewed the newcomers as
brash, youthful, and naive. Eventually, of course, the liberals would win.
But in 1959 they were just a nuisance.

Kennedy's 1960 election gave Democrats total command in Washington and seemed to herald the conquest of the upstart '58 liberals. But the
truth is somewhat less idealistic. For one thing, the Democrats' net loss
that year of twenty-one House seats—including the defeat of nineteen of
Rostenkowski's freshmen colleagues, many of them from "swing" districts in the Midwest that Republicans had long held—gave party leaders
less room to maneuver. "The Kennedy-Johnson ticket had no sweeping
mandate from the voters," Lawrence O'Brien, JFK's chief congressional
strategist, said many years later. "Few if any members of Congress owed
their election to the new President's political coattails."[9] As his first key
test, Kennedy turned his attention to adjusting the House's power levers.
With the president-elect's encouragement, during a December 1960 meeting in Palm Beach, Florida, Rayburn agreed on an attempt to weaken the
conservatives' grip on the Rules Committee, the scheduling panel that had
become a graveyard for many Democratic proposals. If he and his allies
failed, the new president would be severely undercut and his program
would face a grim future. In what became a titanic struggle in the days
immediately following Kennedy's January inauguration, the moderate
and liberal Democrats prevailed on a 217 to 212 vote and added new slots
for two mainstream Democrats on the Rules Committee. All but one of
the sixty-four Democrats voting against the expansion were from the
South. The reformers gained vital support from twenty-two Republicans,
mostly liberals and moderates from the Northeast.

The outcome was, wrote Bolling, "the end of the beginning" in the reformers' efforts to overhaul the House; for the first time they had made a
committee more accountable to the majority party's wishes.[10] But Ros-

tenkowski had reservations even then about the reformers' agenda. Before the crucial vote he was standing at the rail in the back of the House chamber with "Judge" Howard Smith of Virginia, the legendary chairman of the Rules Committee who leveraged his position as a legislative gate-keeper. Smith wanted him to oppose Rayburn's bid to expand his commit-tee, Rostenkowski recalled. "He said, 'You're Tom O'Brien's fellow and he thinks a lot of you.' . . . He pointed to Sam Rayburn and said, 'That man never asked me for anything that he didn't get [at Rules]. But the secret is, he didn't ask for much.'" Rostenkowski's decision to back Kennedy was easy in this case because he was with Rayburn. But the resistance by many Democrats and hard-fought victory sent a clear warn-ing to the new presidential team. "The memory of this fight laid a re-straining hand on the Administration's legislative priorities for some time to come," wrote the historian Arthur M. Schlesinger, Jr., who was a Kennedy White House aide.[11]

While the election of the nation's first Catholic president marked a major turning point for the Democratic party, more deep-seated political factors limited the ultimate impact of Kennedy's New Frontier and his mix of party bosses with intellectual and social courtiers. Like many House Democrats, Rostenkowski had a complex relationship with Kennedy and his team. As a young urban Democrat new to Washington, Rostenkowski quickly became pals with other Democrats close to JFK. Those friendships reinforced the already close relationship between Mayor Daley and the Kennedys, which was vital to the 1960 election. The two clans, and the operatives close to each, built a tight and mutually re-warding professional relationship.

Their alliance had officially begun in 1945 when Joseph Kennedy purchased Chicago's Merchandise Mart. The sprawling twenty-four-story downtown building along the Chicago River, previously owned by the local entrepreneur Marshall Field, included ninety-three acres of space for office rent. "Once [Joe] turned it around, with physical changes and spec-tacular merchandising, it skyrocketed in value and became the basis for a whole new Kennedy fortune," his wife Rose Kennedy later said.[12] By 1955 Joe Kennedy was clearing more profit annually on the building than he had put down for its purchase. Within two decades his $12.5 million purchase had soared in value to $75 million.[13]

As one of Chicago's most prominent businessmen, even in absentia, Kennedy moved aggressively to stake his claim in the local power structure. Before Richard J. Daley was elected mayor in 1955, his friendship with Joe led him—as Cook County Democratic chairman—to invite John Kennedy, who had been a senator for little more than a year, to address the party's annual dinner in 1954. Even at that early date, Daley was warming to the idea of an Irish Catholic president. "It was Jack Kennedy's first speech west of the Alleghenies," said Bill Daley, the mayor's son. "Joe helped to arrange it." Shortly after Daley was elected mayor, he chose Sargent Shriver, a Manhattan lawyer who turned to journalism after World War II, to serve as president of the Chicago Board of Education. Not coincidentally, Joe Kennedy had earlier designated Shriver, who was his son-in-law, to manage the Merchandise Mart. In his dual capacities Shriver became the "liaison between the man who ran City Hall and the man who owned the world's then largest commercial building."[14] (In 1968 and again in 1970 Rostenkowski talked up with reporters and local Democrats the possibility of drafting Shriver—who held several positions in the Kennedy and Johnson administrations—to run for the Senate from Illinois. But Shriver, who was the Democratic vice-presidential nominee in 1972, likely would have suffered from criticism as a political carpetbagger and he deferred.)

After his 1958 election Rostenkowski expanded the network by making friends with "Kennedy mafia" members such as Reps. Edward Boland and Torbert McDonald of Massachusetts and Kennedy aides Lawrence O'Brien and Kenneth O'Donnell. At the request of campaign officials, Rostenkowski in 1960 made speeches for the candidate outside Illinois. But apart from the often boisterous camaraderie, his chief interest was local. "Joe Kennedy dealt with Richard Daley," Rostenkowski said. "I was talking to the Kennedy people in Washington. Our main interest was to win Illinois for the Democrats." Among the urban pols, JFK—who was a decade older than the first-term congressman—enjoyed razzing the new guy in town. "Kennedy would kid me that I was too loyal to Dick Daley," Rostenkowski said. "He said I should be more independent. He and the other Kennedy people used to rib me about it." But the young congressman reveled in his insider access. At Kennedy's invitation, Rostenkowski was the only member of Congress among the few dozen spectators in the small CBS studio in downtown Chicago during the first televised presidential debate in September 1960, which became famous as the turning point in the Kennedy-Nixon campaign. "I was the only Democratic politician in the studio," Rostenkowski later said. Unaware of the two candidates' stark differences on camera, he added, "I was under the impression that Kennedy lost the debate."

After Kennedy narrowly won Illinois in November 1960—with major assistance from all levels of Daley's organization, producing a huge Democratic turnout in Chicago that many Republicans and some historians have termed of dubious validity—the mayor staked his claim to national influence. Kennedy's victory made Daley "the most powerful political leader in Illinois' history, and with the single exception of the president, the most powerful politician in the country," Mike Royko wrote, with more than a tad of local chauvinism. "He would assert this power, however, in a way limited only to Chicago. His interest in the workings of Washington were confined primarily to obtaining federal money and laws for Chicago."[15] As the loyal machine operative, young Rostenkowski was always prepared to assist Daley. That helped explain why he was aboard Air Force One in April 1961 when Kennedy flew to Chicago "to talk a little . . . local politics" at the Cook County Democratic dinner.[16] Rostenkowski enjoyed that hands-on contact and Kennedy's success in ethnic politics.

But Rostenkowski was among many congressional Democrats who were less enchanted with the new president's legislative program. JFK's accomplishments on Capitol Hill were limited. His fresh ideas and popularity helped him win passage of modest initiatives that generated public enthusiasm, especially creation of the Peace Corps. When the economy dipped slightly in 1961 he resorted to the recycled New Deal option of public-works assistance to areas with high unemployment. And after a pitched battle with business groups that first resulted in a narrow setback in the House, he eventually delivered on his campaign promise to raise the minimum wage to $1.25 per hour. But Kennedy's more sweeping proposals met a chilly response. The House in 1962 thwarted ambitious programs such as a proposed Urban Affairs and Housing Department plus mass-transit help for the nation's cities.

More important, Kennedy's advocacy of a program to aid elementary and secondary schools suffered a serious setback at the hands of the House's old-line Democratic forces. In retrospect the issue seems modest: should the federal government assist states with funds to supplement teacher salaries and construction of new schools? Some Southern Democrats were appeased when the administration agreed to additional money for low-income areas. But the machine Democrats representing Northern cities that were heavily Catholic proved a bigger stumbling block. For them, none of Kennedy's concessions "were so important as the single question of whether the grants to the states could be used to assist Roman Catholic and other religious or private schools."[17] The first Roman Catholic president was unwilling to open that door following the heated 1960 campaign discussion of whether he would govern independently of his church. Sensitive to his firm pledge that he would not be influenced by his religion, Kennedy refused to buckle. In sending his proposal to Congress, he cited "the clear prohibition of the Constitution" against aid to parochial and other private schools. But the Catholic church's allies on Capitol Hill were not impressed. Ironically the focal point of their opposition became the House Rules Committee, where Democratic leaders thought they had gained control by increasing the number of loyal Democrats. Rep. James Delaney—a backbench Irish Catholic from Queens, New York, who was known "less for the substance of his views than for a mulish streak,"[18] joined with the committee's two arch-conservative Southern Democrats and all its Republicans to bury Kennedy's school-aid bill. Although Rostenkowski's committee assignment kept him out of that debate, his own experience growing up in Chicago made him sympathetic to government assistance for all parents, even if they sent their children to a religious school.

The House's cautious response to Kennedy's agenda wasn't simply a matter of Southern or Catholic intransigence. Many senior Democrats felt cool toward the young president. When the House narrowly defeated a youth "jobs" program in 1962, "the Kennedys lost that bill because they hadn't done the proper work," said Tip O'Neill, who was gaining cachet as the successor in Kennedy's House seat. "In the legislative halls, they didn't follow through in the same manner in which they campaigned."[19] Nor did Vice-President Johnson provide much help in rounding up votes, despite his own proven skill as Senate majority leader in pushing legislation through Congress. "In my judgment, [Johnson] wasn't too active," said Boggs of Louisiana, who became majority whip after Rayburn's death. "I think he was uncomfortable in the vice presidency."[20] JFK's reticence caused grumbling among House liberals who eventually embraced Johnson as more policy-oriented.

Kennedy bequeathed more a sense of energy than of policy. His greatest domestic legacy lay in the seeds he planted for future debates. One that has been historically overlooked came in January 1963 when he endorsed legislation to cut income tax rates for both individuals and corporations. In what became a model years later for Republican "supply-side" theory, his advisers argued that fiscal policy could be an effective tool in stimulating the stagnant economy. Many thinkers in both parties were aghast, but some liberals embraced the tax cut as part of what the influential Bolling then termed "the new economics";[21] although it was not enacted until the following year, the House passed a less ambitious version shortly before Kennedy's assassination in November 1963. On another emerging issue on which he showed himself ahead of Congress, Kennedy framed the public debate on civil rights with his June 1963 proposal to prohibit discrimination in public places and to ensure fair employment practices. That proposal was a prelude to the giant March on Washington two months later in which Martin Luther King, Jr., gave his famous "I have a dream" speech on the steps of the Lincoln Memorial.

It took President Johnson to enact these proposals and other major pieces of Kennedy's social agenda, which earlier had been stymied. Whether they would have been enacted if Kennedy had lived remains one of history's great unanswerable questions. Years later Kennedy's stature defined him as the heroic president who moved the nation to a "New Frontier"; by contrast, Johnson's Great Society became the victim of excessive federal rules and a failed war. In 1983 a *Newsweek* poll showed that three of ten respondents wished that Kennedy were still president; only one in a hundred wanted Johnson.[22] Even among congressional Democrats there was major disagreement over which president was responsible for passage of their party's program. If Kennedy had lived, he "wouldn't have gotten half of it through," said Wilbur Mills, whose position as House Ways and Means chairman placed him in a position to know.[23] "Johnson doesn't get the credit [he deserved]. He had the greatest ability of any president to get things done." Jim Wright of Texas attributed the passage of many Kennedy ideas to both Johnson's legislative skills and his commitment to the martyred President. "He was consumed almost by an obsession, to achieve those things that JFK had asked for and that had not been granted," Wright said. "The nation felt it owed the memory of JFK something. I don't believe that Kennedy would have achieved as much" on his own.

John Culver, a Kennedy friend who rode into Congress on Johnson's coattails in 1964, takes a different view: Kennedy achieved so little because the numbers were stacked against his proposals, especially in the

House, which Culver called "hard, rocky soil." His narrow 1960 election as president had been "a personal mandate," Culver said, but "the political referendum on Kennedy grew only after his death." Once Johnson took office, circumstances became far more hospitable to those ideas, he added. "The mood of the country was to act and be liberal," Culver said. Yet according to *New York Times* columnist Tom Wicker, Kennedy could have strengthened himself as a vigorous liberal and posed more of a challenge to nervous Republicans if he had been more steadfast in challenging the congressional barons. After the sobering Rules Committee showdown, "the liberal new President conciliated with the South," Wicker wrote. "The man who had pledged to get the country moving again through strength in the White House was forced to compromise."[24]

Rostenkowski retained his generational and cultural attachments to Kennedy. Former Kennedy White House aide Chuck Daly recalled a 1964 visit that he made with Rostenkowski and Ed Boland of Massachusetts to the Georgetown home of the still-grieving widow Jacqueline Kennedy, who wanted to hear stories of Jack. "We had a couple of drinks and started to talk about one of Jack's 1960 campaign visits when the nuns were climbing the fence to see him," Daly said. "Danny was crying after he saw [JFK's] kids grabbing Bobby's leg." But Rostenkowski's historical assessment was more sympathetic to Johnson's legacy. "All Kennedy did was to win the [nuclear] test-ban treaty and enact the Peace Corps," he says. "It was all Camelot. It's a shame that Lyndon Johnson doesn't get more credit." Rostenkowski no doubt preferred Johnson's hands-on approach to politics, Chicago style. Members of Congress were like mere stage props for LBJ's initiatives, making few changes before returning the finished bills to the president for his signature. "It was frightening not to be with Johnson, because he knew how to wield his power," Rostenkowski remembers. Years, even decades, of planning and arguments were consummated in days. Democrats, who have struggled since then to figure out what to do next, left virtually nothing undone.

Although historians have focused mostly on Johnson's legislative achievements in 1965 following his landslide election, 1964 was also a time of important accomplishments. "LBJ took the program from JFK and from the congressional Democrats," said Neil MacNeil, a premier congressional reporter at *Time*. "After 1963 had been a year of frustration because Southern Democrats did not want Kennedy's agenda, 1964 became an extraordinary legislative year." The chief victories were enactment of the tax and civil rights bills. As an incumbent campaigning for his own term, Johnson emerged from his national obscurity to pressure Congress aggressively. Although LBJ gave credit to his predecessor, he "wanted to run, not on memories of John Kennedy, but on a current assessment of himself," Richard Bolling wrote.[25] The 1964 election gave liberal Democrats firm control of Washington and made Republicans and even Southern Democrats nearly irrelevant. This time Democrats had a president who would be not only their spokesman but also their paramount legislative leader. True, they lost seven House seats in the Deep South, chiefly due to local hostility to the national Democrats' advocacy of new civil rights laws; that was an ominous precursor to the party's eventual loss of most of the region. But for now most of its members held on. Elsewhere across the nation, unlike 1960, the election produced an overwhelming mandate. Johnson's coattails helped the Democrats win 295 House seats, the most taken by either party after 1936.

An important shift, though it is overlooked today, was the conversion of machine Democrats to a federal agenda. Although Rostenkowski had initially voiced concern that in the 1964 election his working-class white voters might display a "backlash" to political advances by blacks, his concern proved premature. Instead LBJ achieved for Democrats in November a notable though ephemeral success: he unified black and white ethnic voters in the North. That balancing act also provided Rostenkowski one of his biggest thrills. He emerged onto the national stage at the Democratic National Convention in Atlantic City when he seconded the nomination of Hubert Humphrey to be Johnson's vice-president. Rostenkowski was candid in explaining why Johnson asked him to give the brief speech. "I like to think the President does like me," he told a reporter in 1968. "But he was also certainly aware that when I stepped up on that podium on nationwide television, that nice long Polish name 'Rostenkowski' was being displayed at the bottom of the screen. And that Poles all over the country were watching me and thinking, 'What a good Polish name.' "[26]

As with any landslide election, many House candidates unexpectedly prevailed with little electoral experience, just a promise of change. "The country was receptive to the suggestion that a lot of problems needed to be attended to," said John Culver, who was elected from a northeast Iowa district. "People were feeling good and in an altruistic mood, . . . a generosity of spirit that was possible because people felt comfortable." In some respects Culver's story was typical. At age thirty-one, a graduate of

Harvard University and Harvard Law School and a Marine Corps veteran, in September 1963 he left the staff of first-year Sen. Edward Kennedy— his undergraduate classmate—to explore a candidacy for the Republican-held House seat. His father was a Cedar Rapids auto dealer who had been a delegate for Sen. Robert Taft at the 1952 Republican National Convention, but that provided little immediate help. "I got the names of twelve people and systematically went to see them, one by one," Culver recounted. "I talked about our interests in the Democratic party. . . . By the time we were campaigning, Johnson had inherited Kennedy's program and added his own touches." Iowa voters elected five freshman Democrats, including Culver, to the state's seven House seats. "We all campaigned unabashedly and proudly for the Great Society."

By contrast, 1964 was not such a great year for machine Democrats. In the Bronx both Buckley and Healey lost renomination to reform Democrats—one Jewish, the other a patrician Protestant; the challengers won the primary by campaigning against Tammany Hall, the crumbling and discredited party organization. As Johnson's victory opened the Democrats to new voices and brought a high point of popularity, it severely damaged the closed system that had sustained the party in other areas.

The breadth of Johnson's landslide and the large number of new liberal enthusiasts caused conservative Democrats on Capitol Hill to mute their opposition. As had been the case three decades earlier with urban ethnics and Southern Democrats who didn't believe in the New Deal, most Democrats in 1965 stayed with Johnson. Facing LBJ's demands for new programs, Rostenkowski said that he and his cohorts simply fell into line as "the followers of the liberals." But the machine Democrats at most times remained "more like the Dixiecrats," he said. "We were more frugal in spending money" than were the emerging party leaders. Johnson and his ardent flock, nonetheless, boldly and relentlessly enacted the Great Society program in what may have been the most sustained period of legislative action in the nation's history. "He wanted to get everything through as quickly as he could because he didn't know what the future would hold," said Carl Albert, who was House majority leader during Johnson's presidency.[27] Having witnessed the New Deal and how Roosevelt kept an iron grip for only a few years, Brademas said, "Johnson understood that when you've got the votes, you better move." Years later even some Johnson allies second-guessed that he tried to do too much too fast and that Democrats consequently made serious mistakes. "They rushed to judgment," concluded Bolling, comparing Johnson's excesses to the Republicans' overreaction in approving Reagan's economic program in 1981. "His program was good but the content was lousy." But Democrats at the time brushed aside their doubts, assuming they would make needed adjustments later.

By one count, Congress passed eighty-nine major proposals submitted by Johnson in 1965 and defeated only three of them.[28] Among the most prominent were an expanded version of Kennedy's federal aid to public education but with money directed at children—based on need, to skirt the religion controversy, rather than at the schools; a housing program emphasizing low-income facilities and urban renewal; the Voting Rights Act; and the "war on poverty." The results had profound influence on the country, encouraging grassroots community activism that undermined fading political machines at city hall in many communities, an increased role for teachers as a political force, and a greater awareness of the environment, starting with Lady Bird Johnson's highway beautification crusade to remove unsightly billboards. Each of these forces would later prompt extensive second thoughts. But the Democrats were focused at the time on fulfilling their promises; they would let history take care of itself.

1965 saw one of those infrequent sessions of Congress in which a party set aside its usual internal divisions—on ideology, region, and personalities—and achieved results at a dizzying pace. Behind and in front of it all was LBJ. "Johnson brought tremendous energy to the job," Hale Boggs said. "I got the impression that the man never slept. He was, particularly at that time, very close to Congress, and he would see members constantly and would talk to them, persuade them."[29] For Rostenkowski and other machine Democrats, that sense of urgency brought about the unthinkable: a shift of allegiance from their local bosses back home to the national boss in Washington. For the only time during his thirty-six years in Congress, he was awed as he saw a president operate as forcefully as his own mentor, Richard Daley. While attending a White House meeting in which LBJ was pressing Democrats for their support, veteran House Democratic aide D. B. Hardeman recounted, the president "bore down" on some issue. "I was sitting next to Danny. Here Danny came out of the Daley machine and so forth, but the president made one of these points. And Danny leaned over to me and said, 'God, he's tough!' "[30]

Some House Democrats were not so favorably impressed. Johnson wanted them to fear that he knew how each was voting. Tom Foley, a former Senate aide who had defeated a twenty-two-year Republican incumbent from Spokane, Washington, was one of the few freshmen to vote against a bill that would permit the federal government to pay rent supplements for low-income groups. Soon after that vote he and the three other freshman Democrats from his home state were called to the White House for his first business meeting with the president. "The first thing he said was that he wanted to thank me for my support of the rent supplement bill," Foley said, with obvious irony. "He went on and on, listing all the groups that were supporting the bill. . . . He knew I had voted against it. But he squeezed us hard like a lemon." LBJ was famous for giving people "the treatment"—often standing over and peering directly at them in an intimidating way, so that they could not possibly deny his fearsome force or his request for support.

Rostenkowski's switch of focus from Daley to Johnson was timely. As a national figure, the mayor's luster was fading; and his Chicago machine was starting to lose its solidarity. Daley grumbled that some Great Society programs intruded too much into city hall operations. Federal approval was now required to replace a street light on State Street, Daley complained in the 1960s. But Rostenkowski had become mostly a team player on Capitol Hill. "Lyndon Johnson solved more problems than he created," he still believes. And loyalty opened the door to new rewards. The lasting importance of the Kennedy-Johnson years for Rostenkowski was that it became a time for the young lawmaker to climb the political ladder on his own. He was building friendships both with the older power brokers and with urban Democrats who had recently entered the House. He instinctively understood the steps that would bond him to other colleagues. When longtime machine Democrat Bill Green, Jr., of Philadelphia died in 1963, Rostenkowski took custody of Green's heavy, green leather furniture to prevent its return to the congressional warehouse; four months later, when Bill Green III was elected to succeed his father—and eventually to replace him on the Ways and Means Committee—Rostenkowski passed on the chairs. "Young Bill thinks about that a lot," said Jim Healey, who understood that mind-set as the son of another former machine congressman. "It's the personal aspect of the job."

Soon enough Rostenkowski won his first big opportunity to move into the House's power elite. When Tom O'Brien died in April 1964, at age eighty-five, after a stroke and a subsequent illness that hospitalized him for nearly a year, his departure created an opening on the Ways and

Means Committee. For Democrats from most other large states, such a development would produce intense jockeying within their delegation and among other key players on Capitol Hill. But Chicago operated differently. After O'Brien's death, when Rostenkowski sought the Ways and Means seat, "I went to Daley and said that I'm doing all the work" for the city, he recalled. "He said, 'Let's do it.' It was my call because I was already the guy reporting back to the mayor." Although Roman Pucinski—Rostenkowski's distant ally from Chicago's northwest side—also voiced interest in the seat, Daley's endorsement easily clinched the deal.[31] In return for the committee seat, John McCormack set only one requirement for Rostenkowski: he must promise Johnson to support his goal of federal medical care for the aged. That was no problem for the administration enthusiast.

Winning a seat on the twenty-five-member Ways and Means panel moved him to the inner sanctum. For decades the committee had been the House's power center. Its control over the raising of all federal revenues—including taxes and tariffs—plus the spending for health and welfare programs that were directly financed by specific levies made Ways and Means the pulsing heart of the increasingly active federal government. For the most part, its members won their assignments only after senior Democrats concluded that they could make tough decisions. When Rostenkowski joined the committee, more than half of its fifteen Democrats had served in the House since the 1940s; the next-youngest was nearly a decade older than he. They were carefully selected; unlike Rostenkowski, half were lawyers. Due to their age, they represented a fading profile of the party. In 1964, seven Democrats were from the South and five others—including Rostenkowski—were from large cities in the Northeast and Midwest. In those days, before television had entered the House and when the committee's consensus approach rarely made headlines, few Ways and Means members were well known in Washington, let alone elsewhere in the nation.

Established temporarily in 1789 and made a standing House committee in 1802, Ways and Means reigned as the House's most prestigious committee. After its initial responsibility "to prepare an estimate of supplies requisite for the services" of the new nation, the committee rose to legislative prominence because of its authority to set rates for tariffs, the nation's chief source of revenues in the nineteenth century. With the momentous ratification in 1913 of the Sixteenth Amendment to the Constitution, which permitted Congress to levy a tax on individual and corporate income, the committee secured a virtually limitless source of revenues. Its grip over the spending side of the federal budget emerged in 1935 with the creation of the tax-based Social Security program. From there, Ways and Means directed a vast array of other programs and responsibilities, including health-care financing linked to the payroll tax; welfare; unemployment compensation; and interest on the national debt. By the 1980s Ways and Means controlled about half of all federal spending. With the expansion of domestic programs since the 1960s, a large share of expenditures moved from "discretionary" programs—which required an annual appropriation—to "entitlement" programs, whose benefits were permanent and automatic unless the underlying statute was changed; Ways and Means held the purse strings for most of these entitlements.

Ways and Means has always attracted the House's most skillful and politically savvy lawmakers. Seven of the committee's members later became president—from James Madison, who served on Ways and Means during the 1st Congress, to George Bush, a member throughout his four-year House tenure; in addition, eight became vice-president. The committee basked in its influence. According to a committee member anonymously quoted by congressional scholar Richard Fenno, "Ways and Means is powerful around here because it's interpreted as being powerful."[32] Until the 1970s the committee usually acted on a bipartisan, almost clubby, basis. Its decisions were rarely challenged, let alone overturned, on the House floor. Never was the camaraderie stronger than during Rostenkowski's early years on the committee, when Wilbur Mills was chairman. Mills was one of the most powerful members of Congress in the twentieth century. He was also one of the least exciting. He was the sort of gentlemanly technician who would have had a tough time getting elected in today's television-run campaigns. With his husky voice and portly profile, he did not command the attention of outsiders. Among colleagues during the 1960s, however, he was revered. "He seems to have an instinctive knowledge of the needs and prejudices of the individual members and how to cope with them," according to a 1962 profile in the *New York Times Magazine*. From his early years, "He was affable with his colleagues, maintaining good relations with both the southern conservatives and the northern big-city men of his party."[33]

Governance under Mills was nonconfrontational and nonpartisan. A tax lawyer reputed to have memorized most of the code, he mastered the

details of the issues facing his committee and made it his business to secure a broad consensus on most legislation. His colleagues as well as
many reporters agreed he was "the most important man on Capitol
Hill."[34] A self-described "country lawyer" from Searcy, Arkansas, Mills
was anything but a prairie populist. The son of a successful banker, he
attended Harvard Law School and he was elected to the House in 1938
at the age of twenty-nine. After he became Ways and Means chairman in
1957, he set his sights on building support from virtually every member
of the committee. "To reach a consensus in the committee, [Mills] will
compromise, bargain, cajole, swap, bend, plead, amend, coax and unite
until as much of the controversy as possible is drained from the bill, and
as many members of the committee as possible support it," wrote political
scientist John Manley, who found widespread praise among committee
members for Mills's responsiveness to their views.[35] Bipartisanship was
his unceasing goal. That was true even during the Kennedy-Johnson
years, when Democrats could ignore the Republicans and still prevail on
the House floor. But the chairman practiced the politics of inclusion. John
Byrnes of Wisconsin, who was the senior Republican on Ways and Means
from 1963 to 1973, often functioned as Mills's partner. Also a lawyer
without much flair but with more enterprise than Mills, Byrnes was
skilled at cutting centrist deals. The two of them rarely disagreed on a
major committee decision, and most Republicans rarely complained
about Mills. "John was, in a way, the first sergeant of the Ways and Means
company," wrote Barber Conable, a Republican who joined the committee in 1967. "When he saw that the committee had decided what it wanted
to do, thanks to John Byrnes' honest and persuasive ministrations, the
company commander—Wilbur Mills—would appear out of the bushes,
position himself at the head of the column, and the committee consensus
would become the Mills bill."[36]

   In many ways Mills served as both a model and a foil for the young
Rostenkowski. From him the young apprentice learned how to make
tough decisions that were almost never challenged, and how to minimize
partisanship and cooperate with the president regardless of the consequences. Still, Rostenkowski thought that Mills's reputation was exaggerated. Talk that Mills would seek the speakership was "a joke," he said.
"He was a technician. He would go home with the *New York Times* cross-
word puzzle and read the tax code." Reflecting his own yearning for that
simpler time, Rostenkowski added, "There was so much more trust by

members and the leadership in what he was doing." On Capitol Hill, Mills often appeared larger than life. Presidents sought him out, not vice versa. In January 1962 Kennedy left Florida a day earlier than planned so that he could meet with Mills in Washington.[37] Two days after Kennedy's assassination, Mills dined at LBJ's home with the new president and their wives. "There was no business. He just wanted me there. . . . I was surprised when he asked me to come up for dinner, frankly, that quick after he'd been sworn in."[38] The ego-massaging went both ways between Mills and presidents. As chairman, he rarely launched his own initiative. He viewed the prospect of a presidential veto of a Ways and Means bill as an "embarrassment,"[39] he told the House in 1973; in a model admired by Rostenkowski, he never suffered such a rebuke. (Mills died in Arkansas in May 1992, the same month that the state's governor, Bill Clinton, wrapped up the Democratic presidential nomination.)

As liberals gained more strength among House Democrats during the 1960s, Mills fueled growing resentment outside the committee. Led by the increasingly confrontational Democratic Study Group, his critics griped that the committee was dominated by a coalition of Republicans and conservative Democrats, of which he was the architect. The liberals prepared issue briefs offering alternative proposals and explored ways to reduce the committee's influence. In his 1968 book, Bolling proposed the then-radical step of requiring that the Democratic Caucus approve all Ways and Means members every two years to ensure their party loyalty. "No longer could a Speaker blame Ways and Means for not reporting out a tax or medicare bill," Bolling wrote.[40] Although the suggestion gained little support at the time, it laid the groundwork for much deeper cuts in the committee's autonomy. House reformers began to focus on additional sore points. Some objected that the Democrats' method of filling a Ways and Means vacancy paid more attention to experience than ideology; like Rostenkowski, most of the committee's members were chosen for their pragmatic deal-making skills, not their policy views. Other critics sought to deny Ways and Means the virtually automatic protection of having its bills debated on the House floor under a "closed rule," which denied other members the opportunity to propose an amendment.

Some House reformers began to explore the possibility of stripping Ways and Means Democrats of their authority as the "committee on committees," appointing all Democratic members to House committees. That was the work that most intrigued Rostenkowski, just as it had his predecessor, "Sheriff" O'Brien. For six weeks at the start of each new Congress, he and other Ways and Means members would meet with freshmen and veteran members seeking a new committee assignment. A number of factors came into play in the decisions of whom to place where: ideology, ambition, geographic balance, legislative impact. "I loved the give and take," Rostenkowski said. "I loved the maneuvering and the planning." Outsiders rarely challenged the committee assignment process, and most members were grateful for what they got. Reformers complained that this was just one more illustration of how the Ways and Means Committee— and Mills, in particular—had become too much of an independent power. They began a campaign to give Democratic leaders more leverage over committee assignments.

There were other resentments. Many Democrats voiced growing unhappiness with committee members' predilection for currying favor with financial barons—from oil drillers to real estate developers—whose fate was in the hands of Ways and Means in the awarding of tax-code preferences. Brademas recalled that he thought about bidding to fill a committee vacancy in 1965, but he dropped the idea because other members often gossiped that Ways and Means members were involved in shady financial deals. "You just weren't sure what they were up to over there," he said. Although Mills sought to limit special-interest favors by the committee and treasured his reputation for evenhandedness, his door was usually open to lobbyists. He had no patience for the Democratic Study Group and the liberal critics.

The 1965 passage of Medicare was a capstone effort for the Mills committee, in spite of its conservatism, and a noteworthy embodiment of Rostenkowski's early years in Congress. The expansion of health-care services for the elderly had become a top goal of many House Democrats, starting in the late 1950s. Democratic presidents in the 1960s had enthusiastically joined them. For a half-dozen years, however, Mills was the central figure who blocked its approval. Even after Lyndon Johnson's landslide election in 1964 left him no choice, Mills placed his own imprint on the program. Mills later claimed that he opposed Kennedy's plan because it did not go far enough. "What Kennedy had recommended merely took care of the costs, or most of the costs, of hospitalization," Mills said. "They did not take care of the costs of the doctor bill and other related services." After the 1964 election, Mills said, he told Johnson that Democrats would be "the laughingstock of the country" once the public learned that the plan would cover only 25 percent of the elderly's medical costs.[41] But that explanation, by itself, fell ludicrously short of the truth. The path by which Ways and Means came to support an expanded program was far more tortuous and revealing.

Harry Truman had been the first president to propose mandatory national health-insurance coverage, but his plan went nowhere in Congress during his tenure. During the 1960 campaign the Kennedy-Johnson ticket called for expansion of health-care coverage. But Ways and Means continued to stand in the way. Mills and Senate Finance Committee chairman Robert Kerr of Oklahoma won preelection passage of a very modest alternative to the proposed reforms. Under the Kerr-Mills plan, the federal government gave matching grants to the states to finance medical assistance for the aged and the disabled. That program became known as Medicaid. In 1961 Kennedy called on Congress to enact mandatory coverage for the elderly. The fact that his plan was confined chiefly to hospital and home-care expenses was a bow to the omnipotent American Medical Association. Still, Mills became the leading foe of Kennedy's plan; Ways and Means members solidly backed his refusal to bring the issue to a vote. The Senate fell narrowly short in an intensive 1962 effort to pass an alternative plan. Then, in 1963, Kennedy stepped up the pressure by submitting to Congress a first-ever presidential "special message" for aiding senior citizens. The script remained the same: Ways and Means held hearings (including a session on November 22, which Mills quickly adjourned after he learned of Kennedy's assassination), but it took no action. Even pressure from President Johnson had no impact. On June 24, 1964, buttressed by a narrow majority of his committee, Mills capped the frustration of health-reform advocates by "postponing" action on the Medicare bill. Instead he passed in the House a 5 percent hike in Social Security benefits; that bill died in the Senate.

But the dam was close to bursting. "Wilbur started to get a sense that the committee was ready to move," Rostenkowski said. Bolstered by Johnson's landslide in November, administration officials began discussions with allies in organized labor and on Capitol Hill for a more aggressive strategy. With the Democrats' gain of thirty-six House seats, they increased their control of Ways and Means to a 17–8 majority, assuring solid support for Medicare. Finally Mills decided to get out front. He combined portions of three alternatives: the administration's earlier proposal that chiefly covered hospitalization costs; a plan by Republican

John Byrnes to permit the elderly to make monthly contributions to a federal program to provide some insurance for doctors' bills; and the American Medical Association's "Eldercare" proposal for voluntary coverage for senior citizens at a state's option. With technical help from the Health, Education and Welfare Department, "I developed the whole thing in the committee," Mills later said.[42] Then, to assure what many at the time viewed as superfluous bipartisan support, he had Byrnes offer the plan for the new optional "Part B" coverage of the nonhospital bills of some medical specialists; the beneficiaries' contributions would be matched by federal revenues. That move to include Byrnes stunned virtually all observers and was made independently of high Johnson administration officials.

The outcome expanded the Medicaid program more than Kennedy and Johnson had proposed. Liberal Democrats were in no position to complain. The House passed the bill, 313 to 115, on April 8, 1965; four months later, after the House-Senate conference committee included additional hospitalization coverage, Johnson signed the bill into law with Truman seated at his side at the former president's library in Independence, Missouri. Rostenkowski, who stood in the background and received a pen from the signing, was part of the large congressional delegation that flew aboard Air Force One to participate in the ceremony.

Although Medicare became the costliest Great Society program and had the greatest impact on the average citizen, its enactment generated less controversy than did the Voting Rights Act and the War on Poverty. As the master lawmaker, Mills cared chiefly about the perfection of the process. Granted, he set aside obvious misgivings about the program. That made his legislative craftsmanship all the more vital to the success of the Medicare proposal. Indeed, he may have been the only official who understood how the law was assembled. According to Wilbur Cohen—a senior Health, Education and Welfare Department official, who was the Johnson administration's chief expert on Medicare and worked closely with Mills—the chairman asked him to consolidate the proposals before Ways and Means. "The effect of this ingenious plan is, as Mr. Mills told me, to make it almost certain that nobody will vote against the bill when it comes on the floor of the House," Cohen wrote to Johnson.[43]

Serving as legislative partner to the Johnson administration obviously was a pleasing role for Mills at Ways and Means. But despite the Democrats' satisfaction with the 1965 success, which would place Medicare next to Social Security in their "Hall of Fame," Mills later acknowledged some regrets over his inability to anticipate its fiscal repercussions. "We never foresaw what did happen: hospital costs going up," he said in 1987. "Every hospital had to have this expensive equipment—maybe they'd use it one day out of a week—in place of all the hospitals in a community going together and having it in one hospital." The lawmakers also failed to foresee, he added, factors such as inflation, costly damage lawsuits filed against doctors, and the impact of automatic cost-of-living adjustments in many federal programs. But the political die had been cast in the 1964 election. Johnson "had this tremendous loyalty to John Kennedy," Mills said. "He had to enact everything that [Kennedy] has espoused, because he had succeeded him. He had to do it."[44]

Alas for the Democrats, their Great Society bandwagon would stay on track for only a year. Johnson's bid to pass so much legislation in such a short time after the 1964 election ultimately backfired. Under the president's whip, congressional Democrats had neither adequate time nor the ability to carefully consider their handiwork or to fully implement major pieces of the legislative program. "One problem with the Great Society is it grew a bureaucracy whose members were not attuned to the sensitivities of people," said Jim Wright, an LBJ ally. "There was an inexorable tendency of programs to encumber themselves with ever-slower procedures and ever-more paperwork." That problem was compounded by insufficient funding. Plans for the War on Poverty, for example, were so sweeping that perhaps no amount of money could have "fully funded" it. The program "was never tried," complained John Culver. Opposition of conservative Democrats, the economic costs of the Vietnam War, plus "vested" political and corporate interests "combined to smother the Great Society in its crib," Culver said. "It was never given a chance."

The failings resulted in part from the iron grip of seniority. Conservative Democrats used the Appropriations Committee to limit funding. Even with a majority of votes, McCormack lacked the skills to discipline wayward chairmen. "The seniority system was in full throat, and it tended to destroy the best people," Culver said. "It was a crushing political experience." In addition, many new members elected in 1964 lacked the luxury of time. Of the forty-seven freshmen who won a seat that had been held by a Republican, twenty-four failed to return for a second term. The voters' problem, Tom Foley said, was not so much that the Democrats were trying to do too much but that LBJ tried to take too much credit. "The Republican argument was that we were rubber stamps and playthings for Lyndon Johnson and that he treated it as 'my Congress,'" said Foley. "Republicans didn't go after the specifics of legislation so much as the modalities of giving up the independence of Congress." Anticipating the danger, some Democrats began in 1966 to back away from Johnson; but many others remained unabashed supporters, even though they came from "swing" districts. A decade later House Democrats would learn the art of distancing themselves from flawed national leaders. But in 1966 the old politics were very much alive. In that year's elections, Johnson allies shrugged off the forty-seven-seat loss in the House as a normal swing of the pendulum after the Democrats' big win in 1964.

For the surviving Democrats, the high-water mark of 1965 passed quickly. Their years of controlling the House—including the Ways and Means Committee—subsequently became more complex and less productive. Never again would they command such a clear-cut period of congressional activism. But Rostenkowski had learned some key lessons from House insiders and especially from Wilbur Mills. The alliances and influence he developed would serve him well years later when references to Sheriff O'Brien and Gene Keogh would draw blank stares from new generations of legislative rookies. As for the Great Society, Johnson's legacy proved less grand than he had hoped. Overtaken by conflict abroad and divisions at home, LBJ could not sustain public attention or support for his program. "During 1966, the War on Poverty faltered," wrote Robert Dallek, a sympathetic Johnson historian. "It was a victim of expenditures on Vietnam, threatened inflation and economic disarray, and its own internal contradictions."[45] Still, it would be a mistake to call Johnson's vision a failure. At the most basic level, the nation's poverty rate declined and cities from New York to Chicago and Los Angeles eventually made dramatic comebacks, in both their local economy and spirit. Despite their condemnations of Great Society programs, Richard Nixon, Ronald Reagan, and Newt Gingrich—each in his own way—made significant accommodations to LBJ's monuments. Notwithstanding the traumatic remainder of his presidency, the man who ranks among the most skillful congressional leaders continues to shape his nation.

Chapter Three

FIRST BLOODY SIGNS
OF TROUBLE

IN RETROSPECT it is amazing that the Democratic party survived so many severe blows during the late 1960s. The war in Vietnam; civil rights riots in many major cities; the appalling clash between police and protesters during the 1968 convention in Chicago and that year's devastating presidential campaign—each was jarring enough to have unleashed a lasting popular revolt against the party in power. True, Richard Nixon won the White House for Republicans. But 1968 proved to be little more than year fourteen of forty for Democrats in the House. This despite their support for stationing more than a half million soldiers a half world away on behalf of a dubious cause, which led to more than fifty thousand dead and lifelong trauma for countless others. The absence of political repercussions was profound. Incumbency advantages only seemed to increase; in November 1968, at the depth of their party's ignominy, only seven House Democrats were defeated for reelection.

A quarter-century earlier the far more consuming World War II had strengthened public support for FDR and Winston Churchill and their hold on power. Yet the triumph of the Allies saw Churchill and his Conservatives promptly booted out of office; Truman's Democrats were stripped of control of Congress a year later, and the president barely beat the polls to prevail in 1948. By contrast, congressional Democrats never faced serious jeopardy as American military losses mounted. Indeed, when the nation's forces withdrew in the mid-1970s and Communists were victorious in South Vietnam, the Democrats' House majority was as large as it had been during Johnson's heyday, and voters soon elected another Democrat as president.

Rostenkowski, however, suffered ups and downs that more fully illuminate the years from 1967 to 1975. It was a stormy and sometimes bloody time filled with setbacks to him personally and to his style of life, in both Chicago and Washington. As change and disorder erupted around him, the organization man stuck with the rules, the beliefs, and the institutions that had always worked so well for him. As he moved into the middle of intraparty conflicts, however, he was forced to choose sides. In so many of his attitudes, he was obstinate when confronted with challenges and unyielding in the face of threats to his status quo. By 1970, with his political benefactors gone or losing influence, Rostenkowski had little to fall back on to defend himself. It became less of an advantage in Washington to be Richard Daley's protégé or Lyndon Johnson's ally. Rostenkowski's opposition to reforms in the Ways and Means Committee or in the House's internal operations, like his unquestioned acceptance of Daley's police tactics during the 1968 Democratic convention, revealed a closed-mindedness to conditions that many found objectionable. But his party loyalty played out in varying ways. Stubbornness also can be an admirable sign of consistency. When neighborhoods in Chicago, along with those in many of the nation's other large cities, were wracked by racial disorder, he voiced anxiety but did not abandon LBJ's civil rights programs. And when he suffered a wrenching personal setback to his ambitions in the House, he swallowed hard and lent support to his friend, Tip O'Neill of Massachusetts, who won the speaker's job that he earnestly craved. As much of his world crumbled, Rostenkowski stayed alive to fight another day.

When he was riding high in 1967, adversity was the last thing on Rostenkowski's mind. His appointment that year as Democratic Caucus chairman showed that his old-style apprenticeship had served him well. In contrast to later years when caucus members voted on their chairman, filling the slot was still the speaker's prerogative. So John McCormack of working-class South Boston, who had patiently bided his time as a Ways and Means member and spent twenty-one years as Rayburn's deputy before taking over as speaker in 1962, chose Rostenkowski. "He wanted someone friendly to John McCormack," Rostenkowski boasted. With Southerners Carl Albert and Hale Boggs in the second- and third-ranking positions it made sense for the old man to pick a reliable machine Democrat. Rostenkowski also got a big boost from the testimonial of his dinner pal Gene Keogh of New York, who was close to McCormack and served in the mostly ceremonial caucus chairmanship in 1965–1966 before retiring to practice law. Rostenkowski remained forever grateful to McCormack. "He put me on the dance floor," he said. But Rostenkowski's tie to the aging speaker became a mixed blessing. Among other problems, McCormack was the target of Democrats' complaints that his backroom style and scant public-speaking skills were outmoded in a television era. When McCormack and octogenarian Carl Hayden of Arizona, the Senate's president pro tempore, sat together behind President Kennedy or Johnson in a televised address from the Capitol, the two cadaverlike Democrats, who would serve in Congress for a total of ninety-eight years, acutely symbolized a political class out of touch.

Because House Democrats rarely met after Congress convened in those days, the caucus chairman's powers were mostly ceremonial. But days after he took over, Rostenkowski passed the word that he wanted to attend Johnson's regular meetings with congressional leaders. According to a January 1967 note to Johnson from a White House staffer, McCormack took steps to assure that his rising star was included. Rostenkowski also reached out to younger rank-and-file Democrats who were growing restive with McCormack. In tandem with his friend Boggs—a fellow Ways and Means member and Roman Catholic—he began the Thursday morning meetings to encourage more internal dialogue. His idea gained such popularity that, years later, dozens of Democrats would convene "Whip" meetings in the Capitol each Thursday morning to raucously second-guess their leaders and discuss ways to ensnare the Republicans.

But Rostenkowski and the Democratic command were unprepared for the growing internal activism of reformers, liberals all, who wanted to tame the unaccountable power of committee chairmen and of the seniority system that was the core of their influence. The delicate balances that Sam Rayburn had artfully managed began to crumble soon after his November 1961 death. As his successor, the seventy-year-old McCormack was past his prime and engendered nowhere near Rayburn's reverence. He took control of a new Democratic team that was "based on power and patronage—not issues," according to a caustic 1962 analysis by the National Committee for an Effective Congress, a New York–based reform clique.[1] In that prescient report (titled "The Democrats Under McCormack—A House Divided?") the NCEC laid the framework for what became a decade-long liberal takeover. Referring to the approximately ninety Northerners and Westerners in the House, most of whom were "strongly issue-oriented" and held districts that had been Republican bastions before Roosevelt's New Deal, the report said they acted chiefly as "a guerrilla operation" demanding the leaders' attention. What was needed, the NCEC concluded, was to "break the southern and city-machine stranglehold on the power structure of the party."

Unlike college campuses of sixties-era protesters, revolution usually comes slowly in the House. Although its rules and folkways are not so ossified as those of the Senate, the "established order" retains broad discretionary command. In this struggle, young Dan Rostenkowski left no doubt where he stood: he had little patience for reformers and their ideas, which he disparaged as "professorial" and not grounded in practical politics. But as the Vietnam War ground on he was making a futile stand against inevitable change. Reformers who wanted to take more of a national focus gained increasing numbers in the House. By the early 1970s the contest was all but over. Early champions of modernity such as John Brademas of Indiana, Don Fraser of Minnesota, and Morris Udall of Arizona moved past Rostenkowski into positions of influence and greater respect from junior members. Rostenkowski's grand design for power began to crumble as old-style rules and power relationships eroded.

Still, the Vietnam conflict demonstrated how the power elite stubbornly clung to power in the House. Following the House's unanimous endorsement in August 1964 of the Gulf of Tonkin resolution, which gave Johnson military carte blanche in Southeast Asia, it would be many years before the House seriously debated the war. While Senate Foreign Relations Committee chairman William Fulbright began extended hearings in 1966 that cast a skeptical eye on the war's origin and conduct, and other senators sought to shut down funds to support U.S. involvement, the House was silent. The House is supposed to be the "lower" body, akin to the House of Commons, less deferential and more populist than the Senate. But under the Democratic coalition, the reverse was true. Senators, with their confirmation and treaty-ratification powers, took a more active role in seeking to shape the nation's foreign policy. But House leaders and committee chairmen, most of whom stoutly defended Johnson and the Pentagon, could not imagine confronting the nation's chief executive or defying public opinion while several hundred thousand U.S. troops were engaged in battle. (At the time, alternatives to the nation's prevailing anti-Communist views were confined chiefly to a thin slice of the academic community.) The 1960s were, after all, the pinnacle of the "imperial presidency." Most House Democrats—facing the imperative of a two-year term—were disinclined to confront their leader publicly on a paramount issue, even if they held private doubts. "I thought, how could a man be so right on domestic issues and not on foreign policy," said Rep. James Corman, a liberal House activist. But by 1967 public opinion began to turn against the war; in August a Louis Harris poll found 34 percent favored a quick withdrawal. Two months later came draft-card burnings at several sites and a student protest at the Pentagon. Soon Eugene McCarthy entered the presidential campaign against Johnson. Yet Rostenkowski, like most House Democrats, held firm with LBJ on the war.

Increasingly Vietnam posed an economic and domestic distraction. Johnson and other top Democrats could no longer devote their chief attention to fulfilling the Great Society's ambitious promises. In the 1966 elections resurgent Republicans regained more House and Senate seats than they had lost during Johnson's landslide two years earlier. Even in Rostenkowski's Illinois, liberal icon Sen. Paul Douglas, who stuck with LBJ on the war, was soundly defeated by Republican Charles Percy, who played to public doubts. Still, Democratic hawks in charge of the House Armed Services and Foreign Affairs Committees were not interested in public debate. Curiously, it was the Ways and Means Committee that took center stage for the House's first showdown on the war. Partly in response to Wilbur Mills's near obsession with avoiding large deficits, members grew worried about August 1967 projections that showed the 1968 federal budget of $135 billion with a deficit exceeding $29 billion. Johnson had proposed a tax surcharge of 10 percent on all federal income taxes, both individual and corporate, chiefly to pay for the war. But the Ways and Means chairman, as if to prove that his pioneering role in enacting Medicare had not altered his fiscal conservatism, had other ideas. He sought to use the fiscal crisis as leverage to cut domestic spending, including many Great Society programs. "I kept saying to [Johnson administration officials] that the House would pass [a tax increase] if they would agree to some spending limitations," Mills said. "We couldn't pass a bill without a spending limitation and a reduction in federal spending."[2]

But the president strenuously objected, and a lengthy deadlock ensued. Following the election and the return to a 15-10 Democratic majority at Ways and Means, the liberals' brief dominance of the committee ended as the old-time coalition of Republicans and conservative Democrats revived. "Conservatives read the [election] debacle as a mandate to put the brakes on the Great Society program," wrote Joseph A. Califano, Jr., who was LBJ's chief domestic-policy aide. "Their leader was Wilbur Mills."[3] Both Democrats and Republicans believed that the tax surcharge proposal could not pass the House. The wartime showdown between the president and the mighty chairman was extraordinary. "Never before in the Johnsonian presidency has a powerful figure in Congress—and Mills is the most important man on Capitol Hill today—defied and frustrated the President the way Mills had during the past eight months," a reporter wrote of the tax surcharge struggle.[4]

The debate over the surcharge placed Rostenkowski, for the first time in his career, at the center of controversy over taxes. In addition to his new Democratic Caucus chairmanship, he was speaking his mind at Ways and Means. He was reluctant to raise the financial burden on his blue-collar constituents, most of whom viewed the war as a distant abstraction, though they remained patriotic. He was aware also that reservations about a tax increase were, as usual, widespread in the House. As early as January 1967, Treasury Secretary Henry Fowler wrote to Johnson that Rostenkowski "personally doesn't like idea of tax surcharge and thinks that we will have a difficult time getting it through."[5] By October, Rostenkowski told LBJ aide John Roche that because Mills was feeling neglected by the White House, "the tax bill is in very, very bad shape." The House Democrats' continuing objections eventually forced the White House to develop an unusual strategy of bypassing the House—which traditionally starts tax bills—and gaining initial passage in the Senate, which attached a modified version of Johnson's proposal to a minor House-passed excise tax bill in April 1968.

When the president announced that he would not seek reelection, the tax fight was far from over. A House-Senate conference committee reached agreement in May on both the 10 percent surcharge and the demand by Mills for $6 billion in spending cuts for the next year, but Rostenkowski went his own way. He told Barefoot Sanders, the White House chief legislative adviser, that he opposed the deal because the cuts were too large. He joined liberal Democrats in insisting that the House vote for a spending reduction of only $4 billion. In a May 16 memorandum to LBJ, Sanders acknowledged Rostenkowski's influence among Chicago

Democrats. A tentative count showed that five of the nine Cook County Democrats would vote in favor and only one definitely opposed the $6 billion compromise, Sanders wrote to Johnson. "But Rostenkowski, the bell cow, is [opposed] and so told me" according to Sanders. "If he stays with that position, I believe the 8 others will go with him." Ultimately other bosses stepped in. Rostenkowski succumbed to pressure and voted for the tax package with its $6 billion spending cuts. The bill passed. The federal budget would be balanced in 1969 for the final time in nearly three decades. The tax surcharge bill also prompted the first major debate between liberals and conservatives over budget issues. These politics set the stage for Congress to view the federal budget in broad terms, not simply through the traditional prism of thirteen annual spending bills and an occasional tax measure. In seeking to force budget discipline, Democrats opened the door to the sweeping reforms of the 1974 Congressional Budget Act. The future would feature many more House conflicts on tax and spending issues, quite unlike the Mills model.

Despite his hint of independence, "regular" Democrat Rostenkowski remained an ardent supporter of the Vietnam War throughout Johnson's presidency. In those years he enjoyed showing his affinity with Pentagon allies by presiding over the House during the annual military spending debate; party leaders generally grant such an assignment as a reward to loyalists. With a firm gavel, he reached out to Southern allies of the military. His pro-Pentagon credentials were also helpful back home. Many Polish-American constituents were ardent anti-Communists and strongly supported the military campaign. By contrast, his pal Tip O'Neill of Massachusetts became an opponent of the war in September 1967, following his liberal Cambridge district. Not until the spring of 1971 would Rostenkowski break with the House majority and Democratic leaders.

Vietnam was only one challenge for Rostenkowski and other Democrats in the Johnson years. Conflict between neighborhoods and local authorities increased civil rights tensions, which sparked riots in many black communities. For a congressman who kept close tabs on his district, it was one thing to defer to the White House on an overseas conflict but quite different when it came to law-and-order breakdowns at home. In August 1965 a riot incinerated many blocks of the Watts community in downtown Los Angeles, leaving dozens of deaths, thousands of arrests, and hundreds of millions of dollars in property damage. That month, after incidents in Daley's mostly Irish Bridgeport neighborhood, the Mayor outlandishly called it "a matter of record" that "known Communists" had fomented the trouble. Rostenkowski sent a letter to Johnson suggesting that the president "find some pretext to send Daley out of the country for a week or two to defuse the tension."[6]

But Rosty's voters wanted no part of a pro–civil rights regime. They were traditionalists who lived in a neighborhood for life and looked after their own. Helping blacks was not on the agenda. Following the Chicago tensions, White House legislative affairs chief Larry O'Brien wrote a memorandum urging the president to "have Dan drop by in view of the problems that Members of the [Chicago] delegation have had with some recent legislation, caused to a great extent by the Chicago civil rights situation."[7] A year later legislative counsel Jake Jacobsen sent Johnson a brief note, summarizing a telephone call from Rostenkowski, who "talked at some length about the 'touchiness' of the [race] problems and how the white citizens and the police are becoming very aggravated."[8] Even before the Chicago disturbances, Rostenkowski was anxious to make clear to Johnson his Polish constituents' fears about advances made by the black community following the landmark 1964 Civil Rights Act, which he had supported. "There is definitely white backlash" in his district, Rostenkowski told a senior White House political aide. In an August 4, 1964, memorandum to LBJ, Jack Valenti described Rostenkowski's "estimate of the Polish turn of mind" on the eve of that year's presidential election: "They are mostly Catholic but in spite of the [Catholic] Church's emphatic stand on civil rights, they are very much opposed to the Negro advances. The Polish people are real-estate conscious and worry about the value of their homes. He estimates that the majority of the people at the Polish-American Congress are Republican-inclined. . . ."[9] In November 1966 Rostenkowski's Republican opponent John Lesgynski appealed directly to white voters unhappy about civil rights legislation and protesters. A taxi driver and political neophyte, Lesgynski proclaimed the slogan, "a little man representing little people," to appeal to the district's "white backlash" to civil rights protesters advocating open housing.[10] Largely ignoring the attacks, Rostenkowski received 60 percent of the vote, only slightly below his customary share during the 1960s.

Aided by his potent network delivering city services, Daley sought to brush aside pockets of criticism from white liberals and blacks. In his 1967 bid for a fourth term, the mayor looked to Washington for a timely infusion of federal funds to grease the machine with special projects. Increasingly those tasks fell into the lap of Rostenkowski, Chicago's chief liaison to Washington. The congressman got the job done and kept the machine alive at a time when machines were falling in other Northern cities. As outlined in a February 20, 1967, memorandum to Johnson from his aide Larry Levinson, Rostenkowski would not be shy during an "off the record appointment" that had been arranged for that day. Just in time for the city election, according to Levinson's note, Johnson could respond to Rostenkowski that the administration had approved five urban-renewal projects and a mass-transit planning grant. With his high-level Washington help, Daley retained his popularity, including overwhelming support from the city's heavily black wards. "Race problems or not, the Chicago Democrats were doing business as usual," a local reporter wrote.[11]

Still, the city's racial problems festered. In April 1968 the assassination of Martin Luther King, Jr., triggered riots with major damage. The results were not nearly as destructive as simultaneous outbursts in Los Angeles, Detroit, and Washington. But the Chicago disorder was disastrous nonetheless, both to the blacks affected and to Chicagoans' view of themselves. After a helicopter survey of devastated areas, Rostenkowski was stunned by what he saw. "It doesn't look like Chicago," he told reporters. The result also raised serious questions about Mayor Daley's fairness and his boast that Democrats served all communities equally. The police were rough on the rioters. Daley exacerbated the already considerable tension in Chicago when he told a press conference that he had ordered police to "shoot to kill" any would-be arsonist and "shoot to maim or cripple" any looters. The outraged national and local response forced Daley to rescind his instructions the next day.

These growing national and local tensions provided an ominous backdrop for the Democratic National Convention, scheduled for August in Chicago. Even though Daley had serious reservations, President Johnson's selection of the city as host made sense for several reasons. After all, more conventions had been held in Chicago than in any other city in America, ten by the Democrats and fourteen by the Republicans. Daley was enough of an egotist that he welcomed the opportunity to showcase his city and its skill in controlling large crowds. For Johnson, the mayor's "no-nonsense" reputation surely would guarantee order when anti-war protests and racially inspired riots had become standard fare across the nation. To those who feared a breakdown in public safety, Daley said, "As long as I am mayor, there will be law and order in Chicago. Nobody is going to take over this city."[12] At the time neither could have foreseen the disastrous events that would occur prior to the gathering: an unexpectedly bloody offensive by the opposing forces in Vietnam, a ballot-box insurrection against the president by his own party, assassinations of two national leaders, and further urban riots. 1968 was a year, wrote Theodore H. White, that shattered American faith: "the myth of American power broken, the confidence of the American people in their government, their institutions, their leadership, shaken as never before since 1860."[13]

For much of America, from alienated students to fearful adults, Chicago became a focal point of despair and a stage for the seeming ruin of a once-great party. This would be no ordinary convention. In the International Amphitheater, well-organized convention protesters vigorously voiced unhappiness over the nomination of Vice-President Hubert Humphrey and Sen. Edmund Muskie as the Democratic presidential ticket. (Muskie's selection as the first Polish-American nominee for national office was largely overlooked amid the convention chaos.) Outside the hall, with the likes of Tom Hayden, Abbie Hoffman, and hundreds of "yippies" arriving for street disruptions, Daley took a tough line. No permits for sleeping in parks or demonstrating, law-enforcement authorities decreed. Daley built an intensive security network, both at the convention site and in downtown streets. It quickly became apparent that neither side would yield. The result was "the wildest Democratic convention in decades . . . and the bitterest, the most violent, the most disorderly, most painful, and in certain ways the most uncontrolled." It was, Norman Mailer added, "a five-day battle in the streets and parks of Chicago between some of the minions of the high established, and some of the nihilistic of the young."[14] When Daley unleashed cops on anti-war protesters, he became the despised symbol of Democratic failure. And because Rostenkowski was a steadfast lieutenant who sat at Daley's side, he too paid a steep price.

On both sides the tone was set the Sunday night before the convention opened. When roughly a thousand protesters refused to halt their rally at Lincoln Park—three miles north of downtown—after the 11 p.m. curfew, police decided to force them out. "They beat people beyond the point of subduing them. They chased them down and left them bleeding," Mike Royko reported.[15] It was an ugly scene, with police making a target of out-of-town news reporters as much as the anti-war crowd. As the convention opened the next day, violence intensified. "In the ensuing Lincoln

Park fracas that night," Roger Biles wrote, "policemen removed their badges so they could not be identified and then went on another rampage. Attacking demonstrators and bystanders alike, shooting canisters of tear gas, flailing away indiscriminately at men and women, at adolescents and the middle-aged, at clergymen and area residents, the police moved through the park chanting, 'kill, kill, kill.' "[16] At the Amphitheater, Daley downplayed the turmoil. Despite the bloodbath, he was, according to Royko, "trying to participate in a convention as if nothing happening on the street was in any way connected with it."[17] Decades later, time had done little to heal the painful wounds for city patriarchs. The ever-loyal Rostenkowski claimed that the news media "orchestrated" the confrontation in the streets and blamed Eugene McCarthy, the insurgent senator opposing LBJ on a peace platform, for failing to restrain the protesters. The results "frightened" ordinary people, he said. That assessment was similar to the view of another Chicago mayor as the city prepared for another Democratic convention twenty-eight years later: the riots had "nothing to do with the city, per se," nor with his father, Mayor Richard M. Daley told a reporter. "It was a most difficult time for this country. . . . Vietnam tore this country up."[18]

As delegates learned of the violence, many grew enraged. The convention hall became a snarling pit, especially during the Tuesday night debate of proposed anti-war language to be used in the Democratic platform. At one point Daley, seated on the convention floor with the Illinois delegation, signaled House Majority Leader Albert—who was presiding over the bedlam—to end the debate. He moved a finger across his neck in a dramatic sign to silence the speaker. The gesture, captured by television cameras, "graphically demonstrated how the boss was manipulating the convention."[19] That incident deeply embarrassed Albert, the little-known Oklahoman who had been a faithful lieutenant in the House—especially because he failed to constrain the mayhem. "Every attempt to transact orderly business," Albert wrote in his autobiography, "ran headlong into all of the bitterness, all of the divisions and all of the frustrations that our assembly only mirrored. I can only say that it looked and sounded awfully confusing to the presiding officer up there on the rostrum."[20]

Lyndon Johnson, however, saw it differently. Watching on television from his Texas ranch, the lame-duck but still commanding figure grew agitated over Albert's failure to discipline the rowdy convention. During the clamor on Wednesday night, rioting in the streets spread into the convention as anti-war delegates demanded that Daley's police end their attacks on protesters. The anger intensified when Sen. Abraham Ribicoff took the podium to nominate Sen. George McGovern for president. During his speech Ribicoff set off a tirade in the Illinois delegation when he criticized the "Gestapo in the streets of Chicago." Amid televised coverage of the ensuing bedlam, according to Rostenkowski, the president telephoned the podium to demand that someone other than Albert wield a stronger gavel. Rostenkowski was on the platform. Clary Sochowski, his top Washington aide, picked up the call and told Rostenkowski, "the president is on the line." When Rostenkowski took the phone, LBJ told him, "God damn, get order in the hall. Take that gavel." Rostenkowski wouldn't do it. Albert was his boss in the House. Only later that night did he bang the gavel when it was time to adjourn the convention.

As Albert later told the story, "I had done what I thought was a favor when I handed him the gavel to preside briefly and ceremoniously over the delegates assembled in his hometown."[21] After the convention, however, Rostenkowski embellished the incident and his take-command authority, even reversing the outcome of LBJ's call, as he described it to colleagues and others. The peeved Albert heard Rostenkowski's version. "I had forgotten the whole incident by the time the story began to circulate that big Dan Rostenkowski had wrestled the gavel out of the hands of little Carl Albert because only big Dan Rostenkowski could bring order to that convention. If that were so, no one had told me about it at the time."[22] The truth is, only one man could have made Rostenkowski defy the next speaker of the House. According to Alderman Ed Burke, a longtime Rostenkowski pal, "Danny answered to a higher authority. He answered to Richard Daley, not to Carl Albert."

By itself the Albert-Rostenkowski incident was not important. Following a pressure-packed episode, politicians often have differing and self-serving memories. But it became an important piece of a larger tale in which Albert two years later delivered a crushing setback to Rostenkowski by triggering his removal from the House Democratic leadership ladder, and by sending a message that Daley's influence was far less welcome in Washington. As the story has evolved through the years, when Albert took over as speaker in January 1971, Rostenkowski still hoped for appointment as majority whip, the third-ranking Democratic position. Had he gained that post, he likely would have become majority leader and then speaker, quite possibly within the decade. Instead his bad-mouthing of Albert resulted in Rostenkowski's ouster from the top ranks, and shunted a once-promising career into the Ways and Means province. "Danny did not embarrass Mr. Albert at the Chicago convention, but he embarrassed Albert because of what he said after the convention, that he had to take the gavel because Carl couldn't manage the convention," said Jim Wright of Texas, an occasional ally of Rostenkowski. "That was an unnecessary and gratuitous insult."

The saga began in May 1970 when seventy-nine-year-old John McCormack announced his retirement. Many House Democrats greeted the news with relief, given their continuing division and need for revitalization following Richard Nixon's presidential victory in 1968. Largely unnoticed outside Capitol Hill, the slow unraveling of the old-style Democratic party with which Rostenkowski had been so comfortable had reached critical mass. "This was essentially an ideological and generational dispute over the seniority system, fought within the Democratic ranks and caused by a temporary mismatch between the party's senior leadership (overwhelmingly conservative and southern) and its rank and file (increasingly northern and liberal)," wrote congressional scholar Roger Davidson. "By the early 1970s, this internal contradiction had been resolved in favor of youth and liberalism."[23] Most of the key committee chairmen had been in the House since Franklin Roosevelt was president. These Mills-type pacifiers resisted challenges from junior members to take more confrontational stands against the Republican president. Despite his own limited skills, Albert was widely expected to become speaker without opposition. With most Democrats loyal to an orderly succession, he had secured support from most factions.

The battleground for the generational conflict would be the House Democrats' contest to select a successor to Albert as majority leader. Hale Boggs of Louisiana was the front-runner. A Democratic Caucus vote would determine the outcome. Although some liberals objected to placing Southerners in the top two Democratic posts and many had doubts about Boggs's excessive drinking and a recent FBI investigation into charges of his shady dealings with the contractor who had built the parking garage in the House's newest office building, his status as majority whip placed him next in line. If Boggs were chosen majority leader, Rostenkowski reasoned that he had a good chance to be appointed as whip: he was a Northerner, he was friendly with Boggs, and he had Ways and Means experience and credentials as caucus chairman.

To the cocky Rostenkowski, it apparently never occurred that he might encounter problems. Indeed, by machine rules his four years as caucus chairman *entitled* him to appointment as majority whip. "Rostenkowski feels strongly there exists a well of appreciation for the 'fairness' he displayed in presiding over numerous caucuses of House Democrats, especially in the South," wrote a Capitol Hill reporter.[24] He had been evenhanded with reformers who in 1970 had crafted a package of major changes in the House's internal procedures, Rostenkowski said. And by launching the Thursday morning whip meetings, he had expanded participation in leadership activities.

But not all Democrats were impressed with Rostenkowski or his claim as a reformer. "A lot of members did not have much of a relationship with him," said Tom Foley, an ally of the reformers. "Younger members felt he was distant, and they considered him kind of gruff, muscular in his personality, and there wasn't much to tie them to him." In short, by linking himself to the "old guard" when he joined the House, and by failing to extend his hand to many of his own contemporaries, Rostenkowski had failed to build important bridges. "He was not as natural a successor to a leadership position as was, for example, Tip O'Neill or Tom Foley," each of whom had reached out to many lawmakers, said John Brademas.

Oddly, Rostenkowski helped to prepare his own demise by seeking re-election as caucus chairman in January 1971, even though he planned to relinquish the position soon after winning an unprecedented third term. If he had stepped aside pending the caucus's selection of the top leaders, it would have been more difficult for Albert to refuse to appoint him as majority whip. But Rostenkowski wanted to retain the chairmanship so that, with Albert's permission, he could preside over the majority leader contest. "Danny always wanted to have a gavel in his hand," said Jim Healey, his chief Washington aide at the time. Rostenkowski also thought it made sense to retain the chairmanship as "insurance" in case he was not appointed majority whip.

Assured by all the majority leader contenders that they backed him as caucus chairman, Rostenkowski was oblivious to a possible challenge. But he carelessly ignored the first rule of politics: protect your base. (His error was similar to his father's ignoring the threat from Chicago's Polish community in the Democratic primary for alderman sixteen years earlier.) Inexplicably, Rostenkowski prevented the Illinois delegation from endorsing Albert's selection as speaker, even though most Democrats had voiced their fealty and it was apparent that the Oklahoman would have token opposition, if any. Rostenkowski later blamed Daley, saying the mayor objected to selecting a speaker from "such a small state." "The delegation wanted to endorse Albert in the summer of 1970," Rostenkowski said, "but the mayor said, 'not now.' " No doubt Daley had bad memories from the 1968 convention. But if he allowed the mayor's rancor to affect House politics, Rostenkowski deserved the comeuppance. Another factor that exacerbated his ill will with Albert was that two veteran House Democrats from Illinois, Frank Annunzio and Mel Price, were stirring the pot. "I didn't have friends in the Illinois delegation, because I was moving too fast," Rostenkowski said. "Frank and Mel poisoned Albert's mind." He harbored a glimmer of hope that lightning would strike and that Democrats would bypass Albert for speaker, perhaps in favor of Mills.

During the months before the selection of new leaders, Rostenkowski also kept alive the possibility that he might run for majority leader. "If Boggs' campaign had not begun to gain momentum, there is little doubt that Rostenkowski would have announced his candidacy," according to an authoritative account of the contest.[25] Chicago newspapers published reports of questionable veracity that he was seeking support for a leadership bid from conservative Southerners and from machine Democrats who wanted a "strong man" to enforce party discipline.[26] "If the election were held this week, it is popularly conceded that Rostenkowski would get more votes than any other candidate and would probably win a majority on a second or third ballot," claimed one newspaper, presumably based on information spoon-fed by Rostenkowski or his allies.[27] But it soon became apparent even to the ambitious Rostenkowski that he lacked sufficient support for a credible bid.

Still, when Rostenkowski acknowledged two days before Christmas that he would not enter the contest, there seemed little reason to dispute the subsequent news story that "he is likely to be reelected by acclamation if he wants the [caucus chairman] job again."[28] After all, selecting the chairman was not a major issue for most House Democrats. For Rostenkowski, however, the unthinkable was about to happen. When the twenty-member Texas Democratic delegation—thirsting to regain a Democratic leadership seat—met on the eve of the new Congress, they endorsed sixty-year-old Olin "Tiger" Teague, one of their own, to run for caucus chairman. Although the Teague campaign was not well organized, supporters knew that the highly decorated World War II army colonel and

Veterans' Affairs Committee chairman was respected by many colleagues. One of the Texans said, "Danny had served his time," Wright recounted. "Someone said, why don't we nominate one of our guys. Tiger Teague was not at the meeting. Omar Burleson said, 'How about Tiger?'" So Teague was nominated to run against Rostenkowski. As the story goes, Teague was so nonchalant about the episode that he waved his ballot during the voting to show that he had voted for Rostenkowski, assuming he had no chance to win himself.

Astonishingly, Teague won easily, 155 to 91. The reason, said Wright, was simple: "Tiger won because he was more popular than Danny." John Culver of Iowa voiced a similar reaction to the outcome: "Personal popularity transcends ideology in leadership contests. . . . Rosty wasn't that popular. He was Daley's boy and a golden boy. But he didn't have the stature that Daley thought." The contest gave rank-and-file Democrats an opportunity to vent their displeasure over Daley's handling of the Chicago convention. They also wanted to reduce the mayor's influence on Capitol Hill. "There are just an awful lot of anti-Daley Democrats around here," Frank Thompson, a New Jersey liberal, said after the vote.[29] Although he never confirmed his involvement in the caucus vote, Albert bolstered the case that he encouraged the Texans to support Teague, a native Oklahoman. "I was not surprised at all" with the result, Albert wrote with apparent understatement in his autobiography. Most Democrats, he added, supported "a man with enough brains to climb on board a bandwagon while it was roaring out of the station."[30] In hindsight there was another clue that Albert was familiar with the move to oust Rostenkowski. On the night before the caucus vote, an assistant to the parliamentarian—who reported to Democratic leaders—telephoned Rostenkowski and asked whether he was "sure he wanted to run" for reelection as caucus chairman, according to John Salmon, a long-time Rostenkowski aide. "Rostenkowski did not think much of it at the time. The next day it became clear that this was a little tit-for-tat by Albert."

The shattering defeat was one of the lowest points of Rostenkowski's political career. "I sat alone that night with Danny, in tears, and Hale in Hale's office," said Gary Hymel, chief aide to Boggs. As Jim Wright recalled, "Danny said to me afterward, 'Why didn't you tell me and I wouldn't have run?' He said now he was in trouble with Mayor Daley." Not only would Rostenkowski have to explain to an irate Daley how he could have so badly mishandled the vote, but his hopes for winning appointment as whip were now practically nil. As it turned out, Boggs prevailed on the second ballot over runner-up Morris Udall in the five-candidate contest for majority leader, and he kept his promise to request that Albert appoint Rostenkowski as whip—in return for Rostenkowski delivering a sizable number of votes to Boggs in his contest. "Hale wanted Danny as whip," Hymel said. "They matched each other. Both were big-city, ethnic types who believed in organization politics. Each was on Ways and Means; they had a sense of humor and liked to socialize, and both came from humble conditions—although Hale later became haughty." Boggs kept their agreement secret for several reasons: public knowledge would inhibit his ability to win support from other Democrats who wanted the appointment as whip; Rostenkowski sought to preserve the impression of impartiality while preparing for the majority leader contest; and talk of a deal could encourage opponents to criticize "crass, political manipulation."[31]

In the deal between two friends, Rostenkowski fulfilled his end of the bargain more than did Boggs. Some Rostenkowski friends grumbled that Boggs made little more than a perfunctory request. "Hale told me he tried to change Albert's mind, but he wasn't going to throw a tantrum," Hymel said. In any case, Albert almost surely had decided to pass over Rostenkowski. "On the morning after he was chosen majority leader, Hale said that Albert was unalterably opposed," recounted Healey, Rostenkowski's chief aide. Albert gave Boggs a choice of five other names for whip; from that list he chose Tip O'Neill.[32] Before deciding to accept the position, O'Neill gave his friend Rostenkowski the courtesy of informing him of Albert's offer. But that was little consolation. O'Neill had leapfrogged Rostenkowski into the House hierarchy. "Danny was devastated because he assumed he was going to get it," Healey said. "He went through two very tough years after 1970 because he was so disappointed. It was a real low period."

For the crestfallen Rostenkowski, the defeat had a salutary effect. It liberated him from the House Democrats' established order. He was now free to test the political waters. In doing so he joined the shift in Congress from bloc voting to free agency. One early result was his decision to break from party dogma—and even from his district's wishes—on the Vietnam War. The opposition of many young people, including aides on his own Washington staff, focused his attention on the intensifying polarization between generations, Rostenkowski said. By talking with them, "I have come to change my beliefs on the wisdom of our commitment to South Vietnam," he told the graduating class of Chicago's Gordon Technical High School on April 16, 1971. He joined the growing ranks of House members—though still a minority—who sought to legislate a deadline on U.S. participation in the war. "It was a coming of age and showing some independence from the Democratic organization," said John Salmon, the Rostenkowski aide who had graduated in 1970 from Georgetown University. "I would argue with him at night that if he couldn't explain to me why we were sending troops to Vietnam, he should rethink his position." The fact that many conservative Democrats had voted for Teague gave Rostenkowski another excuse to thumb his nose at them. (Still, Rostenkowski during his career usually supported his commander-in-chief, no matter who held the White House. In early 1991 he was among the minority of House Democrats who backed President Bush on the resolution authorizing U.S. military action in the Persian Gulf. "But if Congress must make the decision on whether armed combat is an appropriate action, let me caution my colleagues that we cannot and should not attempt to decide how war should be fought," he told the House.)

The victory by Boggs surprised many Democrats who were expecting that a more junior liberal would win the contest for majority leader. But its significance was mostly as a transition. Boggs, a Rayburn protégé, was moderate on racial issues for a member from the Deep South. He also was renowned for hosting lavish parties at his spacious home in suburban Bethesda. As the years passed, however, Boggs chafed at playing second fiddle, both on Ways and Means and in the Democratic leadership. He became emotionally unstable, according to several members and reporters who dealt with him at the time. "Boggs was nutty because of drugs and drink," said Neil MacNeil of *Time*, who had been a friend. "He claimed the FBI was bugging his office. He was so flaky, I was startled that he won the majority leader race." The curious Boggs saga took a fateful turn in October 1972 when he campaigned for freshman Rep. Nick Begich of Alaska. On a private flight to a remote region of Alaska, the airplane went down; Boggs and Begich were never found. Brademas voiced a peculiar but surprisingly common reaction when he said that the tragic death was "merciful," given Boggs's personal problems. If it had not been the airplane crash, he added, "there would have been another mishap." With Boggs gone, Democrats chose Tip O'Neill without opposition as their new majority leader. Within months he overshadowed Albert as the party's chief strategist. Rostenkowski knew, of course, that fate could have swung in his favor had he not alienated Albert.

As the years passed, the old order faced other threats. Rostenkowski's willingness to challenge LBJ—and Wilbur Mills—on major fiscal policy and to embrace the anti-war cause showed the erosion of party discipline. Riots in the streets and undeclared wars that generated years of domestic protest—plus broad public awareness of such events—inevitably led to a breakdown of politics-as-usual. The reform movement in the House grew from "the desire to spread the power around," said Tom Foley. Insurgent forces were gaining added strength to challenge Ways and Means. Fueled by the Vietnam War's unraveling of Democratic cohesion and by public divisions over the merits of the Great Society, House reformers targeted the committee as an antiquated bastion that frustrated party goals. They centered on three major projects: (1) the effort spearheaded by the Democratic Study Group to weaken unaccountable House figures who also were frustrating liberal legislation; (2) a bipartisan attempt to reorganize the House's complex committee rules for dividing jurisdiction; and (3) awakened by the tax surcharge turmoil in 1967–1968 and fueled by President Nixon's 1973 spending impoundments that rebuffed Congress, a House-Senate move to strengthen legislative authority over budget procedures and to impose more discipline. In each case, Ways and Means was a leading target.

Each of these projects received major inspiration from Richard Bolling, the Missouri Democrat who had been a Rayburn ally but had lost influence in the 1960s after he wrote two caustic books about the need to reform the House and the Democratic party. Bolling probably did more to shape the House as an institution than did any other member in the last half of the twentieth century. "The greatest member of the House in modern history who never became speaker," said Democratic Rep. David Obey, who later picked up the reformers' torch. By the 1970s Bolling's critiques had unleashed major pressures to make the House more responsive to demands for party cohesion and agenda-setting. "Dick Bolling thought that Ways and Means had too much power, and he was a very dominant figure at the time," Rostenkowski later said, with an air of resignation. As the appeal of the New Frontier and the Great Society gained strength among national Democrats, liberals gained numbers, experience, and influence in the House. But Southerners and machine Democrats did not go gently.

Rostenkowski loathed Bolling as a pompous intellectual who sneered at Ways and Means and its consensus-building. Their animosity was personal and long-standing. "Bolling hated Mills and the Ways and Means Committee because we had too much power," Rostenkowski said. In large measure, the conflict dealt with style more than substance—chiefly Bolling's resentment that most Ways and Means Democrats placed a lower priority on Democrats' partisan needs than on accommodating special-interest pleaders. Rostenkowski was hardly the only member who clashed with the often supercilious Bolling, who was quick to remind colleagues of both his intelligence and his close relationship to Rayburn. Even Brademas, who described Bolling as a mentor, said, "There was an Olympian attitude that was off-putting." But by 1973, after McGovern's landslide defeat by Nixon, and with exhaustion setting in among the antiwar crowd, Albert recognized the need for assistance and called on Bolling for important assignments.

During the early 1970s there were few outward signs that Wilbur Mills's grip was slipping or that he was concerned about the threat. He worked closely with Treasury officials in President Nixon's first term to win enactment of two major bills: the 1969 Tax Reform Act (a measure that was filled with technical changes but also included modest tax cuts for both individuals and businesses) and the 1971 Tax Reduction Act (which was largely a response to Nixon's call for wage-and-price controls to combat rising inflation). For those who were watching closely, however, pressure for internal changes was mounting. After lengthy debate, Congress passed the 1970 Legislative Reorganization Act, which sought to impose discipline on committee chairmen. It included a requirement to make public all recorded committee votes plus a provision to permit a majority of the committee—not simply the chairman—to convene a meeting. That law also encouraged, but did not require, that all committee meetings be held in open session. This small step led to greater strides toward party accountability, as Bolling had advocated in his reform critiques. In 1971 the Democratic Caucus changed its rules so that seniority was no longer mandatory in the selection of committee chairmen. That year Democrats also agreed to permit a vote to approve any committee chairman; two years later that provision was made mandatory, including the option of a secret ballot. The caucus also approved a "subcommittee bill of rights," which gave subcommittee chairmen control over their ju-

risdictions and calendar of activities, plus greater authority to hire and supervise their staffs.

At Ways and Means, however, Mills taunted the reformers by refusing
to create subcommittees or to respond to liberal views. The Democratic
Caucus responded with a new rule, directed at his committee, to encourage additional House debate: if fifty Democrats wished to offer an amendment on the House floor, the caucus could decide whether to instruct the
Rules Committee to permit debate and a vote on such an amendment. In
May 1974 Mills objected in vain when the caucus voted to permit House
votes on two amendments directed at the oil industry; each was sponsored
by a liberal Democrat on Ways and Means. Mills was suddenly in the unaccustomed position of coping with challenges from junior members of
his committee and from House leaders. It got worse. The caucus in 1973
had approved another rules change that required committees to conduct
their meetings in open session unless its members voted to close the
doors. Although Ways and Means members in the next two years continued to make their key decisions mostly in private, the pressure to work in
the sunshine had the unintended consequence of increasing lobbyists' access to the panel's deliberations. Open meetings, several members said,
altered the atmosphere just enough to create problems.

Probably the most serious peril to Ways and Means came from the bipartisan Select Committee on Committees, which promoted changes to
rationalize committee jurisdictions and more evenly apportion the
House's workload. Chaired by Bolling, the panel launched a direct assault
on the archaic structure and on chairmen who continued to use their powers to thumb their noses at their party and its embrace of LBJ's Great Society. The select committee's chief target was clear from the start. In July
1973 Bolling said that the domain of Ways and Means was "so vast that it
can't possibly be handled by a committee that doesn't have subcommittees."[33] Bolling's panel called for a major cutback of Ways and Means influence, including a loss of most health and foreign-trade issues. As it
turned out, the Select Committee prompted a revolt among House power
brokers because its recommendations would have disrupted other committees as well. Many insiders, including Rostenkowski, worked in the
Democratic Caucus to prepare a modest alternative that left Ways and
Means jurisdiction mostly intact. After lengthy skirmishing, which featured little public airing of the Ways and Means controversy, the House in

October 1974 approved the narrow Democratic Caucus alternative. Bolling and the reformers would gain their revenge, however, less than two months later.

The attack on Ways and Means was abetted by Mills's behavior. The once-omnipotent chairman was behaving erratically, both personally and in his legislative work. Much like Boggs, he showed signs of succumbing to what had become the House's drug- and alcohol-laden culture. In public settings he was able to preserve his aura of invincibility; privately, however, many colleagues worried when they saw the impact of medication he was taking for chronic back ailments. "He clearly was having trouble with his back and taking painkillers, conventional and unconventional, and I think he finally underwent some kind of temporary personality alteration," wrote Barber Conable, a Republican on Ways and Means.[34] Years later Mills acknowledged that he had begun to drink heavily in 1969—in part to ease his back pain—and his judgment became impaired. "Toward the end, I do not even remember one meeting I had with President Ford at the White House," he said.[35] In 1972 he ran a half-hearted and hopeless campaign for the Democratic presidential nomination, in which he sought to focus public attention on tax and health-care issues facing Ways and Means. "The fact that the wise and realistic Mills now seeks the presidency against impossibly long odds evokes astonishment on Capitol Hill," columnists Rowland Evans and Robert Novak wrote.[36] Also that year he sponsored and secured passage of a 10 percent benefit increase for Social Security recipients, a budget-buster that would soon require a major payroll tax hike to assure the system's solvency. He suffered his final and devastating collapse in late 1974, a fling with a burlesque dancer known on stage as Fanne Foxe; within weeks he careened with her from a midnight automobile escapade through Washington's Tidal Basin to an onstage appearance at a seedy strip joint in Boston. It resulted in Mills's hospitalization and gave critics of Ways and Means their opening. Within weeks many of the old traditions at Ways and Means were tossed onto the trash heap of history.

Whether a physically fit Mills could have resisted the challenges to his committee remains an intriguing question. He built consensus conservatively, keeping a disproportionate share of Southern and moderate-to-conservative Democrats as committee members even as the ideology of most Democrats moved to the left. Wrote one scholar, "By the mid-1970s, the political climate in the House was such that Mills's centralized, consensus-oriented leadership regime and the committee's autonomy and extensive authority would likely have come under attack even if the Arkansas Democrat had spent all of his evenings in 1974 home studying the tax code."[37] But could a handful of skillful politicians have kept the two parties, including the young ideologues, working together? A quarter-century later, amid more polarization and much less public happiness with governance, the old-style Ways and Means Committee evokes fond nostalgia.

Rostenkowski learned a lot from Mills about legislative leadership. He drew from those lessons to shape his view of Ways and Means as a blue-ribbon committee that made tough decisions and usually prevailed. But his assessment is not wholly rapturous. "I loved Wilbur Mills," he said. "But I thought his reputation was overrated. He was a technician. He didn't have the talent opposing him on the committee that I had constantly. . . . There were not as many lobbyists or reporters." The tight control exercised by Mills ultimately sowed the seeds for vast changes, including diminished influence, for Ways and Means. For Rostenkowski, a familiar leadership model had been destroyed. But as he moved up the committee's ranks, new opportunity soon would beckon.

Chapter Four

THE NEW BREED AND THE LIMITS OF REFORM

THE 1974 ELECTIONS, by sending seventy-five fresh-faced and assertive Democrats to the House, were the turning point for the majority party. The arrival of the "new breed" launched the second half of the Democrats' forty-year control. But the midpoint of their era proved to be far more than a historical marker. The entire tone of the institution changed. The old House in which party loyalists or often obscure hacks came to Capitol Hill and bided their time for many years until they could exercise real power—the House in which Dan Rostenkowski had been so comfortable—suddenly became a distant memory, though it had not entirely disappeared. "The authority no longer rests solely with the speaker or even with the committee chairmen," Rostenkowski said at the time. "It is now more widely dispersed throughout the House."[1]

Nurtured by a decade of growing public cynicism toward government, the freshmen brought a new spirit to the House. Spurred by the double-barreled wound that Republicans suffered in the 1974 election because of that year's recession—unemployment, at 6.5 percent, was the highest since 1961—and public outrage after President Gerald Ford in September granted a pardon to Richard Nixon for his Watergate-era crimes, they comprised the largest freshman class in a quarter-century. They featured an impatience bordering on irreverence, scorn for the House's traditions and precedents, and an eagerness to open government's back rooms to public view. In the preceding 20 years freshmen usually were seen and not heard when the House debated legislation or held hearings. Now the new members flaunted their attacks on apprenticeship and reveled in their disdain for seniority. They even created their own autonomous freshman-class organization within the Democratic Caucus. To retain their authority, once-imperious committee chairmen would have to pay homage to the most junior Democrat. Reluctant or unable to reach out, they failed. In an outlandish turn of the tables, the caucus in January 1975 ousted three veteran House barons: Edward Hebert of Louisiana at Armed Services, Wright Patman of Texas at Banking, and Bob Poage of Texas at the Agriculture Committee. (On December 3, under pressure, the ailing and humiliated Wilbur Mills had announced that he would surrender his Ways and Means chairmanship when the new Congress convened.) Granted, each of the four chairmen was from the South. And they were very senior: the four had served in the House a total of 154 years, including 41 years in their chairmanships, and their average age was 74. But the rebellion was not simply a purging of mossback conservatives. The 81-year-old Patman, for example, had been an ardent populist renowned for his attacks on Wall Street and on the Federal Reserve Board's high interest rates; he was ousted because many rank-and-file lawmakers complained that the autocratic chairman balked at spreading responsibilities among committee members.

The Democratic newcomers contrasted sharply with the large classes elected in 1958 and 1964, many of whom lost reelection after one term in which they did little more than provide dependable votes for the large House majority. Rather than fall into lockstep with a House that was hostile to internal reform, many freshmen elected in 1974 claimed a mandate to restore public confidence in government and to change how Washington worked. By background they were very different from young Dan Rostenkowski, the local politician, or John Culver and Tom Foley, the former congressional aides. Instead the activist freshmen featured Bob Edgar of Pennsylvania, who had been a Protestant chaplain; Toby Moffett of Connecticut, a Ralph Nader activist; Phil Sharp of Indiana, a political science professor; and Tim Wirth of Colorado, an environmentalist and policy guru. Some called them quiche-and-salad Democrats, with blow-dried hair, in expensive tailored suits. They viewed Rostenkowski and his pals as relics from the 1950s, akin to the fins on a Cadillac. Rostenkowski still ate steak and drank gin in noisy restaurants; his penchant for rubbing broad shoulders on the golf course and his frosty demeanor left a big chill with the new breed. Certainly the new freshman class had the usual panoply of members with a personal or family background as legislators. But even those—such as Christopher Dodd of Connecticut, Stephen Solarz of New York, and Henry Waxman of California—were less likely to be respectful, standpat politicians. Born in anti-war activism, they were in a hurry to make an impact. For Rostenkowski, an amicable newcomer was Marty Russo, a tough thirty-year-old Italian kid from Chicago's southern suburbs who would soon become an important ally. But also from Illinois were do-good reformers Paul Simon from downstate and Abner Mikva, who was first elected to the House in 1968 by defeating an eighty-six-year-old Daley-backed incumbent but later was redistricted by the machine out of that south side seat, forcing his move to the northern suburbs.

Suddenly the House was energized to challenge the old ways of doing business and to increase congressional influence vis-à-vis the White House. During the first half of their era of House control, Democrats agreed that the president, regardless of his party, should initiate governmental activism. But in the wake of their widely praised impeachment inquiry, when the House led the nation through the crisis that ended with Nixon's resignation in disgrace, the lawmakers now believed they could seize the initiative in reshaping national policy. The impeachment episode raised the public's consciousness of the long-ignored House and increased the members' self-confidence. They no longer would be content with tinkering at the margin on policy or exchanging legislative pork and other favors. (Nixon's impeachment was yet another example of the vast gulf between Rostenkowski and the junior Democrats. Although it received little publicity at the time, he reportedly joined a bipartisan group of House members who explored a plan to give Nixon immunity from prosecution for Watergate crimes. But he dropped the effort, he told a reporter at the time, because "lots of people agree with me that we don't want to see a President of the United States go to the penitentiary, but nobody wants to put his name on a piece of legislation."[2] Ironically, according to the news report, House Republican leader John Rhodes objected to the immunity deal, asserting that "no man is above the law." A month later President Ford created a firestorm when he pardoned Nixon from his crimes.)

The "Watergate babies" provided the numbers and the energy to finish transforming the House. When the Democratic Caucus met in December

1974 to prepare for the 94th Congress, the reformers ratified long-sought objectives such as a separate secret ballot to approve each of the twenty committee chairman and each chairman of the thirteen Appropriations subcommittees, plus steps to assure that junior members would receive choice committee assignments. In truth, some veteran reformers resented the brash new crowd and the news media's implications that the Reform Era had begun in November 1974, not years earlier. As in any institution, however, the former neophytes gained a sense of entitlement as they learned the ropes and began to shape the place in their own image. Years later, survivors of the Class of 1974 would face comparable tensions with other freshmen classes. Meanwhile, the Watergate babies and the House Democratic establishment would have to learn to get along with each other. This time they didn't have Sam Rayburn, let alone Lyndon Johnson, to help them.

In this brave new world, Dan Rostenkowski's relentless return to influence might at first seem puzzling. He had hitched his wagon to the fading bulls of what turned out to be a bygone era. His sanctuary in the House's old elite had crumbled—though, in truth, he had not been much of a player since Carl Albert's assumption of the speakership four years earlier. He had little interest in the rambunctious newcomers or their grandiose blueprints for what ailed the House and the nation. So why did he soon find himself with more power than he had ever held before? For one thing—despite the reformers' intentions—seniority, savvy, and stubbornness still mattered. As a senior Democratic lawmaker, Rostenkowski wasn't shy about flexing his clout, especially after the 1976 election of Jimmy Carter as president gave Democrats an opportunity to enact serious legislation. Another big opening came with Tip O'Neill's takeover as speaker and Rostenkowski's adept efforts in the battle royale to choose the new majority leader. Even the abandonment of his delusion that he could return to Chicago as mayor had positive career implications because it ensured that his future lay in Washington. In a House where apprenticeship was no longer a hallowed value, upstarts such as David Obey and Dick Gephardt made lots of noise. But by making modest stylistic accommodations, old-timer Rostenkowski decided that he could show them a trick or two. Most important for Rostenkowski, the revolt in the Democratic Caucus gave him what sometimes doesn't come in life: a second chance. This machine pol didn't muff it.

At Ways and Means, which had survived as a refuge for the traditionalists, Rostenkowski faced a turnabout that was more sweeping than any-where else in the House. Consider how much change took place so quickly at the panel whose members had long prided themselves on their stability. For decades they had conducted their business quietly, colle-gially, and usually without the harsh partisanship that was now pervading the House. Suddenly all of that was smashed. First, Mills was replaced as chairman by Al Ullman of Oregon, who had been widely regarded as an amiable but obscure and ineffectual member whose conservative views were out of step with most Democrats. "Ullman didn't have the ability of a Mills or Rostenkowski to get legislation through," said James Corman of California, a key Ways and Means Democrat during the 1970s. "I don't know if he wanted to do much."

Second, to assure that the committee would be more responsive to the Democratic Caucus, the reformers expanded its size from the clubby 25 members—which it had been since 1919—to a less manageable corps of 37 members. With the Democrats' gain to 291 House seats in the 1974 election, that meant an increase from 15 to 25 Democrats at Ways and Means. Of the 12 new Democrats chosen for the committee, 4 were first- or second-termers, and 2 others had just returned to the House after they had lost reelection in 1972. Such an influx of inexperienced and elec-torally vulnerable members previously would have been unthinkable; Mills and the House barons had insisted that Ways and Means members be reliable legislators and politically secure at home. Their backgrounds too changed considerably from the old days. The 12 newcomers included only 3 Southerners—two liberals and a former leading White House aide to Lyndon Johnson; from the North, Daley-nemesis Mikva of Illinois and Otis Pike, a maverick from Long Island, were very different from the ma-chine Democrats who once were recruited for the committee.

Third, the Democratic Caucus stripped Ways and Means Democrats of their authority as the "committee on committees," which had allowed them to designate committee assignments for all Democrats. That power—a favorite of Rostenkowski's—had given Ways and Means mem-bers major leverage. Now the leadership-dominated Steering and Policy Committee gained the authority to appoint all Democrats to committees.

Fourth, a new House rule required each legislative committee to es-tablish at least four subcommittees; that requirement was aimed directly at Ways and Means, where Mills had defiantly resisted decentralization of power.

Finally, without public fanfare or understanding by most members, the Congressional Budget Act of 1974 took full effect the following year. Among other things, the new law created a competing center—the Budget Committee—to shape fiscal policy. It set limits on the Ways and Means Committee's authority to initiate tax or spending legislation that did not comply with the annual budget already approved by Congress. Ironically these changes and others all came only a few months after Ways and Means Democrats had breathed a sigh of relief that they had survived the assault on their clout by Richard Bolling's proposed committee reforms. Now the Mills Era was truly dead.

Many new members who arrived in the House in the 1970s had gained their political education from the reform proposals Bolling had pushed. But in Rostenkowski's view, the Democratic reformers and their changes went too far in weakening the House's committee system. "Rostenkowski was distressed that the old ways were gone and he was sure enough that the new way was wrong," said John Sherman, a former magazine reporter and veteran congressional aide who in 1981 became his press secretary. Although the reformers who took over the Democratic Caucus did little to revive Bolling's abortive 1974 plans to overhaul the House's committee system, he lived to see Democrats embrace many of his new-age ideas. "He had the perspective and the ability to take the big view," said Dick Gephardt, whom fellow Missourian Bolling quickly identified and promoted as a rising star after Gephardt was first elected in 1976. "He could relate the present legislative situation to the needs of the party and could get members to pull back from their infighting."

Rostenkowski, whose more instinctive legislative style contrasted with Bolling's cerebral approach, never reconciled himself to the changes. The mere mention of Bolling's name would often launch him into a tirade. He opposed Bolling's changes not only procedurally, as an unwarranted attack on the Ways and Means Committee, but also politically, as an attempt to transfer more control to liberal Democrats.

Under its new activist chairman Philip Burton of California, the reinvigorated Democratic Caucus moved quickly in 1975 to encourage passage of the liberals' legislative agenda. High on the list, not surprisingly, was a cutoff of all U.S. military aid to South Vietnam and Cambodia. That won House approval in March, just as those two governments were on the verge of collapse. Another issue was the liberals' long-standing demand to repeal the energy industry's oil-depletion allowance, which Ways and

Means had long protected. Although Rostenkowski voted with most Democrats for this tax change, he was uncomfortable with what he viewed as the legislative chicanery by which it won approval on the House floor and with the young turks' Establishment-rattling cries. Nor was he alone. Old-style Democrats soon rebelled, and King Caucus faded. "Traditionalists hated Burton's aggressive leadership," wrote his biographer. "It was one thing to make chairmen accountable or spread power among younger subcommittee chairs. It was quite another to bypass the committee system entirely and use the Caucus to make policy."[3]

But the reforms had a classic unintended effect for Rostenkowski. For the first time in his sixteen years in the House he would chair a subcommittee, permitting him to set his own agenda and to move legislation at Ways and Means. As the committee's new No. 3 Democrat—behind Ullman and Jim Burke of Massachusetts, a Rostenkowski pal of limited skills but a staunch ally of organized labor who opted to chair the Social Security Subcommittee—Rostenkowski in 1975 faced a choice of chairing either the Health Subcommittee or the Trade Subcommittee. Although it received little attention at the time, his decision was a revealing sign that he intended to become a more active player in the new House. To chair the Trade subcommittee, as some friends advised Rostenkowski, would have played well in Chicago's expanding business community and with the state's industrial and agricultural sectors, which increasingly depended on overseas commercial dealings. With enactment the previous year of legislation overhauling the nation's international trade laws for the first time in decades, however, trade would move to the back burner on Capitol Hill for the next few years. Health-care issues, on the other hand, were emerging as a prime focus of discussion, especially among activist Democrats and their liberal allies who eagerly sought a national health-care system for all Americans. With the growing scale and complexity of medical issues, Congress was becoming more involved in writing the rules for the high-finance world of hospitals, doctors, and other parts of the health-care system.

By choosing the Health Subcommittee, Rostenkowski found himself in the center of swirling legislative conflicts—chiefly the Kennedy-Corman plan for national health-insurance coverage, which was backed by organized labor. As a moderate Democrat who had helped to enact Medicare in the 1960s, he was open-minded about further expansion of the federal government's health-care role. But he moved more cautiously

on those issues than many Democrats wished during his four years as subcommittee chairman. For many reasons, some of them related to his opposition to federal regulation of local hospitals and to his affinity for other
influential health-care interests, such as the American Medical Association based in Chicago, Rostenkowski resisted vast changes. By tempera-
ment, as well, he was not the type of legislator who took the lead in
advocating major federal programs. Even after he gave up the Health
Subcommittee chairmanship in 1979 and focused more broadly on tax
and other spending issues, however, health-care would remain one of his
inescapable preoccupations. In later years, despite his reservations about
increasing the role of government, he often was more inclined to support
sweeping changes in health care than were other prominent Democrats.

Suddenly Rostenkowski had gone national. To lead the subcommittee
he had to shift his attention from chiefly Chicago-based problems. Although he long had shown interest and skill in the House's internal machi-
nations, he needed to concentrate more than ever on legislative details.
Like others on Ways and Means, Rostenkowski could no longer rely on
Mills to make legislative decisions and to assure that the committee had
sufficient support in the House. When Rostenkowski tapped John Salmon
to handle the subcommittee's staff work, the cocky aide—who had joined
Rostenkowski's staff five years earlier—bluntly told him, "I'll go to work
if you go to work." The new subcommittee chairman, despite some lack
of confidence that he could master the complex policy problems, took up
the challenge. He did not want to be embarrassed. "This was the first time
Rostenkowski really worked," recounted Salmon. "At first he was gun-
shy because he didn't know the issues. But once he was well briefed, he
saw that he could be a player." As became the trend across Capitol Hill,
the added staff at the post-Mills Ways and Means Committee meant that
members faced less of a burden to resolve the policy issues among themselves. Salmon and other aides claimed that they gradually brought Rostenkowski into the twentieth century as a legislator. Typically they were
more knowledgeable about the intricacies of policy issues; but they often
suffered from political naiveté or a failure to relate to constituents on their
bosses' home turfs.

Rostenkowski now worked more closely with the House's eager junior lawmakers. The rules, however, had changed. Unlike Mayor Richard
J. Daley or Sheriff Tom O'Brien, to whom he had dutifully reported when
he was first elected, Rostenkowski could not simply expect or demand

loyalty. He had to respond nimbly and often reluctantly to the new forces taking shape among Democrats and across the nation: open government, a decline in the deference to the presidency, and increased partisan divisions. As the years passed, he slowly joined the crowd and grew more supportive of an expansive role for the federal government. Jack Lew, a longtime Tip O'Neill aide who dealt closely with the Ways and Means Committee and later became Office of Management and Budget director under President Clinton, explained, "As Rostenkowski grew to care about broader issues, he and the newer generation of Members ended up in the same place—working to create a better economy and standard of living." In the legislative world, after all, all that really matters is the votes. "Everything else is just bullshit," in the memorable words of Frank Annunzio, another Chicago machine Democrat who had limited legislative abilities but a streetwise approach.

A defining moment in the struggle among House Democrats followed the 1976 election when they selected a new Majority Leader. Tip O'Neill ran unopposed in the caucus to replace the ill-fated Carl Albert, who retired that year as speaker, ill-equipped to cope with the House's generational tremors. But the unity for O'Neill could not mask the turmoil within the party. Many factors—geography, seniority, and personal relationships, among others—came into play in the battle to replace him as majority leader in the No. 2 Democratic post. The jockeying was hard fought. In the end the old-style Democrats narrowly won. Rostenkowski played an active role in the internal maneuvers and found himself in the good graces of the winner.

Choosing a horse in the contest might have seemed obvious for Rostenkowski, at least in retrospect. Jim Wright of Texas was running against Bolling and Burton. (John McFall of California, the majority whip for the previous four years, also sought the position; but his distant fourth-place finish on the first ballot eliminated him from the contest, in which the candidate with the least support on each vote was dropped until someone won a majority.) Wright had been the most conservative of the three in his policy views. And Rostenkowski had been comfortable with Wright's style of coalition-building, both within his own party and with the Republicans. As a senior member of the Public Works Committee, who was in line to take over its chairmanship in 1977, Wright had been helpful on projects that sent vital federal dollars to Chicago. On the other hand, said fellow Ways and Means member Jake Pickle of Texas, Rostenkowski had "some reservations" about Wright. In part he harbored grudges against the Texas delegation for his unexpected loss of the Democratic Caucus chairmanship to Tiger Teague in 1971. Deep in his heart, Rostenkowski still believed that he, instead of O'Neill, could have been ruling the roost. And despite their intramural differences, Rostenkowski and Burton got along personally as two burly, urban politicians who were eager deal-cutters; even though they were adversaries, the two talked regularly during the lengthy campaign—"going over names and discussing vote counts," said Jim Healey, Rostenkowski's aide.

Wright formally entered the contest in July 1976, after Bolling and Burton each had been campaigning for months. After months of quiet maneuvering, Wright stepped forward because, he later said, "I was aware of bad blood between Burton and Bolling and I felt that I could get the supporters of either" in a final showdown. Even at that point, significant numbers of Democrats had not committed to either front-runner. Once Wright became a candidate, his success in winning Rostenkowski's quick support was vital. An important element in that decision was the tacit signals that O'Neill and Leo Diehl, O'Neill's chief aide, sent to Rostenkowski; as the presumptive speaker, O'Neill welcomed Wright's candidacy, if only as a step to curb the crafty Burton, whom he disliked and distrusted. Rostenkowski also correctly concluded that a Wright victory likely would open the door for him to regain a leadership position. He sensed that a Burton victory would be a final blow to the old elite; under those circumstances, Rostenkowski understood that he was highly unlikely to have sufficient connections to be rewarded.

As it turned out, Rostenkowski assisted Wright at three critical points during his campaign. Early on he invited Wright to a breakfast meeting with Mayor Daley in Chicago. "We met in a little room at a downtown hotel," Wright said. "The mayor said he was for me and said he would call some other mayors." According to several accounts of the contest, Daley's endorsement proved crucial when some of those big-city mayors urged their local House members to back Wright. Among them was New York Mayor Abe Beame, whose support came after Daley "reminded him that Wright had rounded up the votes to prevent New York from going bankrupt."[4] (During a financial crisis in the mid-1970s, the city pleaded to Washington for loans to bail itself out; despite widespread resentment of the haughty New Yorkers, Congress and President Ford reluctantly went along.)

A second key move was Rostenkowski's secret deal with Burton to switch some Burton supporters to Wright on the second ballot so that Bolling would finish at the bottom in the three-man contest; both the Burton and Wright camps feared that the more centrist Bolling would pick up enough extra votes to prevail against either of them in a two-man contest on the final ballot. The move was especially calculating for Burton because he held a significant lead after the first ballot, and Wright had trailed Bolling by 4 votes for the second spot. "Burton and I conspired to defeat Bolling on the second ballot," said Rostenkowski. The ploy worked, but just barely. On that second ballot Burton had 107 votes, Wright had 95, and Bolling was forced out after he won only 93.

As they were lining up to submit the third ballot, Rostenkowski saw that his friend Thomas Ashley of Ohio had written Burton's name on his paper. When Rostenkowski urged him to support Wright, Ashley responded that the Texan had no chance of winning. But Rostenkowski told Ashley that he was wrong and urged him to make the switch. "Wright doesn't have a chance," Ashley shrugged, "but if you want me to vote for him, I will."[5] Ashley crossed out Burton's name and wrote Wright's instead. The final count was 148 for Wright to 147 for Burton. With such a razor-thin result, of course, any number of last-minute actions could have been crucial and several were. But Rostenkowski won his just reward. With O'Neill's support, Wright named him the Democrats' chief deputy whip. O'Neill had earlier made a commitment to give the whip position to John Brademas of Indiana, Rostenkowski's freshman classmate, whose more liberal voting record and cerebral style provided a better balance to Wright. Nonetheless Rostenkowski's rehabilitation was on course in the post-Albert era.

While House Democrats were selecting their new leaders, Rostenkowski unexpectedly confronted a major decision at home. On December 20, 1976, the seventy-four-year-old Richard Daley died of a massive heart attack. After more than twenty-one years of following the dictates of their legendary mayor, for better and worse, Chicago and its Democratic lieutenants were forced to choose someone to serve in the unenviable role as his successor. For Rostenkowski, the loss was like the death of a parent. "Mayor Daley was a man who could put you down in a second, and he could also make you soar to heights you never believed you could attain," he said in a eulogy delivered to the Cook County Democratic organization. "Mayor Daley sometimes scolded. But when you were feeling low, he would really come through. You remember, I had an election in the United States Congress with a very disappointing result [a reference to the 1970 loss of his leadership position]. The phone rang. I got on the line, and his voice said, 'Danny, what did they do to you? What can I do for you, Dan?' That was the kind of man he was."[6]

After the tears, this was the political moment Rostenkowski had long been awaiting. He wanted to be mayor, he had said many times before and after Daley's death. But there was a big problem: a loyal lieutenant couldn't just have the job, as in the old days. In effect, he wanted the bosses to hand it to him on a platter. "Rosty made no serious moves, except for the little stories in the press," said Alderman Richard Mell. "He may have been waiting to be called, but it doesn't work that way." The problem was that "there is no Prince of Wales rule," said local political scientist Paul Green. Daley was unwilling to anoint his successor or to step down himself. So, with the "Boss" gone, Rostenkowski needed to move quickly. Instead he dithered as the Democratic aldermen selected one of their own as interim mayor. The low-key Michael Bilandic, who represented Daley's heavily Irish ward on the city's south side, promised that he would be a caretaker who would hold the seat until a special election. But a few months later Bilandic decided that he liked the job, and he won election to serve the remainder of Daley's term—defeating Alderman Roman Pucinski, who ran strongly in the city's Polish neighborhoods, and Harold Washington, then a young state senator and an emerging leader in the black community.

For Rostenkowski, perhaps the best excuse for his failure to run was that the upheaval in Washington made for bad timing. But as in 1970 when Carl Albert denied him the whip position, he seemed diffident about making his own case. "He didn't put together the deal himself," Bill Daley said years later. "He could have done it if he had moved quickly. No one else could do it for him. . . . But I don't think it was a burning issue in his heart, in contrast to being speaker." In his heart of hearts, Rostenkowski probably did not relish the spotlight, increased job demands, and difficult racial challenges that faced an urban mayor at that time. In Chicago some of his peers snickered. "You know, it's a damned shame—Danny's such a nice guy," a ward committeeman said in the late 1970s. "And if he just wasn't so lazy he wouldn't have to stay in Washington. He could become somebody big in Chicago—maybe even mayor!"[7] But, as Bill Daley added, "the city was much better off having him as Ways and Means chairman." Rostenkowski later claimed to have no regrets.

In Washington, where they had regained complete control, Democrats found that their internal conflicts were far from over. Nobody bore the brunt of Rostenkowski's criticism more than the savvy and blunt-spoken David Obey, who moved to the forefront of the reform movement after he was elected in 1969 to fill a vacant House seat in Wisconsin that Republicans had held for several decades. And nothing better symbolized Democrats' problems than Obey's clashes with Rostenkowski, which grew in the mid-1970s and rarely subsided for the next two decades.

Obey's hometown of Wausau in central Wisconsin was less than thirty miles from Stevens Point, where Rostenkowski's grandfather Peter had lived before moving to Chicago, a fact that both lawmakers said they never discussed. No matter. Rostenkowski was uncomfortable with Obey's political breeding. Their disagreements played out on many levels: he viewed Obey as too liberal in his ideology, too hostile to business interests that had built a cordial relationship with many Democrats, too eager to reform the House's organization, too inclined to challenge presidents of both parties, and—perhaps most important within the House— too willing to expand the ethical rules that guided members' professional and personal lives. Obey, of course, had just the opposite impression of Rostenkowski: a big-city, back-room dealer who responded to the commands of others and was unwilling to change his often simplistic approach to issues. Worse yet for Rostenkowski, Obey had more insider skills and determination than did Richard Bolling, the reform patriarch. "I can't live with David Obey," Rostenkowski told a group of scholars in 1994. By then it was too late. "I have nothing in common with Wausau, Wisconsin—absolutely nothing."

Obey challenged the way in which many politicians conducted their own business. "If David Obey goes home and makes a town meeting, maybe he will have a beer," Rostenkowski said. "If I go home, I have to go visit two or three restaurants, shake hands with people, let them know I am in town." Obey led a charge to strengthen the ethics rules that imposed limits on gifts, including meals, that House members could accept from outsiders. Meanwhile Rostenkowski was increasingly rubbing shoulders with and doing favors for corporate chiefs and spending less time with grassroots constituents. Obey, who described himself as a "progressive," wanted to return the Democrats to their heritage of representing common folks. "The contrast was between Main Street and Wall Street," Obey concluded. Like the conflict between the Kennedy admirers and the Johnson allies during the 1960s, the divisions between Rostenkowski and his kind, opposed to Obey and his, festered and ultimately became ruinous.

The selection of O'Neill and Wright, if anything, only intensified the party conflict percolating below them. The reformers had suffered a huge setback with Wright's victory. With O'Neill's tacit encouragement, they shifted their attention to such procedural issues as the administration of the House, financial disclosure requirements for members, and limitations on their sources of outside income. Obey chaired two House task forces that O'Neill created in 1976 and 1977 to address those problems. "Few members are willing to spend the time, energy, and political capital to strengthen and improve the House so it can play its proper role," said Fred Wertheimer, who as Common Cause president worked closely with Obey. Long after the House in 1977 approved rules drafted by Obey to restrict how much outside money members could earn, Rostenkowski publicly spoke against the changes and sought to undermine them. (A larger group of lawmakers who preferred the old system's limited rules encouraged Rostenkowski but were unwilling to go public.) Even though he had no outside job, as did some lawmakers, the Chicago Democrat objected to this kind of paternalism and to an elitist attitude that lawmakers could not be trusted to earn additional money that, he firmly maintained, they richly deserved. As he later complained, "Why do I have to live and abide by the rules that [Obey is] writing for Wausau?"

With the financial demands of four daughters and few apparent resources to support a more upscale style of living, Rostenkowski said he needed the outside money that he earned from speeches; of course he did not mind the embellishments that often accompanied the travel. But Obey and the reformers prevailed on that issue. The new House rules imposed a limitation of 15 percent in additional money that members could earn in honoraria beyond their House salary, which was then $57,500; Rostenkowski was one of only thirty-one House Democrats to vote against the restriction. (In 1989, when Congress voted itself a roughly 40 percent pay raise to $125,000, it finally agreed to eliminate virtually all sources of outside earned income.)

Obey met stiffer resistance when he proposed reforms to strengthen O'Neill's authority as the new House speaker. With the increased size and complexity of the House bureaucracy, Obey and others contended that the speaker needed additional management tools. But Obey's recommendations, such as the designation of an administrator to run the House's non-legislative affairs, were torpedoed by members who insisted on maintaining the House's often arcane system of baronies, such as the clerk, sergeant at arms, and doorkeeper, who provided personal favors for insiders. The old spoils system remained intact. If Obey had got his way, Democrats might have avoided severe problems with internal House operations years later.

BY 1979, two years after O'Neill became speaker, the reform movement had ground to a halt. There were several reasons. Bolling's grand design for a leadership-directed House ran into the familiar jealousies and organizational clashes from competing power centers—committee chairmen, the Democratic Caucus, and the ever-assertive Watergate babies. After ousting the aged conservative Southern chairmen and increasing the number and influence of subcommittee chairmen, erstwhile reformers began to enjoy the fruits of their new influence. A prime example came at the Commerce Committee when Henry Waxman of California in 1979 successfully challenged the more senior Richardson Preyer of North Carolina for the chairmanship of the influential Health and the Environment Subcommittee. Waxman's victory—which he achieved with the help of lawful campaign contributions to other Commerce Committee Democrats who made the selection—became an important illustration of how skillful junior members could influence major policy issues in a manner that would have been inconceivable when Rostenkowski entered the House. Waxman later became a major player writing legislation ranging from the 1990 Clean Air Act to a series of laws expanding medicaid eligibility for lower-income recipients. But this entrepreneurial style made it increasingly difficult for O'Neill and other top Democrats to set a course and to impose discipline on their often-warring factions. Waxman had power, and he wasn't about to relinquish it. In the nation, Democrats in the late 1970s also faced the scourge of huge increases in inflation and interest rates, exacerbated by escalating oil prices. Many of these difficult issues found their way to Rostenkowski and his colleagues, old and new, at the Ways and Means Committee.

In the post-Watergate House, Ways and Means became a prime example of the breakdown in discipline. In part because the committee under

Mills had been so averse to reforms, the pace changed radically after the Arkansas Democrat was forced to step down in 1974. "A chairman can't wheel and deal as in the past, because decisions are openly arrived at," said reform advocate Abner Mikva in 1978, a year before he resigned as a Ways and Means member to become a federal judge. (Later he was White House counsel to President Clinton.) "When it was a closed process, everyone could be mysterious and it was a chairman-oriented committee. Now, with thirty-seven individuals, it is a much healthier, though different, process." The decline in the panel's consensus-building tradition, however, made legislating more difficult and less predictable. Ways and Means members were "more likely to exploit the opportunities for position taking, credit claiming and distributing benefits to individual constituencies and organized groups," wrote Randall Strahan, a scholar who has studied the committee.[8] And increased activism within the Democratic Caucus made it more difficult for the two parties to join hands in the kind of bipartisanship that had characterized the committee when Mills was its chairman.

The results of those divisions grew more pronounced after Carter took office. When he sent the committee proposals in 1977 for his ill-fated tax rebate of fifty dollars per person and a major package of energy-tax increases and incentives for energy efficiency, Republicans termed them gimmicks and intrusive. More important, Ways and Means Democrats were more willing to go their own way, regardless of the new president's wishes. The feelings were mutual. "My impression is that the president pays little attention to anyone in Congress, including Al Ullman," said Rep. Barber Conable of New York, who became the committee's senior Republican in 1977. With increased partisanship on both sides of the aisle, and without Mills diligently building a coalition, legislative success became elusive.

As successor to the legendary Mills and in the face of the reformers' demands to make the committee more responsive to Democratic dogma, Ullman faced a virtually impossible task in any case. But he compounded his difficulties by deliberately underscoring his contrasts with his predecessor. Where Mills saw his role as patiently steering the committee toward consensus, Ullman often proposed options at the start of committee deliberation. He led, in effect, by trying to set a public example. "I see my role as altogether different than chairmen used to see theirs," he said in a snide reference to Mills. "They were worried about image and not losing any bills and not bringing a bill to the floor unless they had all the votes in their pocket. . . . I see my role as one of leadership and trying to expand the thinking of Congress in new directions in order to meet the long-term needs of the country." Instead of Mills's approach of accommodating the concerns of as many committee members as possible, Ullman was more hands-off toward building internal agreement. Although he was usually a loyal Democrat and was popular in the back rooms of Congress, "he didn't have the leadership ability" to move legislation, said Bill Frenzel, a Minnesota Republican who served on Ways and Means. Even those closest to him conceded that Ullman's shyness made him anything but a natural politician. He preferred to work in the open; unlike Mills and Rostenkowski, he was not gregarious or a gifted deal-cutter. "On occasion, he'll ask for support, but once you give him an answer, he will leave you alone," said Joe Waggonner of Louisiana, the leader of the committee's conservative Democratic bloc during much of the 1970s. "I'm aware of no arm-twisting." Rostenkowski called Ullman "a 9-to-5 guy" who did not "mingle" with committee members. "He was a nice person—not that I'm not[!!]—but he didn't have the hammer" in dealing with other members.

Ullman's approach created severe problems for Speaker O'Neill, whose chief aim was to gain quick House passage of Carter's legislative agenda. The chairman, by contrast, was more selective in endorsing the president's proposals, and he objected to tight schedules that made it difficult for his committee to work its will at its own pace. "Tip interpreted Ways and Means as too conservative" when Ullman was chairman, Rostenkowski said. That problem was not solely Ullman's doing. The fact that the committee was less of a liberal stronghold than was the Education and Labor Committee, for example, was a legacy from the Mills era, when the chairman sought Democratic members who were chiefly dealmakers rather than ideologues. During the Ullman years the panel retained its conservative tilt: of its twenty-five Democrats in 1977, ten were from south of the Mason-Dixon line. But that would not satisfy the new speaker. His doubts about Ullman's loyalty and effectiveness led O'Neill to create an ad hoc committee to coordinate the handling of Carter's energy proposals in 1977, circumventing Ways and Means to assure that the House would pass the president's plan by summer. A few months later O'Neill took a similar approach by creating an ad hoc panel from three House committees to manage Carter's welfare-reform proposal. As it turned out, Ullman's strong opposition led to the demise of the welfare bill in Ways and Means, despite earlier favorable action by the ad hoc committee. "Al didn't totally trust me," said James Corman, who chaired the ad hoc welfare panel. "He felt I would bring out legislation that would be too liberal." The energy bill, by contrast, finally was enacted in November 1978, after months of Senate debate and lengthy House-Senate discussions that made major revisions in Carter's proposal.

With all these changes, Rostenkowski's position as chief deputy whip and a senior member of Ways and Means—plus his insider skills—propelled his return to the center ring in the revamped House. To monitor Ullman, O'Neill tapped Rostenkowski to become his eyes and ears at Ways and Means. The liaison made sense not simply because the two men shared a close friendship and their urban background and education. Perhaps more important, O'Neill admired Rostenkowski's political talent. Democrats in Boston were chronically factionalized when O'Neill entered politics during the lengthy reign of the legendary Mayor James Michael Curley. "In Boston, the Irish were so numerous that they could organize themselves around individuals, as with tribal chieftains," said Ralph Whitehead, a former Chicago journalist who has written widely about urban politics. "Contrast that to Chicago, where the Irish built a countywide organization and they became the brokers. . . . Democratic organization politics in Chicago were designed by the noncharismatic for the noncharismatic. Within that culture, Dan Rostenkowski was very charismatic and personable." That analysis helps to explain the admiration that O'Neill voiced for Rostenkowski's ability to "read the House"— understanding the ever-shifting views of its members and knowing when it was time to act. "If you ask me: 'O'Neill, can you read the place?' well, I'm afraid the answer's got to be no, I can't," the speaker told a Harvard University class soon after he took the House reins. "Of course, it doesn't make any difference, 'cause I've got a friend who knows how to do it, so he does it for me. Danny Rostenkowski. Of Illinois. I don't know how he does it, but he does it."[9]

Likewise, Ullman looked to Rostenkowski for his contacts with House leaders and for his proficiency at reading the House's mood. As a conservative Westerner with virtually no experience in hardheaded Democratic politics, the insecure chairman was a novice at moving legislation and lining up allies. Rostenkowski the insider, by contrast, used his one-on-one strength with other politicians to adapt more easily to the tumultuous changes occurring within the House. With these cross-pressures, he sometimes found himself caught in an awkward predicament between his usually nonpartisan chairman, who took an evenhanded approach to issues, and his longtime friend, who was driven by a partisan desire to get the job done as speaker. "Al is practical," Rostenkowski said at the time. "Tip would like to pass the president's program, but he does not have as good a grasp on the committee."[10]

These tensions illustrated the shifting dynamics among senior Democrats in the wake of House reforms. Despite Ullman's independence, it was hardly unusual for a Ways and Means chairman to want his own imprint on legislation. But O'Neill's assertiveness in scheduling and defining issues for House debate was a stark change from the more passive Albert and McCormack, his recent predecessors. With their rules changes during the early 1970s and the ouster of three committee chairmen in 1974, members of the House Democratic Caucus had made it clear they were on the move. They wanted their chairmen to toe the line on important legislation, and they gave the speaker a mandate to be more forceful in overseeing the committees. Yet, as soon became clear, the Democrats' new rules had their limitations. Unlike many state legislatures where party leaders have virtually unchecked authority over the selection of committee members and their legislative output, the new system did not empower the speaker to dictate results.

O'Neill's problems with Ways and Means reached a low point in 1978 when the committee drafted a tax bill in response to Carter's call for tax reform. During his 1976 campaign debate with Ford, Carter had criticized the income-tax code as a "disgrace to this country . . . a welfare program for the rich." But the pragmatic Ullman had privately urged candidate Carter to abandon his effort to repeal major tax breaks for business. And he was disappointed that Carter failed to offer proposals that were popular in the business community. Twice rebuffed, the chairman vowed to get his way on tax policy. The outcome was a bitter setback for Democratic reformers. It was like the old days at Ways and Means: a coalition of Republicans and moderate Democrats crafted its own alternative. The centerpiece, which shaped the tax debate in Washington for more than a decade, was the plan sponsored by Democrat Jim Jones of Oklahoma and Republican Bill Steiger of Wisconsin to reduce the maximum tax rate on capital gains from 49 percent to 35 percent. Ways and Means approved the original measure on a 25-to-12 vote; the opposition came from the panel's liberal Democrats, who complained that the cut was a giveaway to the wealthy and business. Although they initially sided with Carter's call for a more progressive tax code by directing more cuts toward the middle class, Ullman and Rostenkowski soon realized that a majority was moving in another direction; so they ultimately abandoned the president and played key roles in steering the bipartisan coalition's bill.

When the two men met with Carter and urged him to abandon his tax-reform plan because it lacked support at Ways and Means, the president was not pleased. "I found through bitter experience," Carter wrote, "that *any* tax proposal—including our welfare and tax reform packages—attracted to Capitol Hill a pack of powerful and ravenous wolves, determined to secure for themselves additional benefits at the expense of other Americans. . . . We were never successful in focusing sufficient attention on them to implement this important reform."[11] The measure passed and Carter signed it. The Ullman-Rostenkowski partnership with the conservative coalition bitterly disappointed O'Neill. The result was not what he had in mind when he asked Rostenkowski to be his liaison to Ways and Means. Kirk O'Donnell, O'Neill's top legislative adviser, placed the blame chiefly on Ullman, complaining that he was "not a strong enough leader."

Passage of the 1978 tax bill at a time when their party held a 2-to-1 House majority, was a crushing blow to liberal Democrats. The setback sent a strong message to Rostenkowski and other tax writers that many of the new breed of Democrats, despite their much-heralded independence and reform posture about tax-code "fairness," bore striking similarities to old-style Democrats when it came to coalition-building. "Most of the problems of the country have to be solved on a bipartisan basis, and I've felt we perhaps are a little too partisan on such things as our budget policy," said Democrat Jones, when asked about the coalition that he and Steiger had built. (The widely respected Steiger died of a heart attack, at age forty, in December 1978.) Jones, who had been a senior White House aide to Lyndon Johnson, criticized O'Neill and other Democratic leaders as "not responsive" to conservative Democrats' fiscal views. Although Rostenkowski publicly muffled his criticism of Carter and O'Neill, the 1978 vote also showed him that the liberals could not deliver the votes when the moment of truth arrived. The result would profoundly affect his own strategy once he became Ways and Means chairman.

Another major showdown during the Carter presidency gave Rostenkowski even more reason to keep his distance from the liberals if he wished to pass legislation. The issue was health-care costs—specifically, Carter's proposal to restrict the soaring fees for hospital services; those costs were increasing at 15 percent annually, more than twice the overall inflation rate. What grabbed Washington's attention was that the expenditures compounded the growth in the federal budget for the aging under Medicare and for the poor under the Medicaid program. Calling for a formula to limit revenue increases for 6,000 affected hospitals, the White House sought a 9 percent lid on their added costs in 1978 and smaller increases in following years. Among the steps envisioned by Health, Education and Welfare Secretary Joseph Califano, the plan's chief architect, were restrictions on the construction of new hospitals and on purchases of expensive new medical equipment; he claimed, for example, that the hospitals had 100,000 more beds than the nation needed. "If we would only curb the appetite of the hospital industry, we could free up vital resources to tackle prevention and early treatment of conditions before they deteriorate to a point requiring hospitalization," Califano told a House hearing in May 1977. Although the Carter administration's proposal fell far short of national health-care proposals from Sen. Edward Kennedy and organized labor, it was the most serious health-reform initiative submitted to Congress since the 1965 enactment of Medicare. If hospital cost containment were enacted, so the argument went on both sides of the debate, it would open the door to sweeping federal regulations throughout the health-care industry.

The task of sorting out the competing policy claims and the political merits of the Carter proposal fell chiefly to Rostenkowski, the Health Subcommittee chairman. His Ways and Means panel was more centrist than either the liberal-leaning Senate Labor and Human Resources Subcommittee chaired by Kennedy or the conservative Senate Finance panel chaired by Herman Talmadge of Georgia. Rostenkowski's initial reaction was positive. "I feel that we will do something this year," he said shortly after Carter submitted his plan.[12] But he voiced an important warning: his experiences with Chicago hospitals showed him that it would be "pretty difficult" to require them to limit their spending if their cost of products and services continued to increase without controls. And Califano's proposals took few steps to address that underlying problem. Rostenkowski also signaled that nothing would happen without strong presidential initiative. Especially in the wake of the administration's mishandling and subsequent abandonment of its proposed tax rebate in early 1977, Rostenkowski doubted that Carter had made a firm commitment to his health-care proposal. Nevertheless O'Neill was applying heavy pressure on Rostenkowski to act quickly on Carter's plan. "Tip wants a bill to support the president but he leaves the details to the committee," a Rostenkowski aide said at the time. " 'Just get me a bill,' Tip said."

Rostenkowski grew more cautious by summer. In July, when his sub-committee began to draft a measure, the chairman introduced a series of amendments designed to address the hospital industry's worries, including exemptions for small hospitals and a more generous formula to determine a hospital's revenues. But the revisions were not enough to break the logjam that had developed. Several subcommittee members were reluctant to cast votes that would provoke their local hospitals, which remained adamantly opposed. With his thirteen-member subcommittee (including nine Democrats and only four Republicans) close to evenly split on several issues, Rostenkowski deferred the moment of truth in the hope he could find a compromise. But when he and Salmon proposed an alternative—with voluntary compliance for hospitals and a longer phase-in of the 9 percent growth ceiling—Califano turned them down. Califano was so angry, he later wrote, that he called Rostenkowski's alternative "the Rostenkowski hospital tax of $50 billion" because of the additional costs it would impose on patients.[13] As he sought to convince proponents of Carter's plan that they needed to lower their expectations, Rostenkowski pressed ahead with his scaled-back plan to impose federal controls only if voluntary compliance failed to lower hospital costs.

As prospects for a bill faded, Rostenkowski found himself the bearer of bad tidings to the White House. The moment of truth was at hand after O'Neill called late one night at his Wisconsin summer home to pass on a complaint: as Rostenkowski recalled, the speaker sighed, "Danny, what are you doing to Joe Califano?" A few days later the president summoned Rostenkowski to an Oval Office meeting with Califano and several senior White House sides. "I walked in," he said, with a smile, years later. "I said to them, 'It's Daniel in the lions' den.' They were busting my buns for saying that the plan could only be voluntary." But he insisted he lacked votes for anything stronger—and he was right. Carter's plan died from a failure of presidential leadership coupled with Carter's inability to speak to lawmakers on their terms, Rostenkowski said.

The ill will was mutual. "He [Rostenkowski] had the utmost contempt for most of Carter's staff, particularly congressional liaison Frank Moore," Califano wrote.[14] Like many other Democrats, Rostenkowski doubted that Carter and his aides understood how to accomplish his goals. "Jimmy Carter once asked me to go to Camp David with my wife," said Rostenkowski, delivering a metaphor to explain the failure of the hospital cost-control proposal. "I called LaVerne and I said we were invited to Camp David [for the first time], and she said that would be nice." But the logistical predicament was that Carter also wanted Rostenkowski to join him the next day for a speech in St. Louis, and Rostenkowski then would have to fly immediately to Wisconsin for another appearance. "LaVerne said all that flying would be unbelievable." He turned down the visit, explaining it this way: if LBJ had been president, "Johnson would have called LaVerne and he would have arranged for my trip to Wisconsin. That would have been different." The point of the story: Carter's failure to reach out to members of Congress and to accommodate their problems made them less willing to comply with his legislative demands.

When the 95th Congress adjourned in October 1978, Rostenkowski still had not brought the health-care measure to a vote in Ways and Means. (The House Commerce Committee, after a lengthy debate that summer, passed by a one-vote margin a Republican-sponsored alternative that retreated to the hospitals' plan for voluntary cost-cutting.) The struggle offered important though largely overlooked insights into the handling of other health-care plans years later by House Democrats, especially by Rostenkowski. First, he and other Ways and Means members viewed these proposals, in part, through the prism of medical practitioners who were politically active in their local districts. Second, the lawmakers wanted the executive branch to give them only the broad outlines of a proposal. But, third, they sought the administration's cooperation in hammering out the details. Finally, as all sides repeatedly have been told, the policy scope and financial dimensions of proposed health reforms have made it virtually impossible to satisfy the many competing interests.

Still, that did not end Carter's cost-containment saga. After the 1978 election the retirement of four of the nine senior Ways and Means Democrats prompted a reshuffling of subcommittee chairmanships. Rostenkowski decided he had had enough frustration at the Health Subcommittee, so he chose to chair the lower-profile Select Revenue Measures Subcommittee, where he eventually won House passage of dozens of relatively minor tax bills. With the more liberal Charles Rangel of New York replacing Rostenkowski as Health Subcommittee chairman, Democrats decided to make another attempt to pass Carter's health bill. Even though Rostenkowski was not directly involved, the Democrats' continuing failure later would have repercussions for him. This time, however, the problem was more than simply a deadlock at Ways and Means. With hospital costs continuing their 15 percent annual spiral, Carter maintained his assault on the entire industry, warning that the nation's economic and social future was at risk. The cost of health care is "rising so rapidly it jeopardizes our health goals," he stated in an April 25, 1979, message to Congress. After months of delay, most Ways and Means Democrats agreed to a jury-rigged proposal that called for voluntary steps by the hospitals but provided for standby federal controls on most hospital operations, starting in 1980.

Moving that bill to the House floor proved to be a short-lived victory for Carter and his allies. After another four months of squabbling among Democrats, the House in November gutted the proposal and instead passed a meaningless call for a national commission to study hospital costs. That proposal died in the Senate. In retrospect, the striking feature was not so much the 234-to-166 vote in favor of the anemic alternative but the names of the chief cosponsors. In the reform House, where smart young lawmakers could gain major influence, the authors of the plan to gut Carter's proposal were obscure second-termers who were on their way to greater fame: Democrat Dick Gephardt plus Republican David Stockman of Michigan, who would emerge two years later as the budget-slashing Office of Management and Budget director under President Reagan.

For Gephardt, who was becoming a major player in the House, his initial venture into high-stakes politics would become a moment of considerable regret. Years later, after he devoted countless hours as a Democratic leader to crafting more ambitious health-care plans and benefited from the learning experience of his 1988 presidential campaign and his populist slogan "It's your fight, too," he would chalk up his opposition to the Carter plan to youthful indiscretion, among other factors. In 1979, however, he harshly criticized his party's dogma and its leaders. Rather than impose federal regulations, Gephardt embraced support for vouchers to encourage competition by health-care providers and insurance systems, the type of free-market option for which he would later attack Republicans. Carter's price controls would "treat symptoms and not causes," he told the House. "It is a system of permanent bureaucratic controls. . . . It provides no element of reform in the system or any commitment to seek such reform." Citing his own experience on Ways and Means, he advised House members to spend more time "knocking heads in committee to come up with bipartisan coalitions" rather than "frittering our time away" rewriting bills on the House floor. Gephardt's implicit criticism of chairman Ullman—and of Rostenkowski, the next-senior Democrat—demonstrated the unhappiness by new-breed Democrats with what they considered their leaders' failure to develop a coherent program independent of the White House's wishes. "The committee system suffers because we are so fragmented," he added at the time. Yet demands by junior members such as himself for a more open House had contributed to that splintering of authority, as Rostenkowski and others had warned.

To Rostenkowski, Gephardt's independence amounted to an unacceptable breach of responsibility. Carter and his aides had earlier dismissed Rostenkowski's warning that they could not rely on Gephardt's support. His own early experience soured Rostenkowski because he felt that Gephardt spent too much time seeking to cut deals and impress others outside Ways and Means—with the Democratic Caucus, with lobbyists, with the news media—rather than earning his apprenticeship at the panel, as Rostenkowski and others had done as junior members. "The chemistry was never there between the two of them," said a Democrat who closely observed them at Ways and Means. "They came from different planets and different times." Although they were only thirteen years apart in age and had both grown up in blue-collar urban communities in the Midwest, these two Democrats became legislative opposites, in much the same way that Rostenkowski and Obey clashed on House ethics and internal operations. In contrast to Rostenkowski, who knew John Kennedy and his cronies as congressional colleagues, Gephardt's chief contact with JFK came through the television screen during the 1960 campaign, when he was an undergraduate at Northwestern University, a few miles from Rostenkowski's home. Their generational contrasts help to explain Gephardt's preoccupation with imagery and message development, subjects for which Rostenkowski had little aptitude or patience.

The Gephardt-Rostenkowski clashes went beyond mere issues or personalities. The two men had fundamentally different views of the legislative process, which often would divide Democrats when Rostenkowski chaired Ways and Means. As a protégé of Bolling, Gephardt thought that

Democrats needed to spend more time in informal and wide-ranging discussions, which were designed to produce policy agreements apart from the narrow confines of committee bill-drafting. With his seemingly endless patience, he could sit around a table for hours or days listening to diverse viewpoints and hoping he could devise a position that would satisfy the group's consensus. In the Rostenkowski school, by contrast, politicians operated on the premise that leaders talked separately or in small groups with their colleagues to determine what was important. After they had heard enough, the bosses handed down solutions that they believed should be acceptable to a sufficient number. Although many of the reformers resented such diktats, the old-timers' experience was that endless discussions of complex issues were cumbersome and often failed to arrive at an acceptable common ground. Gephardt and his friends also professed discomfort with Rostenkowski's practice of greasing his deals with favors to financial backers. As Gephardt and Rostenkowski showed during the debate over containing health-care costs, stylistic differences usually proved less important than how a lawmaker voted when the crunch came. In this case, neither method proved successful. But the Carter bill was only the start. Gephardt and Rostenkowski would play out their contrasting styles on many more occasions—ending with the futile collapse of the sweeping health-reform initiative from the next Democratic president, Bill Clinton.

By the 1980 election Democrats had begun to come to grips with how much the House had changed in the preceding six years. Although they had not resolved their conflicts, Rostenkowski and his allies understood the stylistic and substantive challenges presented by the Obeys, Gephardts, and others. The chairmen were beginning to comprehend that their wish was no longer viewed by rank-and-file lawmakers as a command. For their part, the reformers occasionally acknowledged that a discussion must end and someone must attempt to impose order. For Speaker O'Neill the task was not only to referee these endless clashes but also to force closure on issues that he deemed crucial. In short, the House had changed radically from the slower-paced, seniority-dominated institution that had marked the first twenty years of the Democrats' reign. But one constant endured. The Democrats had such a large and usually comfortable majority that they could deal with House Republicans as and if they wished. For the most part that partisan dominance also persisted in the Senate. As for the president, with his economic and foreign-policy woes,

Carter endured a nasty primary battle in 1980 with Kennedy. And a big field battled for the Republican nomination. But congressional Democrats had shown that they could survive and do business no matter who was president. And even though Republicans would win their fifth of the eight most recent presidential elections, Capitol Hill remained in the Democrats' firm grip. So in the spring of 1980 there was little expectation that these broad dynamics would soon change. Few Democrats in Washington paid serious attention to Ronald Reagan, the former Hollywood actor who had served two terms as California governor before leaving Sacramento as the darling of the nation's conservatives. They assumed that Republicans only nominated presidents—Eisenhower, Nixon, and Ford—who had proved that they could do business in Washington on a bipartisan basis. Soon enough, all that and more changed drastically.

Chapter Five

MR. CHAIRMAN
CONFRONTS
MR. PRESIDENT

FOR MANY HOUSE DEMOCRATS the 1980 election produced the worst of all worlds. For starters, Ronald Reagan overwhelmingly ousted Jimmy Carter from the White House. With the new president's proposed tax cut promising massive budget change, the Democrats' economic policies were shattered. And unlike the Senate, where Democrats' loss of control left them with few legislative duties, they retained nominal authority in the House where their committee chairmen were in the Reagan revolution's line of fire. Even with their loss of thirty-three seats, some Democrats hoped they could retain influence with their 243-to-192 majority, the same margin they held when Nixon became president. But Reagan's background differed greatly from the earlier Californian, who had served fourteen years in Congress and as vice-president and had a keen appreciation of federal policy complexities and Capitol Hill politics. The new president was more committed to junking the status quo.

Within weeks it became clear that Reagan's economic program would win House support from a coalition of Republicans and conservative Democrats. Worried Democratic leaders began to fear the loss of their House majority if they did not get their act together. "It's important that we stop fighting among ourselves," Rep. Tony Coelho of California, the House Democrats' chief campaign strategist, said shortly after Reagan took office. "If we lose the House majority in 1982, we're really down the tubes."[1] Quite simply, Democrats were on the defensive. And many of the old guard were ill-equipped to deal with the radically changed setting. Tip O'Neill was "in a fog," proclaimed Rep. Les Aspin of Wisconsin, a leading Democratic rebel. With their speaker buffeted by the reelection defeat of several top lieutenants, many others shared that view. Republican firebrands were more caustic, exulting that the hefty O'Neill was a metaphor for the federal budget: both, they claimed, were "big, fat and out of control."

Among the Democrats' election casualties were four House committee chairmen, including Al Ullman of Ways and Means. He had helped to dig his own political grave in Oregon by endorsing a national value-added tax as a tool to reduce a then-paltry federal deficit. Although he disavowed during the campaign his prior sponsorship of the proposal, Ullman's vision that "we need more taxes . . . [is] pretty well out of touch with the district," said Republican challenger Denny Smith.[2] Ullman's greater responsibilities on Capitol Hill also left him less time to spend in his rural and increasingly conservative district. Still, Ullman's defeat shocked the House. Only once before, following the Republicans' "Do-Nothing" Congress in 1948, had a Ways and Means chairman lost reelection. In that case the Democrats' seventy-five-seat gain had given them the House, and the Republicans could sit back and heal their wounds. This time the discredited majority was forced to rehabilitate itself on the run.

As the most senior Ways and Means Democrat behind Ullman, Rostenkowski normally would not have hesitated to replace him as chairman. John Salmon, his chief aide at Ways and Means, awoke him in a 2 a.m. telephone call to Chicago with a glib, "Good morning, Mr. Chairman." But the boss didn't appreciate the phone call or the premature congratulations, Salmon recalled. As it turned out, Rostenkowski faced a complex decision that he pondered for weeks. Because John Brademas of Indiana had lost reelection, Tip O'Neill needed a new majority whip. As deputy whip, Rostenkowski also was next in line for that position, both formally and as O'Neill's favorite. He was torn. The Democratic Caucus rules did not explicitly prohibit him from taking both positions, as he desired. But his pal O'Neill and leadership ally Jim Wright told him that one job was difficult enough. "Danny was upset that we would not let him do both," said Wright, who faced a similar dilemma in 1976 when he passed up the Public Works Committee chairmanship to move into the leadership. "We said it had to be one or the other." (Until 1930 the senior Ways and Means Democrat also was his party's floor leader. But power in the House had grown both more complex and participatory.)

When Rostenkowski returned to Washington the week after the election, he asked Salmon and Jim Healey, his top political aide, to detail the pros and cons of each post. As Rostenkowski's issues guru, Salmon was so sure of the decision that "I thought it was a charade and walked out." Although he agreed with Salmon's conclusion, Healey was more circumspect. "I wanted Danny to be chairman because it was a greater challenge, and he has the ability to rise to a challenge, even more than I had thought," said the former congressman's son. "Plus I thought he had a better chance to become speaker after being chairman because he could prove himself from another position, rather than being whip, which was viewed as a hack position." Still, despite the appeal of Ways and Means, Rostenkowski loved life as a party leader, and he had soaring ambition. As Democratic whip he could deal with a broader range of problems and members while making fewer complex legislative decisions than did the Ways and Means chairman. Indeed, as a junior member in the 1960s he had worked closely with Hale Boggs to strengthen the whip office by organizing the weekly meetings where members could blow off steam about their leaders. As he had witnessed, especially after becoming a subcommittee chairman in 1975, slots below the speaker were less demanding—politically and intellectually—than were most committee chairmanships, which required a grasp of issues and an ability to build coalitions. Later, said a confidant, Rostenkowski often voiced second thoughts about his decision, especially when O'Neill leaned back in his speaker's chair puffing on a cigar and the chairman grumbled that he was working ten times harder than his Boston pal.

More than any other House position, speaker was the job Rostenkowski had always wanted. In Chicago, of course, the "Boss" held the only job that really mattered. Since 1931, when John Nance Garner became speaker, the No. 2 slot was each Democrat's route to the top. If Rostenkowski took the safer route of whip, he would be only one notch below Wright. O'Neill, then sixty-eight, would likely return to Massachusetts within a few years. But what about Wright? In December 1980 the Texan turned fifty-eight, and he was in good health. For fifty-two-year-old Rostenkowski, it might be a long and frustrating wait playing second fiddle. "If he had taken whip, he would have been speaker," said Tom Downey of

New York, who became a close Rostenkowski ally at Ways and Means. "But he saw the leadership ladder was not moving fast." Besides, as chairman, Rostenkowski would immediately gain vast influence and perquisites on Capitol Hill. "Tip wanted me to be the chairman," Rostenkowski later said. "It had a higher public profile. No one knew who the whip was." And, depending on how events unfolded, who knows what might lie ahead after O'Neill or Wright moved on?

Rostenkowski also agonized over whether he had the smarts to be chairman. Despite his bravado and his desire to get things done, he was insecure about the job. "My confidence level for dealing with the tax code in the beginning was very low," he said. With three years at Loyola, he was not even a college graduate. Mills, his role model, was a Harvard Law School student who understood and cared about tax-code details. "I'm not a tax lawyer or an economist," he said in a 1981 speech, proudly but guardedly. "I'm a politician. I count my strength as being able to spot a problem, find the best options, choose the best, build support around it, count votes and carry it from one end of the political obstacle course to the other."[3] For such a Chicago-style pol, choosing the whip position would have been the safer, more predictable route. "I talked to a number of people who knew him well," said a former House Democrat who had been a Rostenkowski friend. "They said it was a difficult decision. The question was, did he have the intellectual security and self-confidence. . . . Even with staff, Rostenkowski had not dealt with issues and was not known for a blazing intellect."

For every plus, there was a minus. If he took the committee route, Rostenkowski understood that he would become one of the Democrats' top guns for Washington's influence-peddling lobbyists to see in Ronald Reagan's Washington. Yet by moving into a more parochial position he would remove himself from the Democratic Caucus's power loop. And still another dilemma: if he took the chairmanship, could he win the eventual contest for majority leader that almost surely would lie ahead, most likely from a liberal like Burton, or a reformer in the Bolling mold, or someone like Foley who could combine those two qualities? A decade earlier Rostenkowski experienced the pain of being knocked off the leadership ladder. In the back of his mind, no doubt, was the thought that a bird in the hand was worth two in the bush. Tom Foley understood the dilemma that Rostenkowski faced. He had chaired the Agriculture Committee since 1977 and was O'Neill's next choice if Rostenkowski decided not to become whip. "At the time, people thought I was crazy to give up the Agriculture chairmanship," said Foley, a lawyer and former Senate aide who had more legislative expertise than Rostenkowski. "I didn't give it much thought. . . . Inside the House a committee chairmanship can be inhibiting because other chairmen do not welcome you [another chairman] challenging them." True, the Agriculture Committee lacked the clout of Ways and Means; and, compared to Rostenkowski, Foley was more congenial—a useful asset for a cajoling whip. "He told me that he wanted to be speaker," Foley added. "He felt he wanted to kick ass and I was not decisive enough. . . . He might have been a strong speaker. But there was a question of whether he could be elected." As when he decided not to run for mayor in 1977, Rostenkowski spurned risk-taking.

There was yet another complication to the mix. If Rostenkowski decided to become whip, Sam Gibbons of Florida was next in line to chair Ways and Means. Unlike most Southerners, Gibbons was a liberal and a reformer. And Gibbons had forever stamped himself as a maverick when he ran a futile campaign against O'Neill for majority leader after Hale Boggs's 1972 disappearance in Alaska. His legislative work also marked Gibbons as unreliable. "Gibbons becoming chairman at Ways and Means was a major reason why Danny did not take the Whip position," said a member close to Rostenkowski. O'Neill apparently did not raise this problem explicitly with him, but Rostenkowski surely knew that Gibbons would not be the hard-nosed chief that Ways and Means needed—or that O'Neill wanted. (As Rostenkowski was reviewing his options, Gibbons also bruised some feelings when he passed the word within Ways and Means that he already had selected the top committee aide for his chairmanship.) After six disastrous years under Ullman, and facing a popular Republican president with a bold agenda about to come before that committee, other Democrats surely told Rostenkowski that he could not pass the Ways and Means baton to the weaker Gibbons. As it turned out, as No. 2 to Rostenkowski for more than a decade, Gibbons suffered from the chairman's disdain while he toiled in obscurity on international trade issues. Indeed, Gibbons's ineffective performance years later as Ways and Means chairman in the final months of the House Democrats' majority confirmed his opponents' doubts.

So, with assurance from Salmon that he was equipped to do the heavy lifting as the Ways and Means staff director, Rostenkowski told O'Neill that he would cut the deals. His decision to take Ways and Means was deeply personal. "He knew he would have hated himself if he had not taken the position," said another Rostenkowski ally. Finally he had completed his lengthy apprenticeship and was ready to take charge. "He decided he would break out of the Washington stereotype of him as a Polack," a friend said. At a bittersweet dinner of Democrats at Washington's posh Jockey Club on the night of Reagan's first inaugural, a bipartisan group of friends cheered as Rostenkowski climbed onto a chair and joyfully sang, "Danny, Danny, Danny, who ever thought he'd chair the Ways and Means Committee." In his ever-calculating manner, Rostenkowski also won some deal-sweeteners from O'Neill before agreeing to the chairmanship. He gained additional prime work space for Ways and Means meetings inside the Capitol plus a leadership staff slot for Healey to remain as his liaison to the Democrats' inner circle. The new chairman, in short, looked to maximize the perception of his power.

But his initial performance proved disastrous. Like other top Democrats in early 1981, Rostenkowski was ill-equipped to handle the Reagan onslaught. And his failings were all the more exposed in the highly publicized showdown over the administration's tax-cut plan. True to his experience and training, he thought he could find a compromise. Instead he got rolled by the new guys on the block. Worse, his attempts to gain support in the House succeeded chiefly in adding huge costs to the final version of the tax cut. It was an embarrassing defeat, similar to his lost leadership position a decade earlier. But under pressure to produce, he rebounded more quickly this time. As Washington eventually settled into its customary routine of posturing and deal-cutting, Rostenkowski took charge. Applying a lifetime of his mentors' lessons, he grew comfortable as chairman. The early disappointments soon turned into bipartisan coups that showed the Reaganites they would have to deal with him. Within two years the grumbling over his accomplishments was coming from both political extremes.

To suit his style as chairman, Rostenkowski quickly reorganized the committee and placed his imprint on its operations. In earlier decades, leaders of Ways and Means and the Senate Finance Committee had relied heavily on the professional staff at the Joint Committee on Taxation, an unusual hybrid that had the sole task of providing expertise to the tax-writing panels. Its aides kept in close contact with their Treasury Department counterparts and usually tried to diminish the political pressures on tax issues. That style suited the usually bipartisan Wilbur Mills, who basked in legislative details and faced few threats. But the less-confident Rostenkowski was no policy maven, and he did not believe in sharing control. As chairman, he wanted his chief aides to be accountable to him alone. With the Republicans' Senate takeover after 1980, he also doubted that the joint committee could serve two masters. So, although he agreed to retain the committee and its staff, he added a new layer of tax experts to Ways and Means. With Salmon in charge of the overall operation, he named veteran Ways and Means aide Rob Leonard to supervise the expanded tax staff. The joint committee's staff director would now, in effect, report to Salmon when it came to House business—a radical change inside the often priestly world of tax politics.

From the start, Rostenkowski displayed several traits that remained consistent during thirteen years as chairman, regardless of the issue, the president, or the politics. Win or lose—and he certainly suffered his share of setbacks—Rostenkowski was a consensus-builder who worked the committee's center. Like Mills, he closely monitored other committee members, patiently probing to see whether and where a majority surfaced. Likewise, he had no interest in moving a bill to the House floor that was not assured of passage. He sought to avoid extremes that had no chance of enactment; not for him were the liberals' latest fads on taxes, trade, health care, or the other major issues facing Ways and Means. He played his cards close to his vest and, not surprisingly, displayed a Chicagoan's deal-making instincts. Chuck Daly, the former Kennedy White House legislative aide, recalls a visit to Rostenkowski in his Capitol Hill office to seek a tax-law change on behalf of the Chicago-based Joyce Foundation, where he was president. "It was a small change in a big bill," Daly said. "Danny said he would do it, and he did. . . . I never met his staff, and I didn't have to lobby anyone." Rostenkowski made a point of contrasting himself to Ullman, who led the committee with a light hand and was never troubled by a setback. Whenever the committee finished work on a bill during O'Neill's years as speaker, Rostenkowski typically informed him immediately of the result and requested support.

But there were also vital contrasts to committee operations as they had been under Wilbur Mills. Rostenkowski typically did not embrace a detailed set of views to guide debate. "Mills dominated the committee because of his command of the tax code," said Robert Reischauer, who worked closely with Ways and Means as director of the Congressional Budget Office. "Rostenkowski commanded the committee through his political judgment and his ability to make a deal." As chairman, his job was to satisfy demands within the House and with the president so that he could enact legislation. "He was driven by a desire to legislate," said Rob Leonard, the tax expert who was a chief Rostenkowski aide for nearly two decades. "He wanted ink on the parchment," referring to the bills sent to the White House for presidential signature. Like many modern lawmakers, Rostenkowski did not agonize over policy nuances; it was the staff's responsibility to make sure that the words made sense and that the papers were straight. Conceding that he was no expert on the intricacies of tax or social-welfare policy, he hired well-versed aides who were fiercely loyal to him. They were no-nonsense guys—and, by the end of his career, a few women. He gave them broad leeway to shape legislation, leaving for himself the political judgments and actions that were required to pass the proposals. "Is it good law?" was his directive to his aides. "I want that on my tombstone."

Typically Rostenkowski made his tactical decisions sitting around an office table following a discussion with his advisers (usually without other House members) in his inner sanctum. Although the aides sometimes clashed personally, they played it straight with one another and the boss. "His staff was excellent," said Barbara Kennelly of Connecticut, a Ways and Means Democrat. "They worked night and day and were totally dedicated to him. They listened to him. . . . But they wanted to keep the reputation of Ways and Means, and they did not want to steer it in the wrong direction." They spent much of their time reviewing options with other committee members and attempting to balance competing interests. "He reacted better to verbal briefings so that he could listen, absorb, and raise questions," said Rob Leonard. Rostenkowski did not spend much time reading memos of more than a couple of pages. "He acknowledged in many ways that he was not a technician and that much of this stuff was indecipherable without the help of staff," said Joe Dowley, who served as Ways and Means staff director from 1985 to 1987. "But he was willing to work at it." Like Dowley and Leonard, most of Rostenkowski's top aides stayed in Washington after they left his Capitol Hill staff, typically becoming downtown lawyers earning far greater compensation from corporate clients.

Rostenkowski's years as chairman were complicated by growing partisanship in both parties. The schism resulted from factors that extended far beyond his purview. Starting in the late 1970s, young activists—such as Democrat Dick Gephardt and Republican Newt Gingrich—seeking to shape the nation's debate made the task of back-room operators like Rostenkowski far more difficult than for their predecessors. In his later years as chairman, he often was more comfortable with mainstream Republicans and their views than with those of his own party. Still, most House Republicans, embittered by their perpetual minority status, viewed Rostenkowski as a menacing symbol of the majority's autocratic procedures. Even within his own party he was not universally revered. Many Democrats, young and old, grew frustrated that his deal-cutting prowess did little to encourage new ideas or to bolster a party in dire need of new blood. "He had no policy commitment," protested a Democratic insider. "The emphasis on getting out a bill and the arm-twisting made him come up short on substance where he could have had an impact." And despite occasional attempts to rebuild the big tent at Ways and Means, he lacked Mills's proclivity toward bipartisanship. Perhaps the most significant difference from the Mills-led committee was that Rostenkowski, when he became chairman, was forced to deal with a conservative and ideologically aggressive Republican president at the same time Republicans also controlled the Senate. All too soon his legislative mentor's world became an anachronism.

FOR ROSTENKOWSKI and House Democrats, the trauma of the Reagan presidency arrived quickly when Republicans submitted their sweeping tax-cut plan. That proposal became the 1980s' most significant enactment. Its advocates promoted it as the centerpiece of their effort to place more money in the American consumers' pocketbook. Crafted in the economic down-cycle of the late 1970s by congressional Republicans—led by Rep. Jack Kemp of New York and Sen. William Roth of Delaware— and advocated during the 1980 campaign, the proposal slashed tax rates for most individuals by 10 percent a year for the ensuing three years. And it included major incentives for businesses, featuring accelerated depreciation for plant and equipment investments. Fiscally the proposal was designed to permit growth in the federal government while it promised the elixir of a balanced budget. Critics complained that these goals were mutually inconsistent. The bill was "a riverboat gamble," conceded Senate Majority Leader Howard Baker, a Tennessee Republican. But usually cautious Republicans united around the plan and were in no position to withstand Reagan's pressure to make a quick start and to boost the faltering economy. Many liberals and others came to view the 1981 tax bill as the Republicans' cynical attempt to force the federal budget into a permanent deficit so that they could slash spending on the Democrats' favored social programs. It was the "starve the beast" style of governing, wrote Sen. Daniel Patrick Moynihan, in which "a crisis was being created [by the Republicans] by bringing about deficits intended to force the Congress to cut back certain programs."[4] What seems unmistakable is that Republicans convinced a compliant Congress to take the legislative candy before swallowing the painful medicine of spending cuts. But Reagan and his allies could take neither all the credit nor all the blame. Despite their repeated criticism of the tax cuts, many Democrats were willing accomplices in that exercise. And the Ways and Means Committee contributed more than its share to the excesses. For Rostenkowski, the result would mark an embarrassing start as chairman.

What became knows as the "bidding war" was born of ultimately irreconcilable goals for the tax bill: Rostenkowski wanted to pass a less sweeping version on the House floor, but his deal-cutting failed to draw a clear enough partisan contrast. He handed out favors to sway undecided House members, but the chairman's clout paled beside that of the new president. Compounding his problem, he struggled to cobble together a consensus among fractious Democrats in the face of a virtually unified Republican party. His mission proved futile. "The Democratic Caucus didn't know whether to do good or to look good," lamented Dennis Eckart of Ohio, a freshman House Democrat in 1981. In those early months, as they struggled to cope with the new president's policies, they failed at both objectives. Many Democrats believed a big tax cut was irresponsible and they should simply oppose it. But a few Democrats supported the Reagan plan while many others feared the partisan consequences of voting against it. In addition, Democrats were divided over legislative strategy. Some believed they simply should make their case and reconcile themselves to a Reagan triumph, at least for the short term. Indeed, the House and Senate approved in the spring a three-year budget plan that envisioned enactment of the big tax cut. But conceding defeat was difficult medicine for other House Democrats, including Rostenkowski, who were accustomed to getting their way. The result was that he lost control of a major bill for the first and last time in his tenure as chairman. "We didn't know what we were doing," conceded John Salmon, Rostenkowski's top aide. Adding to his problems, the new Ways and Means chairman was forced to comply with a tight deadline from O'Neill, who didn't want Republicans to accuse him of delaying House action on Reagan's tax-cut proposal. "The speaker's view was that the voters had voted for change, and he would not use his parliamentary tools to thwart the will of the public," said Kirk O'Donnell, O'Neill's chief political adviser. "He had a four-by-six-foot schedule for action mounted on an easel near his desk. That was very uncharacteristic of him." Complying with that calendar was the House Democrats' only success—such as it was—during the early months of 1981.

With the Democrats' recent budget debacle fresh on his mind, Rostenkowski was intent on avoiding a similar setback on the tax bill. He already had decided, probably unrealistically, that he could do business with the new president. On the day after Reagan took office, Rostenkowski met with him at the White House. "I was brought into the Oval Office by [Vice-President] George Bush, an old friend," he recounted in a February 1981 speech to Chicago business executives. "I sat down, and the first observation I made—and perhaps the most significant—was that we are both new to the job. And we both want to pull this economy out of the rut." In that speech Rostenkowski made clear that he wanted to cooperate. "Let me say, up front, that the Ways and Means Committee will pass a bill to cut taxes for both businesses and individuals." In hindsight, many Democrats later contended, he should have repackaged Reagan's across-the-board tax proposal so that its cuts would have mostly benefited the middle class. Ultimately Democrats would pursue that course in challenging the alleged unfairness of Reagan's policies. But it took time for them to settle on that approach. Instead Rostenkowski countered with an alternative modeled on the Kemp-Roth proposal, featuring a 5 percent cut in 1981 and a 10 percent cut the following year; Reagan and congressional Republicans had trimmed their plan to a 25 percent cut in income-tax rates during the next three years. Rostenkowski discussed the terms of a possible compromise with top Reagan administration officials and with congressional Republicans, when each side was wary of forcing a showdown. For a few weeks some senior Republicans thought that his split-the-difference approach might prevail. After he met Rostenkowski in late May, Senate Finance Committee chairman Robert Dole added, "If it's left to us, I think we can probably work out an agreement."[5]

But the negotiations probably were doomed from the start. Many Democrats griped that Rostenkowski was moving too close to the Republican plan. Even O'Neill told reporters that talk of a Rostenkowski-Dole deal was "vastly overstated." When Reagan responded that he would not retreat from his three-year proposal, bipartisan prospects disappeared. Instead Rostenkowski added several baubles in an attempt to win conservative Democrats' votes. Those features included increased exemptions for estate and gift-tax filers, liberalized capital-gains provisions for home owners, extended tax credits for small businesses, and new benefits for Americans working abroad. "In his usual, careful manner, [Rostenkowski] had his staff draft additions that were designed to attract a variety of special interests," according to Barber Conable, the senior Ways and Means Republican. "He asked, and was given, a pledge of support for each adjustment to his package."[6] Then, just before the committee's final vote, Democrats added their biggest and most controversial provision: significant tax relief for oil producers, a measure designed to capture the same Southern Democrats who had been siding with Republicans on budget votes—but hardly appealing to middle-class taxpayers. Gephardt, a leading proponent of Rostenkowski's consensus-building approach, played an active role in crafting that deal within Ways and Means. Chastened by criticism after working with Republicans in 1979 to assemble an alternative to Carter's health-care plan, he confined his deal-cutting this time to the Democrats. Rostenkowski preserved the unity of all Democrats except for Kent Hance of Texas when Ways and Means approved the bill on July 22. But that did not end the bidding war. Republicans now responded with their own trinkets, adding benefits on the House floor for charitable institutions and for the oil industry. In the end the vote in the House wasn't close. With White House aides coordinating a blitzkrieg lobbying campaign, Republicans won the support of forty-eight House Democrats. The July 29 vote for the Reagan plan was 238 to 195. On his first major test as Ways and Means chairman, Rostenkowski had been badly outmaneuvered. With the Senate firmly backing the three-year tax cut, the Reagan revolution on federal fiscal policy became a reality.

Many Democrats were dejected over how they had lost. Rather than engage in Rostenkowski's high-stakes bidding war—which raised the tax cut's cost to the federal treasury to $750 billion over the next five years—they regretted they had not fought Reagan's plan more directly. Rep. Morris Udall of Arizona, a champion of the liberals, offered a clear-cut alternative: a modest one-year tax cut that Democrats backed, 139 to 104. Although his plan received little publicity outside Capitol Hill, Udall said it had two advantages: it would balance the budget in fiscal 1982 and it would permit Democrats to make a sharper case against Reagan's big tax cuts. "Many of us were really unhappy about the bidding war in the Ways and Means Committee and thought we should stand on our principles," Udall said. "Even if we had 'won,' it would have been on a Republican bill." But the Democratic dissenters decided to withhold public criticism because of "turf problems and past personality differences with Danny," Udall confessed. Ironically, Rostenkowski in April 1981 proposed such a limited one-year tax cut. But he intended that approach as a bargaining chip for later negotiations. For many Democrats, the result revealed Rostenkowski as too eager to seek victory at any costs, too willing to accept the terms of debate set by the Republican president, insufficiently attuned to the Democrats' needs at a time of shifting partisan roles, and naive about his prospects. "Rosty was convinced until the last day that he had it won," Udall said.

Years later he would continue to suffer criticism on the tax-cut bill. "Danny wanted to win and not to fight the excesses," said Jim Wright. "We should have offered a much more limited and targeted cut to make us more competitive in the world markets. . . . I didn't see the profit in defeating the president's plan with something so close to the president's plan." As the years passed, top aides to O'Neill and Rostenkowski conceded that they should have done more in 1981 to dramatize the issues of income-tax "fairness" and the federal deficit. "We tried to win when it wasn't in the cards that we could win," said Jack Lew, the former O'Neill aide. "Our failure was not in reaching out to the Republicans but in failing to let the Republicans win." (Years later, when he was a top official in the Clinton administration, Lew showed his skill in achieving budget victories.) At the time, however, most Democrats on Rostenkowski's committee agreed with their chairman's strategy. As the House's tax-writing experts, they were unwilling to walk away from the fight. "Ways and Means Democrats concluded that we can't face a loss that would create God-knows-what result," both for the nation's politics and for the economy, said Rep. Bill Brodhead of Michigan, a liberal Democrat on the committee. On a more personal level, the inexperienced Rostenkowski worried that the press would criticize him for losing on his first big bill. Even in hindsight he was never convinced he had made a mistake. His job as chairman, he believed, was to move the ball forward. He did not wish to hand over his duties to others, nor did he care to see his committee's handiwork upstaged on the House floor. "I wanted to pass legislation," he said of the tax-cut debate. "The conservative Republicans and liberal Democrats wanted it all their own way. . . . But, as Lyndon Johnson said, you have to open the door to get it ajar. That was pretty much my position."

The 1981 tax-cut debate damaged Rostenkowski in another way. An informal group of Democrats had challenged him, chiefly with Udall's alternative. Many of these liberals, with backstage help from Obey and the Democratic Study Group, had battled him during the 1970s on the House's organizational reforms. True, Rostenkowski heard little second-guessing from O'Neill, who was slow to respond to the insurgents' pleas to draw the partisan lines aggressively against Reagan. But Obey was enraged that the Ways and Means chairman sold out Democratic principles of protecting the middle class. And Democratic campaign impresarios like Tony Coelho grumbled that Rostenkowski was not sufficiently attuned to electoral imperatives, starting with their attack on Reagan's proposed changes in Social Security benefits. By the end of 1981 many of these Democrats had reconciled themselves to the reality that they no longer could dictate results. "We have realized our duty is to be the loyal opposition and force Reagan to explain what he had done," Rep. Patricia Schroeder of Colorado said at the time. Much as he sought to wield power and to encourage consensus, Rostenkowski disagreed. But it was clear that he could not command his own party on Ways and Means issues.

Even though the tax bill was the most humiliating defeat that he suffered as Ways and Means chairman, the battle offered insights on how Rostenkowski would run the committee. Most important, he expected to be the boss. All information and decisions flowed through him. Rostenkowski met with his committee Democrats—both individually and as a group—to learn what they needed in a bill and then to assure that their vote was secure; he briefed O'Neill and his lieutenants to be certain of their support; he discussed possible deals with Treasury Secretary Donald Regan and chief White House aide Jim Baker; he met with Bob Dole or Ways and Means Republicans to gauge their interest in bipartisanship. In all these contacts and more, Rostenkowski demanded control. He wanted to know what everybody was thinking. "All politicians hate surprises," said Rep. Bill Frenzel, a Minnesota Republican who served with him on Ways and Means for sixteen years. "Rosty was a great politician." The reason that he abhorred surprises, said Rep. Bill Gradison of Ohio, another veteran committee Republican, was that he "wanted to know where the votes were. . . . He would much rather that someone oppose him as long as he knew ahead of time." The 1981 tax debate also was an important measure of Rostenkowski's passion for bipartisanship. Even though the intensifying conflict usually made that goal unattainable, he wistfully recalled how much easier it was for Wilbur Mills. "He often spoke in private conversations about how unhappy he was that the committee had changed and become more partisan," Gradison said.

As chairman, Rostenkowski relished the art of the deal. His quest for coalition-building kept lines open to the chief executives of large corporations and trade associations. Although he gave Chicago-based groups an especially friendly ear, he liked to rub shoulders with the rich and powerful from across the nation—both in Washington and in more hospitable resort locales. Sometimes those meetings provided him an ulterior benefit, such as a lawful honorarium of a few thousand dollars, which he could recycle to various Chicago projects. But Rostenkowski also believed that the tycoons' support was useful to his legislative goals. "He loved the notion that corporate executives would come and sit in his court," said Sen. Byron Dorgan of North Dakota, a former Ways and Means member. And, to be fair, he also solicited the support of big union officers. "He had friends in business and labor," Frenzel said. "The Daley system was to encourage cooperation."

Nowhere was Rostenkowski's coalition-building more apparent than in his dealings with the executive branch. "He had an old-fashioned view that the President of the United States is an important guy and that members of Congress have a responsibility to deal with him," said another Democrat. His respect for the aura of the White House—which was enhanced by his dealings with Presidents Kennedy and Johnson—was a product of his awe for Mayor Daley, who was not shy about exercising the tools of his office. Like many frustrated legislators, Rostenkowski coveted a president's power to make a decision without securing the approval of half of his 435 colleagues. Of course, during the Reagan and Bush presidencies he knew he would need their support to enact legislation. During those years, however, many congressional Democrats took a decidedly different view; the post-Watergate members, in particular, showed far less deference to the president. Rostenkowski's desire for cooperation also contrasted sharply with the attitude of John Dingell of Michigan, the Energy and Commerce Committee chairman, who was

Rostenkowski's frequent adversary over turf within the House. Dingell, another Polish American who could be a fearsome foe, showed greater regard for the institutional prerogatives of Congress; he loved, for example, to hold lengthy hearings where he could torment officials of various agencies. But his legislative legacy was much slimmer. Rostenkowski's deference to Republican presidents also reflected his days in Springfield, including Daley's approach. "It was not a mean partisanship," said a Rostenkowski ally. "He didn't screw the Republicans or shame them."

Yes, but. Rostenkowski had a long memory when somebody burned him. So it would not take long for him to seek—and gain—a measure of revenge for the 1981 tax fiasco. "Losing the 1981 bill made him even more determined to do the job right," said Ken Bowler, a leading aide at Ways and Means. When Senate Republicans acknowledged their excesses and sought to repair them, Rostenkowski was pleased to assist. Within a few months it became obvious that the Reagan tax cut had gone too far. First, the president and Congress failed to deliver the tough medicine that both sides had promised in the budget package. Reagan in September 1981 proposed $58 billion in spending cuts; Congress approved $2 billion. Even most Republicans maintained a business-as-usual approach, rejecting efforts to kill pork-barrel projects such as expensive dams. The budget chickens were coming home to roost. In a startling confessional, Office of Management and Budget Director David Stockman voiced profound doubts about Reagan's "supply-side" economic theory and the prospect of balancing the budget. "None of us really understands what's going on with all these numbers," Stockman told reporter William Greider. "There was a certain dimension of our theory that was unrealistic."[7] Although Stockman later sought to explain that he had intended to talk "off the record," his explosive comments were a stunning repudiation of the Reagan budget strategy, of which he had been the chief architect. Most damaging of all for Republicans was economic reality. By the end of 1981 the nation was mired in a deep recession: unemployment peaked a year later at 10.8 percent. Instead of progress toward a balanced budget, the federal deficit soared in fiscal 1983 to $208 billion—6.3 percent of the gross national product, its highest level since the depression.

Rostenkowski was quick to say I told you so. "No one ever told us that a full-blown recession was to initiate the supply-side miracle," he told a meeting of American Stock Exchange officials in November 1981. He also sent a clear message about who must take the initiative to fix the nation's economy. "It's going to take a bit of tongue biting and political moxie," he said then. "But the president must face the fact that the tax bill went too far." When Reagan and his accomplices in 1982 confessed that reality, Rostenkowski reinforced these lessons in the danger of overreaching and the value of compromise. He would not discuss a tax increase, he said, until at least nine of the twelve Ways and Means Republicans agreed on precisely what they would support. According to Conable, the House GOP members "clearly could not satisfy his requirement."[8] So, taking an unusual procedural step to evade the constitutional requirement that the House initiate tax legislation, Rostenkowski eagerly deferred to the Republican Senate. That handed the ball to Bob Dole, who earlier had swallowed his doubts about Reagan's three-year tax plan. After several months of dallying, the Senate approved a broad range of business and individual tax increases, including the elimination of several tax deductions. In working with the White House to restore about one-third of the previous year's cuts, Dole generated deep-seated hostility from many GOP conservatives; the plan led House backbencher Gingrich to call Dole "the tax collector for the welfare state." Democrats, of course, were delighted by the turn of events—both the Republicans' intramural clashes and their acknowledgment that in 1981 they had overplayed their hand.

The 1982 tax deliberations strengthened Rostenkowski's partnership with Dole, his counterpart at the Senate tax-writing committee and mitigated some of the political damage that Rostenkowski incurred in the 1981 showdown. Despite their differences on many issues, the two chairmen were deal-cutting legislators who respected each other's candor and conciliatory style. "Dole and Rostenkowski learned to trust each other," said John Salmon. As they demonstrated on both the 1981 tax cut and the 1982 tax increase, they were in much closer agreement than were the partisans on each side. "They both liked to work things out," said a Dole confidant. In a news report when both were chairmen, the *New York Times* referred to "the general good feeling between the two tax titans" and the optimism that "the Dole-Rostenkowski teamwork" would produce a compromise.[9] Many years later Rostenkowski voiced regret that Dole's skills translated so poorly in the rigors of a presidential campaign. "I'd feel comfortable with Bob Dole as president," he said privately in May 1996, when it was clear that Dole would be the Republican nominee to oppose Clinton.

THE HIGH POINT of Rostenkowski-Dole cooperation during Reagan's first term was the 1983 enactment of major Social Security reforms. Culminating two years of tortuous political posturing, the legislation rescued the retirement system within weeks of its likely insolvency and averted the popular firestorm that surely would have been unleashed. The incident was instructive on several counts. On an issue that Democrat campaign strategists were milking for partisan benefit, Rostenkowski resisted external interference with what he considered an appropriate legislative response. Still, when O'Neill insisted that he would dictate the Democrats' handling of the issue, Rostenkowski acquiesced as a loyal soldier. It was the speaker's job to set the tone for Democrats in opposition, all agreed. Finally, when it came time for the key players to make their deal, Rostenkowski was at the center of the bargaining. As with his 1981 tax-cut setback, he found himself on the opposite side from many liberal Democrats. This time, however, he was patient and understood that he could prevail without dictating the timing. The Social Security showdown represented his emergence as a legislative titan.

One of the peculiar features of the Social Security debate in the early 1980s was that Ways and Means Democrats already were seeking to resolve the system's dire financial plight before the Reagan team began to take similar steps. Indeed, if Rostenkowski had had his way, the problem would have been fixed without the high-stakes brawl that ensued during the next two years. But Reagan's ham-handed attempt was too tempting for key congressional Democrats to ignore. As Republicans were painfully reminded, Social Security is the third rail of American politics, which can ruin anyone who does not handle it very gingerly. Still, its problems had begun to require increased attention by Ways and Means. The agreement by Nixon and Mills in 1972 to provide an automatic annual cost-of-living adjustment for beneficiaries fueled financial distress for the system, especially when inflation rates soared during the late 1970s. Responsible lawmakers understood that they had no choice but to fix the problems. In 1977 President Carter and the large Democratic majorities in Congress agreed to changes that Carter said would keep Social Security solvent for the next fifty years. Because his advisers severely underestimated inflation and overestimated economic growth, Carter was too optimistic by forty-four years. Despite its shortcomings, however, the changes showed a course toward cooperation in enacting painful but essential changes that increased payroll taxes for nearly all American workers and reduced benefits for recipients. Then, in 1981, Ways and Means embarked on a similar rescue mission. With Rostenkowski's approval, Social Security subcommittee chairman Jake Pickle quietly prepared a bill that featured a gradual increase in the retirement age from sixty-five to sixty-eight. Based on the 1977 precedent and his panel's unanimous approval, Pickle expected prompt House action. But he failed to reckon with a major change in political dynamics. This time the Democratic House saw an opportunity to make mischief for a Republican president and Senate.

At first the Reagan administration also overlooked the partisan implications of the Social Security rescue. Although the president did not embrace Pickle's proposal, Stockman and other top officials agreed to include Social Security cutbacks in their budget plan. With the need for spending cuts to balance his big tax cuts and still achieve Reagan's balanced-budget goal in 1984, Stockman sought quicker fixes than those recommended by Pickle. "I'm just not going to spend a lot of political capital solving some other guy's problem in 2010," Stockman said.[10] Instead he looked for shorter-term savings, chiefly by reducing benefits for early retirees—those starting to collect at age sixty-two. But Stockman severely miscalculated the reaction. "The early retirement cut was the first major break in [the Reagan administration's] string of successes and became a target for liberal attack," according to a study of the legislation. "In his haste to avoid a GOP economic Dunkirk, Stockman had created his own Social Security debacle."[11] Desperately seeking to slow Reagan's bandwagon, O'Neill and other Democrats launched a fierce attack on the administration's proposal. Characterizing Reagan as "stonehearted," O'Neill called the proposal "despicable" and "a rotten thing to do."[12] Although he doubtlessly opposed the substance of the administration's plan, the speaker also was "looking for an opportunity to counterattack" Reagan's broader program, including his budget plan, said O'Neill aide Kirk O'Donnell. With their campaign strategists fearful that Republicans could win the House in 1982, Democrats could ill afford restraint. "The ball has been lofted right to us," Coelho said in the summer of 1981. "We've taken it and we're running with it. . . . We're not going to fumble it. It is without doubt our big issue today, and there's no close second."[13]

Although most Democrats welcomed O'Neill's "fairness" campaign against Reagan's program, his attack caused dismay at the Ways and Means Committee. "Tony Coelho's role was to get a majority in the

House and to make Social Security a political issue," said the scornful Salmon, Rostenkowski's top Ways and Means aide. "We wanted to deal with the issues." In contrast to the chairman's focus on getting results, the speaker's priorities featured Democrats' partisan interests. With Rostenkowski set to move Pickle's bill to the full committee, O'Neill told his friend to stop. The chairman wasn't happy, but he bit his tongue. "Rosty never liked to play politics with Social Security," O'Donnell said. "But he went along because O'Neill was the party leader, and the speaker saw this issue as a way to drive a stake through the Republicans." Postponing action on Pickle's proposal, Democratic leaders turned the Social Security spotlight toward the Reagan administration's excesses. With a series of House votes during the late spring and summer of 1981, Democrats managed to undermine Reagan's plan and to weaken significantly the president's popularity.

The demise of Reagan's proposal did not solve the financial crisis, of course. With the president and Congress deadlocked, cooler heads in late 1981 sought to unravel the political mess. Their answer was to create a bipartisan fifteen-member National Commission on Social Security Reform to prepare recommendations; the chairman was Alan Greenspan, who later would chair the Federal Reserve Board. With its diverse membership from the two parties and from the private sector, the commission sought to define the problems and to identify options. Not coincidentally, the panel's deadline was the end of 1982—after the election, so that Democrats could remind voters of Reagan's earlier proposal and so that Republicans could avoid further opportunities for Democratic mischief. Although he was not in a position to veto the unconventional scheme, Rostenkowski didn't like it. He and Pickle were the only major congressional players on Social Security who objected to serving on the commission. To them the study was redundant. Ways and Means members from both parties already knew what was needed, even though the politics prevented them from taking those steps.

After Democrats gained twenty-six House seats in the 1982 election, aided by the recession plus Social Security politics, Washington finally ran out of excuses for ignoring the problem. And Rostenkowski felt free to complain about his party's handling of the issue. " 'Political football' is a pretty hackneyed phrase, but I can't think of a better way to describe the political battering Social Security has taken over the last year and a half," he said a few days after the election. "All I can say is, the scrimmage ended last Tuesday. The real game is about to begin." But Greenspan's commission failed to meet its deadline; it lacked the muscle to force the two key sides—the lieutenants for Reagan and O'Neill—to cut a deal following the election. Not until January 1983, with the clock on Social Security's bankruptcy ticking close to midnight, did the same players begin serious negotiating that finally produced an agreement after more than a week of hard-nosed talks. The final deal was similar to the Democrats' 1977 rescue: further payroll tax increases, a six-month delay in the 1983 cost-of-living adjustment, and some taxing of benefits for upper-income Social Security recipients. Rostenkowski's immediate role was limited to granting his assent in a Saturday afternoon telephone conversation during which he and O'Neill—who were at a golf tournament in Palm Springs, California—received a report from the speaker's aides in Washington.

Rostenkowski's real contribution to the final agreement was far greater than was publicly acknowledged, either at the time or later. "We worked out a bipartisan plan before the 1982 election" among a handful of Ways and Means members, said Bill Gradison, the Ohio Republican. That agreement provided the outlines of the plan that the key players accepted in January. John Salmon echoed that view and provided more detail. As far back as August 1982, at Rostenkowski's direction, Salmon and top aides on the Ways and Means Social Security subcommittee "sat around and talked about scenarios" for a deal. Later several Ways and Means members took a postelection trip to several Caribbean nations, in what also turned out to be an important mission to salvage congressional approval of Reagan's beleaguered initiative of trade assistance for the region. During lengthy discussions with Ken Duberstein, Reagan's chief congressional liaison, Salmon outlined the elements of the package that the Ways and Means staff and members had informally endorsed. "After the trip it was decided to have the negotiators sanitize the agreement and to shift the blame," Salmon recounted.

But the Reagan and O'Neill negotiators were unwilling to approve one key piece of the Ways and Means package: the gradual increase in the Social Security retirement age, which was a centerpiece of the package assembled by Pickle in early 1981. Because top AFL-CIO officials fervently opposed that change, O'Neill rejected the proposal and tacitly encouraged opposition by Rep. Claude Pepper, the aging Florida Democrat who championed senior citizens. Pickle believed just as strongly that raising the retirement age was vital to the package. But despite Rostenkowski's steadfast support for his subcommittee chairman, Pickle could not be certain that Rostenkowski would confront O'Neill on the issue when the House debated the rescue package. "I couldn't get Tip to move," Pickle said. But his fears proved unwarranted. "Danny supported our proposal at a critical time," Pickle added. "He always supported his subcommittee chairmen. That's the first principle he learned from Richard Daley." On a 228-to-202 vote, with only 76 of 268 Democrats siding with Pickle and Rostenkowski, the House on March 9, 1983, agreed to increase the retirement age to 67. With support from more than 90 percent of House Republicans, Rostenkowski secured the type of bipartisan coalition that prevailed when Mills had been chairman. The House then passed the bill, 282 to 148; in the face of Pepper's lonely opposition, Democratic leaders decided they could not wring any more politics from Social Security.

With enactment of the Social Security bailout, Rostenkowski relished the return of Ways and Means to its House preeminence. And he had staked out his claim as one of the House's most powerful figures. "The main characteristic of Dan's leadership was that he was intensely proud to be Ways and Means chairman," Pickle said. "He guarded the committee's reputation like a bear. He could be hard for the Democratic leaders to deal with because he felt that his committee had more character and discipline and that it was more important than the other committees." Because Rostenkowski coveted the speaker's job, there was surely an ambivalence to his dealings with O'Neill and, soon, with his two Democratic successors. Had he become speaker, he probably would have softened his reverence for the Ways and Means Committee. But the chairmanship was all he had, and it wasn't such a bad consolation prize in any case. Rostenkowski's stubborn independence bruised the egos of some other House Democrats, especially those who were more focused on political demands. On occasion, as with the 1981 tax cut, he lost. More often, as with Social Security in 1983, he won. And sometimes, as on the 1982 tax increase, he made an impact in indirect ways. In each case he called most of the shots for House Democrats.

These initial battles offered important clues to what lay ahead. As the House grew more and more partisan, chairman Rostenkowski often found himself swimming against the tide. "I was a pragmatist," he said. "I tried to get what I felt was possible. . . . The liberals never knew when to take the ball" to make a score. Because he wanted to be a player who got results, he concentrated on seeking accommodation with Republican presidents rather than catering to his own party's parochial needs. But mounting partisanship often made consensus-building more difficult, even in a case like Social Security where the need was unmistakable. Democratic reformers, whom he had steadfastly opposed in the 1970s, had taken control of the House and the party; those who wanted to return to old-style politics faced an uphill road. "Rostenkowski always talked about how we are the 'Cadillac of committees,'" said Tom Downey of New York. "He overstated the point a bit. He remembered the committee in its best, collegial days under Mills." As the years passed, the changes in the House eventually forced Rostenkowski to abandon some of his bipartisan instincts. "When Dan assumed the captaincy, he made a strong point that he wanted a majority in each party," said Republican Frenzel. "But he failed to do that. . . . The House was becoming more polarized. And the Democrats were driving that." But partisanship, of course, is a two-way street. Although Rostenkowski tried to open doors to Presidents Reagan and Bush, their actions often contributed to the congressional brew that made it impossible for the chairman to emulate Mills, even if he had the skills to follow in his mentor's footsteps.

Rostenkowski met additional turbulence when he began to take the lead on national issues to make his mark as a lawmaker. During Reagan's second term and beyond, as the chairman became more confident and assertive, he inevitably offended Democrats on his left and Republicans to his right. But he typically saw their opposition as the price of getting results. Finally he had become the big man among Washington's tax-writers. That was vindication for Rostenkowski, whose politics proved more enduring than did the skills of reformers who had earlier taken his measure. Despite the many changes in Congress, he was intent on running the committee like an old-fashioned boss.

Chapter Six

WHEELING AND DEALING
TO MIDDLE GROUND

DURING ROSTENKOWSKI'S CHAIRMANSHIP, the Ways and Means Committee faced never-ending demands that kept the panel in the spotlight. For a week or a month, members might work to tame the federal deficit, then shift to historic tax-reform plans. Proposals to reduce international trade barriers—or contrasting legislation to protect U.S. industries from competition—might be followed by complex schemes to reform welfare or expand health-care coverage. In many cases, proposals were initiated by White House strategists who demanded a speedy response. But frequent tension between Republican presidents and the Democratic-controlled House placed added pressures on Ways and Means to develop its own initiatives. Consequently the committee faced challenges that would have been alien a decade earlier. Never during his chairmanship did Wilbur Mills encounter a gimmick to implement a five-year schedule to reduce the federal deficit; such a proposal would have been as unlikely as dictating what percentage of an automobile's parts must be U.S.-manufactured. Although Rostenkowski rarely embraced such novel ideas, they became standard fare during his Ways and Means reign.

On most issues Rostenkowski used a similar modus operandi to secure a majority on Ways and Means business. First he held preliminary discussions to identify the views of Ways and Means members, especially problems that might generate opposition on the committee. Then the chairman conferred one-on-one to discuss changes that members demanded before they could support the proposal. Finally, especially if Rostenkowski agreed to accommodate a member, the chairman required a pledge of unwavering support for the overall bill. His style was based on deal-making notions that have become old-fashioned, almost corny: "It takes two sides to make a deal," in his view. Once it is struck, "a deal is a deal"; so woe unto anyone who broke that word. Such informal rules bore "the unmistakable imprint from his apprenticeship in the Chicago Democratic machine," wrote Randall Strahan in his study of Ways and Means.[1]

Settling in as chairman, Rostenkowski became larger than life, especially to Ways and Means colleagues. He sometimes play-acted in asking their price for supporting legislation. "Once, we were in a dark room, and he asked me in the voice of Don Corleone [from the *Godfather* movie], 'What do you need, kid?' to support the bill," recounted Mike Andrews, a Texas Democrat who joined the committee in 1986. "I told him what I wanted. He said, 'You got it.' . . . Danny ran the committee the old-fashioned way, with loyalty, trust, and his word." Even when members figured out some of Rostenkowski's tricks, they had few opportunities to challenge him. "Once, when it was my turn to go to [room] H-208 in the Capitol for a meeting, he took out his negotiating book and listed the four things he could do for me," said Byron Dorgan of North Dakota, who served for a decade on Ways and Means before he was elected to the Senate in 1992. But Dorgan wasn't grateful for the gifts. "I said that the first two he had already given to other members." Rostenkowski later told Dorgan that he was "the only one to break my code." Then there was the promise to Ray McGrath, a New York Republican and frequent ally of the chairman. "I will be with you until the end," Rostenkowski told McGrath during the tax-reform debate in 1985, when Empire State lawmakers demanded to retain the deductibility of state and local sales-tax payments. During Rostenkowski's final negotiations with Reagan administration officials, the chairman late one night reluctantly abandoned that promise in order to salvage the broader deal. Alerted to the concession, McGrath sought out Rostenkowski the next morning to ask whether the rumor was true. According to McGrath, he responded, "Ray, I told you I'll be with you until the end. This is the end."

Of course, committee members' demands often clashed. Or the cost to the Treasury of favored baubles might far exceed budget strictures. One lawmaker's "good government" might be anathema to a colleague or—worse yet—to the president. Any chairman must resolve such conflicts and convince members to support what he claims is the best attainable compromise, even if they consider the result inadequate. "It was a marketplace," said a veteran Rostenkowski aide. "All members had their own list of what they wanted and some other things they put on the table that were less important. The problem was to divine everybody's price and not spend a dollar more than was needed. That had to be matched up with fiscal and tax-policy considerations." Although he handled most committee contacts himself, Rostenkowski invited a few Ways and Means Democrats into his inner circle, to solicit their advice and to make assignments for dealing with other House members. "The people who liked him understood that he needed information," said an aide. Probably the most reliable friends were Tom Downey of New York, Ed Jenkins of Georgia, and Marty Russo from the southern edge of Chicago. Each was first elected to the House in the mid-1970s and had gained respect among various factions. "We gave him a lot of news that Rostenkowski didn't want to hear . . . on legislation or his personality, for example," Downey said. They also gave him a useful bridge to junior members whom he knew barely, if at all. In a House of 435 members, he needed a lot of help. Noncommittee members would jokingly confide, "Danny spoke to me today," said Jake Pickle of Texas. Even with some Illinois neighbors he felt no need to learn their names if they lacked influence. "It was four or five years before he knew who I was," said Dennis Hastert, a Republican from the Chicago suburbs who was first elected in 1986 and became House speaker a dozen years later.

Rostenkowski's close relationship with his committee members permitted him to stay current with the Capitol's latest gossip. To succeed he needed a precise understanding of their political interests—both within the House and in their home districts. He also required mutual confidence and trust. By deftly granting technical provisions or local favors in exchange for members' commitment to the overall proposal, he cultivated a cohesive and loyal team. "He was the ultimate master: games-player, strategist, bully," Downey said. "He had a better feel for members—a street instinct, a sense that you reward your friends and punish your enemies." Although his image was often fearsome, even among colleagues, Rostenkowski could be quite convivial. He encouraged teamwork by organizing informal get-togethers of Ways and Means members. Given the relentless schedule pressures of their job, that could be difficult. In part he resorted to a technique from his early days in the House, when machine

Democrats would assemble for dinner at a fancy downtown restaurant. His favorite was Morton's, a Chicago-owned franchise in Georgetown which featured large cocktails, huge steaks, and a robust ambiance; needless to say, that was Rostenkowski's kind of place. He was enough of a regular that Morton's *maitre d'* reserved a special table for him on most weekday evenings. In contrast to the days when he was the junior member who responded to the old-timers' stories and tricks, now Rostenkowski was the host and chief raconteur. "We had dinner at least three times a month and shared anxieties and family information," Downey said. The chairman also built loyalty with committee-sponsored trips—often known as junkets—to other nations, where participants would explore local problems and conduct occasional sight-seeing. (In an embarrassing incident during a supposed review of U.S.-Caribbean trade problems, Rostenkowski's group was captured by ABC investigative cameras amid merrymaking on a beach in Barbados.) And he organized bipartisan weekend "retreats" for committee members outside Washington, where the stated purpose was to focus on emerging policy issues. Such sites usually included a golf course and other facilities to promote social contacts. Although outsiders might criticize these get-togethers as ethically inappropriate or professionally inconsequential, a high-level participant praised them. Robert Reischauer, who participated as Congressional Budget Office director, thought the forums were "unusual for Congress in creating an environment in which members could learn without cameras in front of them"; they were especially useful, he added, given the "amazing lack of informal contact among members."

"He had a pride in the committee," said Barbara Kennelly, a Democrat from Connecticut. "Members off the committee wanted to get on. Those on the committee were very proud to be there. That's where the action was. . . . Danny liked Ways and Means. And he was not willing to take his foot off home plate." That clannishness sometimes caused bad feelings among other House members. Some complained that he took too narrow a view of politics inside the House. Others criticized his lusty grab for issues or his gratuitous attempts to flaunt his power rather than to advance the broader interests of Democrats or the House. But that was a common trait among committee chairmen. Such rivalry often frustrated Democratic leaders; when it came to protecting their jurisdictional turf, Speaker Tom Foley said in a fit of pique, chairmen drew distinctions "with the dedication of medieval monks." Another House Democrat complained that "Rostenkowski's view was personal. . . . He didn't brook interference with his bills." Although he might not fully grasp all the policy nuances, friends and foes agreed that Rostenkowski's political instincts usually were sharp.

One classic insider tool that he used to promote discipline was the Democrats' committee-assignment process. Although the 1974 reforms stripped this power from Ways and Means, Rostenkowski developed new techniques to influence the results. Reveling in the deal-cutting, he kept a close eye on who wanted what. He also formed alliances with others who served on the Democratic Steering and Policy Committee; the party caucus usually rubber-stamped its recommendations. He worked closely with burly ex-Marine Jack Murtha of Pennsylvania, another renowned wheeler-dealer, to allocate perquisites between their two states and to collaborate on deals with other Democratic insiders. "We never lost one," said Murtha. "Most members never even knew what we were doing. We did it all inside the room" where the selections were made. Rostenkowski had advantages in the recruitment process: a chairman's views were crucial for a member who sought a new assignment, and senior members tended to scratch each other's back. "Putting people on committees is the foundation for being able to operate in the legislative arena of the House," he said. "Yeah, I was good at it. I was the only one at Steering and Policy during the 1980s who had done it earlier at Ways and Means."

Rostenkowski applied several criteria for prospective Ways and Means members. He wanted them from relatively safe House districts, so that they would be less reluctant to cast dicey votes that might get them in trouble back home. In his years as chairman, only three Ways and Means Democrats were defeated for reelection, each of them in 1992 when incumbency was losing its cachet with voters. He wanted as many views as possible woven into his consensus, a goal that had many facets. He wanted to ensure, for example, that conservative Democrats were adequately represented on Ways and Means, as was the case when he joined the committee in the 1960s. He struggled to preserve the regional balance even when Southern Democrats were switching parties or becoming too conservative for their Northern colleagues. With Jenkins of Georgia, one of the House's most conservative Democrats, he had "chemistry," said a chief Rostenkowski aide. "When Jenkins was off the reservation, he would tell him why." In 1992, after Jenkins retired, he recruited Bill Brewster of Oklahoma to join the committee to advocate the conservative viewpoint. "If you become a liberal, I'll kick your behind," the chairman told Brewster, whom he had barely known during Brewster's first two years in the House.

Rostenkowski also sought members who would be loyal, especially to the committee and its chairman. He wanted to be sure that new members endorsed his deal-cutting approach. For that reason he vehemently opposed selecting freshmen for his committee, contending that they had not yet proved their loyalty or skills. He prevailed on that point until 1993 when Democratic leaders, over his objection, succumbed to pressure from the sixty-three-member freshman Democratic class. But he didn't bend too far: the sole first-termer was from Chicago.

Although the assignment process usually worked well for the chairman, success was not guaranteed. One of his embarrassing setbacks came when Kent Hance of Texas enlisted as the chief Democratic sponsor of Reagan's 1981 tax cut. Rostenkowski and other top Democrats, including Jim Wright, had selected Hance that year to fill a committee vacancy only after he had sworn loyalty on key issues. Following Hance's apostasy, Rostenkowski won a measure of revenge by barring him from Ways and Means foreign travel and by stripping the wheels from his chair in the committee's hearing room; Hance left the House in 1984 and switched parties a year later.

One of Rostenkowski's rockiest relationships was with Dick Gephardt, the Missouri Democrat who gained a seat on the committee in 1977 as a thirty-five-year-old freshman and soon became the leader of the "new breed" Democrats. As became clear during the late 1970s, when he spearheaded the defeat of President Carter's proposal to regulate hospital costs, Gephardt did not play by the old House rules—the loyal soldier awaiting his turn—as Rostenkowski had done. But that was only the start of their friction. As each gained more influence, Gephardt and Rostenkowski developed something of a love-hate relationship. Rostenkowski was the chairman who wanted to exercise power on his own terms, without direction from others in the House. Gephardt believed in building consensus from the bottom up, without regard to seniority; he wanted to be more responsive to party members outside the committee system. "They had a difficult relationship," said Dorgan, who dealt closely with both. "Rostenkowski saw Gephardt as a golden boy who liked starched shirts and long meetings."

Their dealings grew even more strained as Gephardt gained national prominence. In 1985 he became chairman of the House Democratic Caucus. But, in contrast to the hand-picking of Rostenkowski for that position in 1967, Gephardt won the office in a contest in which all House Democrats were eligible to run and vote. Gephardt worked to make the caucus more active in weighing political options and shaping public debate. As he ran from meeting to meeting, the shirtsleeved Gephardt made little effort to mask the reality that he was a young man in a hurry. To the surprise of no one in the House, he launched in early 1987 a grassroots campaign for the 1988 Democratic presidential nomination. That was another big difference from Rostenkowski's early world, when local bosses awarded presidential nominations. Still, when Gephardt announced his candidacy before cheering thousands at the St. Louis Union Station, Rostenkowski gave a rousing introduction and endorsement of the candidate. "I think he'd make a hell of a president," he told the flag-waving crowd. A top Gephardt adviser was "stunned" by the chairman's action. To friends who questioned his support for a frequent adversary, Rostenkowski simply responded, "He is on my committee, of course." Aside from demonstrating his loyalty at Gephardt's big moment, however, the embrace had little effect on the campaign—or on politics in the chairman's hometown.

Gephardt's overweening ambition helps to explain why Rostenkowski grew peeved with this rising star. Even though he remained a Ways and Means member, Gephardt worked with others to develop competing Democratic power centers. As the most influential spokesman for the new breed of post-Watergate Democrats, he was constantly on the move. He worked with small groups of colleagues to develop new ideas in areas from international trade to health care to the federal budget. In addition, Tip O'Neill assigned Gephardt to chair task forces that were designed to rally rank-and-file Democrats behind bills that faced problems on the House floor. Gephardt also sought to use the Democratic Caucus to shift the party from the left toward the center. He helped to assemble many of those "neoliberal" ideas in widely circulated caucus publications referred to as "The Yellow Brick Road," which he saw as an opportunity to help reshape the Democrats' national message so that eventually they could regain the White House. But what Gephardt allies described as earnest consensus-building was viewed by many other Democrats as naked self-promotion and the abandonment of ideals.

Rostenkowski didn't like Gephardt, said a Democrat who watched them closely for many years. "He was an upstart at Ways and Means and a grandstander on some issues. . . . Their differences were in generation and style more than substance." In part their problem was that the trim, neat, blond-haired Gephardt acted like the Eagle Scout he had been as a St. Louis youth, while the hefty and disheveled Rostenkowski was the old-style, gruff pol who came across poorly on television. But the deeper-seated difference between them was that Rostenkowski played politics by the old rules; this bull did not welcome advice from the new kid on the block. Gephardt, by contrast, was eager to shake up the established order. He used high-profile publicity campaigns that ran counter to Rostenkowski's conciliatory style. On trade issues, for example, Gephardt was a prime supporter in 1983 of "domestic content" legislation to require manufacturers to use up to 90 percent of American-made parts for each car sold in the United States. Rostenkowski opposed that proposal, which was pushed by the United Auto Workers union; much to Gephardt's regret, Rostenkowski helped to derail the measure in the House. For a short time in 1985 he signed onto another Gephardt-initiated proposal to add a 25 percent surcharge on imports from any nation that enjoyed a large trade surplus with the United States and permitted unfair trade practices. But Rostenkowski backed away from that proposal, which clearly was targeted at Japan, when it generated strong criticism from trade experts.[2]

Gephardt's efforts, ironically, paved the way for Rostenkowski's most celebrated accomplishment during his thirteen years as Ways and Means chairman—passage of the 1986 Tax Reform Act. Moving that bill to center stage also was a success story for Gephardt, even though he was barely in the picture during the heavy legislative lifting. He had taken the lead in 1982 when he cosponsored with Sen. Bill Bradley of New Jersey what became known as the Bradley-Gephardt bill. Their proposal eliminated most deductions and other major preferences in the income tax code in exchange for lowering the top rate to 30 percent for individual taxpayers—a huge drop from the 50 percent maximum for high-earners that had been written into the 1981 tax cut. Although he was less instrumental to the new tax-reform measure than was his more famous partner—the former New York Knicks basketball player—Gephardt exploited the proposal to broaden his own appeal with the national audience.

For Rostenkowski the eventual enactment of the Bradley-Gephardt plan was a vital accomplishment on several levels, policy as well as politics. Although he deferred to Reagan on the broad outlines, Rostenkowski took control of the deal-making once the president unveiled his own tax-

reform plan. In Ways and Means he crafted details to fit his personal lean-
ings. He used the bill's framework to appeal to the middle class and to
place various business sectors on a more even keel. Then he added features to accommodate numerous political friends. If the enactment of the
1981 tax cuts was the law that had the single greatest impact during the
ensuing decade, the 1986 tax reform was the preeminent model of bipartisan cooperation on legislation that responded to the public interest.
Within the House, Rostenkowski emerged from the battle as the dominant
legislative force. He clipped the wings of the pesky Gephardt and gave
the prodigy few opportunities to become a major player in the wheeling
and dealing on the proposal. By eclipsing Jim Wright, who was about to
replace O'Neill as speaker, Rostenkowski also signaled that he would not
readily surrender influence. With Republicans he sought cooperation but
more often on his own terms. In short, Rostenkowski became the master
legislator on tax reform by deftly combining old-style politics with a
smattering of new-age techniques.[3]

Under inauspicious circumstances for Democrats, the 1984 presidential campaign raised the curtain on the tax-reform debate. In January Reagan ordered the Treasury Department to submit a plan after the election to
"simplify the entire tax code so that all taxpayers, big and small, are
treated more fairly." In his reelection campaign he often cited the issue.
Perhaps surprisingly, Democratic presidential nominee Walter Mondale
turned down pleas from Bradley and others to make tax reform a centerpiece of his own campaign. Although many of his supporters embraced
the elimination of tax breaks for the wealthy and big business, Mondale
rejected their pleas. The proposal "never even got serious consideration,"
according to a review of the tax-reform battle. "The ultimate reason that
Mondale avoided tax reform, a reason that was rooted in the nature of the
campaign itself and that overshadowed all other reasons, was this: Mondale was a campaign of the special interests."[4] With Reagan winning
forty-nine of the fifty states, the Democrat obviously could have benefited
from such fresh ideas.

If the progressive Mondale opposed tax reform, would Rostenkowski,
whose quarter-century in Washington had made him comfortable with
special-interest groups, express similar reluctance? Well, yes and no. As a
Democratic coalition-builder, he had sought to keep under his party's big
tent as many viewpoints as possible. Consequently tax reform should
have flashed red lights for Rostenkowski. Its premise was to inflict pain

on many narrow groups and their favored tax provisions in order to grant benefits to the public as a whole. When he unveiled his plan, Reagan told the nation that it "will free us from the grip of special interests and create a binding commitment to the only special interest that counts—you, the people who pay America's bills." But Rostenkowski put aside his personal views; he realized he had a pivotal role in determining the fate of tax reform. As someone who revered the presidency throughout his career, he did not wish to be responsible for killing the president's proposal. Given Reagan's landslide reelection, Rostenkowski feared that Democrats placed themselves at peril if they did not respond seriously. "When he asks the American people for help, it's amazing how the people blindly trust any president," he said in an early 1985 interview, proudly pointing to photographs on his office wall of the seven presidents with whom he had served since 1959. "In my own living room, when I was arguing [on television] with President Reagan during the tax-depreciation debate, my youngest daughter told me the president was very convincing." Many Democrats disagreed with Rostenkowski's handling of Reagan's plan. "He paid just a bit too much deference to presidents," said Dennis Eckart of Ohio. But Rostenkowski believed that tax reform had considerable merit. "Much of it is a Democratic dream." He brushed off his critics, most of whom were outside his committee, and concentrated on showing that he was a strong chairman who made things happen. "Danny was the ultimate pragmatist," said Bill Gradison of Ohio, a Ways and Means Republican throughout the Reagan-Bush years. "He was not an ideologue."

As the tax-reform debate heated up following the 1984 election, Rostenkowski was careful to let Reagan move first. "If he leads, we'll follow," the chairman said. He wanted to make sure that the president backed the package before committing himself or his own party. Especially on the controversial features of the proposal, Rostenkowski wanted to limit the Democrats' exposure. But he also made clear his own view that the concept made sense, much as Gephardt and Bradley had argued. "We must all reckon with the increasing public frustration with our tax system," he told New York City tax specialists in February 1985. "So there's a strong case to be made for starting the long march toward a simpler and fairer code." For Rostenkowski personally, tax reform also offered the opportunity for redemption. After four years as chairman he had overcome both self-doubts and skeptical colleagues as to whether he could meet the challenge. Now he hoped to prove that he had the technical skills to lead Congress on such an important measure and the strength to make the necessary compromises and face down powerful interests, both on and off Capitol Hill. "Everyone recognizes my authority as chairman of the Ways and Means Committee, and I don't want to abuse it," he said in an interview. "I want people to say I played tough politics but also was a respected chairman." Within weeks Reagan's aides began to unveil their plan's outlines. Although it restored some business tax breaks that had been dropped by the purer tax-reform option prepared by Treasury Department officials, the new top rate of 35 percent for individual taxpayers was bound to generate public support.

The biggest stumbling block Rostenkowski faced was the ambivalence of most House members. Like most Republicans, Democrats professed to agree with the general goal; but the devil was in the details, typically those that affected the interests of businesses and workers in their districts. "Like everyone else, I agree with 80 percent of the goal," said Jim Jones of Oklahoma. "But the problem is that no one's 80 percent is the same." Many Democrats also were more leery than was Rostenkowski of joining Reagan on such a major issue. "Democrats must show what we are for," said another Democratic lawmaker. "We can't say, as Rostenkowski does, that it's Reagan's issue and we'll help enact his bill." Majority Leader Jim Wright, in particular, strongly opposed tax reform. He objected to setting the top income tax rate so low that it could adversely affect the budget deficit; he also feared the proposal's damaging impact on Texas, especially its oil and savings-and-loans industries that historically benefited from tax breaks. But Rostenkowski was fixed on placing Ways and Means at the center of the action. "We want to be part of this from the beginning," committee member Kennelly said at the time. And other Rostenkowski allies wanted to position Democrats to share the credit for success on the tax-reform measure—while avoiding blame for possible failure to act. Mostly Rostenkowski believed that Reagan's support made the bill too good to turn down. "To my knowledge, Ronald Reagan never broke his word with me on the bill," he said later. "I asked him to promise me not to nit-pick. . . . I knew that he didn't know the details anyway."

Rostenkowski indicated the Democrats' cautious balancing act when he responded to Reagan's nationally televised May 28 address by delivering his own carefully crafted eleven-minute appeal. It was an important occasion for Democrats, especially because of their recent unhappy history on tax issues. The response became Rostenkowski's magic moment in the national spotlight. Using a text drafted by his press secretary John Sherman and then polished by Democratic consultant Joe Rothstein (who also worked to place the chairman in the most favorable camera and lighting angles), Rostenkowski was conciliatory as he highlighted his party's contribution to the debate. "Trying to tax people and businesses—everyone—fairly," he told the nation. "That's been the historic Democratic commitment." Replicating the approach he had used at the 1964 Democratic convention to nominate Hubert Humphrey for vice-president, he also reached out to the workingman in his speech. Citing his own "Polish neighborhood" in Chicago, he recalled that most workers, including his parents and grandparents, didn't like taxes. Reagan's proposal, he continued, could redeem the Democrats' "long-standing commitment to a tax system that's simple and fair" and that also gives "real relief for middle-income taxpayers." Although Rostenkowski emphasized that Democrats would not rubber-stamp the proposal, especially if Reagan yielded to "special interests," the chairman concluded the speech with a personal appeal to the "silent majority." Write him a letter to show their support, he urged. "Even if you can't spell Rostenkowski, put down what they used to call my father and grandfather, Rosty," he said into the camera. "Just address it to R-O-S-T-Y, Washington, D.C."

His brief speech was a resounding success. Within days his plea had generated more than 75,000 letters. The previously obscure congressman became something of a folk hero. His aides produced "Write Rosty" bumper stickers that were distributed across the nation. Although he did not overshadow Reagan's performance, Rostenkowski made tax reform a bipartisan cause. "You have to be a legislator with a mind that understands the Rose Garden," was his credo as chairman. "Whatever you do in committee or on the House floor, once you get to the Rose Garden, no one knows what you did." In effect, he said, Democrats should let Reagan take the credit while they wrote the key details. But his Democratic allies' reaction was split. Bradley was elated that the two speeches had focused public attention on the issue. Gephardt, however, emphasized Reagan's shortcomings. "By retaining many deductions and preferences, the Reagan plan is not designed to simplify the tax code as Bradley-Gephardt does—it merely shifts the preferences around," Gephardt said. "What President Reagan is going to propose is not tax reform but tax retreat." Gephardt's statement caused teeth-gnashing at Rostenkowski's camp. But it gave cover to Democrats who had reservations about tax reform. It was an omen of the difficulties facing the Ways and Means Committee.

The ceremonial launch of the debate provided only a brief lift for tax reform. Once Rostenkowski convened several weeks of Ways and Means hearings, the focus shifted from the zealous reformers to the narrow interests who were concerned with Internal Revenue Code minutiae. Status-quo advocates used the hearings to sound alarms about change. Among more than six hundred witnesses who testified during thirty days of hearings, most voiced complaints and many quickly gained allies on Ways and Means. By the time the House recessed in August, the opposition had run the gamut: state and local governments griped that their constituents would no longer be permitted to deduct local taxes on their federal tax returns; many businesses opposed elimination of the investment tax credit, even though the change was a tradeoff for lower corporate rates; specific industries such as oil, timber, and pharmaceuticals feared the loss of tax breaks they had exploited for decades. Although a survey of Ways and Means members showed that at least twenty-five of the committee's thirty-six members were prepared to approve some version of tax reform, many favored major changes in Reagan's plan. But for every tax code preference that was restored to the bill, sponsors would have to propose compensating revisions. The responsibility to make the whole proposal come together weighed heavily on the chairman. "There are three key players on the committee," said Frank Guarini of New Jersey, a Ways and Means Democrat. "They are Rosty, Rosty, and Rosty. He can't dictate what happens, but he's very influential and respected as a leader because of his knowledge, persuasiveness, and understanding."

Rostenkowski understood the challenge he faced. Despite the positive response to the May 28 televised speeches, the average voter barely understood tax-reform nuances. With his committee under siege, Rostenkowski needed to bolster support. One effective tool was his private early-morning meetings with Ways and Means members and their chief aides, where Rostenkowski probed their reaction to controversial provisions and the options for modifying them. In a manner reminiscent of the committee under Mills, the members sipped coffee around the long table in the cozy library behind the committee's cavernous hearing room. These bipartisan meetings would turn into hard-nosed discussions of tax-reform complexities. Bob Matsui, the California Democrat, recalled that the sessions were useful for encouraging "an exchange of views and much more candor than during the hearings." Rostenkowski sometimes used the closed-door meetings to invite big-name guests—such as New York Gov. Mario Cuomo, General Motors chairman Roger Smith, and Treasury Secretary Jim Baker—to provide more candid assessments than were available in the often stylized procedures of a public hearing, where television cameras and reporters' notebooks discouraged probing exchanges. With these private discussions, Rostenkowski narrowed the differences among members on controversial issues.

When lawmakers returned to work after Labor Day, tough choices lay ahead. "A lot of the early enthusiasm faded after members started to learn the details," said Joe Dowley, who was the committee's top aide and Rostenkowski's confidant during tax reform. Rostenkowski decided he had no choice but to measure the committee's interest. From the start it wasn't easy. "The bill had several wakes but no funeral," Rostenkowski recalled. The committee held lengthy debate, even on amendments that should have gone down quickly. The first moment of truth came in mid-October when the committee unexpectedly approved an amendment by Ronnie Flippo, an Alabama Democrat, who wanted to expand—not reduce—tax breaks for big banks. With adoption of what he viewed as a "killer" amendment, Rostenkowski angrily gaveled the committee into recess so that members could reflect. "The Flippo vote was the culmination of a lot of jitteryness," Dowley said. "We knew very well that we had a problem with the bill as a whole. The Flippo amendment was only a stalking horse." With only one of the thirteen Ways and Means Republicans voting against the proposal, Rostenkowski could have walked away and said that Reagan failed to control the Republican side. "That was one of my darkest days," he said. It was also a stressful time in his personal life: his daughter Stacy was very ill in Chicago with kidney problems. The accumulated pressures left him exhausted and brought him to tears in private. But Rostenkowski was stubborn, a useful trait in legislative deal-making. "Danny felt an ethnic pride that he was going to do this," said Tom Downey. "He had a great quality—both a blessing and a curse—that once you begin a journey, you continue with it, even in sweaty-palms time." So Rostenkowski leveraged Flippo's amendment to show committee members that their credibility was at stake. Even Flippo soon conceded that his amendment was a mistake. When Ways and Means reconvened the next week, he worked with Rostenkowski to win support for a scaled-back version. Finally, it appeared, the committee had turned the corner. With his shrewd instincts, Rostenkowski brought the members to realize that they had no escape from the tax-reform debate and that they must pull their oars together to reach the goal.

As Ways and Means members grew more committed, Rostenkowski tapped lieutenants to lead small bipartisan task forces to resolve several of the thorniest problems. For example, on the arcane issue of tax-exempt bonds for local governments, Rostenkowski designated Jake Pickle to oversee the effort. When Matsui proposed what proved to be excessive local benefits, "Joe Dowley saw how much we were losing and he croaked," Matsui said. So several aides met overnight and prepared a compromise package that Wyche Fowler of Georgia offered the next morning. The task force approved the deal. That was typical of how Ways and Means handled the bill in the crucial days of deliberation. To boost loyalty, Rostenkowski carried a large notebook that listed the special provisions each member wanted in the bill. In the final days he often opened that book as he pleaded with members for their support on controversial provisions. "He was fair, more so to his allies," said Barbara Kennelly. "That is how it works, especially to get good legislation."

Rostenkowski discovered, however, that his attempt to cater to the middle class had created a big problem: House Republicans complained that the reduction in taxes paid by individuals would be balanced by higher taxes on business. Even though Reagan was their president, many Republicans had been unenthusiastic about tax reform from the start. And Democrats had insisted on so many changes that Republicans found even more to dislike. "Republicans felt that we had been taken to the cleaners," said Bill Frenzel. Adding to the dilemma, Reagan aides had stayed in closer touch with Rostenkowski than with most Republicans during the committee's work, Bill Gradison noted. Their unhappiness peaked as the bill moved to the House floor in early December. To the shock of both Rostenkowski and the White House, Republicans voted overwhelmingly against a procedural motion for the terms of the House vote on the bill. "The mistake by Jim Baker is that he dealt exclusively with Rostenkowski and ignored the House Republicans," said a party insider. The defeat of that proposed rule posed an interesting twist. Now Reagan was forced to rescue Rostenkowski's tax-reform bill. The president visited Capitol Hill for a rare, closed-door speech to the House Republican Conference; other GOP leaders began twisting arms to support the measure. A major player was Minority Leader Bob Michel of Illinois, Ros-

Dan Rostenkowski entered the family business of politics in 1952, when he won a seat in the Illinois legislature. His father, a longtime Chicago alderman and Democratic ward committeeman, gave the twenty-four-year-old a head start. (Chicago Sun-Times)

Richard J. Daley, mayor and Democratic "boss" of Chicago from 1955 to 1976, took a special interest in Dan. "Mayor Daley could put you down in a second," Rostenkowski recalled, "and he could make you soar to heights you never believed you could attain."

As a young Catholic in Congress, Rostenkowski felt close to
John F. Kennedy and his political team. But he was disappointed
by JFK's limited achievements. "It was all Camelot," he later said.

Rostenkowski was
awed by Lyndon
Johnson's political
muscle. When the
president bore down
on an issue during a
White House visit by
House Democrats, the
disciple of machine
politics whispered,
"God, he's tough!"

With his friend, House Speaker Tip O'Neill, Rostenkowski resisted Jimmy Carter's legislative agenda and disdained his political incompetence.

As chairman of Ways and Means, Rostenkowski unsuccessfully challenged Ronald Reagan's tax cuts, then sought common ground with the new president on many issues. The 1986 Tax Reform Act slashed rates and eliminated many loopholes.

Although he basked in his friendship with George Bush, Rostenkowski was disappointed by their limited success—though their work on deficit reduction helped force budget discipline.

Inside this drab building on Chicago's near northwest side (opposite), Rostenkowski provided "one-stop shopping" for constituents seeking federal assistance, local government help, or political favors. (Chicago Sun-Times)

Rostenkowski had a shaky relationship with Harold Washington, Chicago's mayor from 1983 to 1987. But he used his influence to deliver federal dollars to the city. And, said a Rostenkowski ally, "he never asked for credit." (AP/Wide World)

When Bill Clinton became president, Rostenkowski became part of the Democratic team pushing legislation—here working on the deficit-reduction plan with (to his right) Clinton budget director Leon Panetta, House Speaker Tom Foley, and Senate Majority Leader George Mitchell. (AP/Wide World)

With members of the Ways and Means Committee, Rostenkowski was blunt in seeking support and willing to offer inducements. Here his target was Charles Rangel of New York, later the committee's senior Democrat. (AP/Wide World)

Rostenkowski met with many Chicago organizations pleading for federal help, but toward the end of his career he paid a price for failing to heed warnings that he was losing touch locally. (Chicago Sun-Times)

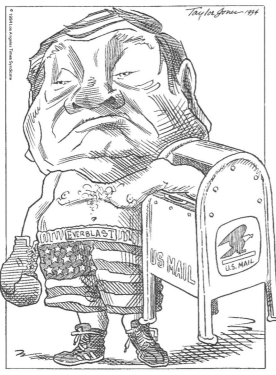

Federal prosecutors accused Rostenkowski of using his official allowances to pay for sixty armchairs from the House stationery store, which he stored in his basement and intended for friends. After his indictment, he asked, "Why are the chairs there if not for us to purchase?" (Chicago Sun-Times)

The centerpiece of the seventeen-count indictment against Rostenkowski was the charge that he exchanged official stamps for personal cash at the House post office. (Los Angeles Times Syndicate)

Following his arraignment, Rostenkowski insisted that he would be vindicated. When he later pleaded guilty, his attorney, Dan Webb, said his client had been "singled out." (AP/Wide World)

Despite the adversities at the close of his career, Rostenkowski's legislative record and his personality marked him as a towering congressional figure in the last half of the twentieth century.

tenkowski's pal who had joined him in many drives between Chicago and Washington during their early years in the House. "We've had a long friendship," Michel said later. "But you also can't deny how important is his knowledge of the system." The tax-reform package returned to the House floor a few days later with only small changes. On the second try, Republicans voting for the procedural rule increased from fourteen to seventy. Democratic support held firm. At long last the elated Rostenkowski had scored his victory. He felt, he said at the time, like General Patton after V-E Day in May 1945, "knowing the rest of the war will be fought in another theater."

House passage, of course, was scarcely the final step. Tax reform endured a "Perils of Pauline" struggle at the Senate Finance Committee, similar to the travails at Ways and Means. The contrast was that Finance chairman Bob Packwood of Oregon initially lacked Rostenkowski's enthusiasm for the bill. After seeing his own committee nearly kill it, Packwood—with vital support from Bill Bradley—stunned his committee with a bill that set the top rate for the wealthiest individuals at 27 percent, compared with 38 percent in Rostenkowski's final version. When the Finance Committee and the Senate ultimately passed something close to Packwood's version in late June, Rostenkowski and Packwood took command of the difficult House-Senate conference to craft the final deal. Rostenkowski launched the final negotiations by voicing a willingness to accept a top rate close to 27 percent. In return he insisted on paring many tax breaks that had survived the House or Senate bills. That would tip the tax writers' "distribution tables" so that the benefit of tax reform would go chiefly to the middle class, not to the wealthy. "Our commitment to a bill that lowers rates while broadening the tax base is stronger than our allegiance to any particular part of either bill," he warned on the eve of House-Senate negotiations. "To the extent we give to special corporate interests, we must take from middle income earners."

As Rostenkowski, Packwood, and their aides came under intense pressures from special interests, they stepped up to carry the day for tax reform. Having come this far, they understood that failure was not an option. Besides, they had an additional tool to coerce the critics. As had become a tradition on tax bills, the chairmen could hand out "transition rules"—special benefits typically targeted to constituents, companies, or communities in the states or districts of key members. Often these provisions were legislative gobbledygook, which only true insiders could decipher or connect to a particular patron or interest group. "In the case of an individual who is a beneficiary of a trust which was established on December 7, 1979, under the laws of a foreign jurisdiction . . ." read a provision inserted in the tax-reform bill. Some beneficiaries were easier to identify: they included the owners of the Cleveland Indians and the Miami Dolphins, who won tax breaks for their new sports stadiums, and the Commonwealth Edison utility company, which happens to be based in Chicago. Rostenkowski played hardball on these provisions. When David Martin, a junior Republican from upstate New York, asked for a transition rule to benefit a hydroelectric plant in his district, Rostenkowski telephoned Ray McGrath at his Long Island home on a Saturday afternoon to ask whether Martin would vote for passage of the bill. In response to McGrath's query, Martin said no. "He didn't vote for the bill or get the help for his plant," McGrath later noted. To critics, such provisions were little short of graft. "The people who wrote the tax law either say they do not know how it got there, or are not talking," reported a muckraking critique of how Congress writes tax law.[5] To Rostenkowski, however, transition rules long ago had become an unavoidable—even necessary—part of tax politics, and he was not about to sacrifice his power to dispense such plums. Besides, he contended, these measures' cost to the Treasury was minor compared to the public benefit of the entire bill. Victory on tax reform was not merely for the taxpayer, Rostenkowski added, it was also a triumph for bipartisanship. "The political process worked," he crowed as House-Senate negotiators finished their work. "The center held."

But the outcome did not cheer everyone. Perhaps the unhappiest was Jim Wright, for whom Rostenkowski was campaign manager in his 1976 contest. Over the years their alliance had cooled. As a Texan the majority leader had several grievances on tax reform. In addition to fears about the loss of long-standing benefits for the oil and gas industry, Wright saw signs that the state's real-estate explosion was ending at the same time tax reform was expunging many provisions that had been a boon to those investors. "It brought on a hell of a recession in Texas," Wright said years later. "It set up the failure of real property and its decline to the point where the savings and loans found that their collateral would not cover the loan." For Wright, those weren't the only problems. As a populist architect of national Democrats' attempts to draw the lines between the two parties more sharply, he opposed the Reagan-Rostenkowski blurring of those differences. Wright wanted to build more progressivity into the income tax code so that working-class voters could see that Washington was giving them a better deal than the wealthy received. And with the federal budget deficit mushrooming, Wright contended that higher taxes on business should be used to reduce the Treasury's debt, not to lower taxpayers' rates. "I asked Tip where would we be when we need more money," Wright recounted. "Tip said, 'Jimmy, that will be your problem.'"

Wright's strongest objection may have been to Rostenkowski's handling of tax reform on the House floor. After the Republicans' nearly unanimous opposition brought defeat on the first procedural vote, Wright strenuously opposed giving Reagan a second chance. "We had [tax reform] beat after the rule was defeated," Wright lamented. "It was a horrible mistake for Tip to allow Danny to sit down with Jim Baker," the Treasury secretary, to discuss how to secure Republican votes. Had he been speaker, Wright added, he would not have granted tax-reform supporters another opportunity.

At the time Rostenkowski did not talk much with Wright because his objections were well known. With O'Neill having announced that he would not seek reelection in 1986, Wright had begun to carve a more active role as heir apparent. His opposition to tax reform, consequently, also posed an internal risk for the Ways and Means chairman. "Danny resented that I was not as willing as Tip was to let him make policy on taxes," Wright said. But Rostenkowski was not intimidated. To the contrary, he sent clear signals that he wished to challenge Wright for the speaker's office. And he appeared to keep alive his prospective candidacy well beyond the time when he had a realistic chance to win. As in 1970 when he withheld support from Carl Albert's unopposed bid to replace the retiring John McCormack, Rostenkowski again scorned the imperative to fall into line behind the speaker-in-waiting.

WHEN ROSTENKOWSKI sought to exploit his role in tax reform, his ambition generated a rapid response from the ever-vigilant Wright. The Texan quickly realized that Rostenkowski's "strategy would be to ride tax reform to the speakership," according to a Wright biographer. "The people around Wright grew increasingly impatient—and nervous."[6] In a preemptive move, Wright decided in late January 1985 to canvass all House Democrats to ask whether they would support him for speaker. The response was highly favorable, claimed Wright's team. He even won substantial support from what would have been Rostenkowski's base. "In Illinois, Wright got the immediate commitments of over half the delegation," according to Wright's findings. "In Ways and Means, he got exactly half."[7] After his blitzkrieg, which lasted less than a week, Wright staged a Capitol press conference to proclaim that he had already locked up enough votes to assure victory when House Democrats selected O'Neill's successor after the 1986 election. He took the early initiative in order to "clear the air and see who your friends are," Wright said. But Rostenkowski dismissed the claim as far too premature. Wright's fate "will be determined by his performance," he said at the time, "and he has egg fields to walk over."

Although Rostenkowski continued to talk publicly about running against Wright, he never mounted a serious bid where it mattered: in talks with House members. Even when a handful of Rostenkowski's allies and senior aides began to lay the groundwork for a campaign for speaker, he did not seize the opportunity. "I did some work," said John Sherman, his press secretary from 1981 until 1986. "He knew that." Despite his talk and his occasionally strongly felt conviction that he would be a better speaker than Wright, Rostenkowski was unwilling to challenge the front-runner. "I was very disappointed that he didn't run," Sherman acknowledged. The ambivalence bore similarities not only to his 1970 fiasco with Albert but also to his failure to step up to the plate and run for mayor after Daley's death in 1976. Rostenkowski realized that a bid for speaker would require a grueling campaign with no guarantee of success. He could not count on a committee of bosses to declare him the most worthy contender, as had been the case decades ago in Chicago and in other places where Democrats assembled. Might he have fought and won? Perhaps. Did he show a lack of political courage? Probably. But he surely realized that a challenge to Wright would risk everything, including his Ways and Means chairmanship.

The factors weighing against Rostenkowski were in fact overwhelming. For more than a half-century every Democratic speaker had previously served as majority leader. Like others in his situation, Wright had been unwaveringly loyal to the top man, sometimes in difficult circumstances. And he had worked hard to convince colleagues that he was the best man for the job. To have a shot, Rostenkowski probably would have had to depict Wright's Southern base as out of step with the party. And he would have cited his own skills. "As speaker, he would have redefined the party," said an admiring Ways and Means colleague. "And he would have created discipline where we needed it." Given his own moderate predilections, however, Rostenkowski would have had his own problems in securing support from liberal Democrats. And in contrast to Wright, Rostenkowski had not reached out to build goodwill with many colleagues. "I never thought of Danny as seeking popularity. He was more interested in being powerful," Wright said. He "did not have a reservoir of goodwill" with many members at that time, added Tom Foley, who was campaigning to succeed Wright as majority leader. "To take on a sitting leader, he needed more than the loyalty of friends." Still, by artfully building coalitions with candidates for other slots, Rostenkowski might have tested his vaunted skills at insider deal-making. In addition to his own allies from the committee, he might have expected friendly words from his pal O'Neill. And there could be no guarantee how Wright would respond to the pressures of a challenge.

Rostenkowski faced another difficulty in mounting a challenge to Wright: the relentless demands of his chairmanship. In late 1985, at the same time he was consumed with moving the tax-reform bill through the House, he also was working on the Democrats' response to the Senate-passed Gramm-Rudman-Hollings plan to reduce the federal deficit, which had risen to the then-astronomical level of $221 billion in fiscal 1986. In approving that bipartisan proposal, with the Reagan administration's support, the Republican Senate sought to impose a timetable to wipe out the federal deficit by 1991. At the core of that proposal (which the Supreme Court later determined was unconstitutional) was a deficit-reduction schedule that could trigger automatic across-the-board cuts in most federal spending, including many entitlement programs under Ways and Means jurisdiction. Rostenkowski and most committee Democrats strongly opposed that provision. But they recognized they probably lacked the votes to kill it in the House, especially if they failed to offer an alternative. "What began to create our coalition was the reality that the votes ultimately would be there in the House to pass some form of Gramm-Rudman," said Leon Panetta of California, who later became House Budget Committee chairman and President Clinton's chief of staff. Coming on the heels of Reagan's landslide reelection, the budget debate was a time of great peril for Democrats.

As chairman of the House-Senate conference that hammered out the final compromise on the deficit-reduction scheme, Rostenkowski encouraged pragmatism in coordinating the House Democrats' response. Among other changes they added several programs for the poor to the list of exemptions from the threat of across-the-board spending cuts. Staff experts also fine-tuned what critics contended were the potentially blunt edges of the new budget mechanism. The result was "the first time in the Reagan era there was close cooperation among the key committee chairmen and leadership staff" in preparing a Democratic alternative, said a senior budget aide. Although Congress and Reagan later decided to suspend Gramm-Rudman-Hollings, and the law failed to achieve its sponsors' stated goals, the 1985 experience helped to set a framework for more successful deficit reduction by both parties in the early 1990s.

With his commonsense attitude, Rostenkowski was appalled by the continuing growth of the deficit. Less willing than many Democrats to call for tax increases, especially in the face of Reagan's opposition, Rostenkowski advocated what he considered sensible steps to cut spending. "We're a bit like the binge eater who keeps promising that he'll go on a diet but never quite manages to translate his hope into reality," he said in an October 1985 speech. "We do, however, know that the country is increasingly anxious over huge deficits and is demanding more than just another promise of reduction." His growing preference during the 1980s for spending cuts over tax increases raised the hackles of many liberal Democrats who complained that he was unwilling to impose pain on the wealthy. But he responded that he was being both politically realistic, during an era of tightfisted Republican presidents, and fiscally sensible, given the consistent spending increases of the preceding two decades. Rostenkowski also displayed his fiscal restraint by cooperating with House Budget Committee chairman William Gray, a Baptist minister from Philadelphia who spearheaded a campaign to show that Democrats stood for greater budget discipline. Under pressure from the Budget Committee, which was exercising its power under the 1974 Congressional Budget Act to set an annual fiscal game plan, Rostenkowski became more responsive in the mid-1980s to reducing the escalating growth rate in Medicare and Medicaid programs. In contrast to the late 1970s, when he resisted Carter's proposal to contain the inflationary spiral in health-care costs, Rostenkowski began to encourage belt-tightening by health-care practitioners. In a Mayo Clinic speech in Minnesota in August 1985 he described "a continuing need for government restraints" in health costs. "Faced with the competing claims of a relatively small number of affluent doctors and a large number of sick senior citizens, Congress will side with the elderly nearly every time," he warned the medical professionals.

The 1986 elections changed Capitol Hill's dynamics in several ways. First, the Democrats scored an eight-seat gain in the Senate, regaining control there for the first time under Reagan. No longer would House Democrats be the lonely defenders of their principles against attack from Reagan and his Senate allies. In addition, the unraveling of what became known as the Iran-contra scandal—in which the Reagan administration allegedly funneled covert U.S. arms to Iran in exchange for funds that were shipped to anti-Communist rebels in Nicaragua—resulted in lengthy congressional hearings that severely weakened Reagan, who already was a lame duck. Finally, Jim Wright's takeover from O'Neill produced a speaker who was more assertive in defining the legislative agenda and less respectful of presidential prerogatives. At Wright's initiative the House and Senate quickly passed and overrode vetoes of public-works bills that Reagan had stifled a year earlier. Wright also laid out a lengthy agenda of economic legislation to show that Democrats were in charge and ready to address the nation's needs with more activist government. "Now, it is up to us to show that we are prepared to govern," Wright told Democrats following the election.

For Rostenkowski the Democrats' resurgence was a mixed blessing. With O'Neill's usual assent, he enjoyed his role as chief spokesman on the many issues controlled by Ways and Means. But other House and Senate Democrats now competed to speak for the party, which might complicate Rostenkowski's pursuit of bipartisanship with the Reagan team. Perhaps the most difficult challenge he faced was sorting out an arrangement with Wright. Even before Congress convened, the new speaker resurrected his opposition to tax reform by advocating a delay in promised tax-rate cuts for the wealthy. He was quick to meddle in the turf of a chairman who valued his autonomy. "Jim Wright wanted to be more involved in the work of the committee," said Rob Leonard, who in 1987 took over as Ways and Means staff director. "Mr. O'Neill and Mr. Foley had a higher level of trust in the work of the committee, both the policy and the politics." Rostenkowski reacted quickly. Pleading for realism, he told Wright "to decide whether to make a political statement or to have an accomplishment." Nor was that all. Wright also hoped to move quickly on an international trade bill to strengthen the nation's economic power overseas. That proposal, which died in the Senate after House passage in

1986, raised Rostenkowski's objections to its protectionist features. And he issued perhaps his most stinging rebuke of Wright when he condescendingly said in a late 1986 interview that the new speaker could not understand the difficulty of passing legislation because in thirty-two years in the House he had never been a chairman. "The rules by which we play are so complicated," Rostenkowski said. "He has to sit and referee if he wants to be visible."[8]

With Wright's ascension, Rostenkowski found himself under attack from critics emboldened to stifle his bipartisanship and his secretive operation of Ways and Means. Some were unhappy about the propensity of Rostenkowski—like his predecessors as Ways and Means chairmen—to bring bills such as tax reform to the House floor under a "closed rule" that permitted few if any members to offer amendments during the debate. "The committee got arrogant under Rostenkowski and felt they didn't have to think about the views of other members," said Barney Frank, a Massachusetts Democrat. Rostenkowski "cared only about the committee and failed to run traps on floor, so he sometimes got into trouble," said a business consultant with lengthy experience in dealing with Ways and Means. But others who watched him closely, notably the committee Republicans, contended that Wright shortened the Democrats' leash on the independent chairman. As the years passed, said Frenzel, Rostenkowski's role increasingly became that of "the good loyal Democrat."

In Wright's two-plus years as speaker, Rostenkowski sometimes bowed to his party leader, but often he was as independent as ever. A brief review of three conflicts that preoccupied Ways and Means in 1987–1988 shows an enhanced pragmatism in what was probably his most productive period as chairman. When Democrats demanded partisanship on their major trade bill, Rostenkowski sought to meet them partway but eventually prevailed. Where he saw the opening to cooperate with Republicans on expanded Medicare coverage, he moved. And when his committee had an opportunity to place its own stamp on welfare-reform legislation, he seized it. Contrary to the conventional wisdom that not much happens in Washington during a presidential election year, Congress worked actively on these bills well into 1988 before sending them to Reagan for his signature. "Enactment of any one of these bills—trade reform, catastrophic health insurance, or welfare reform—would be considered a major accomplishment in any Congress," he said in a February 1988 speech to

Harvard University's Kennedy School of Government. "We have a chance to enact all three. My point is not that the Congress is working perfectly. In fact, its record on the deficit is not very good. But it is taking incremental and important steps in addressing many other important issues." True, as the two parties made little progress on the budget stalemate, Rostenkowski paid less attention to the endless jousting over the spiraling deficit. All told, however, the bottom line was surprisingly positive.

On the trade bill Rostenkowski again clashed with activists in his own party instead of with the opposition. Gephardt's efforts to curry favor with organized labor in 1987, while he was pursuing the presidential nomination, brought on a nasty conflict with the Ways and Means chairman. Gephardt sponsored an amendment that required the United States to close its trade doors to countries that enjoyed a large surplus resulting from unfair trade practices. With the steady increase in the nation's trade deficit and the accompanying loss of millions of domestic manufacturing jobs, he argued that the president needed additional tools to force other nations to open their markets to U.S. products. But Rostenkowski was not impressed, as he showed in a sharp rhetorical jab at Gephardt. "I am not trying to please [AFL-CIO president] Lane Kirkland," he told a National Press Club audience in March 1987. "I'm trying to write legislation that will be signed by the president."[9] Influenced by corporate executives in Chicago's international business environment, Rostenkowski also grew hostile to what he termed "the porcupine policy of trade—roll up in a ball and show your quills."

But with Wright firmly on Gephardt's side, Rostenkowski was no longer able to stiff-arm labor. As Wright packaged Ways and Means provisions with sections drafted by other House committees, he and his advisers rewrote major pieces. Then, as the bill moved to the House floor, Gephardt filed new language to strengthen its enforcement mechanism against nations that continued to run large surpluses with the United States. Although "the vote had become one as much of symbolism as of substance," according to a study of the trade legislation, the battle lines were drawn in a way that pitted Wright and Gephardt against Rostenkowski, Foley, and most Republicans.[10] Wright was "apparently determined to pull out all the stops on Gephardt's behalf."[11] Not surprisingly, Rostenkowski was displeased; but he did not wage a full-fledged fight. Once he realized that Wright had embraced Gephardt's initiative, Rostenkowski took a light-handed response that "served to set him apart from the more heavy-handed approach adopted by Wright."[12] On a 218 to 214 vote, the House passed Gephardt's amendment, with Democrats divided 201 in favor and 55 against. True, Rostenkowski suffered an unaccustomed rebuke. But in his biography of Wright, author John Barry makes clear that Rostenkowski could have found the votes to turn the tally his way. Instead the chairman held back "as a peace offering to Wright and a sign of his strength."[13]

As Rostenkowski understood, the House's April 1987 vote was hardly the final step for Gephardt's amendment. In the Senate a bipartisan coalition overwhelmingly rejected the House-passed trade sanctions. By the time a House-Senate conference began serious negotiations on the bill, it was the spring of 1988. With Gephardt's presidential candidacy a victim of insufficient funds and an outsider's message that seemed jarring for a congressional insider, his amendment no longer enjoyed a partisan imperative on Capitol Hill. For labor's allies, instead, the new hot-button priority was a proposal to give workers sixty days' advance notice of a plant closing. As for the harder-line trade position, the Reagan administration had taken other steps to satisfy its critics, including measures to mandate closer cooperation with Congress on trade policy and presidential retaliation against nations with large U.S. trade surpluses. After suffering a high-profile setback in the earlier House vote on the Gephardt amendment, Rostenkowski ultimately prevailed on decisions that really mattered.

On the question of welfare reform, the 1988 debate was nowhere near as partisan or public as Gephardt's trade plan. With Rostenkowski's guidance, Ways and Means helped to produce the most comprehensive overhaul of laws affecting assistance to the poor in at least a quarter-century. Following the failures to enact major reforms proposed by Nixon and Carter, the 1988 proposal succeeded by carefully tracking the middle ground between Reagan-led conservatives and liberals who took their cue from Sen. Daniel Patrick Moynihan. Both sides agreed that local welfare agencies were rife with waste and abuse and were not adequately serving their intended beneficiaries. Under prodding from many governors (led by Bill Clinton of Arkansas, who became friendly with Rostenkowski during the handling of the bill), they called for sensible administrative changes for welfare recipients.

Although Rostenkowski was unfamiliar with many of the policy details, and the program was not high on his personal agenda, his direction proved vital in the bill's tricky path to enactment. When Texas Democrat Mike Andrews had a "heart-to-heart" talk with Rostenkowski and Downey, advising that the bill would not pass the House because conservative Democrats were unhappy with its cost, the chairman ordered a 10 percent spending cutback. With only a handful of Republicans in favor, the measure passed narrowly, 230 to 194. For Rostenkowski, welfare reform was an important initiative to bolster public confidence; in part he believed that government had a responsibility to assist people who needed help. "Poverty is this country's dirty little secret," he said in explaining why Congress needed to reform the welfare laws.

To critics who complained that Rostenkowski spent too much time dishing out tax breaks for the wealthy, the welfare-reform debate was a rare effort to improve a federal program to aid the poor. "Rostenkowski was instinctively more conservative on economic issues such as the deficit," said Downey, whom Rostenkowski designated to handle the measure. "But he was instinctively more liberal on social issues like welfare." Downey cut most of the deals that produced the final agreement in private negotiations with senior Reagan aides. Although Moynihan had long been a leading expert on welfare policy—as a Harvard University professor and as an aide to Presidents Kennedy, Johnson, and Nixon on the issue—and provided much of the intellectual firepower for the proposal, he was less skillful in the legislative deal-making. A notable feature of the welfare bill, which Reagan signed, was that it encouraged recipients to find training assistance and jobs. Both liberals and conservatives widely applauded its new requirements that absent parents—usually the father—provide money to support their children. Under Republican pressure, the bill failed to add much spending for state and local programs. But it did not include the kind of punitive measures—such as a ban on single mothers living alone and strict time limits for welfare recipients— that the Republican-controlled Congress and President Clinton agreed to in 1996, much to the dismay of many welfare advocates in his administration.

On what became known as the catastrophic health-insurance bill, too, Rostenkowski sought to improve an important program without adding significantly to the huge federal deficit. (Under the complex budget rules of the 1980s, congressional committees were required to assure that new programs or benefits were "paid for" by commensurate changes, either spending cuts or tax increases.) Like the welfare bill, the Medicare changes were written largely in closed-door negotiations between the Reagan administration and bipartisan leaders in Congress. But in contrast to welfare recipients, the elderly were far more sophisticated politically—more assertive in protecting what they already received, and demanding of new benefits. The outcome triggered one of Rostenkowski's biggest controversies. Indeed, in several respects the catastrophic health-insurance debacle marked the beginning of the end of his successful reign.

The impetus for Medicare changes came from the Reagan administration. Secretary of Health and Human Services Otis Bowen—a former family doctor and governor in Indiana—launched the proposal to address the acute problem of families forced to disburse many tens of thousands of dollars for the costs of "catastrophic" illnesses for the elderly. "Let us remove a financial specter facing our older Americans—the fear of an illness so expensive that it can result in having to make an intolerable choice between bankruptcy and death," Reagan said during his 1987 State of the Union message. For legislators like Rostenkowski who had witnessed the creation of Medicare nearly a quarter-century earlier, coverage of catastrophic and other long-term illnesses would finish their earlier work. But, as in the past, they knew that the challenge was financial. Given budget pressures, both parties agreed that there was no choice but for senior citizens to pay for this additional care through their Medicare premiums. Bowen's original proposal called for adding $4.92 to the $17.90 premium that the elderly already paid each month for Medicare; in exchange they would be eligible for up to one year of hospital care, and their annual personal expenses for all Medicare-related services would be limited to $2,000. At a time when Washington could provide no free lunch, it seemed like an equitable deal. "For the first time, the nation's elderly will be protected against the enormous costs of a catastrophic illness," Rostenkowski said as the bill neared enactment. "And for the first time, the elderly population will finance its own expanded benefits."

After the House and Senate overwhelmingly passed the final version of the bill, Reagan signed it into law at a Rose Garden ceremony on July 1, 1988. Although Congress included an additional Medicare premium of up to $800 annually for the most wealthy recipients—estimated to be married couples with at least $90,000 in income—the new law essentially adopted Secretary Bowen's self-financing framework. Despite widespread congratulations among policymakers, however, from the elderly came an undercurrent of dissatisfaction. Their longtime congressional champion Claude Pepper objected that the measure should have been more comprehensive, including coverage of long-term home care. Pepper's efforts were encouraged by the National Committee to Preserve Social Security and Medicare, a private organization founded a few years earlier by James Roosevelt, son of President Franklin Roosevelt. That organization, which typically relied on direct-mail campaigns that made alarmist claims to senior citizens, warned that the new bill would increase Medicare costs for all beneficiaries. "Letters arrived on Capitol Hill by the thousands, a testament not only to the deep public feelings but also to a series of organized campaigns," wrote an author who covered the conflict. "A special tax on senior citizens! Have you ever heard of anything so outrageous?" read one of the mailings.[14] Well, yes, that had been a foundation of Medicare from its start. But that didn't satisfy Roosevelt's group, which argued that the elderly should not pay a tax for their additional benefits. In a survey of its members in late 1988, 51 percent responded that they objected to paying for catastrophic health-care benefits.[15]

Rostenkowski was unimpressed with the critics' arguments. "Here we had a Republican president willing to support a major expansion of the Medicare program and some Democrats wanted to risk losing the bill by overreaching," he told a Chicago audience two months after the bill's enactment. "I didn't want to risk this incremental but significant improvement in health-insurance protection for the elderly." Faced with the prospect of getting Reagan's signature on a bill to authorize $5 billion in added annual benefits, "I wasn't about to call him a piker and demand a $30 billion bill." But his desire to pass a law may have blinded Rostenkowski to the bill's defects and the opposition from senior-citizen activists. "Common sense was overwhelmed by the desire to be fiscally responsible," said the Congressional Budget Office's Reischauer. With only a slim fraction of the elderly population receiving benefits for which nearly all of them were paying, support for the bill was unsustainable, he added. "Rostenkowski's view was that we are giving you retirees something. But it turned out to be a political mistake because those who benefited were not well organized or public."

Although Rostenkowski's comeuppance would come soon enough, at the end of 1988 Reischauer's fears were not widely shared on Capitol Hill. After a year in which Congress had enacted three major laws initiated by the Ways and Means Committee, Rostenkowski and his members were justifiably proud. They had found ways to deliver greater benefits to the people and had rejected demagogues across the spectrum. They also had won Reagan's signature on each proposal. Rostenkowski's art of the deal had become a reality. "Rosty was willing to swallow a policy he did not like if the big picture was worth the price," said Jack Lew, the former chief aide to Tip O'Neill. If he had to grant a few favors to parochial groups or delay achieving all the goals of a legislative program at once, he was simply being pragmatic. The process and the details weren't always pretty, nor were they predictable. After all, politics is art, not science. And, consistent with his Chicago roots, Rostenkowski's style was marked by considerably more bluster and intimidation than other politicians used. "Official, genteel Washington stands in awe of Rosty," wrote *Chicago Tribune* columnist Clarence Page. "He stands 6 foot 2, more than 200 pounds. He cuts deals. He browbeats. He cajoles. He eats red meat. He drinks Bombay gin, straight, with a couple of little teeny onions in it."[16] But he always operated with the idea that good results outweighed propaganda and public relations. With the end of the Reagan era, however, many of his old ways soon would be jeopardized.

Chapter Seven

CLASH OF CULTURES

AS HIS NATIONAL INFLUENCE GREW, Rostenkowski remained a quintessential Chicagoan—in his hard-nosed political style and tough-guy
physical appearance, and in his affection for his hometown. But as he
made his mark, his relationship with the city changed, for better and for
worse. On the plus side he delivered vital legislation and beneficial federal dollars. As his Capitol Hill workload grew, however, he had less time
or interest to devote to folks in the neighborhoods. Bit by bit, his isolation
deepened. Alderman Richard Mell, a frequent foe who shared many constituents, bluntly described how Rostenkowski's added responsibilities
distanced him from local politics. "When you chair the Ways and Means
Committee, and when you can snap your fingers to make the Lear jets
come to Washington . . . you have less interest in 'Stosh' and his job."
Once he became Ways and Means chairman, said Democratic consultant
David Axelrod, whom Rostenkowski hired for political advice, the congressman was less willing to "jump through the hoops. Because he was a
national politician, he no longer wanted to spend his time at bingo
games." Eventually he paid a heavy price for failing to heed warnings that
he had lost touch back home. "At the end of his career he wanted to be
chairman, not the congressman," one of Rostenkowski's aides lamented.
"He wanted to be appreciated." But that's not the way politics works.
Many constituents who had viewed him simply as "Danny," the local kid,
began to wonder if he had grown too big for his hat size.

Despite his greater stature in Washington, Rostenkowski defiantly retained his Chicago roots. Even when he was busy managing legislation,

he typically spent four or five nights a week at his Evergreen Street home. In contrast to many influential House members who bask in Washington's high living and devote less attention to the needs of folks back home, he kept a spartan apartment about a mile from the Capitol and spent only a few weekends there during his thirty-six years in Congress. (During her infrequent visits to Washington, his wife LaVerne insisted that they stay at a hotel.) Likewise his Ways and Means Committee work often focused on Chicago interests, both business and political, even when the agenda had national or global consequences. In Washington or at home he played by Chicago's hardball rules, basking in the first Mayor Daley's often scornful moniker of "Boss." Perhaps most telling, he retained until 1988 his seemingly minor position as a party lieutenant—Democratic committeeman for the 32nd Ward—in the old-fashioned machine that had become less influential in Chicago political life. So in the 1970 campaign he ordered his two young legislative aides—Jim Healey from New York and John Salmon from Massachusetts—to spend six weeks walking the still heavily Polish streets of his district and meeting the precinct captains. "We were two Irish kids from Georgetown University," Healey recounted. "He wanted us to learn the area and its life-style. Each morning we went to his Damen Avenue office and did the nuts-and-bolts work, like writing press releases for local candidates. . . . Danny said he wanted us to meet everyone and learn what people did. He didn't want us to be Washington people." (To be sure, not all of Rostenkowski's non-Washington hours were spent in Chicago. In the summer he usually spent long weekends at his comfortable house on Benedict Lake in nearby Wisconsin; in winter he made many trips, usually paid for by a lobbyist or benefactor, to fancy golf courses and resorts in warm-weather climes.)

Rostenkowski's attachment to Chicago was rarely understood by those who dealt with him in Washington. During his early years his House critics viewed him as a neighborhood politician who was ill prepared for center stage. Later his preoccupation with his local base seemed like parochialism resulting from an inability to move beyond his community. By the 1970s many colleagues could not fathom why he continued to hitch his horse to a discredited, old-style pol like Richard Daley. But the mystery ran both ways. In Chicago, few of his friends and political associates grasped the extent of his influence or skill as the city's main man in Washington. Even when he used his clout to direct hundreds of millions of dollars in federal grants or tax breaks to important city projects, he rarely tooted his horn; besides, not many citizens would bother to appreciate a politician who sent money to improve sewers hundreds of feet below the local river bed. For Rostenkowski, who placed the greatest value on the judgment of his peers, it was sufficient that the local bosses knew he had delivered. In less flattering terms, some leading figures in that power-conscious but provincial city—who assumed that no job in America was as prominent as the mayor of Chicago—calculated that he stayed in Washington because he wasn't prepared for the "big time." A Chicago friend who was a daily reader of the *New York Times* once told him that the national press gave him far more attention than did the local news media. "She said she can't believe the good coverage I got in the *Times* compared to the Chicago papers," Rostenkowski said. But Rostenkowski shared responsibility for the scant coverage, said Basil Talbott, who reported on politics for the *Sun Times* for thirty-five years. "Once he was elected to Congress, Rostenkowski wasn't interested in Chicago controversies. He felt that the Chicago press was parochial. He was more interested in the *New York Times* and the *Wall Street Journal* as the ways to reach the big money people."

In both Chicago and Washington these flawed perceptions were not entirely accidental. Rostenkowski worked very hard to keep his two worlds separate, even with those who thought that they were close to him. Like a feudal lord, he left "no illusion of equality" among his staff or in his political organization.[1] Other than his two personal secretaries— Nancy Panzke in Chicago and Virginia Fletcher in Washington, each of whom was a close and loyal aide to him for more than a quarter-century— probably no one fully appreciated the individuals and the workload that filled his dual professional lives. And the fact that Panzke and Fletcher feuded with each other because of professional rivalry and contrasting styles made it difficult for them to stay informed of events in Rostenkowski's other universe. (Panzke was a sassy and street-smart hometown product; Fletcher, from rural Virginia, came across as reserved and close to the vest.) But that was the way Rostenkowski wanted it. "These were two different worlds with different priorities," said another senior aide. "It was a control thing." Another veteran staffer observed that Rostenkowski did not want to explain to his Chicago friends, for example, the details of who was doing what for him (or to him) in Washington. No doubt the reverse was true with his Capitol friends.

The result was an odd disconnect between the two busy spheres of his life, which only he could link. On one occasion after he became Ways and Means chairman, a Washington aide recalled, incredulously, Rostenkowski in his Chicago office speaking on the telephone with Senate Finance Committee chairman Lloyd Bentsen about a Capitol Hill deal, while across the desk a seventeen-year-old neighborhood kid was seeking his support for a local job. "He never became a Washingtonian," said Ed Derwinski, the Illinois Republican who shared with Rostenkowski two dozen years in the House as well as a similar age and ethnic background. "In his earlier years he was happier being a ward committeeman than a congressman. . . . He never got Potomac Fever. His heart always stayed in Chicago." (To reinforce that point, Rostenkowski usually kept his watch on Chicago time, even when he was working in Washington.) As late as the 1980s he kept alive news reports that he might return home to run for mayor, even though he did nothing to pursue that goal and had earlier allowed his best opportunity to pass. And periodically he suggested to his Washington cronies that he was ready to retire from the Capitol grind so that he could make bundles of money in the private sector. "He lived two lives," said Axelrod. "In Washington, like Superman, he stepped out of a phone booth and everyone treated him with awe. . . . [In Chicago] he wasn't treated that way. But he didn't expect it."

Eventually, living dual lives caused problems. Rostenkowski's work pattern had raised few concerns when he was younger and Congress was not a full-time job for many of his colleagues. But as years passed, many in the old neighborhoods thought he had grown arrogant and out of touch from rubbing shoulders with corporate big shots, even when he was in Chicago. Likewise he was often maligned in Washington because he sought to maintain his image as a local pol. It was a difficult juggling act, even though his growing accomplishments at both ends were enough to pacify most critics for many years.

Chicago too had changed in important ways in the 1980s, when Rostenkowski was at the peak of his Washington influence. Gone was Boss Daley with his hands-on control of Chicago and the Democratic party; in his place, an ominous instability shook the power structure, followed by the even more shocking election of a black mayor who triumphantly challenged the Establishment. Coincidentally, those years brought a powerful business resurgence to key sections of the metropolitan area, including the Michigan Avenue retail corridor and other white-collar sectors, which replaced the city's eroding industrial core. But as high-rent neighborhoods spread from downtown, many of the traditional bungalow communities lost their ethnic identity and pockets of poverty festered elsewhere. Divisions between rich and poor spread; Chicago was losing its middle class. And some who remained in the old neighborhoods were no longer so respectful of the political elites. Rostenkowski continued his weekly commute to Washington from the home where he had lived his entire life, but the church and the neighborhood were losing their familiar features.

To be sure, Rostenkowski's many Chicago friends—both old and acquired—focused on what their influential pal could do for them. "For the city, Rostenkowski was like one-stop shopping," said Bill Daley, the local attorney and Democratic scion whom President Clinton in 1997 chose as Commerce secretary. "You could go to him for almost anything." As he moved up the House's ranks, Rostenkowski wielded even more clout for the folks back home. Local leaders were less concerned about policy nuances or personal relationships in Washington than in getting their share of the pie—preferably more. Most had a sense that the Ways and Means Committee was important, especially its chairman. But they had little idea what took place behind the doors of Room 1100 in the Longworth House Office Building. "He brought a lot of stuff back," said Mell. "But it never really sank in how powerful he was." Rostenkowski usually wanted to take care of the Chicago crowd. At least he would make the effort. After all, what good was muscle that wasn't flexed?

Rostenkowski dealt with his hometown on several levels. Just as he built a wall between his Chicago activities and what he did in Washington, he also compartmentalized his local services. The priority was taking care of city hall. Although his enthusiasm and personal dealings varied, depending on who was mayor, he retained his old-fashioned approach of securing money for public needs: highways, sewers, schools, and the like. That was what old Mayor Daley had taught the young Rostenkowski when he delivered his weekly report from Washington. But there were additional demands to be satisfied, too. In the corporate partnership that permeated Chicago's governance, Rostenkowski paid attention to the needs of large businesses that were the engines of economic growth—especially when they promised more jobs for area workers. He viewed those corporations as allies in running the city. "I make no apology for my efforts to build a stronger Chicago," he told a 1990 business gathering in Washington. "I wish I had been more successful." There was also the relentless drumbeat of constituent demands on federal agencies—from an application for a public-housing apartment to replacement of a lost Social Security check. As his legislative tasks mounted, he paid less attention to such mundane requests.

Responding to local demands is an essential responsibility of a public official in a representative government. Despite the lore surrounding his influence, Rostenkowski was little different from other congressmen— except, perhaps, for the way he delivered his services. He required that petitioners follow some rules. First, they had to show respect for his office. Except for meetings of Chicago Democrats, he dictated the terms and usually the place of business. "They had to come to him, as people came to his father when he was the ward committeeman," Bill Daley said; "He built himself up by showing that he could get the job done." As Rostenkowski gained influence, "he didn't like to do events in Chicago," said an aide. His public meetings outside Washington were chiefly with business or trade groups on their turf or at a pleasant vacation spot where he delivered a speech. In those cases he usually received money, for his pocket, his campaign fund, or a favorite charity; he guaranteed, of course, that each payment complied with the ethics rules at the time.

Second, he valued hierarchy. Those seeking to do business with the Ways and Means chairman were expected to have done their homework. When Charles Walgreen III, chief executive of the Chicago-based Walgreen drugstore chain, visited Washington to request an adjustment of federal reimbursement rules for his pharmaceutical products, he brought along a young vice-president to explain the technical jargon to Rostenkowski. That was a mistake, because it showed that the "issue was not important to Charlie," said a Rostenkowski aide. Walgreen came up empty because he failed to understand that business was personal for the Ways and Means chairman.

Third, his meetings usually were swift and to the point. "He's the equivalent of Jack Webb in the 'Dragnet' TV show," said Axelrod, the consultant and ex-newspaperman. "He just wants the facts." If Rostenkowski felt that guests were wasting his time, he tapped his fingers on his desk to move the discussion along. Even when he agreed, he usually would nod and elliptically agree to take care of the problem. Corporate executives visiting his office "go in to see him and they come out fast," said Bill Griffin, who was the chief aide to Chicago Mayor Jane Byrne. "He is not a person who will dance you around. It's yes or no."[2]

That gruff, clandestine style sometimes posed problems in Chicago.

In Congress, hierarchy was accepted as a way to do business in a large and unwieldy institution. As chairman, Rostenkowski didn't mind if some House colleagues were unhappy with him as long as a majority supported him in a showdown. By contrast, in rough-and-tumble Chicago, political players often held grudges against their adversaries. And the local news media gave more attention to those conflicts than to the details and results of arcane congressional debates. So while he won little credit locally for his accomplishments, Rostenkowski frequently found himself the critics' target for his parochial efforts to help friends and for alleged "sweetheart" deals he won for himself. Citizen activists kept drawers stuffed with yellowing files of his misdeeds. The headlines frequently were hostile: "2 Area Dems Get Big Special-interest Gifts," the *Chicago Daily News* reported in 1977 about large campaign contributions to Rostenkowski and his pal, Marty Russo; that same year the *Tribune* ran a story, "Rostenkowski Renting U.S. Office from His Sisters"; in 1986 the *Sun-Times* headlined, "Rosty Dealt a Windfall Profit by Pal."

Whatever their validity, such charges helped to explain why so many voters saw him as just another venal politician. For years Rostenkowski privately dismissed such charges as false, irrelevant, or both. But he made little effort to repair negative impressions or to sell his positive deeds. Unlike most of his colleagues in the 1990s, he refused to hold local press conferences or to hire a press aide to focus on his accomplishments for his constituents. "Although he went out of his way to tell the governor and the mayor what he was doing, there was a side of him that said it was up to the public to know about his activities," said Rob Leonard, his Ways and Means staff director for six years. Until the end of his career, these shortcomings were not a political problem largely because Rostenkowski did not face serious challengers for reelection. But when he finally confronted credible opposition, he found himself in a deep ditch.

In the 1980s, though, he was still a precious asset for city officials struggling with painful federal cutbacks while they contended with fierce battles at city hall. After Daley's virtually unchallenged twenty-two-year reign, the city was battered by political conflict that resulted in four elected mayors during the dozen years following the death of the "Boss" in December 1976. In unconventional fashion for Chicago, Michael Bilandic lost the primary for renomination in 1979 and Jane Byrne, his maverick successor, was defeated in a Democratic primary four years later by Harold Washington—who died of a heart attack in 1987 and was replaced more than a year later by forty-six-year-old Richard M. Daley, son of the late mayor, who had been serving as Cook County's prosecutor. The political struggles of those years were brutal, varied, and unending. The city became known as "Beirut on the lake": the mayor versus the aldermen, the reformers versus the machine Democrats, and, most disruptive of all, blacks versus whites. During this turbulent period Rostenkowski was a tower of stability. "He made sure the city got its fair share, no matter who was mayor," said Bill Daley. "Danny felt that he had to help the pathetic amateurs in the mayor's office because he had a love for the city." Even with his shaky relationship with Harold Washington during the five years he served as the city's first black mayor, Rostenkowski pledged allegiance to what remained of the crumbling power structure. His most enduring local contribution throughout that period was to deliver badly needed federal dollars, either in direct cash or through tax breaks. "He did more for the city than anybody else," said Edward Burke, the veteran chairman of the City Council's finance committee. "But he never asked for credit. He just went to the mayor. That's the way it's done in Chicago." Said political scientist Paul Green, "During a decade of chaos, he became an insurance policy for the city."

After he became Ways and Means chairman, Rostenkowski assigned many of his duties in the Democratic organization to Alderman Terry Gabinski, the chief lieutenant in his Chicago office. Instead, the pols turned to the congressman as their "go-to guy" in Washington. As Reagan sought major cuts in federal aid to the cities, for example, Rostenkowski became a prominent defender of urban-assistance programs. With talking points from the mayor's office, he often lobbied the White House budget office and other congressional barons to protect funds for Chicago. "He was willing to broker certain programs to save highway, housing, and other public works spending," said Ron Gibbs, a chief aide to Mayor Washington. Although those programs were often controlled by committees other than Ways and Means, Rostenkowski's leverage increased simply because he was the House's most powerful chairman. And he wasn't shy about using his clout. He devoted special attention in the 1980s to securing roughly $450 million to resurface and widen the Kennedy Expressway, the heavily traveled interstate that crawls around his home en route from downtown to O'Hare Airport and the northern suburbs; the rehabilitation provided two thousand local jobs. Those funds resulted largely from his one-on-one deals with the Public Works Committee chairman.

But Rostenkowski delivered not only conventional pork-barrel projects to his city. The grateful Marilyn Katz, a leading national advocate for low-income housing and community development programs, offered an insight on his effectiveness. A Chicago native, Katz had been a street protester during the 1968 Democratic convention; she boasted that Daley assigned a guard to monitor her at the time. Later she was an aide to Harold Washington when he was elected mayor. From the start she viewed Rostenkowski as a "powerful curmudgeon" who was on the opposite side from her on most issues. But circumstances changed later when, from her Chicago public affairs office, she developed a tax-law change to permit corporations to invest in the construction of affordable housing. "The proposal revolutionized how cities built housing," Katz said. "Instead of large housing projects owned by outsiders, the new tax credit gave the benefit to local nonprofit companies."

After Rostenkowski and others helped to enact her plan on a temporary basis in the 1986 tax-reform law, renewing the provision caused recurring headaches. "We couldn't get anywhere with Rosty," she said. "We were one group of many" who wanted his help on tax benefits. When Katz was seated near him on an airplane from Washington to Chicago in 1990, she recalled, "I screwed up my courage to tell him who I was and that I wanted to talk about the low-income housing credit." Rostenkowski gruffly responded, "If it's so important to Mayor Daley, let him talk to me." So she went to Daley, and the mayor assured her of his support and said Rostenkowski would follow. Daley proved correct. In 1993 Rostenkowski kept his promise and Congress made the tax credit permanent. "Rostenkowski made it happen," Katz said. "He heard regularly from Daley. He met with the local groups. He got good staff work. He delivered. " The result was the construction of approximately 2,000 new housing units annually for Chicago and nearly 200,000 across the nation. "If you wanted to get something done for the city, Rostenkowski was the guy," Katz said.

The 1986 Tax Reform Act gave Rostenkowski an unusual opportunity to benefit Chicago businesses. Tom Sneeringer, who had become his legislative director for issues not under Ways and Means jurisdiction, worked with local groups seeking special provisions in the sweeping bill.

Sneeringer met with several dozen local representatives and included their requests in a large red binder. "All Chicago interests were treated well, but not all of them got what they wanted," Sneeringer said. Perhaps fifty provisions in the final bill, including ten to fifteen for the city itself, were drafted to benefit Chicago in some form. Among those that received publicity at the time was a "grandfather" exemption from the new law to grant continued tax-exempt financing for prospective new stadiums for the Chicago White Sox baseball team and the Bears football team. Few residents of the sports-crazed city could complain about that. (The tax-reform law included similar provisions for stadiums in several other cities.) In another example, which extended well beyond the city limits, Rostenkowski added a roughly $80 million benefit to entice the Chrysler Corporation to build an automobile factory in the downstate Bloomington area by exempting the new facility from the bill's elimination of investment tax credits and its depreciation reductions. "Getting the commitment early was a key element in the deal" with Chrysler, an aide to Gov. James Thompson told *Crain's Chicago Business*.[3] Rostenkowski received harsher criticism for his tax exemption for an elite class of commodity traders at the Chicago Mercantile Exchange. As a result of campaign contributions and speaking fees from exchange members and other Chicago business groups, the benefit went only to "Dan Rostenkowski's commodity-trading constituents in Chicago," according to a study of tax rip-offs.[4] Rostenkowski defended his provision as a remedy for unfair punishment that a federal court inflicted on taxpayers who took advantage of a widely used loophole during the 1970s.

"If done in the open, these things would not have been allowed to happen," Chicago citizen-activist Tom Gradel complained. That's a fair point. But Rostenkowski kept Chicagoans equally in the dark about his constructive actions on their behalf, to which his critics paid little attention. A prime example was "Deep Tunnel," the massive project to upgrade the Chicago-area reservoir and sewer system. The $4 billion system was designed to keep raw sewage from entering the Chicago River and Lake Michigan while also preventing the flooding of basements across Cook County. Many of the tunnels flowed hundreds of feet below Rostenkowski's district north of the downtown area. Political officials and engineers for the Metropolitan Water Reclamation District, which supervised the project, relied on Washington for two major ingredients: roughly two-thirds of Deep Tunnel funds came from the federal budget, chiefly through the Clean Water Act; and federal rules set increasingly strict standards for construction and operation of the huge facility.

Citizens typically take government public works projects for granted, except when they break down or when there is an emergency. That is especially true with sewers, which operate out of public view. "People don't remember if there is no flooding," Rostenkowski said. "They would rather read the sports page." But frequent Midwest storms, compounded by suburban growth and the Chicago River's winding route, made the city vulnerable to sewer problems. When they occurred, newspapers sometimes reported a few details of Deep Tunnel and its funding sources. But the local congressman usually was not mentioned in these stories. For example, following a heavy rain in 1993 the *Sun-Times* reported that before the first phase of Deep Tunnel was opened, "It was always the same messy story after a bad rainstorm. Sewers would overflow into riverways, beaches would close and a water advisory would go into effect." Fortunately that was no longer the case, the report noted. But water district officials used the storm to plead for an additional $450 million for reservoirs "to hold the type of fast-falling stormwater that hit the city on Monday."[5] The story quoted the eager press secretary to Republican Rep. Henry Hyde, who served a suburban district adjacent to Rostenkowski's but had little influence at the time with House appropriators. It was another case in which Rostenkowski saw no need to solicit favorable news coverage.

Most local officials took for granted his efforts on Deep Tunnel. "The money to accomplish the project came from Rostenkowski," Alderman Mell said. "But nobody thanks him for it." On Capitol Hill, Rostenkowski and his aides made it a constant priority. For more than a dozen years until House Democrats lost their majority, the annual decisions for public works spending were made chiefly by Tom Bevill of Alabama, the chairman of the Appropriations Subcommittee on Energy and Water Development. Not surprisingly, Bevill had little interest in Chicago's sewers. On occasion, however, when officials of the executive branch questioned Deep Tunnel, or when tight budgets left little money to finance every worthy project, the Ways and Means chairman made a plea to Bevill. "The board in Chicago would give me direction and I would start trading" on Capitol Hill, Rostenkowski said. In those cases his appeal was more likely than requests from other lawmakers to carry weight. And Rostenkowski wasn't shy about flexing his clout as Ways and Means chairman.

Deep Tunnel officials were grateful. "I met on a fairly regular basis with Rostenkowski and his staff," said Hugh McMillan, the reclamation district's general superintendent of Deep Tunnel. "He was extremely significant. First, his position allowed him to bargain with others in the House and Senate. Second, he had the advantage in Washington that our effort was totally bipartisan. Third, with our input he could argue on behalf of the project and never fear contradiction." Rostenkowski's 1994 re-election defeat was a setback for Deep Tunnel, McMillan conceded, because the mostly junior members of the city's reorganized congressional delegation "don't have the power of position" on Capitol Hill. For McMillan that was a polite way of saying that Chicago's surviving lawmakers were less inclined than was Rostenkowski to safeguard the program. "Interest now is more ephemeral," he added. "You can't put a name plate on a sewer. There is not the political return."

ALTHOUGH ROSTENKOWSKI was usually steadfast in representing the city, Harold Washington's tenure as mayor was a difficult time for the congressman. Washington's 1983 election and his conduct in office posed a direct challenge to the regular Democratic organization of which Rostenkowski remained a leader. The relationship between the two men deteriorated to the point where they often refused to communicate for weeks. When Ron Gibbs, who ran the mayor's office in Washington, sought to relay information, the chairman demanded to hear directly from the mayor. "Rostenkowski would say that Gibbs was not senior enough and that the mayor himself had to kiss his ring," said a Rostenkowski aide. "The chairman wanted to know if Harold really cared." No doubt the proud Rostenkowski did not like to be taken for granted; he also resented that Washington—who had won the Democratic primary with only 36 percent of the vote against Jane Byrne and young Rich Daley, and then was elected narrowly over an unknown Republican—found a way to gain the office that he had so long coveted for himself. "He was a big accident," Rostenkowski said. "He didn't necessarily like me. But he trusted me to play fair with him." For his part, the frequently disorganized mayor—who had served one undistinguished term in the House before his unexpected election to city hall—saw little reason to pay homage to a former colleague who had cavalierly ignored him, as he did most other freshmen. As the new boss of Chicago's Democrats, the mayor had unrealistic expectations that all party officials would defer to his leadership, as they had historically.

Gibbs's task as the city's chief federal lobbyist was particularly difficult because it was the position that Rostenkowski had defined for himself during the previous quarter-century, even after Mayor Daley's death dimmed much of its luster. "I explained [to Rostenkowski] that I didn't want to take away anybody's power but to facilitate the expression of Chicago concerns in Washington," said Gibbs, who had held several jobs in Washington. He noted, for example, that no city official had a list of all federal money that Chicago received annually. The mayor wanted to elevate the office's profile because "he hoped to organize a national urban agenda as a spokesman for urban America," Gibbs said. That made sense for Mayor Washington: with Reagan as president, liberals were struggling to find their voice on the political stage, and the new mayor was eager to play a role. But the approach offended Rostenkowski, if only because it was such a change from Daley's indifference toward the crowd inside the Washington beltway. Mayor Washington's ambitions also irked Rostenkowski because at the time he was looking to cooperate with Reagan. With the mayor denouncing virtually all administration policies, the Ways and Means chairman was on shaky ground back home. Reagan grew so unhappy with Washington's attacks that he asked Rostenkowski to get the mayor to soften his criticisms, Gibbs recalled. Given their limited communication, such a plea was not in the cards—nor would Washington have taken it seriously. Meanwhile the relentless political wars continued in Chicago between the mayor and the regular Democrats, who in 1983 retained a narrow City Council majority.

Gibbs and Sneeringer tried to get along at the staff level, but the two leaders failed to establish even the semblance of cordiality. A typical example of their frigid relations came during the tax-reform bill when Rostenkowski asked the mayor for information on the likely location of the two proposed sports stadiums. "I asked him where the Bears stadium would be," Rostenkowski recalled. "He did not want to tell me. I hung up. He called back two minutes later and gave me the information. . . . He was afraid his people thought that I'd screw him." Fundamentally their struggle was over control, said liberal lobbyist Marilyn Katz. "Rosty was willing to send money to Chicago. But it was a question of who controls it. Control is everything in politics, regardless of race."

The relationship took a further nosedive in early 1987 when Rostenkowski supported regular Democrat Thomas Hynes, running as an independent in what became a futile challenge to Washington's reelection.
Although white Democrats failed to rally effectively behind a single
opponent to Washington, racial divisions continued to plague Chicago
politics. And Rostenkowski was not immune to the jockeying. In the
autumn of 1987 Washington quietly launched a search for a candidate to
make what would have been an unprecedented Democratic primary challenge to Rostenkowski. The maneuver never transpired—largely because
the stocky Washington died suddenly of a heart attack the day before
Thanksgiving in 1987, a few weeks before the filing deadline for the next
year's primary. Such a bid would have been doomed to failure, if only because the mayor remained highly unpopular in Rostenkowski's district.
Still, the chairman was not accustomed to such effrontery on his home
ground.

THE STYLE of Rostenkowski's political headquarters had changed little
from what he had learned at his father's knee. At the heart of the local
office was its constituent service operation, which tended to the gamut
of individual problems. Although the younger Rostenkowski eliminated
Thursday night meetings, each Monday evening his office saw a few
dozen residents seeking assistance. At those meetings, which typically
ran from 7 until 10 p.m., local citizens could go to one of three small
rooms at his Damen Avenue office, depending on whether their problems
involved the federal government, the city, or the local Democratic
organization. "A ward committeeman's job was like that of a concierge,"
said local political scholar Paul Green. "The job was to listen and
expedite." Rostenkowski himself spent little time on that kind of
work. "Dan was the outside man," said Terry Gabinski. The protégé
began to replace Rostenkowski at meetings to prepare Democratic slates
for other offices. Even on federal topics his precinct captains increasingly
dealt with Tom Sneeringer and Virginia Fletcher in Rostenkowski's
Washington office. The Ways and Means chairman spent his Chicago
time mostly with top brass. "Chicago is so tightly knit that he saw directly
who he needed to see, whether it was the mayor or corporate executives,"
Sneeringer said. "Some were suitors. Others were friends he saw socially."

But nuts-and-bolts political life and demands were changing on

Chicago's northwest side. Initially Rostenkowski hoped to relinquish in 1984 the Democratic ward committee seat that he and his father had held for a half-century. "He said he was too tied up to continue with Chicago's Democratic politics," Gabinski said. "But we said he had to run." His decision to seek another term did not stop thirty-one-year-old Luis Gutierrez, a cab driver's son and a former social worker for the city's family services department, from challenging Rostenkowski for committeeman with "a spirited campaign" in the ward, where the Hispanic population had grown nearly to a majority.[6] Because Gutierrez—a Puerto Rican—was a strong supporter of Harold Washington, his candidacy posed a difficult choice for the mayor, who ultimately gave the challenger a late and tepid endorsement. Although Rostenkowski received 77 percent of the vote, the contest was a harbinger of growing jeopardy. Two years later a federal judge forced a redrawing of aldermanic lines to create a new Hispanic-majority ward, which Gutierrez won. In 1992 Gutierrez would easily win a new heavily Hispanic congressional seat that spanned both the north and south sides of Chicago. Rostenkowski bitterly resented the feisty upstart. But the challenge brought home to him how demographic shifts were reshaping urban America.

In other ways, too, his old community was transformed. With many of the area's longtime residents gone to the suburbs and replaced by new immigrants, many of them Hispanic or Asian, Rostenkowski's ward office—like St. Stans Church—witnessed a radical change in its ethnic base. By the early 1990s the area that had once been overwhelmingly Polish was now only about 25 percent so, many of them elderly. Many Poles left the busy urban streets for the quieter suburbs because of "gentrification," which increased the resale value of their properties and forced up rental rates as yuppie professionals sought homes closer to their downtown offices. In 1988 Rostenkowski finally stepped down as Democratic ward committeeman. Gabinski—who already had served nearly two decades as an alderman—won the companion position. Rostenkowski "didn't feel as comfortable keeping the position because he was not able to be as involved," Gabinski said. "It's very unusual for someone voluntarily to step down as ward committeeman. Usually they keep the title and let someone else do the work."

A few traces of the old neighborhood survived. In 1988 a local Polish group called "Li'l Richard and his Polka All Stars" recorded a rocking tribute, with a polka harmony, to the local kid who made it in the big time:

Danny Boy, Danny Boy,
Danny Rostenkowski.
He's our boy, he's our man,
Danny Rostenkowski.

He's our Ways, he's our Means,
Danny Rostenkowski.
Let's all yell, shout like hell,
Danny Rostenkowski.

ROSTENKOWSKI EAGERLY HELPED local corporations get their share
of the federal spoils. "There is no question that he helped his friends,"
said Alderman Edward Burke. "That's what a congressman is supposed to
do." His favored beneficiaries—many of whom he socialized with at golf
courses or fancy restaurants—included leaders of Chicago's huge financial enterprises, such as the Chicago Board of Options Exchange and the
Mercantile Exchange. Leo Melamed of the "Merc" was a frequent visitor
to Rostenkowski's office. The Chicago Board of Trade—a federation of
the city's corporate titans—also kept in close contact; its chairman, Tom
Donovan, had been the senior political aide in charge of patronage for the
first Mayor Daley.

It wasn't only Chicago activists or muckraking journalists who criticized these close connections. The House's Democratic Study Group issued several reports in the 1980s that complained about unfair tax policy
that benefited only the few. "Democrats must show what we are for," said
a liberal Democrat, in a common refrain. Although the DSG usually did
not attack Rostenkowski directly, there was no doubt he was a prime target. But he had no apologies. "I am not ashamed of representing these
people, as I would not be ashamed of saying I represented cows if I was
from Wisconsin or I represented oil if I was from Oklahoma," he told a
1994 dinner with political scientists in Washington. "The idea that press
from the Midwest would criticize us for bringing home pork. I mean,
what do they want?"

Sometimes he intervened chiefly to flex his political muscle. "He did
not help [local companies] as much as people thought," said Bill Daley,
Rostenkowski's longtime confidant who represented many major corporations as a senior attorney and often received legislative favors from his
pal. "The best situation for a Chicago company was to show they were

being screwed, compared with a company in New York or Los Angeles that was getting preferred treatment. . . . Danny personalized everything." When a corporate chief visited him at his office, Rostenkowski's aides often prepared a one-page profile that listed the boss's salary and military record so the congressman could measure his guest. "He felt he was operating at the mega-CEO level," said Tom Sneeringer, who wrote many of the profiles. "He also wanted to know how much the CEO was ripping off his company." Rostenkowski romanced them so that the corporate executives, in turn, would share information with him and press the flesh with other lawmakers. "A good lobbyist tells you what is possible and what is not," he added. "They know that when they fudge, they won't see me again. When they came to see me, there was no bullshit with Rostenkowski." Still, as he demonstrated on tax reform, Rostenkowski often helped major Chicago-area institutions such as Zenith, the Commonwealth Edison utility, and Northwestern University. "Rosty was always there for big Illinois interests," said one of the state's leading politicians. "He could muscle a lot of stuff through."

Others rightly claimed that his reputation for delivering benefits was overblown. Despite his power, Illinois failed to measurably improve its low ranking among the states in per capita spending by the federal government. "He was powerful," said Tom Gradel, who in the 1990s organized two Democratic primary challenges to Rostenkowski. "But that was overplayed, and the negative aspects of his chairmanship were played down." Some endemic factors limited Rostenkowski's influence on broad federal spending: the climate and geography of Illinois were a poor fit for military bases, and its boundaries included only a modest share of natural resources requiring Washington's support. And, as Rostenkowski often contended, Northern politicians were slow in grabbing their share of federal pork-barrel spending because Southerners were more effective in exploiting the seniority system.

Critics attacked Rostenkowski's dependence on business friends for political contributions and speaking fees. Before the House decided in 1989 to ban lawmakers from speechmaking honoraria—in exchange for raising their salaries from $89,500 to $125,000—members were allowed to receive a maximum of 30 percent of their salary in additional income; more than that they were required to donate to charity. For several years during the 1980s Rostenkowski was the House's leading recipient of honoraria, far exceeding the 30 percent ceiling. Good-government advocates had a field day. From 1980 to 1990 "Rostenkowski pulled in $1.7 million in speaking fees or honoraria from businesses and organizations with an interest in tax legislation," according to a study of the alleged abuses.[7] The authors, who failed to mention that Rostenkowski was permitted to retain less than 20 percent of that total, listed the top twenty contributors to "Rostenkowski's plentiful honoraria." At the top were Blue Cross–Blue Shield, the Chicago Board of Trade, and the Public Securities Association, a nationwide organization of large brokerage firms that includes many Chicago-area members. With his abundant fees, Rostenkowski became the caricature of the pocket-stuffing pol. "If Wall Street poured billions of dollars into leveraged buyouts, hostile takeovers and mergers in the 1980s, it invested just as enthusiastically in Washington," the authors wrote. And the chief recipient was "the one lawmaker who more than any other determines the structure of America's tax system—Dan Rostenkowski."[8] He was the poster boy for Washington's public-interest groups fighting to eliminate the honoraria.

Yet there was another part of the honoraria story that most critics ignored. When his fees exceeded the 30 percent limit, Rostenkowski usually steered them to charitable organizations in Chicago, such as favorite hospitals and his St. Stanislaus Kostka Church. In 1984 he paid $120,000—all of it from honoraria—for four new clocks and the construction and rewiring of the church's surviving north tower. He also directed nearly $50,000 to landscaping and other projects at St. Stans. "He is our largest single contributor," said Father Joe Glab, the church pastor. But that was only the start. Rostenkowski led a fund-raising drive for a new wing of the city's Mercy Hospital, which was dedicated in 1990 as the LaVerne and Dan Rostenkowski Outpatient Surgery Center. In exchange for his tax-law assistance to the Chicago-based Joyce Foundation, Rostenkowski asked only that several foundations give $2,000 grants to St. Johns' Academy, where he had attended high school, said Chuck Daly, the foundation's president. Rostenkowski also made smaller contributions to community organizations—the Polish Museum of America, a homeless group, an amateur football team, and others. "Among congressional philanthropists, no one can match Rostenkowski," *Newsweek* reported in 1988. But even that mostly complimentary article had a hostile and unproven twist when its final sentence concluded that "the biggest boost" from the contributions goes to Rostenkowski's "political fortunes."[9] Over the years Rostenkowski did not seek wide publicity for his charitable gifts because he had concluded that no good deed would go unpunished.

Of course Rostenkowski's dealings on behalf of Chicago financiers were not always charitable. And the local news media often highlighted some of those connections. But even in those so-called scandals, other facets of the story were sometimes overlooked. One long-running saga involved the aid that Rostenkowski steered through Ways and Means during the 1980s to underwrite construction of a huge private housing development in a redeveloped area three blocks west of the Chicago River and the city's financial district. Among the chief developers of the Presidential Towers project—which featured four forty-nine-story apartment buildings for middle- and upper-income tenants—was Dan Shannon; a well-connected accountant and Democratic insider, he was Rostenkowski's longtime friend and financial adviser. The new complex was designed as a catalyst for rehabilitating the city's near west side, which had been ridden with slums. For years, as other real estate developers balked at investing their dollars, the site had deteriorated into a skid row.

The Presidential Towers chronology placed Rostenkowski on the defensive way beyond his hometown. The *Wall Street Journal* termed the luxury apartment complex "a monument to clout" that was "built on a foundation of uncommon government favors—big ones" at the same time Washington was reducing aid for low-income public housing.[10] The *Journal* article detailed Rostenkowski's sponsorship of a provision in the big 1982 tax bill to permit investors in the Towers to deduct contributions on an accelerated basis. At the same time Congress was closing the depreciation loophole for most other housing investments across the nation. "The exception granted Presidential Towers will save investors in the project an additional $7 million over five years, assuming the investors are in the 50 percent tax bracket," according to a 1983 report. "The wealthy businessmen and doctors involved in the project already stood to save $20 million in taxes from depreciation alone during the period."[11] According to the *Journal,* the typical financier had to put up only $5,414 in after-tax dollars to reap an estimated profit of $160,000 to $210,000. The plan attracted 590 backers in $100,000 tax-exempt mortgage bonds guaranteed by the federal government. The project also boosted "Shannon's credibility as an investment promoter."[12] But Rostenkowski voiced no regrets. "Anything I did for Presidential Towers, I did for the city," he told a reporter.[13]

Despite many millions of dollars in federal tax benefits for Presidential Towers, rentals failed to meet expectations. After the first units opened to the public in 1985, the development became the victim of the high interest rates and reduced values that plagued real estate nationwide in the late 1980s. When the sour economics forced developers to drop their rents, they were unable in early 1990 to make their $1.5 million monthly mortgage payments to HUD. As a result the owners were forced to default on their federally insured loan, which had grown to $171 million. In offering an additional $16 million to rescue Presidential Towers, HUD Secretary Jack Kemp included requirements to benefit low-income tenants, which the developers termed unacceptable. It took another four years until the owners finally concluded a refinancing deal with the Clinton administration. HUD Secretary Henry Cisneros called the new arrangement for Presidential Towers, with 7 percent of the units available to low-income renters, "an excellent example of . . . cooperation among governmental, private-sector and non-profit advocates."[14] Rostenkowski's adversaries were not assuaged. "Presidential Towers is an economic disaster foisted on the taxpayers by the developers and their friend, Congressman Dan Rostenkowski," said Dick Simpson, a political reformer who challenged him in the 1992 and 1994 Democratic primaries. "The main economic benefits of the project have gone to Rostenkowski and the developers. Federal taxpayers have been stuck with the bill."

But the tale eventually turned as the area surrounding Chicago's Loop became hot commercial property. In 1995 Chicago's wealthy Pritzker family, owners of the Hyatt Hotel chain, made a $14 million investment to gain control of the partnership that owned the towers. The apartment buildings became a success story that appeared likely to turn a profit on the federal government's initial investment. And it grew into the redevelopment centerpiece for Chicago's west side. By the summer of 1996 thousands of visitors passed Presidential Towers on their way to the Democratic convention at the nearby United Center, the newly constructed mecca that is home for the Chicago Bulls and other entertainment. Several television studios, including headquarters for the Oprah Winfrey program, were among the businesses that within a few years converted skid row into a bustling area, including many popular restaurants. "When the corporations and companies in the area saw a private developer building four towers at market rate—even though subsidized with government funds and loans—it increased faith in the development potential of the West Loop," said Bob Wiggs, executive director of a seventy-eight-year-old community and business group that has its office in the complex. "It was a visible sign as the towers rose that the place was alive, not a dumping ground."[15]

Amid civic pride over the rejuvenation spurred by Presidential Towers, news stories continued to depict Rostenkowski as the sleazy politician. "The project aroused suspicion when, with the help of then-U.S. Rep. Dan Rostenkowski, it finessed" various federal laws, the *Tribune* reported in 1996, more than a decade after his intervention.[16] Yet the history of the Towers makes clear that his role was essential to its financial success. "Despite all of our criticism, the project anchored economic development on the west side," said Marilyn Katz, the liberal lobbyist. "That's the nature of political debate." No doubt critics make a good argument that Rostenkowski circumvented long-standing policy by changing a federal law to dish out special privileges to his friend. That kind of abuse arouses citizen contempt of government. In such cases, politicians often respond, critics fail to consider whether the contribution to revitalize a once-seedy neighborhood was worthwhile and, if so, whether any other public or private-sector initiative could have achieved that goal.

If the Presidential Towers controversy was an annoyance for Rostenkowski, a 1989 incident at a local senior citizens center was a more harrowing sign of the changes in his once-sheltered political world. Although most of the news media quickly forgot the August protest, the national attention it drew was strong evidence that his influence had become a liability—for himself at home and perhaps for other Democrats. The episode on Milwaukee Avenue in the heart of his neighborhood was part of nationwide protests over the controversial catastrophic insurance law. He steadfastly defended the 1988 law, but as complaints gained traction on Capitol Hill, support for the new benefits dwindled. Given his aversion to take seriously opponents of any kind, it was surprising that Rostenkowski agreed to spend a morning on their home ground with protesters of the new health-care law. "I didn't want to go," he said years later. "I saw no value with the meeting. . . . I went only because a representative of the AARP (American Association of Retired Persons) asked me to talk with an executive committee of a few members." Persons familiar with the ugly incident contend that it was fueled by a small group of local political organizers intent on making mischief and gaining attention. Regardless, network news coverage of Rostenkowski's skittish reaction sent warning signals that political barons were no longer immune to challenge.

The local group discussed its grievances with Rostenkowski at the Copernicus Senior Citizens Center, a meeting place on the city's northwest side where the elderly gathered to play cards and share lunch and gossip. Without consulting his Chicago staff—who had little familiarity with the topic or the protesters—his Washington aides arranged the meeting. But they ignored a clear warning of something unusual when Ways and Means press secretary Jim Jaffe unexpectedly received telephone calls from national television networks interested in the event. "Those calls raised the questions of how the reporters had learned about it and what the protesters planned," Jaffe said. "It seems to me that the event was a setup" to embarrass Rostenkowski. But Jaffe and others did not investigate at the time. In any case, the chairman met privately with the group for more than an hour at the Copernicus Center. The senior citizens complained that they should not have to pay for the new Medicare benefits for long-term illnesses and that taxpayers should share the financial burden. Rostenkowski defended the self-financing law and explained why the nation's high budget deficit required that relatively wealthy senior citizens pay a tax to finance the program. Both sides vigorously aired their views, but the discussion was otherwise uneventful.

To Rostenkowski's surprise, when the meeting ended a related group of senior citizens with protest signs was waiting outside the center. This larger group had been organized by Jan Schakowsky, executive director of the Illinois State Council of Senior Citizens, which was working to expand its influence on progressive issues. "They were into organization-building with the seniors, and they found a convenient target," said a veteran Chicago liberal activist. "Rostenkowski became a piece of their reality." (In an interesting twist, Schakowsky was elected to Congress in 1998 from Chicago's North Shore, adjacent to the district once held by Rostenkowski. During the campaign, she successfully disassociated herself from a federal criminal investigation into her husband Robert Creamer's alleged financial wrongdoing as executive director of Citizen Action of Illinois, another liberal group.)

For the protesters, the Ways and Means Committee was a distant abstraction. The job of their powerful congressman, they argued, was to represent their interests. "To these people, he was no king, no committee chairman," according to a narrative of the scene. "He was just Danny, their longtime congressman, the guy who ran interference for them if the federal bureaucracy screwed up their benefits and the reliable pol they could count on to show up at the Pulaski Day parade."[17] As Rostenkowski tried to make his way through the nearly two hundred people after the meeting, he made what he later called a "foolish" mistake by stopping at a television camera to talk to a local reporter. A smaller group of protesters then circled him and his car and driver waiting outside the center to speed him away. Although some regular visitors cheered him, the organized protesters "taunted him with shouts of 'Chicken!' 'Coward!' and 'Rottenkowski,'" and demanded that he speak with them about the new law.[18] But Rostenkowski had no interest in further conversation and moved toward the waiting Chevrolet. "These people are nuts," he muttered into a television microphone as he squeezed into the car and ordered the driver to get moving. But there was nowhere to go. The protesters had surrounded the car. When the young driver desperately sought to move ahead, the vehicle came directly into contact with Leona Kozien, a sixty-nine-year-old white-haired lady with a flowered shirt. When she mounted the hood of the car and stared directly through the windshield at Rostenkowski, while other protesters began pounding on the windows, he decided he had had enough. "Forced either to sit and wait for the crowd to disperse or make a break for daylight, the wide-bodied Rostenkowski bounded from the car and headed for a gasoline station two blocks away," according to a news report. "The seniors followed him—which freed up the car to move. It arrived at the station, Rostenkowski jumped in and, with tires squealing, drove away."[19] Most of the event was captured by the several television cameramen who had conveniently arrived at the scene.

When CBS network news reported the incident that evening, the Milwaukee Avenue protest quickly became more than a local firestorm. The symbolism of the congressional chairman running from a few frail senior citizens became a sorry metaphor for the decline in American politics. "What's smart about jumping out of your car and running away from old people who think they're getting shafted by Congress with this here catastrophic health tax?" wrote *Chicago Tribune* columnist Mike Royko.[20] Rostenkowski later dismissed the incident as insignificant. "I wasn't scared," he said. "And I was reelected with no problem." Indeed, later that day he played golf and had dinner with Bill Daley. "Most politicians would have said it was a major crisis," Daley said. "But he didn't think it was a problem. When I learned about it, I told him it was. . . . Some call it arrogance. Some say it's 'out of touch.' " Like several other allies, Daley thought the incident should have been avoided. It demonstrated to them that Rostenkowski, increasingly shielded by his Washington staff, "misunderstood local problems." It also revealed the problems resulting from the wall he had built between his Chicago and Washington staffs.

Rostenkowski responded that the protesters—not he—were out of touch with public sentiment. More than a year later a group of protesters came to Washington and told him they had been wrong in urging repeal of the health benefits for the elderly. Ignoring his staff's caution to steer clear, Rostenkowski said, he told the erstwhile protesters, "Go fly a kite," and he scolded them because "they didn't have faith in me." As for warnings that the Copernicus Center showdown revealed he had lost touch with constituents, Rostenkowski agreed that he no longer had time to spend "holding as many hands" as when he was a young politician. But the matter was blown out of proportion, he said. "I never viewed myself as a very important guy," he added. "Billy [Daley] thought the Ways and Means chairman being punished would be a national incident. I kind of laughed at that." True enough, the protest was staged and included a tiny share of Rostenkowski's constituents. But the new dynamics of citizen education meant that Rostenkowski and his successors needed more ways to communicate with an increasingly volatile electorate.

Rostenkowski's dwindling ties to his local ethnic community was another warning signal. As in the past, he sought to provide practical help, such as demanding the hiring of a Polish-speaking staff assistant at the Social Security office on Milwaukee Avenue; and he continued to direct charity to many community organizations. But he showed growing disdain for ethnic influence, which remained a vital part of the city's politics. The opportunity to have become the first Polish mayor "would have been nice," he said later. But the declining share of Polish voters in Chicago, plus Rostenkowski's focus on Washington, among other factors, made that dream unrealistic. During the 1980s and early 1990s he had a chilly relationship with Rep. Bill Lipinski, who served an area on Chicago's south side with a large share of Poles. Focusing chiefly on his district's needs, Lipinski kept his distance from House politics. Dealings between the two men all but ended when Lipinski publicly endorsed Rostenkowski's opponent in the 1992 Democratic primary.

Although Rostenkowski kept a couple of friends who were Polish, his social circle became "a roomful of Irish," said one of his veteran Washington aides. As "a second-generation mainstreamed American, . . . he felt neither defined or confined by" his Polish roots.[21] In part that was because so many Irish-Americans remained atop the city's political and business hierarchies. And as many American Poles became more conservative, both socially and politically, relatively few remained prominent in Democratic circles. "Danny had to struggle to keep his support among Poles," said Father Glab, the pastor of St. Stanislaus Church. "Part of his political success story is that he did not depend solely on Poles. . . . He didn't show favoritism to the Polish community."

Rostenkowski's belief in cultural assimilation also diminished his interest in strictly Polish activities. It was a telling fact that each of his four daughters shortened her name to " Rosten," as he had done as a youth after his father sent him to St. John's Academy. (Rostenkowski reclaimed his full surname when he decided to seek elective office in 1952.) "I did it for them," he said, with no hesitation. "Why saddle them with the 'k-o-w-s-k-i'?" Many Poles believed it was easier to get a job outside their community if they downplayed their nationality. The old Polish community waned: the membership list of St. Stanislaus fell, and the magnificent church became a fading relic. In the mid-1990s only about a fourth of its members were Polish; many Masses were conducted in Spanish. On the grand boulevard of Milwaukee Avenue, a few butchers continued to sell their aromatic kielbasas and pierogi. But most of the old storefronts were taken over by Mexican merchants; a stone's throw away, homes and small businesses in the "port of entry" neighborhoods were owned by struggling Korean immigrants, then the Vietnamese, and so on, in Chicago's grand melting-pot tradition. Some whites moved into gentrified neighborhoods; in most cases they were not Poles.

In one area Rostenkowski displayed genuine pride in his Polish heritage: the tribulations of his grandparents' homeland. From his early years in the House he privately sought to lift the yoke of Communist oppression from Poland and to improve that nation's bleak economy. Although he was not as publicly outspoken as other Poles in Congress, he met occasionally with Polish embassy officials and discussed with the State Department steps to encourage progress in Poland. As head of a delegation of friends and other officials, he represented every American president from Kennedy to Clinton at the Poznan international technical fair, held periodically in the heartland of Poland. But it was the Solidarity movement under the charismatic leadership of ex-shipyard worker Lech

Walesa that reawakened Rostenkowski's enthusiasm. "He was awed by Walesa," said Ed Derwinski, the former Illinois congressman who became an assistant secretary of state during the 1980s and dealt with Rostenkowski on Polish issues. After Walesa became president in 1990, Rostenkowski advocated additional investment by the American government and businesses; he was instrumental, for example, in convincing President Bush to forgive 50 percent of Poland's debt to the United States. During an emotional speech by Walesa in 1989 to a joint session of Congress, when the then-leader of the Solidarity Union received a hero's welcome, colleagues said Rostenkowski was in tears as he recalled both his own ancestors' sacrifices and the recent overthrow of communism. But the dealings between the two men were not always easy. A Rostenkowski aide recounted a meeting at Solidarity headquarters in Gdansk when the congressman and the Polish hero pointed fingers at each other after Walesa resented Rostenkowski's lectures on the need for Poland to take steps to increase the confidence of American corporations.

As in so many of his other activities, Rostenkowski retained a commonsense approach on behalf of causes from Warsaw to Milwaukee Avenue. Often he bulldozed ahead, running roughshod over obstacles in his path. For several decades he usually got his way. By the end of the 1980s, however, the cultural dynamics and the respect for order in which he had been nurtured began to change, especially in Washington. As bipartisanship eroded, the legendary chairman's life became more arduous—politically and, later, personally.

Chapter Eight

EROSION OF
DIVIDED GOVERNMENT

IN THE WORLD of Rostenkowski—as in the larger domain of Congress—no single model existed for the management of far-ranging legislation. In several respects his handling of the momentous 1990 budget deal ran counter to his own modus operandi on important issues. Much of his work on that measure took place outside Ways and Means and required him to adapt "new breed" techniques of playing to the media; also, and surprisingly, in the end he became an adversary of his friend in the White House. In his later years as chairman, as national politics became more confrontational, Rostenkowski was forced to abandon some of his comfortable old ways. "As 1990 began, Dan Rostenkowski was a frustrated man," according to Jim Jaffe, his longtime Ways and Means press secretary. "He was ready to lead, but others weren't willing to follow."[1] Still, some aspects of his approach were familiar—his desire to look at the big picture, his goal-oriented persistence, and his focus on building a majority in whatever manner possible. And the budget deal shaped his attitudes that characterized the close of his chairmanship: his focus on the federal budget deficit became pervasive, he gained greater self-confidence to go his own way to achieve his goals, and he showed the flexibility to respond to changing circumstances. Although the budget outcome won little credit at the time, and the resulting public dismay helped to shatter prominent political careers, the budget agreement may have done more to eliminate persistent federal deficits and to move the nation toward prosperity in the 1990s than any other public or private-sector action.

Budget negotiations in 1990 were dramatic proof that politics often does not follow a logical script. The 1988 election of George Bush—a fellow traveler in Washington bipartisanship—should have enhanced Rostenkowski's productivity. Instead, unlikely as it seemed at the time, the switch from Reagan to Bush shattered consensus-building between the Republican White House and the Democratic-controlled Congress. The two parties became entangled in bitter warfare. Virtually any initiative became a supreme test of wills. Compounding this tension was growing public hostility toward Washington's business-as-usual in the face of an economic downturn, plus eroding confidence in the nation's leaders. Even though Reagan and Tip O'Neill had disagreed bitterly, each had the savvy to lead his own party and the strength to impose order. Their successors had a deeper understanding of many issues, but the new president and Democratic leaders failed to exercise as much command. That change proved especially troublesome for the Ways and Means Committee, where bipartisanship had long been the watchword. Despite Rostenkowski's willingness to play partisan hardball, as chairman he increasingly sought common ground.

The chairman basked in his friendship with the new president. Unlike Reagan, who ran for president by attacking Washington and kept up that drumbeat even while serving as chief executive, Bush was a local fixture. His father had been senator from Connecticut. Young George, after moving to Texas, served two House terms before losing a Senate bid in 1970; but he returned to chair the Republican National Committee and direct the Central Intelligence Agency. Meanwhile he remained a regular paddleball player at the Rayburn House Office Building gym. Rostenkowski became a friend during Bush's Ways and Means service in the late 1960s; they learned the ropes together when Wilbur Mills was in his prime. "I liked Bill Clinton, but George Bush was my friend," he said years later. Soon after Bush became president, the two privately reveled in the Oval Office over how far they had come. "He looked around and said to me, 'Jesus Christ, Danny, I'm President of the United States,'" Rostenkowski recounted. "He was like a kid in the toy store." He could identify with Bush's awe; despite contrasting cultural backgrounds, both men were sons of successful politicians. He also was impressed by his pal's moderate penchant. When Bush sought to distance himself during the

1988 campaign from Reagan's harder edges, the chairman was confident they could do business. Indeed, he told colleagues he had voted for Bush against Michael Dukakis, the Democratic nominee. "I love George Bush," he said in a mid-1989 interview. "I think he can be a great president because I honestly believe that George Bush will, when the time comes, make the right decision."[2]

For Rostenkowski, the priority was the federal deficit, which in 1989 had exceeded $150 billion. That was 30 percent less than the $221 billion of 1986. But, in a favorable economy, Rostenkowski was dismayed that there seemed to be no end in sight to annual twelve-digit deficits, which from 1981 to 1989 tripled the federal debt to nearly $3 trillion. "The next president and the next Congress will have to face the twin legacies of the Reagan presidency: a national debt in excess of $2 trillion and a social safety net that has endured eight years of neglect," he said in a postelection speech at Northwestern University. "The main issue for us next year is whether we're going to duck and dodge or finally face the cold facts and try to make a realistic response."

Alas, the two old friends ran into a pack of problems. Bush lacked his predecessor's charisma and strong convictions. Whatever Reagan's shortcomings, his rhetorical rigor made it easier for him to make concessions without offending the conservatives who dominated the Republican party. By contrast, Bush's less secure grip and inarticulate style created serious handicaps. At the 1988 convention, when he needed to demonstrate his contrasts to Dukakis, Bush made a promise that would haunt his presidency. "Read my lips," he said in what became his campaign mantra. "No new taxes." Many politicians sought ways to muffle this kind of promise, once elected. "There's a big difference between being a candidate and being the president," Rostenkowski warned. But Bush supporters took him seriously—probably more so than his advisers intended. When the president tried to abandon his promise, true believers blew the whistle.

Other partisan problems emerged in early 1989 after the Senate rejected—on a nearly party-line vote—Bush's nomination of former Sen. John Tower as secretary of defense. Bush responded by selecting Dick Cheney, the highly regarded House Republican who was minority whip. Cheney's quick confirmation forced Republicans to select a new No. 2 leader. In an epic showdown against a foe backed by Minority Leader (and Rostenkowski pal) Bob Michel, the winner by a two-vote margin was Newt Gingrich, the backbench Georgian who was unknown nationally but who excited many Republicans because he promised to end their perpetual minority status. His selection would have a profound impact on the House. Meanwhile, when a staff report of the House Standards of Official Conduct Committee (commonly known as the Ethics Committee) charged Speaker Jim Wright with sixty-nine violations of House rules, it was only a matter of time until he was forced out. Conflicts ranging from his disagreement with the Reagan administration's Central America policy to a botched pay raise for members of Congress had angered rank-and-file lawmakers in both parties. With his reservoir of goodwill depleted, members were no longer willing to extend Wright a broad license of authority. "Not enough members felt a debt so that they would bleed for him," said New Jersey Democrat Robert Torricelli. That left Wright little choice but to announce his reluctant departure. Days before Wright's resignation, Majority Whip Tony Coelho unexpectedly quit the House in the face of separate financial-conflict charges.

To replace their two deposed leaders, House Democrats chose Tom Foley as speaker and Dick Gephardt as their new majority leader. Senate Democrats too made a big change in 1989, selecting George Mitchell to replace Robert Byrd as their majority leader. Each majority leader now held a partisan view of tax policy and a propensity to insist on his convictions. The changes also mirrored broader shifts within Congress. For House Democrats, Gephardt's move into the leadership ranks and his inclusive habits symbolized the spreading of influence to the most junior members. But he quickly found, to his regret, that those changes created real problems as he tried to get things done. By then, of course, it was too late to turn back the clock.

For Rostenkowski, the House changes were devastating. Even though he had clashed fiercely with Wright during his two years as speaker, the two men shared a deep understanding of power and a reverence for the House. When a shaken Wright returned to his office after announcing his resignation, the first telephone call came from Rostenkowski. After his friend reminisced about House changes, Wright responded, "The institution certainly has. . . . I remember when you came here, Danny."[3] With Tom Foley replacing Wright, Rostenkowski had less reason to fear the speaker's second-guessing. But Foley's cautious style meant that Rostenkowski could not rely on the leadership for as much help. "Tom Foley was a weak speaker who was incapable of making decisions," said Sen. Byron Dorgan, the North Dakota Democrat. "Dan Rostenkowski was everything that Tom Foley was not." The combination of Wright's departure, Gephardt's elevation into the leadership, and Michel's loss of influence to Gingrich among House Republicans meant that House leaders and senior committee members could no longer dictate results. The consequences of a misstep had become more acute. And the political world, including the press, was less forgiving.

It didn't take long in 1989 for Rostenkowski to suffer the kinds of legislative setbacks he had not experienced since his disastrous first year as chairman. The first predicament was Bush's proposal for a lower tax rate on capital gains—those taxes chiefly on the profits from sale of stocks and other investments. Democrats attacked the cut, which most regarded as an undue benefit for the wealthy. Rostenkowski, too, publicly opposed Bush's plan, partly because of his desire to preserve the delicate balances in his 1986 tax-reform package. Privately, however, he was inclined to deal with his friend, the president. "At a White House meeting in mid-April," wrote Lawrence Haas, "the chairman offered to get Bush a one-year cut in the capital gains rate."[4] In return Rostenkowski saw an opportunity for a larger agreement to rescue domestic programs, chiefly those that would benefit big cities. He also made clear his hope that Bush would agree to a major reduction in the deficit, which would require him to breach his no-new-taxes pledge. In early June, a week after Wright announced his resignation, Rostenkowski told reporters he would consider a capital-gains tax cut as part of a budget package. The wheeler-dealer was back in the saddle.

Most Democrats, however, were less willing to trust or accommodate Bush. And Republicans, confident they could find the votes to pass a capital-gains tax cut without the baggage of less attractive provisions, saw no need to cut a deal with the chairman. So three weeks later, as defeat seemed imminent, Rostenkowski withdrew his offer. But his equivocation reinforced centrist Democrats who were inclined to collaborate with Republicans. "Some of it was a mystery to me," said Rob Leonard, the Ways and Means staff director. "I remember being somewhat surprised that he gave a signal to some Democrats that he would not strongly oppose" a capital-gains tax cut. To Rostenkowski's embarrassment, six Ways and Means Democrats joined with the thirteen Republicans to create a narrow majority among the thirty-six members. Their proposal was similar to his own suggestion. Rostenkowski had opened the door to a capital-gains tax reduction, said Ed Jenkins, his Ways and Means ally, who led the push for change. Intriguingly, Rostenkowski a few weeks earlier had backed Jenkins's futile challenge against Gephardt in the Democratic Caucus contest for majority leader. "The tougher the issue," he told House Democrats, "the more you want Ed Jenkins in the room." The master of Gucci Gulch had lost his touch and his control. His on-again, off-again positioning left "the usually shrewd Chicago pol [acting] like a puppy dog to Mr. Bush, weakening when his pride and vanity were stroked by the President," the *Wall Street Journal* reported.[5] By 239 to 190, the House passed the bill prepared by the conservative coalition at Ways and Means. The result was a stinging rebuke to Rostenkowski.

The once-indomitable chairman suffered another blow when, emboldened by the Chicago protesters who had won headlines by blockading him, opponents of the catastrophic health-insurance law succeeded in their yearlong campaign to repeal the measure. Rebuffing Rostenkowski's search for a compromise that might salvage the new program—including a letter from Bush saying, "It would be imprudent to tinker" with the new law—the House took the unprecedented step of rescinding recently enacted benefits. Exacerbating Rostenkowski's woes, the reinvigorated Republican minority embraced Gingrich's strategy of manning the partisan barricades, even at the price of conflict with their own president. Although the Senate was more willing to preserve the catastrophic-insurance program in some form, avid health-care reformers were forced to throw in the towel once they realized that the votes had turned against them. Only fifty-seven House members, including Rostenkowski, held firm in November against repealing the law that was enacted with sparse opposition little more than a year earlier.

In the catastrophic-insurance debacle there was plenty of blame to go around: (1) seniors were too greedy in refusing to share the financing of a new benefit; (2) architects of the new law unwisely imposed higher fees before most payees received benefits; and (3) advocates, working mostly behind closed doors, failed to explain their intentions. Bush's election also removed the executive branch's chief boosters of the new law at a crucial time. Despite pressure from die-hard supporters, most lawmakers concluded that the new program was not worth salvaging. "Rosty was too proud to say that he made a mistake," said Dennis Hastert of Illinois, a leading Republican on health-care issues long before he became House speaker. More simply, most members were unwilling to gamble that the protesters spoke for only a small constituency. "I defended my vote to a local seniors group by explaining it on a blackboard," said Ways and Means Republican Ray McGrath. "I convinced every person in a room of four to five hundred that it made sense. . . . Unfortunately, few other members understood the bill well enough to do that. That was a failure of the political end at Ways and Means. But nobody paid attention." For disciples of old-fashioned deal-making, growing cynicism about politicians had struck home. "My head is bloodied, but I'm not bowed," Rostenkowski told a magazine reporter, who wrote that the "leadership vacuum" created by Wright's fall was "making it tough for once-dominant figures such as Rostenkowski to maintain discipline."[6] More than most Democrats imagined when they abandoned Wright, they were paying a price for their independence.

Repeal of the catastrophic-insurance law soured lawmakers on sweeping health-care plans. Rostenkowski had observed a similar result when he chaired the health subcommittee debating President Carter's unsuccessful cost-containment plan; now a new generation in Congress was reminded that health-care legislation sounds better in theory than it does in the icy world of political reality. Failure had consequences. Although Rostenkowski and other lawmakers in the 1980s made modest changes in Medicare to reduce spiraling federal budget increases and to require more efficient delivery of services of physicians, hospitals, and other health-care providers, the program's cost grew from 5 percent of the federal budget in 1980 to 10 percent in 1995—a huge increase. "The health-care system is broken, and we lack the discipline to make the tough decisions needed to fix it," Rostenkowski told a Washington meeting of the American Hospital Association in January 1990. Subsequent events would justify his pessimistic appraisal.

The dual setbacks in 1989 were all the more embarrassing because Rostenkowski had scheduled for July of that year a major celebration to showcase the influence of the committee and its chairman. The ostensible rationale was the panel's bicentennial. In fact, even its own official chronology shows that the select Ways and Means Committee existed for only a few months in 1789; not until 1794 was the committee established with formal jurisdiction. (As it turned out, 1994 would have been an inauspicious year to celebrate Rostenkowski or Ways and Means.) Notwithstanding that detail, he arranged the celebration because, he said, "I thought it was a good way to study our past, celebrate our history, and think about our future." He spared little expense or modesty. He wanted to show that Ways and Means was the No. 1 House committee. In his introduction to the 526-page official history, Rostenkowski asked readers to "forgive me for some self-indulgence, but I think this history is fascinating."[7] The publication's detailed narrative of issues and players that have paraded across the Ways and Means stage is one of the few books published by the Government Printing Office that is filled with color photos on glossy pages.

Business and labor groups contributed almost $800,000 to pay for the commemoration and—as many of them acknowledged—to curry favor with Rostenkowski. "Everyone wants to be on the good side of the chairman of this particular committee," said a spokesman for American Express, which was among nearly two dozen firms that contributed $25,000 each to finance the July gala.[8] More than half the money went to Steven York, a professional film producer who was hired to assemble a one-hour documentary history of the committee. Rostenkowski wanted York to produce a high-quality program that could be aired nationwide on public television. The resulting production included original depictions of a nineteenth-century lawmaker traveling to Washington, and film clips from the committee's back-room dealings on tax reform. As it turned out, the program was not widely aired by the Public Broadcasting Service. York acknowledged that its appeal was diminished because local stations were aware that Rostenkowski had a hand in its creation. York's work did receive a sympathetic audience, though, during an elaborate dinner celebration at the committee's Capitol Hill hearing room. Hundreds of guests included former members such as President Bush and Wilbur Mills. At the private affair—emceed by Cokie Roberts, a prominent congressional reporter and the daughter of Hale Boggs—Bush fondly reminisced about his Ways and Means years. In response, Rostenkowski put aside his prepared text to reach out to the president with a healing message that "we can work it out."

Despite his 1989 woes, Rostenkowski was looking to sink his teeth into what had become Washington's most intractable dilemma: the budget deficit. Unconventionally for him, he moved out front in shaping the debate and challenging others to follow. He approached the topic with a gambler's swagger as he bullied his House colleagues and Bush to get serious. Although he never received the public credit that came his way on tax reform, his role was vital in creating what may be the most substantial budget deal between the president and Congress in the nation's history.

But it wasn't easy. Given both parties' earlier failures to deliver on their promises, and Rostenkowski's limited experience in pressing a legislative initiative from the start, his efforts took time to gain momentum. Indeed, the entire 1990 deficit-reduction exercise was jury-rigged, exhausting, complex, and alternately disappointing and exhilarating for Rostenkowski and other key participants. Bush and Congress frequently came close to failure during the months-long enterprise. And surely, partisan benefits were minimal for proponents in both parties. Although it won little praise on enactment or during the next few years, the agreement proved crucial in turning the nation away from the huge budget deficits of the 1980s. As it turned out, the 1990 deal was Rostenkowski's only major legislative success during the Bush administration.

Although they eventually reached a deal, the Bush-Rostenkowski budget politics were elaborate. First the chairman ratcheted up the pressure on his friend to act on responsible terms. Eventually he was gratified when the president said he was willing to negotiate a tax increase and all other elements of a budget deal. Later he was miffed by last-minute White House shenanigans. On Capitol Hill the factional fighting was worse than ever. Many liberal Democrats were furious with Rostenkowski's concessions to Bush. Among Republicans, Gingrich staged a crucial walkout from the negotiations. Those moves and others would have long-term repercussions. They helped to explain why the 1990 deal became the final bipartisan gasp between a Republican president and a Democratic Congress. Despite many complications, Rostenkowski and others kept their eye on the deficit-reduction target. Ultimately they succeeded.

His vehicle, immodestly, was the "Rostenkowski challenge." In a series of early 1990 speeches he described the problem and outlined his alternative. His starting point was that the federal deficit had increased steadily from $73 billion in fiscal 1980, with only an occasional small downward blip. "It is time to stop the silliness," he told oil and gas executives. "I am asking you to demand that your elected Washington officials get serious about deficit reduction, face reality and come up with some credible options." His proposal featured a one-year freeze on all domestic spending, a 3 percent cut in defense spending, and tax increases for the remaining 40 percent of the package; initially he called for higher income taxes on the wealthy plus tax hikes on gasoline, tobacco, beer, wine, and pollutants. By requiring increased taxes, he hoped to provide cover to the reluctant Bush.

Rostenkowski received some encouragement from senior House Democrats, including Budget Committee chairman Leon Panetta. From the start, however, the dynamics were anything but favorable. Most Democrats were in no mood to compromise unless Bush disavowed his 1988 campaign promise in taxes; that made the already dubious Republicans even more skeptical about a tax hike. Meanwhile the deficit-reduction targets that Congress had set in 1985 as part of the Gramm-Rudman-Hollings law had become unattainable, even with the 1987 amendments. The projected deficit of $159 billion would far exceed its updated $74 billion ceiling for fiscal 1991, the Office of Management and Budget announced in mid-1990; absent changes, the balanced-budget law would require draconian federal spending cuts. "The annual budget battle had been reduced to political theater, a circus of illusion that often placed Rostenkowski in a peripheral ring," according to Jaffe. "The public was becoming distrustful of and disgusted with politicians. Rostenkowski believed the voters had a point and felt some shame, although he believed that he personally had done all he could."

As he prepared to issue his challenge in early March, key players in both parties were heading irresponsibly in the wrong direction. While Bush proposed a new and larger version of his capital-gains tax cut, Democratic Sen. Daniel Patrick Moynihan of the Finance Committee weighed in with proposals to cut Social Security taxes in direct repudiation of the rescue package that he, Rostenkowski, and others had devised in 1983 with the Reagan White House. "If there was an Academy Award for the worst idea of year, we'd be watching a very tight race here," Rostenkowski bitingly remarked about the two alternatives. Meanwhile the House and Senate Budget Committees proceeded with business-as-usual debate on the next year's budget outlines. On mostly party-line votes, Democrats endorsed slashes in defense spending and increases for domestic programs, but they rejected additional taxes unless Bush took the first step. Demands for wide-ranging deficit reduction generated little interest.

Rostenkowski seized the opening with an initiative that combined policy detail and public-relations bravado. He used the *Washington Post*'s Sunday news analysis section to get attention. "The logical place to start was the Outlook section . . . which was something of a bulletin board for policy wonks," Jaffe wrote. Jodie Allen—the Outlook editor who happened to be a hawk on the need to fix the budget mess—"liked the thrust of Rostenkowski's piece and began to polish it, by totally rewriting it." Headlined "Cold Turkey: How to End the Deficit in 5 Years," Allen gave it page-one coverage on March 11.

"Here's my challenge," the congressman wrote. "Adopt my plan to fix the budget deficit—or come up with a better one. But any competitor will have to measure up to what my plan offers: No smoke and mirrors; no 'feel good' promises or slide-by budgeting; no picking out one or two small-potato items that wouldn't make a perceivable dent in the deficit, leaving the hard part to be worked out later by a 'budget summit.' Just solid proposals—including some that I, as a Democrat, traditionally opposed—that produce substantial, incontestable savings calling for modest sacrifices by nearly every American."[9] As Jaffe wrote, "No ox went ungored." Rostenkowski got additional bite when his staff secured an appearance for him that Sunday morning on "Face the Nation," the CBS television program. "Whether or not my colleagues will support it or not I don't know, but somebody has to start saying it," he told the interviewer. "People are way ahead of us. All you have to do is talk straight to the American people and they will respond."

The most positive response to the challenge came from the White House, where Rostenkowski had alerted officials about his piece. "Basically we think there is some room to talk here," press secretary Marlin Fitzwater said. Bush privately welcomed his old friend taking the lead. When he first informed Bush of his plan, "the President assured Rosty he would not . . . dump all over him," wrote Richard Darman, the Office of Management and Budget director in the Bush years.[10] But an anonymous White House official, who apparently did not get the message, told the *Post* that the Bush-Rostenkowski friendship was "a big piece of" the administration's decision to give the proposal "a little respect."[11]

Reaction from leading Democrats was, if anything, less favorable. Moynihan, doubtlessly peeved by the slap at his proposed cut in Social Security taxes, suggested that Rostenkowski's proposal would not balance the budget as claimed. Senate Budget Committee chairman Jim Sasser dismissed the plan on the following Sunday's "Face the Nation" program. "I don't think it's going anywhere, frankly," he said. But, gradually, inklings of progress emerged. In late April, Rostenkowski told reporters he had had "several encouraging conversations with the White House." Although he gave little detail, he said Bush's team wanted assurances that additional revenues would be devoted to deficit reduction, not new spending. Rostenkowski responded with a proposal to change congressional budget rules to assure such a result. But he warned against excessive posturing: "The year is short and the clock is running."

Finally, in early May, Bush called the top four congressional leaders to the White House for an unusual Sunday meeting to discuss his concern about the weak economy and the rising deficit. That session launched high-level negotiations on the budget. Would he have taken that step without pressure from Rostenkowski? We can only guess. Surely, adverse economic news and the prospect of legislative gridlock helped to force the president's hand. Still, although Democrats exulted when Bush said he had "no preconditions," Republicans' unwillingness to concede the need for tax increases gave the talks a halting start. In part the GOP stance was a negotiating ploy. Given the mutual mistrust and the obvious intent of Rostenkowski and other senior Democrats to demand new taxes, Republicans insisted on their point until Democrats agreed to major spending cuts, at least in principle. "I want to see real change" in spending, Gingrich told an interviewer in mid-May. "Then, let's talk about taxes."[12] The rambunctious minority whip was trying to stiffen Bush's backbone.

The first major breakthrough came on June 26 when Bush issued a brief statement that agreement on a budget package required several components, including "tax revenue increases." The bipartisan congressional leaders agreed on that position, he added. Rostenkowski applauded Bush's comment as "an important step in the right direction." But rank-and-file reaction was less favorable than the negotiators had hoped. Angry House Republicans approved in mid-July a formal declaration opposing "new taxes and all tax rate increases." Many Democrats turned up the heat on Bush by saying that tax increases should be imposed only on the wealthy. Gloating about the Republican splits, other Democrats said they were surprised by Bush's willingness to move their way. "We could not have anticipated that our strategy would work as well as it did," said Sen. Wyche Fowler, the Georgia Democrat. As negotiators dispersed for the August recess, Rostenkowski said he was pleased that his challenge "broke the ice." But the principal evidence of progress, such as it was, came from the GOP's internal squabbling. At the end of the recess, Gingrich told a conservative audience that he could not support a budget package unless it included tax cuts to encourage economic growth.

Rostenkowski was growing restless about the negotiations' slow pace and their format. With Congress only a few weeks away from adjournment for the November elections, he feared that a deal would leave committees little time to add their own flourishes. Although he relished high-level deal-cutting, Rostenkowski worried that his Ways and Means members would resent their exclusion from the process. Many things could go wrong—and ultimately they did. When negotiations were moved to Andrews Air Force Base outside Washington, in hopes of minimizing distractions, it became all the more difficult to gauge the reaction of rank-and-file members to a potential deal. "The process was terrible," said Rep. Henry Waxman, a California Democrat and key player on health-care spending. "It replaced a thorough airing of views in committees with a closed-door summit." Rostenkowski also found that the effort to craft a deal made it difficult to assign final credit or responsibility. And, quite simply, he preferred to hold the gavel. Without it he had less control of the discussions.

In unpredictable ways the leaders finally achieved the broad goals that both sides had sought. Only hours before the fiscal-year deadline that would have triggered huge spending cuts, a still smaller group of negotiators—House Democrats were represented by Foley and Gephardt—announced late on September 30 that they had an agreement. Although Rostenkowski loyally supported the deal, the result was not what he had in mind. The negotiators' package provided the outlines for $500 billion in deficit reduction during the next five years, as he had urged. But he objected to the budget assumptions and to recommended procedures for crafting those details. "The budget summit has done major violence to congressional procedures," he told the House. The result "disenfranchised" most members and was "demeaning" to the Ways and Means Committee, he complained. "You can count me out" if White House officials assumed that he would clear decisions with them, he added.

The deal had other problems. Rejecting Rostenkowski's call for income tax increases, negotiators instead tinkered with the tax code. Violating his commitment to tax-code simplicity, their agreement added complex limitations on deductions for many middle-income taxpayers. And the call for hefty premium hikes for Medicare beneficiaries seemed unwise following repeal of the catastrophic-insurance law. Still, Rostenkowski said he would vote for the initial deal so that the process would continue. As it turned out, the centrist course was an impossible sell. Criticism came from all directions. Liberals, led by David Obey, objected to cuts in programs directed toward low-income groups. Conservatives, led by Gingrich, said that tax increases—no matter how small—were unacceptable. Members of all stripes objected to the convoluted process that led to the deal. "This is a poor way to run a government," Rep. Richard Durbin, an Illinois Democrat, said at the time. Finally the deal collapsed. On a 179-to-254 vote, with a majority of each party opposed, the House turned down the package on October 5, a month from Election Day. "This is a sad night for this House," Rostenkowski lamented.

But the fight was far from over. What followed were the Democrats' resurrection and Rostenkowski's revenge. In effect he threw up his hands at the Republicans' unwillingness to forge a balanced agreement, as he had urged since debate on a capital-gains tax cut more than a year earlier. His alternative gained quick approval on virtually party-line votes in committee and on the House floor. It featured several soak-the-rich provisions, including a 10 percent surtax on millionaires and an increase in the highest income tax rate to 33 percent from the 28 percent that had been set in 1986. It also trimmed cuts in Medicare and spending programs for the poor that had been outlined in the earlier agreement. House passage, by a 227-to-203 vote, was a conspicuous turnabout from the bipartisanship and White House cooperation that Rostenkowski had sought for nearly a decade. His mixed feelings over the earlier deal were overtaken by glee. "Today, the House of Representatives bit the bullet and did what needed to be done," he said following the October 16 vote. "My colleagues accepted the Rostenkowski challenge. . . . Once again, Members of Congress can be proud of themselves—and our institution." A few rough edges of the House-passed bill were tempered by the time the Senate and a House-Senate conference committee completed action on October 27, three weeks after collapse of the first budget deal. Bush signed the bill with reservations but with an understanding that Republican rebels left him no choice but to accept the Democrats' bill if he wished to avoid a legislative collapse.

Stylistically the process was a disaster: five months of bipartisan negotiations proved to be largely a waste of time, as Bush and congressional leaders lost touch with rank-and-file lawmakers. Even with widespread Republican griping, however, the final package included major steps toward budget discipline: firm caps on spending for domestic discretionary spending programs during the next five years, significant cost-savings from entitlements not directed at senior citizens, and a net 2 percent increase in tax revenues, which fell chiefly on the wealthy. (Buried in the final package was a provision close to Rostenkowski's heart, exempting U.S. loans to Poland from spending controls.) The real deficit impact was obscured for years—first by the adverse budget impact of the Persian Gulf War and the recession, both in 1991; later because neither party wanted credit for a law that was so politically reviled. By 1998, however, politicians in both parties suddenly were forced to adjust to the more welcome problem of a budget surplus. Finally it became clear that the "Rostenkowski challenge" and other pressures that led to the 1990 law—by setting into place additional deficit cuts in President Clinton's 1993 tax increases and Speaker Gingrich's 1995 belt-tightening—had begun to reverse a decade of big deficits.

For Rostenkowski the outcome of the budget battle was uncharacteristic in several ways. After jump-starting the negotiations, he was pushed to the outside, only to pick up the pieces of the shattered bipartisan deal later. After enduring a decade of liberal Democrats' criticism that he had been too accommodating to Republicans, he was chiefly responsible for injecting partisanship into the budget package that Foley, Gephardt, and Panetta negotiated with White House officials. And, finally, Bush and congressional Republicans were forced to accept a budget deal that was far less tolerable than what they could have won months earlier. In ways that Rostenkowski could not have planned, he outsmarted both his Democratic critics and Bush. "He started as a statesman and became more of a politician," is how a senior Democratic aide described Rostenkowski's role in the 1990 budget debate. "Sometimes he didn't understand the nuances of policy," said Bob Reischauer, who directed the Congressional Budget Office at the time. "But he had common sense. . . . He would scrunch his eyes and say that he and the American people don't understand that." In this case, Reischauer added, Rostenkowski understood that there was no choice for the federal government: it needed to pay more of its bills.

The budget struggle left a bitter taste that would linger for the remainder of Bush's term. "It was a dreadful experience for everybody," said Bill Frenzel, the Ways and Means Republican. True, few incumbents lost their seats in the 1990 elections. That was partly because the budget horseplay came too late for challengers in either party to exploit. Nor could voters easily conclude whom they should blame. So insiders in both parties did not suffer the consequences until the election two years later. But there was a more immediate result in the aftermath of the legislative struggle.

Bush and his aides quickly stepped back from cooperation with Congress. Speaking a few days after the elections, White House chief of staff John Sununu displayed the administration's arrogance of the next two years when he gave lawmakers the back of his hand: "If Congress wants to come together, adjourn and leave, it's all right with us." Despite all the naysaying, however, Rostenkowski concluded that the years of budget battles had been worthwhile, even if the cost had frayed bipartisanship and his friendship with Bush. "What's at stake here?" he asked rhetorically, as the House was about to approve the final agreement. "Nothing less, in my opinion, than American self-respect."

THE FINAL TWO YEARS of Bush's presidency were the least productive period of Rostenkowski's chairmanship, though not for lack of opportunity. Following U.S. success in the Persian Gulf War, Bush's approval in public opinion polls soared to 91 percent. But both parties had become embittered by persistent partisanship. When a triumphant Bush addressed an enthusiastic Congress in early March 1991, after securing an end to Gulf War hostilities, he could have rallied the lawmakers—and the nation—to address virtually any national problem. Improvements in education, energy self-sufficiency, health care, or national defense were only a few of the worthy goals that Bush might have set. Instead the president curiously decided to spend his political capital by urging Congress to get moving on two narrow goals, crime reduction and transportation funding; he proposed little change in either area, nor did he accomplish much with these Washington perennials. Ultimately the successful Gulf War operation had little impact on U.S. legislative politics. But Bush's caution would backfire in the next year's election.

The inertia did not affect only bipartisan relations. Both parties seemed dispirited and unable to focus on new initiatives to address national issues. Bush's retreat from his "no new taxes" pledge, and his inability to address what he mockingly described as "the vision thing," left Republicans without direction. The Democrats' apparent inability to produce a credible presidential candidate in 1991 increased the Republicans' cockiness to defer major initiatives until after Bush's expected reelection. The greater surprise was congressional Democrats' failure in 1991–1992 to shape the national debate—either to challenge Bush directly or to help themselves prepare for the election. Their focus was health care, especially in the wake of the catastrophic-insurance debacle. Their imperative became more compelling in late 1991, when the previously unknown Harris Wofford won a special election for a Pennsylvania Senate seat by showing the issue's strong appeal; during his campaign Wofford emphasized the need for improved health-care services for all Americans. On Capitol Hill, Democrats tried. But astonishingly they failed to prepare a health-care proposal or rally public interest behind the goal. During much of this two-year period, Gephardt and Senate Majority Leader Mitchell spearheaded intensive party efforts to prepare alternatives. Their failure had major consequences for Democrats and for Bill Clinton after the 1992 election. The health-care maneuvering also offers insight into Rostenkowski's difficult relationships with party leaders, especially Dick Gephardt.

In the late 1970s the Rostenkowski-Gephardt clash over Carter's hospital cost-containment proposal was less personal than in later years, if only because they were not as familiar with each other. Their disagreement was simply a part of the larger Democratic mosaic. During the mid-1980s the differences between the two grew more consequential. Now each was a leader in the House and in the Democratic party. And Gephardt was seeking to redirect Democratic policies and images, both to help the party regain influence and to advance his own presidential interest. Rostenkowski, of course, concentrated on passing legislation. Each achieved some success. After Gephardt became majority leader in 1989, Rostenkowski was forced to deal with him as a peer. Still, the chairman dismissed what he viewed as the younger lawmaker's modest legislative skills and media grandstanding. Gephardt's relentless efforts to build Democratic unity became another irritant to Rostenkowski, whose legislative pragmatism required that proposals have some future with a Republican president. For example, Rostenkowski delivered a backhanded compliment when he said in a late 1990 speech that Gephardt once was among the few members of Congress with expertise on health issues. "But when he geared up for a run at the White House, I suspect he quickly realized that health [policy] couldn't be simplified to the point where it would play politically," Rostenkowski said in a comment laced with ridicule. During the 1990 budget debate, he added, Gephardt "evaded" the need to address the Medicare problem. As intraparty squabbling, these remarks were unusually caustic.

Gephardt, with his popularity among rank-and-file members and his career-long tendency to downplay criticism from other House Democrats, turned his cheek to the attacks. In 1991 his goal was to unify Democrats behind a core of health-care legislation to be sent to Bush. Gephardt and his allies believed they could bridge the Democrats' various approaches for improving health-care coverage. By the spring of 1992 he voiced confidence that they would soon succeed. "I want to make sure that we can get 218 Democrats" to support a plan, he said in an interview. "I am optimistic that we will do that. . . . All incumbents are challenged and have to demonstrate that they are dealing with important issues." Despite wishful thinking and extensive effort, however, neither House or Senate Democrats could produce a plan. In hindsight their splits proved the need for leadership from a president of their own party.

House Republicans, meanwhile, focused on a more parochial Democratic failing. Inspired by Gingrich's harsh critiques of Congress, the GOP upstarts turned their attention to a festering sore that would prove ruinous for many Democrats, including Rostenkowski. Their probing of the obscure House Bank raised the curtain on what had become a ticking time bomb. Revelations exposed the decay from the Democrats' forty-year rule of the House. Indeed, the nonreview of those operations was intentional. "Oversight would have been seen as an attack on vested powers," conceded a Democratic insider. But the gross lack of accountability made the bank a vulnerable target in a chamber where the "get-along" mentality had become pervasive. Years earlier federal investigators privately urged senior House officers to fix the problem. But the leaders and their subordinates were reluctant to remedy the internal bungling. In the first place, they considered it a minor affair. Nor did they wish to interfere with what many members viewed as a well-earned perquisite. So failure to correct small foul-ups mushroomed into a crisis that blew the lid off the insular Capitol. As for Rostenkowski, who was exonerated in the bank scandal, it revealed a more serious underlying problem: the pampered attention that he sought and expanded as a convenience to colleagues became a national scandal.

The House Bank was an impropriety the average citizen could understand. For reporters it was much easier to describe than the federal budget or health-care policy. On its surface the abuses were as straightforward as a bounced check. For its members, the bank provided protection against overdrafts—often involving many thousands of dollars—that most customers could not obtain at a commercial bank. According to the General Accounting Office's investigation, 325 House members (269 current and

56 former lawmakers) had written 8,331 bad checks in the 12 months after July 1, 1989. But these privileged consumers paid no penalty. Nor were the bank's problems of recent vintage. In similar audits over many years, the GAO had uncovered thousands of bad checks. The chief responsibility rested with Jack Russ, the sergeant at arms who had done favors for many influential members during nearly a quarter-century as a House aide. When several freshmen Republicans exposed juicy details of how the bank operated, the reaction was explosive. "We have a crisis in the U.S. House of Representatives," John Boehner of Ohio told the House. "The time has come to thoroughly examine the conduct of this House." Following an investigation, the House Ethics Committee revealed in April 1992 the list of violators, which quickly became a media cause célèbre. That inquiry led U.S. Attorney General William Barr to appoint a special counsel who probed dozens of the worst violators but brought no indictments against House members. In October 1993 Russ pleaded guilty to three felony counts, including embezzlement of public funds.

The public furor over cronyism left Rostenkowski little political cover. Although he had written no bad checks at the House Bank, two factors linked him to emerging details of House sleaze. First was his friendship with Russ, whom he actively backed in 1983 when Russ was first elected sergeant at arms. For years Russ had chauffeured Rostenkowski around town, especially on trips to nearby National Airport. "He had all these officers at his beck and call," said Gary Hymel, the former senior aide to Hale Boggs and Tip O'Neill. Rostenkowski also used Russ's office in the Capitol as "a place to hang out and be involved," Hymel added. Even after he became Ways and Means chairman, he retained an inordinate interest in the House's internal offices. It was in his blood. He viewed the operations of the House as Richard J. Daley had run Chicago's Democratic organization: power meant patronage and control. "Like a boss in a ward, he worked hard to get jobs for his friends," said Rep. Tom Downey, Rostenkowski's young lieutenant. "He wanted to make sure, for example, that they would not talk to reporters" about what they saw or heard about members. (Downey claimed he had no interest in the operation of Russ's office, even though his wife worked there. But he was defeated for reelection in 1992, in part because of his 151 bad checks at the House Bank.) Rostenkowski's continuing ties to House aides of questionable skill and integrity were all the more perplexing because he selected senior Ways and Means Committee aides who were highly regarded for their principles and ability. The dichotomy is reminiscent of Rostenkowski's efforts to separate his Chicago political world from his Washington policy sphere, much as Daley ran distinct offices at city hall and in the local Democratic party. For Rostenkowski "there was a bifurcation between professional staff, whose judgment he valued, and his political staff, whose role was to make his physical environment easier," said one of his Ways and Means aides.

The other factor complicating Rostenkowski's life in 1992 was a federal investigation of the House Post Office. In the public's mind the two probes often blended. But they were quite different matters. At the post office, prosecutors alleged that lawmakers were ripping off the public, chiefly by selling for cash large amounts of stamps they received for official purposes. In recent years most House members had made little use of their postage-stamp allowance because their franking privilege allowed them to send unlimited separately addressed envelopes without routine postage. So news reports of Rostenkowski's stamp purchases created a furor on Capitol Hill, where his $55,000 total between 1986 and early 1992 was the highest for any member. Still more ominous was the May 1992 disclosure that a federal grand jury had issued subpoenas for his office records dealing with stamp purchases. Initially he dismissed any suggestions of wrongdoing, telling reporters, "I am interested in learning what this is all about." Later his aides explained that he used the stamps because the Ways and Means chairman required many mailings with special postage. Eventually the criminal investigation—initiated by Jay Stephens, the Republican-appointed U.S. attorney for the District of Columbia—became the centerpiece of Rostenkowski's 1994 indictment. But as he struggled to carry on routine duties, continuing revelations exposed unsavory details. As with Russ, Rostenkowski had been instrumental in 1972 in securing the House postmaster plum for Robert Rota.

For Rostenkowski, about the only good news from the investigations was that most of the allegations were not publicly reported until after the 1992 Illinois primary campaign in which he sought what became his eighteenth and final term in the House. But that March 17 contest was yet another example of how Rostenkowski's world was crumbling around him. For the first time in his forty-year career he faced a well-organized and astute opponent: reform Democrat Dick Simpson, a political science professor at the Chicago campus of the University of Illinois and a former city alderman who had been a publicity-seeking nemesis of the Daley organization and the remnants of the Democratic machine. In challenging the high-powered Ways and Means chairman, Simpson assailed Rostenkowski's brand of politics. "You have a choice between a Chicago ward boss run amok in Congress and a public servant," Simpson told a campaign gathering in a neighborhood living room. "We have to change Congress. It has become a corrupt institution that is pulling down the whole country."

Simpson was encouraged to run because the 1991 redistricting tore apart Rostenkowski's northwest side district. With Illinois required to lose two seats by the nationwide reapportionment that takes place after the Census count every ten years, at least one had to come from the city's white neighborhoods. The line-drawing generated a double jeopardy for Rostenkowski. Along with the shrinking Polish-American population, he also was forced to contend with the loss of Mexican-American neighborhoods that had taken over large chunks of his former district; those mostly safe Democratic voters were assembled as part of a new House district with Hispanic-majority population. The change dropped the Hispanic population of Rostenkowski's new district to 13 percent compared with the previous 42 percent. The oddly contorted lines of the Hispanic district meandered into the city's south side, where it had the added effect of forcing two other white Democrats—Bill Lipinski and Marty Russo—to run against each other in a redrawn district. Russo, who had been Rostenkowski's ally on Ways and Means and spent much less time than did Lipinski in tending to neighborhood politics, was overwhelmingly defeated. With most of the city's Democratic leaders, including Mayor Daley, supporting creation of the new Hispanic district, Rostenkowski had little choice but to go along. Adding to his pain was that Luis Gutierrez, who easily won the new district, had been his menace since 1984, when Gutierrez challenged his reelection as Democratic committeeman for the 32nd Ward.

Redistricting moved Rostenkowski's district in two diverse directions: (1) to the east, the liberal, economically upscale neighborhoods that ran along Lake Michigan from Lincoln Park to the northern edge of downtown, and (2) to the west, more conservative communities adjacent to O'Hare Airport, northwest of the city limits. (Those suburban neighborhoods had been represented by Democrat Frank Annunzio, seventy-seven, who decided to retire rather than challenge Rostenkowski.) Each new area posed problems—and opportunities—for him. In the yuppie neighborhoods that were Simpson's base, Rostenkowski's old-style politics were out of place among transient voters with few local roots; and Simpson reminded voters in this area of Rostenkowski's earlier opposition to abortion rights. But many of these upper-income residents were sophisticated enough to appreciate a Ways and Means chairman's clout and his ability to deliver local services. "He doesn't apologize for his style," said State Rep. Ann Stepan, a lakefront-area leader who backed him. "He says that he knows he is gruff and that he is who he is."

The other new part of Rostenkowski's district included many blue-collar voters who had lived in Chicago's Milwaukee Avenue corridor and moved to more comfortable suburban Cook County; unfortunately for Rostenkowski and the Democrats, many of these voters had grown more conservative and Republican as they left the city. Roman Catholics in this area who continued to vote in the Democratic primary preferred Rostenkowski's more conservative views on social issues. But Simpson appealed to many of these blue-collar workers by criticizing Rostenkowski's free-trade views, which were opposed by organized labor. "Rostenkowski shouldn't be there anymore," said truck driver Jim Troccoli. "He doesn't even know what's happening in his own town." National cynicism toward politicians was hitting home. "On the northwest side he was a symbol of public discontent with Washington," said David Axelrod, Rostenkowski's consultant. "He lacked a connection to the day-to-day anxieties and hopes of their community."

All these changes resulted in nearly 60 percent of the voters being new to Rostenkowski's revamped district. Many knew little about him; of those who had heard of him, large numbers were unfavorably impressed. According to his campaign's own polls, barely 30 percent approved of Rostenkowski a couple of months before the primary; for most incumbents that would be fatal. Even to those close to him, his prospects in the primary campaign were perilous. "Times had changed," said Thom Serafin, a Chicago corporate consultant who worked with the campaign on communications strategy. "People wanted politicians with a warmer feel. But Rostenkowski did not look to get media attention. All he wanted was to sit in his sweats at home and telephone his friends." Although he retained his strong physical condition, he was losing the enthusiasm for the once- or twice-a-week flights from O'Hare to Washington.

Rostenkowski relied on his advisers for two key ingredients to survive the 1992 primary. First he used radio advertising and a blizzard of mail to introduce himself to voters unfamiliar with his record. "I have learned what I should have long ago remembered . . . that if I don't toot my own horn, no one else will," he said at the time. In his first encounter with costly campaigns, Rostenkowski spent about $800,000 against Simpson. Ignoring both his opponent and his own work as Ways and Means chairman, he talked mostly about what he had done for the city. Seeking to make a virtue out of necessity, the Axelrod-produced radio advertisements did not sugarcoat his rough edges. "I've made a lot of people angry because I speak my mind," Rostenkowski said on one spot. "That's the Chicago way, and I'm not going to change. But to tell you the truth, when it comes to fighting for our community, you have to be tough to win." Mail appeals were targeted to neighborhoods and demographic groups. "He had never done such mailings before," said Serafin. "He didn't want to be part of the process that had bastardized American politics. . . . We talked results." Even though Rostenkowski viewed the cost of such mailings as "obscene," Serafin added, they successfully introduced his record to many voters. He also received street-savvy help from allies of Mayor Daley, who extended his father's loyalty from the 1950s. Axelrod, for example, was the mayor's media adviser. Alderman Terry Gabinski, Rostenkowski's longtime local lieutenant, also collected chits from other Democratic loyalists. But Gabinski too was unaccustomed to a competitive Democratic primary.

Simpson's campaign rested on his belief that old-fashioned precinct organizations had become obsolete and that voters were ready for change. As an urban politics scholar, he saw an opportunity to exploit public hostility toward Washington. "Polls show that this is the first election in which people are prepared to dis-elect their Congressman," he said in a campaign interview. "The hostility results not only from the overall trend but also because of specific action that [Rostenkowski] has taken." From Simpson's cluttered campaign office, Tom Gradel distributed to reporters packets of his extensive research that documented how Rostenkowski had lost touch with the common folk. Simpson's indictment ranged from the congressman's support for the controversial Presidential Towers apartment complex to his campaign's deep pockets filled with money from Washington's special-interest groups. As the House Bank scandal expanded in the final days before the primary, Simpson also sought to exploit public anger, even though there was no direct link to Rostenkowski.

But Simpson had too little, too late. Rostenkowski won the 1992 primary with 57 percent of the vote. He benefited from his obvious superiority in resources—financial, organizational, and communications—and from Simpson's lack of recent campaign experience or connections (he had not held office since the 1970s). Gradel, the challenger's aide, found it difficult to get news coverage for Simpson because of Democratic presidential and Senate primary contests that were held on the same day and "because Rostenkowski has the myth that he is important to the city of Chicago." Rostenkowski was relieved: he had survived his first serious political challenge and had done so on his own terms. "I'll be going back, recognizing [the voters] renewed my contract," he said in his victory statement.

It wasn't a totally happy triumph. He continued to face unpleasant legislative ordeals and the ominous federal investigations of House operations. At age sixty-four, Rostenkowski had plenty of other reasons to call it quits. Under the federal election campaign law, 1992 was the final year that retiring House Members could legally pocket any surplus that remained in their campaign fund. In Rostenkowski's case that would have been more than $1 million. He also was approaching the age when it would become difficult for him to serve as a lobbyist or consultant to businesses that deal with government. With his Ways and Means experience he was highly marketable and could make far more money with a more relaxed and private life. He gave serious consideration to retiring that year. "He and I talked in advance of the campaign about not running," said Republican Bill Gradison, who quit the House soon after that year's election to become president of the Health Insurance Association of America. "But he said he did not want anyone to think that he quit" in order to pocket the money in his campaign account. At roughly the same time, Rostenkowski mused on the House floor with Minority Leader Bob Michel that both should retire in 1992 and set up a Washington consulting firm with their savvy aides. "It was all conjecture and in a kidding way," Michel recounted. But both understood that "big bucks were to be made," Michel acknowledged. Rostenkowski was severely tempted. "His instincts were to go" to private life, said John Sherman, his former press secretary. "But there were a lot of pressures on him to stay." Friends of Bush, for example, hoped that Rostenkowski would work closely with the president once he was reelected so that they could fix Medicare and Social Security for the next generation. And, as was the case a dozen years earlier when Rostenkowski became Ways and Means chairman rather than whip, many Democrats did not want the chairmanship to pass to the independent Sam Gibbons of Florida, who remained next in seniority. "I should have taken the $1 million," Rostenkowski said years later. "But I didn't want to leave under the cloud of 'Rostenkowski took a golden parachute.' I wanted to keep the reputation that the kid from the northwest side of Chicago broke through and showed that he could legislate."

Rostenkowski's decision to remain in the House would have huge and painful consequences. But the course of events would take some unusual twists during his final two years in elected office.

Chapter Nine

TRYING TO TAKE CLINTON'S HAND

FOR DEMOCRATS the 1992 election marked the best of times and the worst of times. After a dozen years on the outside, they basked in regaining the White House. With their House and Senate majorities, finally they were again positioned to press their own agenda. But they quickly encountered problems. First, President Bill Clinton, the former Arkansas governor, was not one of their own. He was elected, as were many politicians in 1992, by running against Washington. During the primaries, amidst the House Bank scandal, he aired a commercial criticizing a pay raise for lawmakers—most of whom were Democrats. "Back in 1990, I was attacking the way Congress was doing its business," he boasted in a televised March interview. "I ran the first ads against the congressional pay raise in this campaign. I have been for change."[1] Congressional Democrats swallowed their objections when Clinton pointedly distanced himself from them at their national convention and during the fall campaign. "It doesn't bother us," said Sen. David Pryor of Arkansas, in a limp pre-election defense of his longtime friend. "From one politician to another, we understand the environment in which he is working."

The outsider-insider contradictions weren't the only challenge facing Democrats as they prepared to take charge. After twelve years as Arkansas governor, Clinton was familiar with many policies and their nuances. He and his wife, Hillary Rodham Clinton, were expert not only because of their official dealings with issues in Little Rock but from their longtime work with national advocacy groups. Indeed, they had separate power bases in Washington before the 1992 election: Bill chaired the centrist Democratic Leadership Council, and Hillary chaired the liberal Children's Defense Fund. Yet the Clintons' early actions revealed that they were remarkably unprepared to take the initiative in the White House. The problems resulted in part because neither Clinton nor his party offered during the campaign a clear sense of direction beyond improving President Bush's record in addressing public needs. Clinton spent his first several months struggling to salvage his poorly designed package to stimulate the economy and reduce the federal deficit. Then, Democrats were stymied by Clinton's overreaching bid to overhaul the nations' health-insurance system. So it was little wonder that voters turned thumbs down on them in the 1994 elections.

Rostenkowski too was scarcely prepared for the 1992 election results. Having abandoned his inclination to retire from the House, he had hoped to work with Bush to fix the nation's major fiscal problems. Managing legislation to expand the government's health-care role was not what he had in mind. Nor did he look kindly on the influx of new Democrats to both the House and the Ways and Means Committee. But the 103rd Congress brought all of that—and much more. For the weary Rostenkowski, it soon became clear, the House that he had first known as a stable institution dominated by its elders had broken down. Likewise in Chicago, his 1992 primary victory did not shut the door to further serious challenges. And, of course, federal prosecutors continued to mine his transactions at the House Post Office. The chairman's passion to control his surroundings, in short, was more and more frustrated.

Problems with the White House were merely the start of the House Democrats' travails. Amid the revulsion over the House Bank's bounced checks, plus the gender-based assaults lingering from the Senate hearings for Supreme Court nominee Clarence Thomas, voters in 1992 sent a clarion call for change. And the 1991–1992 redistricting had nearly doubled the number of black-majority districts in the United States, reducing the ranks of white Democrats from the nation's urban areas, including Chicago. The changes on the House floor were apparent to the eye: thirteen additional African Americans and nineteen new women, most of them Democrats. Once they arrived, however, the newcomers discovered that powerful voices remained committed to their old ways: leaders were often aloof from rank-and-file lawmakers; powerful chairmen fought with one another over turf and legislative minutiae; and neither party showed much interest in bipartisanship. Among other failures, Democrats placed a low priority on demands for campaign finance reform, despite growing public unhappiness with the status quo. Senior Democrats placed a higher priority on the president's game plan for the economy and health care. "Speaker Tom Foley and his team completely misread the message of the 1992 election," wrote Eric Fingerhut of Ohio, a leader of the Democratic freshmen, after he lost his bid for reelection. "They ignored the calls of many freshman Democrats to move quickly on reform legislation, and some of those leaders even ridiculed our efforts and belittled us personally."[2]

Ignoring their generational and stylistic contrasts, the ever-pragmatic Rostenkowski showed a strong early attachment to Clinton, who returned the favor. Despite his long friendship with Bush, during the final months of the 1992 campaign the chairman directed his Ways and Means staff to send thick briefing books to educate Clinton on the complex issues facing the committee. Rostenkowski also advised Clinton in frequent preelection telephone conversations. "Their personalities click," said Beryl Anthony of Arkansas, who served on Ways and Means until 1992 and was a leading Clinton ally in Congress. After the election, Ways and Means Democrat Bob Matsui called the relationship "a marriage made in heaven." Their good vibrations were abetted by Rostenkowski's enduring reverence for the presidency. More than ever, he understood the need for cooperation in order to pass legislation. "For years I have complained about a lack of presidential leadership," Rostenkowski told a Washington audience a week after the election. "Now that there's a real promise of leadership, I plan to be among the most enthusiastic followers." Although he cautioned that Democrats would not compromise their principles, he served notice: "I am suggesting that we try hard to support the president's politics and give him the benefit of the doubt."

Following the grinding impasses during the Bush years, Rostenkowski was quick to level with Clinton. Above all, be "bold," he told his new White House friend. After battling for two dozen years with four Republican presidents and the outsider Jimmy Carter, the chairman wistfully hoped he saw shades of Lyndon Johnson in Clinton's lust for politics and his embrace of government's role in public life. He told Clinton "he should kick Congress in the ass every once in a while," Rostenkowski said privately in early 1993. Nor did he hesitate to define what would be acceptable and what would not work at Ways and Means. Clinton would find it difficult to ignore Rostenkowski, whose committee was the starting point for much of his early agenda—including the free-trade agreement with Mexico, health-care reform, and deficit reduction. Like a friendly uncle, the chairman was eager to help Clinton find his way around town. "The president is a politician," he said at the time. "We will pass his legislation. But it won't be exact." And the president—like many younger Democrats—was charmed by Rostenkowski's beguiling tales about the old days under bygone presidents. The chairman dealt "frequently and comfortably" with the president, said Howard Paster, who was the White House's chief legislative liaison after Clinton took office.

But prospects for success were daunting. In contrast to the elections of Johnson and Carter, when Democrats won more than 290 House seats, they began 1993 with only 258 seats—a 10-seat election loss. That gave several Democratic blocs a potential veto over any Clinton proposal. Conservative Democrats were growing imperiled, especially in the South, where Republicans had gained 8 House seats; they insisted that Clinton not give Republicans cause to revive charges of Democrats' tax-and-spend policies, which had helped to elect Reagan to the White House. But liberal Democrats, strengthened by the growth of the congressional Black Caucus, were eager to reinvigorate government after their bleak 1980s. And the 63 freshman Democrats wanted fast results on issues from the budget deficit to political reform. Conflicts were inevitable. When conservative Democrats in late February charged that the House was moving too quickly on Clinton's $19 billion proposal for a domestic spending stimulus, the first-termers responded with their own call for the House to pass the bill "expeditiously." Something would have to give.

At Ways and Means, Rostenkowski faced unaccustomed headaches, including a radical change in membership. Gone were stalwarts such as Tom Downey and Marty Russo, who lost reelection, and Ed Jenkins, who retired. Their departures were "big losses," said Mike Andrews of Texas, another Ways and Means Democrat. Each had been a reliable lieutenant during Rostenkowski's dozen years as chairman and each was influential with various groups of House Democrats on and off the committee. Of the twenty-four Democrats on Ways and Means in 1993, ten were new to the panel. It would take time for them to fill their predecessors' shoes. The Republicans lost five Ways and Means members, including Frenzel and Gradison, who had worked to build bipartisanship. For the short term, the shifts would increase Rostenkowski's influence, as committee newcomers learned their way. But the changes also injected an element of unpredictability as players took one another's measure. "When you know people, that makes things a lot easier," said Democrat Charles Rangel of New York. Another change was the addition of three Black Caucus members, making a total of five on the Democratic side. Among them was Mel Reynolds of Chicago, a first-termer. The freshmen had demanded Ways and Means seats; Rostenkowski accepted, with great reluctance, the only freshman during his years as chairman—but only on the condition that the newcomer was a Chicagoan, who presumably would be more reliable. As it turned out, Reynolds's career was quickly ended by embarrassing problems that led to his 1995 conviction on felony charges for having sex with an under-age woman.

Rostenkowski's modus operandi also confronted, for his first time as chairman, a Democratic president. No longer would he operate as the virtually autonomous leader of the opposition in dealing with White House minions. Now he was one of many Democrats taking their lead from Bill Clinton, who was eager to call the shots. Even though they seemed to get along well, the new circumstances left Rostenkowski with less room to cut his own deals. "It's as new to me as it is to you," he responded when asked how events might unfold.[3] And there was another consequence, though largely unspoken, of a Democrat in the White House: with the U.S. attorney's investigation of the House Post Office still hanging over him, Rostenkowski hoped that Clinton's selection of a new federal prosecutor for the District of Columbia would defuse the inquiry. Rostenkowski left no doubt of his worry and preoccupation. "My stomach is hamburger," he told the *New York Times* in January. "Thirty-four years in public service, and some yahoo in the post office is saying you took money. I never even thought of these things."[4] The doubts about his future, and the lack of a logical successor at Ways and Means, left Rostenkowski with a smug but anxious sense that he could not be replaced. *Après moi, le déluge*, the French say about an indispensable leader. Soon enough, Democrats would face the consequences of their big man's mortality.

All did not go smoothly after Clinton's decision to set an economic program as his first legislative priority. It took time "to figure out the environment in which we are working," said Vic Fazio of California, who was vice-chairman of the House Democratic Caucus. In the House fewer than one-fifth of the Democrats had served with a president from their own party, and most needed reminders of the requirement for loyalty to their new boss. Clinton's election created some difficulties, Tom Foley acknowledged. Still, they were "welcome problems." Many Democrats lamented, especially in retrospect, that Speaker Foley's frequently passive leadership became a serious problem. Although his affable style and story-telling lore made him well liked by many colleagues and reporters, he lacked the hammer that was essential to effective leadership. Privately Rostenkowski parodied his frequent equivocation. Although Foley had his admirers among Democrats—and, no doubt, Rostenkowski also had many detractors—the speaker's easygoing style and his reluctance to discipline complaining members became added complications for Democrats when Clinton's election forced them to deliver. "Foley didn't give [Rostenkowski] much direction," said Rep. Jack Murtha. The tensions with Foley were all the more striking, of course, because Rostenkowski's 1981 decision to pass up the majority whip position had placed Foley on the ladder to the speakership. At least subconsciously, some pondered how things might have been different if Rostenkowski had been the man at the top.

On Clinton's promise of far-ranging health-care reform, most Democrats agreed that such legislation was vital, but they were at odds on specifics and timing. Aware of the huge challenge, Senate Majority Leader Mitchell wanted to exploit the momentum of Clinton's early months. One option, he suggested, was to merge a health-care plan with the economic program. Congressional budget procedures would give parliamentary protections to the combined measure, Mitchell contended. But Rostenkowski objected to holding one bill hostage to the other. In addition to his usual complaints about senators seeking to dictate legislative process, he worried that the economic package was already a difficult burden for Congress. "Deadlines are distractions," he said in March 1993. "It would be a terrible mistake to act in haste." Given his own unpleasant memories about the 1989 repeal of the catastrophic-insurance bill that had passed with insufficient debate, Rostenkowski did not wish to commit himself to a new health-care proposal until he had seen the details. In addition, the president would require time to educate the nation once he decided on his plan. Debate "will take months rather than weeks," Rostenkowski presciently warned Mitchell and other advocates of quick action. With Foley and most other House leaders unwilling to challenge

Rostenkowski, Mitchell was left isolated, and congressional Democrats made the fateful decision to delay for many months debate on a health-care proposal.

Clinton prevailed in the hard-fought battle over his economic program, but his party paid a bitter price for its divisions and failure to respond effectively to Republican criticisms. The provision for $241 billion in higher taxes over the next five years would cripple Democrats for years to come. Much later, Democrats would resolutely defend their action by pointing to its impact on eliminating the federal deficit and to the sustained economic growth during the mid-1990s. "Since 1993, when we made the tough choice to pursue fiscal sanity, we have revived the economy and counted more than 10 million new jobs," House Minority Leader Richard Gephardt said in a speech a few days after Clinton's 1997 inauguration. Still, the jostling over Clinton's economic program aptly symbolized the changes that had occurred since Rostenkowski's first election to Congress. Bipartisanship was a relic, and budget politics had become fractious and pervasive. Facing no suitable alternative, Democrats followed Clinton's lead much as the Mills-chaired Ways and Means Committee in 1965 took its cue from President Johnson on Medicare. But there were several major differences: Clinton was elected with 43 percent of the vote compared with Johnson's 61 percent; Johnson and Mills secured Republican support in 1965; and, perhaps most important, voters could see the benefits from the creation of Medicare. Although few participants on either side anticipated it in 1993, the stormy passage of Clinton's economic program helped to mark a fateful end to the forty-year Democratic era in the House. "The 1994 election had as much to do with the Democrats' handling of the 1993 economic package as with the health-care debate," said Byron Dorgan, the North Dakota Democrat who moved from the House to the Senate in 1992. "People believed that the bill raised taxes too much."

With bitter residue from the 1990 budget debate and Bush's reelection defeat, bipartisanship would have been difficult to secure for any tax increase. But Clinton all but precluded Republican support when he decided that his first major proposal would be a fiscal "stimulus" to bolster the economy. Ironically the growth rate had surged to 5 percent in the final quarter of 1992, indicating that the nation already had overcome the brief though painful 1991 recession. Indeed, Rostenkowski warned a business group in a December speech that it would be "foolish to propose a short-term stimulus program" if the economy continued to improve. The call for additional spending elicited misgivings from other deficit-conscious Democrats as well. But Clinton aimed his proposal at allies in the cities— low-income groups and other Democratic constituencies that would be adversely affected by his budget plan. Although all but twenty-two House Democrats voted for the stimulus bill on March 18, many supported it chiefly because it was Clinton's first major bill. Only three Republicans voted in favor. With House Democrats simultaneously approving the outlines of their budget package, including the big tax increase, Republicans gleefully revived their attack on Democrats as the tax-and-spend party. The measure soon died as the result of a Republican filibuster in the Senate.

The early budget votes were a precursor that Rostenkowski could expect little if any Republican help on Clinton's tax proposal. Although moderate Republicans on Ways and Means—chiefly Fred Grandy of Iowa and Nancy Johnson of Connecticut—expressed interest in cooperation, Rostenkowski could not meet their demands for much smaller tax increases. For the first time during his chairmanship, Republicans did not actively participate in drafting major legislation. That result increased the leverage of liberals who had often groused that the chairman ignored them in his bipartisan zeal. With the pressure for loyalty, the last thing Rostenkowski wanted was to hear that he had stymied Clinton's program—especially federal deficit reduction. "Who am I to say that I won't support the president?" he asked rhetorically in early 1993.

Despite these constraints, Rostenkowski had room to maneuver on the specifics of Clinton's economic program under the committee's jurisdiction. So as he began his familiar conversations with committee members—in this case, Democrats only—most discussions sought to reduce the sting from the proposed tax increases, especially as they affected members' home states. Bill Jefferson of Louisiana, whose New Orleans district was saturated with tourist-mecca restaurants, organized a nationwide coalition to oppose the proposed decrease in tax deductions for business meals. Clinton's proposed "BTU" tax on energy consumption led Mike Andrews and Jake Pickle of Texas and Bill Brewster of Oklahoma to seek refinements in the administration of the new fee, which would affect their local energy producers. And Mike Kopetski of Oregon pleaded on behalf of aluminum companies from the Northwest, which would be affected by their high use of energy. (Kopetski, a newcomer to the committee, normally would have had little influence with Rostenkowski, but his position was bolstered by Speaker Foley's unusually active intervention for two aluminum companies with large factories in his Spokane-based district.)

In some cases Rostenkowski massaged Clinton's proposal to accommodate committee members. With Foley's encouragement he changed the energy tax to benefit several industries, including aluminum, whose technology required heavy energy use. He made changes only after he also won approval from White House officials. Jefferson and the restaurant owners and employees were unsuccessful; Ways and Means insiders said their coalition was poorly organized and that, in any case, the $16 billion gain in federal revenue from the revised meals deduction was too much to sacrifice. When it came to a tax bill, Rostenkowski was in a better position to accommodate his members if the price was not too high.

The chairman demanded and received support for the overall bill from all Ways and Means Democrats as a price for his concessions. But he and Democratic leaders ran into much tougher sledding than they had expected when the full House debated the bill in late May. Objections came from many directions. For many Democrats, the chief fear was that the Senate would not approve a tax increase anywhere near the amount of the House proposal. They grew all the more worried a few days before the House vote when Democratic oil-state senators David Boren of Oklahoma and Bennett Johnston of Louisiana—mixing home-state interests with a delight in poking a thumb in Clinton's eye—announced their opposition to his proposed energy tax. As it grew apparent that the tax would not survive in the Senate, many conservative House Democrats voiced concern that they would imperil themselves by voting for a controversial proposal that had little chance of enactment. The still-loyal Rostenkowski was not ready to concede. "There is no painless way to attack the deficit," he reminded Democrats. "Too many members of my own party are used to the luxury of having someone from the other party in the White House. They seem to have forgotten that when Bill Clinton was elected, their job description changed dramatically." But partisan pressures created a difficult climate. Management of the bill shifted largely from his control as Rostenkowski could not find effective replacments for former lieutenants Downey, Jenkins, and Russo. With heavy arm-twisting by Clinton and House leaders, the bill narrowly passed, 219 to 213. Not a single Republican voted for the measure. House Democrats had administered a self-inflicted wound.

When the tax bill reached the Senate Finance Committee, it became obvious that the BTU tax was dead and that Rostenkowski's indignities were not yet finished. To replace the lost revenues, Senate Democrats agreed to increase the federal gasoline tax by 4.3 cents per gallon. Because that fee generated only about one-third the revenues of the BTU plan, the Senate dropped other spending features of Clinton's program, including benefits for low-income workers and new tax breaks for businesses. After the Senate passed the bill by the narrowest of margins—with Vice-President Al Gore breaking the tie vote—Rostenkowski was determined to restore in conference much of the House-approved tax increase. Initially he hoped to include some version of the BTU tax, if only to provide cover to the House Democrats who had placed themselves on the line. When Senate Democrats firmly resisted, Rostenkowski demanded several additional cents to the Senate-passed gasoline tax increase. But he ran into firm opposition from several Democratic senators—chiefly Herbert Kohl, a first-termer from Wisconsin—to tampering with the Senate's 4.3-cent increase. During years of facing recalcitrant senators with little or no experience on tax issues, Rostenkowski complained that uninformed mavericks too often interfered with his deal-cutting. "We are always making concessions to help the Senate," he said. But this was perhaps the single most frustrating case for Rostenkowski. "Prima donnas," he called them at the time. He was especially dismissive of Daniel Patrick Moynihan of New York, who had replaced Lloyd Bentsen as Senate Finance Committee chairman and was more skilled in rhetorical flourishes than in legislative deal-making. "Mr. Moynihan, it is said on Capitol Hill, has written more books (16 at last count) than Mr. Rostenkowski has read," the *New York Times* noted. "Mr. Rostenkowski, it is said, is so savvy that he can pick the eccentric Senator's pockets."[5]

Even after deferring to Kohl and the Senate on the fuel tax, however, Rostenkowski encountered more problems when the House-Senate agreement reached the House floor in early August, on the eve of the summer recess. With many Democrats anxious about the Republicans' vocal opposition, support for the bill became more shaky. In the end the House passed the bill 218 to 216, but only after freshman Marjorie Margolies-Mezvinsky of Pennsylvania succumbed to intense lobbying pressure from Clinton, Foley, and others. Likewise the Senate passed the bill only with another tie-breaking vote by Gore. It was a painful process for all Democrats. Rostenkowski was furious with Boren and other Democratic senators who—having once led the rhetorical call for deficit reduction—seemed to resist every politically painful step. "Sure, he has made mistakes," he added, responding to critical comment on Clinton. "But what I see in the president is a man who has had the guts to go where all the clever, Washington veterans were too timid to go." Rostenkowski reserved his harshest criticism for Republicans, who abandoned any bipartisan pretense on Clinton's economic package. "Their goal is obvious—wait until the president stumbles, then move in for the kill," he griped. "This may be shrewd political strategy, but it's no way to govern."

The Republicans' tenacious opposition was masterminded by Minority Whip Newt Gingrich. In seizing control of House Republicans, the shaggy-haired political renegade had all but pushed aside Minority Leader Bob Michel, Rostenkowski's pal who used to pile into the station wagon with him for the weekly drive to and from Illinois. Even before Michel announced in October 1993 that he would retire, Gingrich had made plans to run for GOP leader following the next election, regardless of Michel's intentions. As colleagues who had entered the House when bipartisanship reigned, Michel and Rostenkowski found it painful to see how much that spirit had eroded. "A good part of my success, whatever it may be, has been measured against the goodwill built up over time," Michel reminisced. "You can get much more with sugar . . . than with clawing your way up." His contrast to the confrontational Gingrich was pointed. As the House grew more polarized, Michel became isolated from Republicans demanding more assertive leadership. Gingrich's ascent was another sign of how much the House had changed. But even he did not fully contemplate what lay on the threshold. In one of his few modest moments—albeit unintended—Gingrich a few days after Michel's retirement announcement made himself an "even money" prospect to become speaker in 1996. Yet Gingrich's two-year miscalculation (he won the job in 1994) was probably understandable. He could not foresee how badly the Democrats would mishandle Clinton's health-care plan.

The Clinton fiasco on health-reform started with grand expectations. Democrats wanted to add the third leg to the stool of federal enhancement of Americans' quality of life. First, Franklin Roosevelt in the 1930s had enacted Social Security, with monthly cash grants to ensure that the elderly and the lame would no longer live in abject poverty. Then, in the

1960s, Lyndon Johnson—with crucial help from Wilbur Mills—had secured Medicare for the elderly, which also expanded health-care coverage for the poor through the Medicaid program. Now, another three decades later, Bill Clinton's grand design would complete his party's historic mission with a universal guarantee of health-care coverage. Democrats had prepared for this moment for a half-century. "Our health care system is too uncertain and too expensive, too bureaucratic and too wasteful," Clinton told Congress in September. Americans should be guaranteed "health care that can never be taken away, health care that is always there."

But the president failed to match his lofty ambition and rhetoric with the necessary revenues. Roosevelt and Johnson created new payroll taxes to finance their programs. When Social Security began, Washington took one cent from each dollar of a worker's first $3,000 of income. When Medicare was enacted, it initially imposed an additional tax of 35 cents per $100 on workers. In each case, government later raised the taxes by large sums to pay for added benefits that the public and politicians demanded. By 1993 Social Security and Medicare taxes scooped up 7.65 percent of most workers' salaries to a maximum of $57,900. But each program was a huge success. The elderly were living longer and were better able to support themselves; and most voters supported the programs, even after Reagan and Congress agreed in 1983 to tax increases and benefit cuts to sustain Social Security well into the twenty-first century. In this case, however, Clinton was defensive about increasing the federal budget. He believed he could achieve his health-care security goal without new revenues to the Treasury. Many liberals disagreed. They backed a federal takeover of health-care costs—much as Washington had done for the elderly and as the Canadian government had done with a "single-payer" system for all its citizens. Clinton's advisers brashly but naively concluded that they could achieve cost controls and coverage for all Americans without new taxes, simply by making medical services more efficient.

Like other leading Democrats, Rostenkowski was both pleased and wary. He recognized the historic mandate. "We Democrats have been promising universal insurance for decades, and it's time to deliver," he told the American Association of Retired Persons in February 1993. But he had been chastened by the complexity of the issues and the difficulty of finding common ground. Not only did he recall the repeal of the catastrophic-illness law for the elderly, he also remembered the years of work before Congress enacted Medicare. And he knew that House Democrats had recently spent more than a year inconclusively reviewing options for a broad-based proposal. As he said during a speech a few days after the 1992 election, "we never reached a consensus because we couldn't make the needed compromises." Those lessons convinced Rostenkowski that Democrats must resist the temptation of "putting too much on the wagon until the wheels fall off," said Bill Frenzel, the veteran Ways and Means Republican. Still, imagine how Clinton's presidency might have been different if House or Senate Democrats had prepared the framework of a health-reform package, which they could have delivered to him when he took office.

Rostenkowski sought to share with the new president his experience with health reform. Bill Clinton is "smart as a whip, but he's not about to discover a magic bullet that we're unaware of," he said after the 1992 election. Days before the inaugural, he was part of a small group of senior Democrats who privately met Clinton in the Capitol. At one point the two of them were sitting alone. "I said, 'Mr. President, you are going to engage yourself in probably the hardest legislative agenda you can imagine,'" Rostenkowski recalled. "'If you want my advice, we should focus on one thing and try to solve it. . . . Come up with principles and pass the bill over to Rostenkowski and Mitchell, and have us kick the ball around'" with key members and affected interests. Publicly he underscored the need for "shared sacrifice." In an apt warning both to those who were overpromising and to Clinton's tightfisted approach, he noted that there was no free lunch. "Delivering more services will cost more money." Finally he repeatedly emphasized in both public and private comments that it would take many years for Washington to craft all the details of comprehensive health-care reform. "We may not get it totally right the first time," he said in February. "Whatever we do will be subject to regular legislative revision, just as Medicare has been." Although Clinton advisers said they paid close attention to Rostenkowski's advice, the president and his staff obviously ignored his warnings.

When the president, five days after taking office, appointed Hillary Rodham Clinton to head the health-reform task force, it struck Rostenkowski as an unnecessary risk and a poor choice; critics would be less candid in appraising the work of the president's wife, he feared. As time went on and the task force immersed itself in enormous detail in reviewing options, Rostenkowski grew even more troubled. Not only was the

First Lady conducting her review entirely in private, but she was not reaching out to Republicans or to health-industry groups. Worse, Ira Magaziner, whom the president appointed as the chief White House aide on the project, had little experience in Washington and virtually no background in health-care policy. "I wish he had some dirt under his fingernails," Rostenkowski said of Magaziner, a self-styled wonk who had never worked in government.[6] Magaziner was "completely insensitive to the legislative process,"complained a Rostenkowski aide. Instead of the months-long review, Rostenkowski told Clinton to lay out broad principles and let Congress fill in the details. As rumors spread that the president's reforms would surpass previous proposals, the chairman grew even more uneasy. "Bill Clinton is basically betting his presidency on the enactment of comprehensive health-care reform legislation," Rostenkowski declared ominously in June. "I'm more concerned about the political climate in Washington at the moment than I am the policy choices that will be made by President Clinton." Too many members, he added, want "free votes on the floor that don't cause them any discomfort."

Clinton's delay in unveiling his health-reform plan until Congress completed the economic program put off serious discussion until nearly the midpoint of the 103rd Congress. After the president described the plan in his September 22 prime-time speech at the Capitol, the administration scheduled Mrs. Clinton to testify the next week before several House and Senate committees, starting with Ways and Means. At that appearance Rostenkowski cited her Chicago background and heaped praise on her articulate presentation. "I think in the very near future the President will be known as your husband," he said following her testimony.[7] But the autumn 1993 offensive proved less successful than White House strategists had hoped. Behind the scenes, interminable drafting work postponed formal submission of the plan until November 20, three days before Congress concluded its 1993 session. Ways and Means also was set back by Clinton's request for approval of the North Atlantic Free Trade Agreement, which the United States and Canada signed with Mexico. Rostenkowski spent several weeks engineering side deals with members who sought to protect the economic interests of businesses in their districts. The House passed the implementing legislation on November 17, by 234 to 200, with most Republicans in favor and most Democrats opposed. In building that old-fashioned coalition, Rostenkowski received help from large corporations lobbying for the agreement—creating what one Ways and Means Democrat termed "a countervailing force" to challenge active opposition by organized labor. Truth be told, he would have preferred that kind of consensus-building on health-care reform. But the stubbornness of the Clintons and Magaziner—plus harsh criticism by Republicans— ruled out bipartisanship on health reform. History might well have been different if Clinton had used the NAFTA political model on health reform.

When Democrats finally examined Clinton's health-care plan, they found it to be a nightmare. Magaziner "tried so hard to anticipate every possible consequence of change that the finished plan became a Rube Goldberg system beyond the comprehension of most people," according to an appraisal in the *New York Times*.[8] Probably the biggest problem was the proposed creation of health-care "alliances"—government-organized purchasing cooperatives to give consumers more leverage in bargaining with insurance companies. To avoid new taxes, these alliances would be financed mostly by government "mandates" on businesses to pay their employees' costs. Large employers would be permitted to offer their own insurance coverage to employees, but they would have to pay an additional 1 percent payroll tax to help cover the uninsured. The proposal also called for a seventy-five cent increase in the federal tax on a package of cigarettes. The proposal was a mishmash. Members of Congress found they could not easily explain the proposal to their constituents, a serious omen.

When Ways and Means and the two other House committees with jurisdiction over parts of the bill began working in early 1994, opponents were highly organized but supporters' enthusiasm had waned. "Had Clinton insisted on action in the first three to six months in his term, we would have gotten a bill," said Rep. Jake Pickle, the former Lyndon Johnson aide. "But we waited too long, and we let the opposition build up fears and doubts." Rostenkowski and most Democratic leaders might have backed an early Clinton initiative if it had been clear-cut and simple to understand. Interestingly, one of the plan's chief architects offered a similar postmortem. "We had a historic opportunity, and we blew it," wrote Paul Starr. "The real problem was that time was spent developing a plan that should have been spent negotiating it."[9]

Despite his desire to help Clinton, Rostenkowski was scrupulously evenhanded in managing the House debate. At a crucial moment he broke with the White House script when he said that Clinton's proposal would require "tens of billions of dollars" annually in new revenue when it was fully in place. He also showed his independence when Congressional Budget Office director Robert Reischauer prepared testimony challenging White House estimates of the cost. After anxious Clinton aides got advance warning of Reischauer's views, Clinton placed an emergency telephone call to Rostenkowski to complain that Reischauer was "cooking the books." According to both Rostenkowski aides and Reischauer, the chairman firmly responded that Reischauer had no personal agenda and that Rostenkowski stood by him. The incident was another example of how Congress had changed during Rostenkowski's years. As Ways and Means chairman, Wilbur Mills did not have to worry about protecting a congressional budget expert.

Prospects for health reform fell apart in the spring of 1994. Democrats floundered as three House and two Senate committees worked on Clinton's ambitious proposal and then as they sought common ground. Simply put, reformers could not find a plan acceptable to most Democrats. There were pockets of support for three separate approaches: the single-payer system with increased federal taxes; a managed-competition framework which sought the political center by eschewing federal mandates and encouraging competition among health-care providers; and the complex Clinton plan with its intricate web of federal rules. Majority Leader Gephardt hoped rank-and-file Democrats would move toward the White House plan once they saw that the other two approaches lacked sufficient support. But he was wrong on two key counts. First, Clinton's proposal failed to generate interest on its own terms. Second, a limited alternative backed by conservative Democrats and most Republicans became an attractive option as the months passed and lawmakers sought a proposal that could gain majority support. But Clinton and his team refused to endorse that alternative or to sign on to a parliamentary strategy that might permit its House passage. In the end, Democratic leaders refused to permit a House vote on any alternative.

By early 1994, events were diverting Rostenkowski from the health-care debate and making it more difficult for Democrats to hammer out a deal. In Chicago he again faced a competitive primary to secure nomination for another House term. That contest was quickly followed by his indictment in the House Post Office investigation. Although health-care reform would have been in jeopardy in any case, the distractions facing the House chairman with the most knowledge and experience on health-care issues were major blows to the Clinton plan. The prognosis already was so glum, however, that Rostenkowski's woes merely added to the Democrat's deepening despair. "If Rostenkowski had been there, it would have helped," said Alice Rivlin, who was then Clinton's Office of Management and Budget director. "But it would not have made a whole lot of difference. The process already was too fragmented."

AS THE MARCH 15 Democratic primary in Illinois approached, Rostenkowski could not ignore his legislative responsibilities. But any worthy politician's priority is assuring reelection, and he could hardly take victory for granted. The circumstances were not auspicious. On February 10 he sent two letters to the House Administration Committee, in which he said that some of his House office-supply expenditures "arguably may not have conformed to the committee's rules." Although he did not explicitly concede misbehavior, he included an $82,095 check to reimburse expenses that had been for personal use. "The reimbursement is clearly not an admission of wrongdoing but rather a sign . . . that he is trying to do the right and honorable thing," Rostenkowski attorney Robert Bennett told reporters. By seeking to settle the charges short of an indictment, however, Rostenkowski acknowledged that something was amiss. On February 23, the *Chicago Tribune* reported, Eric Holder—whom Clinton had named as U.S. attorney in the District of Columbia—had informed congressional authorities that "the Rostenkowski probe was in its final stage."[10] The circumstances posed a dilemma for Chicago's Democrats: should they stick by their powerful but admittedly vulnerable lawmaker? Or was it time for them to select a new, untainted congressman? And would any credible candidate step forward to challenge a Clinton lieutenant and a strong ally of young Mayor Daley? For Rostenkowski the campaign became "his last great hurrah," a nostalgic final victory against considerable odds, said political scientist Paul Green. But his satisfaction would be short-lived.

Dick Simpson had been preparing to run for months. After winning 43 percent of the vote in the primary two years earlier, he calculated that he was in the best position to knock off the vulnerable incumbent. Given news reports that Rostenkowski might soon be indicted, Simpson emphasized the apparent wrongdoing. "The perception used to be that Rostenkowski had conflicts of interest," he said. "And that was tolerated because this is Chicago. But now the voters' perception is that he's a crook."[11] Referring to the health-care debate, Simpson charged that hundreds of thousands of dollars in contributions to Rostenkowski from medical and insurance businesses opposed to Clinton's proposal were a major reason why the bill was in trouble. No matter how bad Rostenkowski might be, however, many local Democratic loyalists were not inclined to support Simpson, an academic who had made a career as a political maverick.

But State Sen. John Cullerton—a Democratic organization "regular"—gave voters another choice. Generations of his Irish clan had held high office for more than a century. (At another time in Chicago, the showdown between Irish and Polish leaders would have had deeper significance; but with the decline of white ethnic Democrats in Rostenkowski's redrawn district, the cultural wars had abated.) "No political dynasty in Chicago had been longer lasting than the Cullerton family," according to a local glossary.[12] Starting a few months before the Great Fire of 1871, Edward Cullerton had served forty-eight years on the City Council, a local record. Later P. J. (Parky) Cullerton became a close ally of Richard J. Daley, eventually serving as county assessor. With sixteen years in the state legislature, John Cullerton was a clear threat to Rostenkowski. In contrast to earlier Cullertons, who were notoriously quiet party loyalists, his activism had gained him support from liberals. Because he was in the middle of a four-year term in Springfield, he could retain his senate seat. Aware of the strong public opposition to Rostenkowski, Cullerton expected an easy road to victory. Indeed, a *Tribune* poll in January showed Rostenkowski leading the field with merely 24 percent of the vote against Cullerton, Simpson, and two other opponents; another 35 percent were undecided. Pollsters usually assume that undecided voters will not vote for the incumbent. "I looked at a poll that showed Rostenkowski couldn't win," Cullerton told a reporter. "And I didn't do anything to cause that."[13] Even if he lost, Cullerton believed, a strong showing would position him to succeed Rostenkowski two years later. With Simpson bashing Rostenkowski, according to a news report, Cullerton took "the high road and has tried to run an issue-oriented campaign" on topics such as gun control and education.[14]

Despite their sophistication, both Cullerton and Simpson failed to account for Chicago's tribal politics. Yes, Rostenkowski was badly wounded. But with Mayor Daley's encouragement, other Democrats were willing to help. In some cases they were less interested in assisting Rostenkowski than in advancing their own causes, but the result was the same. Perhaps the most valuable assist came from Richard Mell, who headed one of the city's most effective precinct organizations. Mell was first elected alderman in 1975 when he defeated a candidate backed by Rostenkowski and other Democratic leaders. But an old rule of Chicago politics applied: no permanent friends, no permanent enemies. "I love to be in the action, and I love to win," Mell said. "I worked harder than ever for Dan Rostenkowski in 1994." Why? The answer had far less to do with Rostenkowski than with Rod Blagojevich, Mell's son-in-law, who was then a state representative in Springfield. If Cullerton defeated Rostenkowski, the hard-working Blagojevich might never fulfill his ambition of winning a seat in Congress. So Mell worked with Rostenkowski's hired hands and with Daley's lieutenants to build the primary campaign in little more than a month. "People on the street didn't give us a chance" because of Rostenkowski's legal problems, said Thom Serafin, the campaign's public relations chief. "But Dick Mell was vital to our operation. . . . He was the energy to get others focused." On primary day, Mell said, his organization's several hundred precinct workers helped get voters to the polls.

Winning the 1994 primary demanded that Rostenkowski take unusual steps. First he deliberately limited his campaign to only four weeks. "He waited so long to start for the same reason that you postpone a visit to the dentist," Serafin said. "We knew the campaign would be hard." Rostenkowski relied on longtime friends to work with other political organizations in the city. And he used extensive radio advertising to reach voters. "Leadership we can't afford to lose" was the message that aired repeatedly. He also made carefully selected campaign stops in an effort to show that he was in touch with grassroots voters, many of whom had little sense of his local connections. At most appearances he was dogged by reporters—local and national—who mostly wanted to ask about the House Post Office. Citing his lawyers' advice, he refused to respond. "During a recent week of personal campaigning, the lingering image transmitted by the media was one of Rostenkowski being hounded by queries about the investigation," the *Tribune* reported.[15]

Rostenkowski's reelection appeal was not based on his ability to influence health care, tax policy, and other issues. Instead he ran as a traditional Chicago politician—telling the voters what he had done for them. In hundreds of thousands of brochures mailed to homes, the message was simple: "The best ones let their accomplishments do the talking." Included was a listing of more than three dozen federal grants and other services that Rostenkowski had delivered to his district since 1990; they ranged from $1.9 billion for the Deep Tunnel sewer project to $1.1 million for a residential treatment facility for the homeless. The flyer included four photographs of Rostenkowski on the city streets or meeting with constituents. Nowhere did it include even an indirect reference to his chairmanship or his clout on policy in Washington. His campaign also exploited old-fashioned ethnic appeals. One brochure—with heavy doses of Kelly green ink—heralded his 1988 sponsorship of the Irish Immigration Act, an obscure bill that increased the number of visas to citizens from Ireland, many of them already in the United States illegally. Another four-page flyer, filled with tributes, listed what the congressman had done for the Asian American community.

Clinton provided a vital ingredient for Rostenkowski's success with a Chicago visit just two weeks before the vote. Although he did not formally endorse Rostenkowski during his stop at Wright Junior College on the northwest side (preferring to be "presidential"), he left no doubt of his preference.

Referring to the reluctance of many members of Congress to act on legislation, he added, "The one person you don't have to say it to is Dan Rostenkowski. He gets things done. It's in his bones."[16] He effusively praised Rostenkowski's work in passing the economic package and the free-trade deal with Mexico. "Had it not been for his leadership last year, we would not have done the things that we've done that have got the economy on the right course," Clinton said. Without Rostenkowski, the president added prophetically, "we will not be able to do the things that we have to do to meet our obligations to the future in this coming year, in health care, welfare reform and many other areas." Rostenkowski returned the favor, praising Clinton's leadership on anti-crime and gun-control legislation. Not surprisingly, others criticized the visit. Clinton's praise was "coming dangerously close to interfering with the federal grand jury investigation," Simpson said.[17] Attorney General Janet Reno told reporters a few days before Clinton's visit that she had an opinion about the president's stop in Chicago but would not reveal it. *Tribune* columnist Mike Royko said that Rostenkowski should "feel like a damn fool" for having Clinton "come in here and act as a precinct captain."[18] Still, few doubted that the visit was a big plus in demonstrating the congressman's clout. Asked earlier about his plans by a reporter, Clinton said,

"There is still a presumption of innocence in this country. He has not yet been charged with anything." Another unusual high-level embrace came when Republican Gov. Jim Edgar—recognizing the importance of the Ways and Means chairmanship—called Rostenkowski "indispensable" for Illinois.

Rostenkowski apparently sealed his victory a few days before the election when Cullerton engaged the interest of a well-known Rostenkowski colleague: Rep. Joseph Kennedy of Massachusetts. Cullerton had prepared an anti-Rostenkowski television ad that invoked the memory of Kennedy's murdered father, Robert F. Kennedy. The family did not forget that Rostenkowski had helped a young presidential candidate more than thirty years earlier. "It's very unfortunate that my father's words were used in an ad in an attempt to discredit Dan Rostenkowski," Kennedy responded in a statement. At Rostenkowski's urging, Kennedy telephoned Cullerton and won his consent to drop the ad. Still, Rostenkowski privately was pessimistic about the outcome of the vote. "I conditioned the whole family," he told the *Tribune* a few hours before the votes were counted. "I told them I think we're going to lose this thing"[19] But what he had hoped would be a narrow victory became a blowout. He won 50 percent of the vote to only 30 percent for Cullerton and 14 percent for Simpson, who faded once it became clear he was no longer the chief rival. Given the situation, the winner's bare majority was impressive. Rostenkowski's victory statement amounted to a valedictory. "The critics say I am not perfect and they are right," he told campaign workers. "Ultimately, thousands of voters decided to support me and what I represent. They believe that action is more important than words, that government in Washington can and must work." And he thanked the younger Democrat who had given his campaign a well-timed boost. "I'm proud to be a soldier in the president's march for change."[20]

Rostenkowski's triumphant return to the Capitol would prove short-lived. First he wrestled with the health-reform bill's hopeless plight. Then on May 31, came the indictment that forced him to give up his Ways and Means chairmanship and five months later ended his forty-two-year career.* Under Democratic Caucus rules, the courtroom filing forced Rostenkowski to relinquish the Ways and Means chairmanship. Finally Sam Gibbons of Florida got his opportunity to chair the committee. As Ros-

---

*Details of the criminal investigation and Rostenkowski's guilty plea follow in Chapter 10.

tenkowski and his friends had warned since 1980, Gibbons's performance was less than stellar. Although it was highly unlikely that anyone could have rescued Clinton's plan, the acting chairman added to the problems as Democrats struggled for consensus. Gibbons teamed with Health Subcommittee chairman Pete Stark of California and other advocates of a more sweeping approach. He was a conspicuous contrast to Rostenkowski, who had been trying to build agreement among Democrats by reducing the scope of the bill.

"During the spring, while Danny said everyone should keep their powder dry, he had discussions with Bill Gradison" (who had quit the House to become head of the health insurers' lobby) and other business interests to see if they could put together a bill, said a Ways and Means Democrat. He talked up a limited proposal that he and Treasury Secretary Lloyd Bentsen, the former Senate Finance Committee chairman, had prepared during the Bush presidency; it was designed to assure that individuals would not lose health-care coverage simply because they switched jobs or became ill. "But after the indictment, Pete Stark called Sam and they blew the thing out of the water." White House officials, desperate to move a bill to the House floor, encouraged Gibbons. On June 30 Ways and Means narrowly approved the bill, 20 to 18, with four Democrats opposed. "It became an embarrassment. . . . and terribly painful for Rosty to sit through all that," said Mike Andrews, one of the Democratic dissenters. In contrast to Rostenkowski, "who was always thinking about the next game, Gibbons worried only about the next play," Andrews added. Rostenkowski, who had lost his clout and his enthusiasm to participate, complained that "Gibbons jettisoned the deals he had made with the industry groups."[21]

It was left to Dick Gephardt to try to salvage a majority in endless negotiations among House Democrats. It was ironic, given Gephardt's central role in torpedoing Carter's major health-care initiative. Gephardt sought to return to the outlines of Clinton's proposal, but it was too late. With Clinton slipping in public opinion polls, and with vulnerable Democrats skittish about the looming election, party leaders were poorly positioned to twist arms. "They came to us only in the waning moments before the vote," complained Rep. Dave McCurdy of Oklahoma, whose centrist tendencies moved farther to the right in his unsuccessful campaign that year for a Senate seat. As for Rostenkowski, the loss of his chairmanship and the taint of his indictment left him with little leverage to influence Democratic leaders. Although he made known his willingness to work with business groups in order to generate outside support, Gephardt did not get back to him. But Rostenkowski wasn't shy about second-guessing. "Dick Gephardt was supposed to bring it together," said Rostenkowski. "But he was with the last guy who left the room." During a private meeting with several dozen House Democrats in early August, as Gephardt searched futilely for common ground, Rostenkowski said the handling of the House bill was "out of control." Without criticizing Rostenkowski, Gephardt responded with a defense of Democratic leaders.

In the end, Gephardt and Foley concluded that losing the vote would be more demoralizing to Democrats than simply letting the bill die. That was another point on which Rostenkowski disagreed. "We have an obligation to let these SOBs on the floor vote yes or no and go back to their constituents," he protested. He urged Clinton to warn Democrats that he would not back their reelection if they would not vote for a bill.[22] But it was all to no avail. In the end, said former Rostenkowski aide John Salmon, "Democrats ran out of steam." They had tried to do too much, so they failed to do anything. They found themselves beset by the big egos, weak leadership tools, and deep-seated internal conflicts that had plagued the Democratic majority. It was an ignominious setback both for the party and for the Ways and Means Committee.

The collapse of support for the Clinton plan—which, arguably, was three decades in the making—was a tragedy of historic proportions for Democrats. They had run out of ideas, energy, and public support. "The mistake was in the leadership not telling the president that the emperor has no clothes," said Rep. Dennis Eckart, an Ohio Democrat who retired in 1992. In hindsight many Democrats conceded they should have embraced the less ambitious approach backed by Republicans and conservative Democrats; that incremental bill proved to be the basis for the legislation passed two years later by the Republican-controlled Congress and signed enthusiastically by Clinton. It was a telling comment on his presidency that, despite his obvious interest in health-care reform, the topic now moved lower on the Washington agenda. Republicans, for their part, remained wary. When Clinton attempted in his second term to pass small pieces of health reform, House Majority Leader Richard Armey warned, "What he couldn't accomplish in one giant leap, he's hoping to create with little steps."

Rostenkowski faced one more challenge in 1994: the November election. But he had difficulty concentrating. Like a fighter who had taken too many punches, he was exhausted by the year's events: the primary campaign in March, the indictment in May, the health-reform setback in July. From a campaign perspective, he and his advisers feared that calling attention to him would attract more anti-Rostenkowski voters than supporters. "I made a judgment call about what I viewed as being the best road to pursue, and in my opinion, low key was best," he said in a postelection interview.[23] His lawyers also warned him to keep a low profile; in part they feared that he might say or do something that would adversely affect his legal interests. And he wanted to save campaign money to pay for his lawyers' mounting bills. "There was no campaign," said Serafin, who worked with Rostenkowski on his successful 1992 and 1994 primary contest. He had no full-time campaign staff, broadcast no ads, and sent only one mailing to the district. Besides, it was difficult for Rostenkowski to take seriously his Republican opponent, a neophyte.

Michael Patrick Flanagan, a thirty-one-year-old attorney, had been collecting unemployment compensation for several months before his campaign; his total earnings in 1993 were $8,800. In his first bid for public office he won the Republican primary in March with fewer than four thousand votes against four opponents. "Michael Flanagan has no money, no experience and no connection, but that doesn't stop him from running against Rosty," headlined a front-page article a week before the election in the *Reader*, a free Chicago weekly.[24] Flanagan was hardly an impressive figure: overweight, nerdy-looking, and a fidgety cigarette smoker. But he came across as strangely appealing in a Chicago sort of way. His everyman allure may have been just right for that congressional district in that year. "Who would you want to vote for? The soft-spoken, mild-mannered, inoffensive lawyer, or the deal-making career politician and dark prince of pork-barrel politics?"[25] Besides, Flanagan wanted to cut back the federal government. He viewed Clinton's health-care plan as "socialism."

With opposition to abortion and gun control that contrasted starkly with the views of most of the district's voters, Flanagan would have had no chance in any other year. By mid-October he had raised about $30,000, barely enough to rent a small office and to print a few leaflets. Forget about television, he had no radio advertisements. Running against an indicted congressman, Flanagan was so frustrated with his plight that he issued a press release criticizing the national Republican party for "paying lip service" to his requests for money. Despite what was termed a "thriving Anybody But Rostenkowski movement" that was evident during a walk through the northwest side, a news story reported, "GOP leaders at the national level seem to have written off the campaign"[26] Flanagan complained that Governor Edgar "hasn't done anything" to help his insurgent bid.[27] Then, a few days before the election, Republicans realized that Flanagan might win in the freakish campaign. A late October poll, Republicans said, showed him with a 51 to 30 percent *lead* over Rostenkowski. The national party now gave $55,000 to Flanagan's campaign, and he quickly purchased thirty-second television ads to introduce himself to the voters. Although the ad did not attack Rostenkowski, Flanagan pointedly contrasted himself with the incumbent: "The bottom line is this: If you vote for me, I'll do my best to keep your trust." Still, Rostenkowski publicly dismissed Flanagan as an unknown and called the last-minute Republican advertising blitz an effort to draw press attention.

As soon became clear, it didn't matter that Flanagan was unknown. The election was a referendum on Rostenkowski, and he had been mute. "The best strategy was to keep the focus off the race, keep a low profile, and keep the negatives down," Bill Daley told a reporter after the election. "It was pretty much a personal decision of how he wanted to run."[28] Did he give up? A source close to Rostenkowski said, "The indictment took his heart out . . . and completely undermined his ability to campaign." Still, Dick Mell, the alderman who worked hard for Rostenkowski's victory during the March primary, said he might have won again in November if he had told friends to put together a similar effort on his behalf. "But they never asked me," Mell added. In the final weekend before the election, local newspapers reported that Mayor Daley urged city officials to hit the streets for Rostenkowski. But that order came too late. The reform-minded mayor felt that he could not make a big investment in his indicted friend. The fact that Democrats were running a weak statewide ticket against a mostly incumbent team of Republicans, led by Governor Edgar, added to the local Democrats' lack of enthusiasm. In any case, the outcome didn't matter much to Mell, once he assured that John Cullerton would not challenge his son-in-law's eventual House bid.

When the election results were counted on November 8 they were stunning—on Chicago's northwest side and throughout the nation. Flanagan won 54.4 percent in the district, defeating Rostenkowski by more than twelve thousand votes. The margin was greater than even the most pessimistic Democrats had feared. The jubilant Flanagan instantly became a national celebrity. He told CBS News that voters "have sent the message that they have had all the fun they care to have with the high taxes they pay, the high spending of their government, and the fact that government is too big and costs too much." Flanagan clearly was a beneficiary of that mood, just as Rostenkowski's indictment had become an additional source of national discontent. Democrats suffered devastating defeats across America. Despite being badly outspent, House Republicans gained fifty-two seats and won the House for the first time since 1954. Every House Republican who sought reelection prevailed. In all, thirty-four House Democrats were turned out; they ran the gamut from Speaker Tom Foley and Judiciary Committee chairman Jack Brooks of Texas, a forty-two-year House veteran, to sixteen first-term Democrats, many of whom had naively entered the House in order to reform its ways. The four-decade era of Democratic control came to a crushing end. For years, politicians and professors had wrung their hands about the near impossibility of dislodging long-entrenched members of Congress with their huge fund-raising advantages. In 1994 two well-regarded political scientists with good Republican connections wrote a book that referred to House Republicans as "Congress' Permanent Minority."[29] Now, all of a sudden, the old rules were out the window. Republicans won seats because they had an appealing message: they would change how Congress worked. Democrats' refusal to respond to the public demand for change left them as status-quo advocates. The Democratic era in the House had ended with an implosion. Like a geriatric suffering from many corrosive illnesses, the majority's body simply shut down.

Republicans, of course, were exuberant. But even Newt Gingrich, whose command of the resurgence propelled him to the speaker's chair, paid stirring tribute to Rostenkowski. "I found in my dealing with him that, while he is a liberal Democrat and a big-city-machine Democrat, and we had a lot to argue over, there was a toughness and an integrity in him that I think you had to admire, even when you were fighting him," Gingrich told the Cable News Network on election night. "And I think the last years have been very sad ones. I think it was the right decision for Chicago. I am glad that we have won the seat. But, nonetheless, I don't think you could see somebody who has served their country that long ending their career in that kind of situation without a sense of sadness for them as people, as human beings." Even if Rostenkowski had survived re-election, his indictment likely would have fueled Republican demands for ethics action, including possible ouster from the House. In any case, lacking his senior Democratic seat at Ways and Means, he would have had no constructive role in the new Republican-controlled Congress.

Rostenkowski had little to say about his defeat on election night other than, "I am going to Washington and clean out my desk." In the following weeks he told several interviewers that he was proud of what he and his party had accomplished. "I will match my record of service in the last century against any other member of Congress, and I will prophesy that I would be in the top 10 having done something significant for the nation," he told a Chicago reporter.[30] Interviewers asked him about his indictment, tax policy, and his future. But Clinton's health-care reform plan seemed forgotten by the political community. Most Democrats saw it as a nightmare they hoped would disappear; Republicans wanted to move to their own agenda to change America. Rostenkowski was one of the few politicians who addressed the issue squarely. In his final formal remarks as a public official—a retrospective December 1994 speech to students at Harvard University's School of Public Health—he blamed mostly the president and his aides. He criticized Clinton's plan as "too complex to understand and so riddled with centrist compromise that it was a recipe for political roadkill." A better approach, he added, would have been for Clinton to send Congress "a more radical plan that could have been readily understood by the public and then allowed Congress to amend it in a fashion that would make it more complex and more centrist."

Rostenkowski's health-care reform postmortem overlooked his own legal problems. No doubt the powerful chairman was distracted at a crucial point as he was forced to spend more of his time tending to his interests in Chicago and to his problems with the federal prosecutor. As his speech made clear, however, very little could have been done to rescue Clinton's plan. Once the Democrats had failed so abysmally with their great historic mission, the end of their forty-year control of the House probably became inevitable. After such a long reign, they needed time off. The voters understood and in 1994 cast that verdict. For House Democrats—and for Rostenkowski—the party was over.

Chapter Ten

THE SYSTEM ON TRIAL

"I think I will have accomplished what my dad and mother never thought was going to happen to a kid that they thought was going to be in prison by the time he was 21!"—Dan Rostenkowski (tearfully), House Ways and Means Committee, April 27, 1983.

AT THE CELEBRATION when he unveiled his portrait that hangs with those of other former Ways and Means Committee chairmen, Rostenkowski gave an unusually candid confession of his personal insecurity. Addressing Vice-President Bush, Speaker O'Neill, and other friends and courtiers, he opened a revealing window to the mind-set of latter-day Chicago politicians, many of whom have been forced out of office and to prison because they violated their public trust. Rostenkowski could not have known that he would confront criminal liability a decade later. But many of those who worked most closely with him were not surprised that his career ended in shambles, though they were surely saddened. "Times changed, but Danny was not willing to change with the reforms," said Rep. Jack Murtha. "He was a traditionalist. That's what brought him down."

For many years, Rostenkowski's advisers warned him, he was heading for a fall. They worried that he operated perilously close to the line of legally acceptable behavior. He flirted with danger in his belief that he could play by the old rules in place when he first came to Washington. Because of his scorn for the more rigorous ethics standards, both in the House and at the Justice Department, he ignored warnings that the new

rules applied to *his* conduct. Of course, the events leading to his imprisonment were not inevitable, despite the fears of Joe and Priscilla Rostenkowski. But his downfall became a head-on collision waiting to
happen. When his aides in the early 1980s "discussed some of his legal
problems with him, we warned that he was skating on the edge," said
John Sherman, his former press secretary and confidant. "He responded it
was legal, even though I said it doesn't look good." But what was legal?
That was a major part of his problem. "Dan Rostenkowski came to the
House in the 1950s, and he had a set of rules," said Dennis Eckart, who
served twelve years in the House before retiring in 1992, at age forty-two.
"In the 1990s he used 1950s' rules. The standards changed and he didn't
change with them."

The elements that led to his conviction were tragic and pitiful. On one
level he was "trapped in events beyond his control," as a reporter wrote
during the criminal investigation.[1] A 1991 inquiry into reports of illegal
drug sales in the House Post office took on a life of its own as zealous
prosecutors moved from one target to another, many of which ranged far
from the original reason for investigation. Years later, Rostenkowski
pointed to the comment of Rep. Henry Hyde—the Illinois Republican
who held a neighboring district to Rostenkowski for more than twenty
years and who eventually chaired Judiciary Committee hearings that led
to President Clinton's impeachment. "I have learned only too painfully
what the abuse of governmental power can do to someone's life and career," said Hyde, after federal regulators' lengthy review of a collapsed
Chicago-area savings and loan association where he had been a director.[2]
Rostenkowski was convicted on charges that were picayune compared to
those of the indictment. Although prosecutors indicted him on seventeen
counts for allegedly misusing hundreds of thousands of dollars in official
funds, he pleaded guilty to only two counts. On one charge he illegally
purchased assorted china from the House stationery store, including $200
crystal sculptures of the U.S. Capitol that were inscribed with his friends'
names, which he sent as gifts. The second charge he admitted in court
dealt with the "padding" of his payroll with employees who did little or
no work, aside from routine tasks for Rostenkowski and his family. He
steadfastly maintained his innocence on the broader and more publicized
abuses at the House Post Office, including the claim that he traded official
stamps for personal cash, which was the linchpin for the criminal focus.
Prosecutors never presented their case in a manner that would have

permitted a vigorous cross-examination and defense, let alone a jury's verdict of these allegations.

Perhaps the greatest personal tragedy was that the Chicago pol who had risen to such national influence was brought down by the type of penny-ante abuse that ensnared two-bit local politicians. "Certain of his activities made sense from a Chicago perspective," said former Rep. Ed Derwinski, the Illinois Republican. "If you understand the relationship of ward committeemen, you can understand the mind-set of giving the gifts . . . and maintaining the principle of loyalty." Although federal prosecutors and the handful of journalists who pursued his case were convinced that he was guilty, they never proved that Rostenkowski took a penny for himself. So the big operator on Capitol Hill who could have pocketed from his committee work millions of dollars—legally or illegally—had he really wanted the cash, instead took a fall for a pittance. The chairman who demanded to know the salary of chief executives who visited his office pleading for special treatment was sent to prison for perks that a corporate junior vice-president might have considered piddling.

In a sense, the case of *U.S. vs. Daniel D. Rostenkowski* was the final chapter in the quarter-century clash between Rostenkowski and his archnemesis David Obey of Wisconsin for control of the House and its tribal rituals. For much of that time Obey the reformer sought to eliminate vestiges of graft, part-time legislators, and unaccountable power brokers. Obey's demons were the tools of machine politicians: special-interest influence, back-room deal-cutting, and the House Ways and Means Committee. To good-government types, Rostenkowski symbolized what they wanted to eliminate. His view that members should set their own rules made him a poster child for what ailed Congress, Obey believed. Rostenkowski, of course, had a different view. But he had lost the battles with Obey and the reformers in the 1970s when the House changed the campaign finance law and its ethics rules; the results imposed new disclosure requirements and restrictions on gifts and income from outside sources. "I fought the reformers, but I changed when I had to," said Murtha, the beefy ex-marine who aggressively opposed many of the changes with his friend Rostenkowski. "Danny never seemed to give in. He was too arrogant. That was just him." Obey surely had nothing to do with the criminal investigation of Rostenkowski. In embracing the reformers' premises, however, the prosecutors' case against the chairman for the first time issued a criminal indictment of a House member that was based chiefly on violation of House rules, according to Rostenkowski attorney Howard Pearl.

Two crucial shortcomings help to explain Rostenkowski's downfall. First, as the politician from Chicago's mean streets, he assumed that House rules changes on the use of official funds did not affect him. "Rosty thought a lot of the disclosure rules were chicken shit," said John Salmon, his first staff director at the Ways and Means Committee. "So he stopped asking the questions" about new ethics requirements. Rostenkowski eventually conceded that he disregarded the rules. "I was there thirty-six years," he told a reporter the day after he pleaded guilty. "They changed the rules thirty times. I can honestly say I was not fully cognizant of the rules and where there were changes. Maybe I was brazen, I ignored it."[3] Once he became a committee chairman, he felt he had even more discretion to run his office as he saw fit. Later the departure of loyal but no-nonsense staffers like Salmon and Sherman left few aides who were willing to confront him. "He liked to go first-class, for example, to golf courses around the country, and he felt that the chairman was entitled to respect and perquisites," said a House aide who worked closely with Rostenkowski. "He had a large appetite for companionship, recognition, and consumption. So he demanded attention and respect with the need for sociability." Those cravings and reciprocations of friendship spelled his doom.

Rostenkowski's second major misjudgment came during the criminal investigation, when he repeatedly challenged or ignored the advice of his experienced attorneys. Instead, many friends on and off Capitol Hill convinced him to fight to the bitter end, confident that he ultimately would prevail. Some of those serious tactical mistakes became apparent only in hindsight and after unexpected events, such as the Democrats' 1994 election disaster. Whatever the cause, Rostenkowski—the ultimate deal-maker—bungled the most important transaction of his life.

Despite tougher ethical standards, Rostenkowski could rightly point out that the House had not changed important aspects of its operations. Because Obey failed in 1977 in his efforts to establish an all-powerful chief administrative officer, well-connected political hacks continued to supervise the large House clerk and sergeant-at-arms offices. Likewise members continued to make taxpayer-subsidized purchases in the House, where the stationery shop was closed to the public. The leaders and other top officers of the House obviously knew about and condoned these practices. Rostenkowski, in effect, found himself in a Catch-22 situation where he could be prosecuted for purchases that had the House's imprimatur. Still, ignorance was no excuse for his failure to comply with the House's complex regulations. He simply was unwilling to acknowledge the new realities or to direct his aides to adopt a more ethically pure routine for his office.

ROSTENKOWSKI'S LEGAL PROBLEMS began with a grand jury investigation in mid-1991 into criminal activities in the House Post Office. Investigators discovered that tens of thousands of dollars were missing from the post office, which employed about 150 people; 4 employees were fired, including one for selling cocaine at the site. Early news reports indicated that the investigation was limited to House aides, no lawmakers. But Republicans charged that Speaker Tom Foley and his wife Heather, who was his chief of staff, had failed to oversee the post office or to inform other House members of the problems there. According to one report, postmaster Robert Rota had informed friends that Mrs. Foley "told him to play down allegations of criminality and mismanagement."[4] Republicans also accused a Foley aide of interfering with the Capitol police investigation of the post office. On February 5, 1992, the House passed a resolution that ordered its House Administration Committee to investigate; Democratic leaders backed that action to counter a Republican call for an outside investigator. "The entire cocaine and theft scandal has been handled by the Democratic leadership as a partisan cover-up of their patronage problems," Minority Whip Newt Gingrich charged at the time.

In what became a crucial step, U.S. Attorney Jay Stephens of the District of Columbia convinced three post office employees to plead guilty to embezzlement charges and agreed to drop further charges in exchange for their cooperation. As is common in such an investigation, Stephens saw that blood was in the water, and he unleashed more resources to review the post office. Taking the testimony of lower-level employees to move steadily up the ranks, the prosecutors turned toward postmaster Rota, who in March 1992 resigned under pressure. News reports described Rota as a friend of Rostenkowski, who had helped him two decades earlier to get his job, which required the approval of Democratic leaders and then the full House. Rostenkowski denied that he had more than a passing familiarity with Rota. "Over thirty-six years in Congress, I bet my conversations with him didn't last more than an hour," he said. But Rostenkowski added, "No one gave more to Rota and his staff than I did. I was like a godfather to him. . . . I honestly believed that we should reward people going up the ladder." Another senior staffer in the post office was James Smith, a three-decade employee whom Rostenkowski sponsored in 1989 as the supervisor of accounts, where he administered the supply of stamps. Like Rota—and Sergeant-at-Arms Jack Russ, who mismanaged the House bank—Smith had been a loyal servant of senior Democrats. Their flawed job performances contributed to the Democrats' disgrace. But in exchange for his cooperation with the grand jury, the U.S. attorney's office gave Smith immunity from prosecution.

As prosecutors turned up the heat, newspapers reported Smith's claim that Rostenkowski made "stamps for cash" transactions in which he pocketed tens of thousands of dollars by cashing in stamps at the post office. When Rostenkowski first entered the House, many lawmakers picked up extra dollars from their unused stamps or stationery allowances at the end of the year; but the House in the 1970s toughened its rules to end such practices. If the charges against Rostenkowski were true, prosecutors likely would recommend that his accusers receive a lighter penalty for reeling in the big fish. On May 6, 1992, prosecutors issued their first subpoena to Rostenkowski, demanding his office files. He ridiculed the suggestion of wrongdoing: "I mail a lot," he told reporters. "What's next?" added his spokesman James Jaffe. "How many typewriter ribbons did he buy? This is silly."[5] But, according to the later indictment, the subpoena was not the first signal that Rostenkowski was in jeopardy. On about March 20, the prosecutors alleged, Rostenkowski had told Rota that any legal expenses he incurred would be covered by "a special fund" he maintained. In what became additional elements of a criminal concealment of the facts, prosecutors alleged that Rota in April falsely told congressional investigators that no House members received cash for stamps; also that month, according to the indictment, Rostenkowski and Rota discussed the investigation in a telephone conversation.

For Rostenkowski the next two years were consumed by this investigation: subpoenas from the prosecutors, damaging leaks to the press, strategy sessions with his attorneys, anxiety about the outcome. Although he emphasized business-as-usual as Ways and Means handled legislation, he was distracted and worried. Even the potentially positive development that Bill Clinton's election would bring the appointment of a U.S.

attorney with a fresh view of the case proved to be a fleeting hope once Eric Holder took over in October 1993; he had served a dozen years in the Justice Department's public integrity section handling public corruption cases before serving as a local judge. Rostenkowski's colleagues warned that his plight was serious. "After the 1992 election I urged him not to be sworn in for another term because I thought he had a legal problem," said Murtha.

As prosecutors probed his life and family finances in the kind of detail that he felt no mortal could survive, Rostenkowski grew bitter about lawyers and the legal system. "There were hungry prosecutors and they saw me as a trophy," he said. "It's like putting a notch on the handle of a gun." While firmly maintaining his innocence, he claimed that Rota—his chief accuser—lied in order to target higher officials and reduce his own punishment. Rostenkowski compounded his own predicament by repeatedly switching defense attorneys as he grew unhappy with their advice and their failure to free him of the investigation. Over a two-year period he hired four high-priced legal teams. After the legal process had run its course, he vented his anger. Although he said his comments were "generic," he left no doubt that he was talking about his own experience. "I have a minimum high regard for all lawyers," he said. "They say at the first meeting that we are going to work it out. By the fourth meeting they say the other side is scared. Then, at the sixth meeting, they say the other side is tougher than we expected. Finally, at the tenth meeting, they urge the client to sign a plea bargain."

Of all his attorneys, Rostenkowski became most bitter about Robert Bennett, whose high-profile Washington clients have included President Clinton (in the sexual harassment suit filed by Paula Jones in May 1994, based on his alleged conduct while Arkansas governor). Bennett represented Rostenkowski for almost a year in the period before the indictment, when Rostenkowski obviously hoped to gain an acceptable settlement of the case. In contrast to Stanley Brand and Judah Best—his earlier attorneys, who were chiefly negotiators—Bennett had significant experience as a courtroom litigator. But the relationship between the two men soured: as prosecutors moved toward an indictment, Rostenkowski worried that Bennett's representation of Clinton posed a conflict of interest between his two clients. And the congressman's penchant for control led him to second-guess Bennett's negotiations with the U.S. attorney. Bennett, who has a reputation as strong-willed, reportedly grew unhappy that Rostenkowski was listening to too many advisers. They were "two old bulls in different professions, but in many respects cut from the same cloth—two very strong people," said a Rostenkowski friend.[6]

On July 19, 1993, five days before Rostenkowski announced his hiring of Bennett, Rota pleaded guilty to the stamps-for-cash scheme. In his confession Rota said he had given a "largely untraceable source of illegal cash" to several members of Congress; among them, according to prosecutors, was "Congressman A," who several news reports said was Rostenkowski. "What Mr. Rota did was to place the services of his office, and the United States funds under his control, at the disposal of certain United States congressmen," according to the indictment. "What Mr. Rota got in return was to keep his job as an officer of the United States House of Representatives." Although it did not name him, the Rota guilty plea appeared to leave Rostenkowski one step from an indictment. "It would take an awful lot of explaining to walk away from it now," a federal law-enforcement source told the *Chicago Tribune* at the time.[7] But a review of the prosecutors' case against Rota shows that his confession did not definitively accuse Rostenkowski of the stamps-for-cash deal. According to their statement, Rota provided cash to members in three separate ways: he gave them the cash directly in exchange for stamps; in other cases he gave them cash in exchange for official House vouchers, for which the recipients falsely certified they had received stamps; and he sometimes cashed checks from their campaign accounts—an action that might be illegal but had nothing to do with postage. With Rota's help, prosecutors later charged, "Rostenkowski used a computer-generated list to determine how his stamp purchases for the particular year stood in relation to those of other Members." As they probed the finances of "Congressman A," their interest in Rostenkowski's office and finances extended far beyond the stamps. With evidence from ten subpoenas that they issued over twenty-two months, their focus included leased automobiles that he listed as "mobile offices" for his district, plus his Chicago office space, which was in a building owned by his two sisters. Investigators were "seeking to determine if Rostenkowski has engaged in a broad pattern of self-dealing," according to a news report, which noted that Rostenkowski made no secret of "his open enjoyment of the perks of his position."[8]

These mounting accusations raised implications for the world of Ways and Means. "The investigation of Rep. Rostenkowski has created extreme nervousness, not only in City Hall but among his many allies and supporters in Chicago's corporate community," noted a January 1993 report in a Chicago business newspaper.[9] If Rostenkowski is indicted, said an aide to Mayor Daley, "it would be devastating. . . . He really has, over the years, delivered the goods for Chicago."[10] After Rota's guilty plea, the same publication voiced more anxiety. "Disbelief, denial, grief, anger, acceptance—the emotions normally associated with death are roiling those with close ties to Rep. Dan Rostenkowski, even as they refuse to write his political obituary. . . . There is grief in contemplating what Rep. Rostenkowski has done for Chicago over the last 34 years, and anger that his clout could abruptly disappear for such a stupid reason."[11] But the congressman remained stoic, at least for public consumption. Except for brief professions of innocence and his desire to bring the case to a speedy conclusion, he said little to reporters. Even those who dealt with him privately said he rarely griped about his ordeal. "Many criminal defendants spend a great deal of time bemoaning their fate," said attorney Howard Pearl, who represented him after the indictment. "Rostenkowski was never like that. He never complained. He is the most stand-up guy I've ever seen. . . . He assesses a situation and determines the best practical outcome better than anyone I've ever seen."

On May 6, 1994, the *Tribune* reported that Holder had sent the prospective indictment to senior Justice Department officials for review. "There are a variety of things you have to do at the end of any investigation, and we're in the process of those final things," Holder said.[12] Two weeks later the *New York Times* wrote that Rostenkowski attorneys "have approached federal prosecutors to try to negotiate a plea bargain that would avert a broad felony indictment," with Rostenkowski agreeing to plead guilty to a lesser charge.[13] Under House Democratic Caucus rules, conviction of a misdemeanor would not require him to relinquish his Ways and Means chairmanship. But such an outcome was not in the cards. In their discussions, Rostenkowski and others later said, Bennett urged him—because of the risks of facing broader charges and longer imprisonment—to accept a deal with a felony conviction, a six-month prison term plus immediate resignation from the House. Rostenkowski disputed several press accounts that Holder had agreed to such terms: "It was only an offer by Bennett," he said. "Holder said he would never agree to a deal on six months."

But Rostenkowski's comment is misleading in two respects. First, even though Holder had fully discussed the proposed terms with Bennett, the U.S. attorney could not formally acknowledge his part in the agreement, nor could he receive the attorney general's okay until Rostenkowski signaled that he would accept it. Second, once Rostenkowski rejected the deal in May 1994, Holder could no longer agree to only six months' imprisonment. Although Holder, who took over as deputy attorney general in 1997, has not publicly discussed the plea bargaining, he and his staff surely would have been sensitive to accepting a plea that appeared lenient to Rostenkowski at a time when Clinton had an obvious interest in keeping him on board to handle the health-care reform plan. Although Holder had broad discretion on key decisions in the case, appearances were troublesome. "It is hard to imagine a more delicate, not to say incestuous, situation," the *Washington Post* wrote in an editorial. "A potential conflict of interest exists between the Administration's legislative interests and its law-enforcement responsibilities."[14]

A week later Rostenkowski had two choices, the Associated Press reported. "Resign his seat in Congress, plead guilty to a felony and serve an unspecified jail sentence; or reject the offer and face certain indictment on a broader range of charges."[15] In either case most House Democrats realized that his reign as chairman was finished. "Probably the biggest impact around here is people feeling sick all week," said Rep. Patricia Schroeder. "It's like that little cloud hanging over and you wonder when it will all blow away."[16] They also had a growing fear that disaster loomed in the November election; those concerns deepened after they lost two long-held seats in special elections in May.

For Rostenkowski, of course, the dilemma was more painful. Facing Holder's May 31 deadline on whether to accept the felony plea, his options were stark. If he accepted the deal he would face prison time, and his public career would be done. If he decided to fight, he confronted huge legal bills, more of the grueling ordeal, and a jail sentence that could consume the remainder of his life; even if he prevailed, he faced an uncertain future. On Memorial Day, May 30, he made his fateful decision. "No guilt, no deals," read the statement issued by his office. "I strongly believe that I am not guilty of these charges and will fight to regain my reputation in court. That is a far more attractive option than pleading guilty to crimes that I did not commit." Noting that he would be forced to give up his chairmanship, he concluded wistfully, "I am confident that I will be vindicated and I look forward to the return of the gavel."

At 2 p.m. the next day came the grand jury's stunning news at the federal courthouse near the Capitol. The formal indictment accused Rostenkowski of a scheme "to obtain cash, goods and services, without paying for them himself, for the personal use and benefit of himself, his family and his personal friends; and to conceal and disguise the fact that he was fraudulently causing the amount of the cash, and the costs of the goods and services, to be charged to and paid by the United States as official congressional expenses." According to the seventeen counts, the violations had cost taxpayers more than $690,000 over twenty-two years, most of it to pay employees who performed no work. News reports termed Rostenkowski's disgrace as a dying gasp of old politics. The charges read "like an itemization of the way things used to be in Chicago, complete with ghost payrollers, kickbacks, office slush funds and lots of gifts for political supporters and friends," the *Tribune* reported. But the criminal filing was "also new politics, in the form of federal prosecutors taking sharp aim at the old ways."[17]

At a crowded Justice Department press conference later that afternoon, Holder summarized the government's case: payroll padding, purchase of personal items from the House stationery store that were not used for official purposes, efforts to instruct a witness to withhold evidence from the grand jury, conversion of stamps and official vouchers into cash at the House Post Office, and use of official funds to purchase seven automobiles for himself and his family. "The allegations contained in today's indictment represent a betrayal of the public trust for personal gain," Holder concluded. "In essence, this indictment alleges that Congressman Rostenkowski used his elective office to perpetrate an extensive fraud on the American people. . . . This is not, as some have suggested, a petty matter, but in a larger sense, the true cost of such corruption by elected officials cannot be measured solely in dollar amounts, no matter how high this total. Rather the cost of such misconduct must also be measured in terms of the corrosive effect it has on our democratic system of government and on the trust our citizens have in their elected officials." Responding to reporters, Holder said that Bennett had initiated negotiations on Rostenkowski's behalf, but the prosecutor did not discuss details. He dismissed as "puffery" the view that Rostenkowski was the victim of changing ethical standards. "We're dealing with conduct that is to my mind very reprehensible, very offensive, it's broad in its scope, it's long in its duration, and it seems to me that that kind of conduct was always a problem, was not conduct that was ever accepted," Holder said. "And I suspect that if you talk to Members of Congress and other people, they will say exactly that." Conceding that other House members had bought items at the stationery store or "had a particular staff member not doing all the work that you would expect," Holder said the breadth and duration of the conduct "is what differentiates it from" that of other lawmakers.

Although the stamps-for-cash charges generated the most news headlines, the most detailed accusations dealt with Rostenkowski's office personnel. Between 1971 and 1992, the prosecutors claimed, at least fourteen persons on his official payroll "performed little or no work in his congressional offices" and instead provided personal or campaign-related services for him and his family. Although they were not named, the fourteen were described in some detail. Their tasks ranged from taking thousands of photographs for Rostenkowski in Chicago, including a daughter's wedding, to mowing the grass at his summer home in Wisconsin. Ghost employees included the son of an Illinois state senator who had placed two of Rostenkowski's daughters on the state payroll at the same time (at $48,000 combined), plus tenants in apartments he owned who did little or no official work. The items that he purchased for gifts from the stationery store included approximately 60 wooden armchairs with a painting of the U.S. Capitol on the front and his name on the back, 60 crystal sculptures of the Capitol, 250 pieces of china, and 26 pieces of luggage. (In February 1994 Rostenkowski reimbursed the U.S. Treasury $82,095 for these purchases in an attempt to reduce the charges.) The seven automobiles were leased over a seven-year period from a Ford dealer in Wilmette, Illinois, under a revolving-credit arrangement that permitted him and his family to purchase them later as personal vehicles for a grand total of $5,294. As for Rostenkowski's post office offenses, the indictment listed 12 occasions between 1985 and 1991 when Rota gave him cash in exchange for House vouchers for postage stamps. Although prosecutors charged that he received cash from the post office on other occasions in exchange for previously issued stamps, they gave no dates for such transactions. The U.S. attorney's office signaled its uneasiness about that part of its case when the *Wall Street Journal* reported that Holder told Bennett "in a phone call that prosecutors wouldn't press any charge related to the House post office scandal—the central focus of the two-year probe—if the lawmaker accepted the proposed plea bargain."[18]

The indictment suggested no improprieties in Rostenkowski's legislative activities, despite reformers' frequent criticism that Rostenkowski

dished out favors to pals. Nor did prosecutors claim that he took gifts
from special-interest groups or that he committed tax violations for failure to report income. They presumably had such options, given their
claim that he pocketed income that he did not report to the Internal Revenue Service. Under the tax law, however, taxpayers usually are permitted
to have such charges tried in the federal court where they reside. Although
Rostenkowski sought to have his case moved to Chicago, the Washington
prosecutors objected, citing the inconvenience to themselves and the
many potential witnesses. In nontax cases, decisions on court jurisdiction
rest largely with the trial judge. As expected, Rostenkowski's judge
turned down his attorneys' effort to move the case. Aside from tax-law details, one reason why he wanted the switch, which he did not discuss publicly, was his expectation of a more sympathetic jury in Chicago. "Ghost
payrolling has been a part of big-city politics at least since the birth of
New York's old Tammany Hall, which more than 150 years ago perfected
a process that passed public funds to whole armies of hacks, bums, brutes,
worthies and hopefuls waiting for that next big election," the *Chicago Tribune* reported. "Chicago, of course, has had many variants on the
theme."[19] (The first Mayor Daley once asked, "If you can't help your
friends, who should you help? Your enemies?") With Washington's predominantly black population, Rostenkowski also feared that its jury
would be hostile to a big-time white politician.

Race became another subtle factor in the grand jury filing. Although
most federal court cases are assigned randomly to judges, Holder told reporters at his May 31 press conference that he expected the case to be assigned to Judge Norma Holloway Johnson, a black woman. That was bad
news for Rostenkowski. Because she had handled other litigation related
to the House Post Office, including Rota's guilty plea, court rules permitted her to preside in "related" cases. As she demonstrated with Rostenkowski—and, a few years later, when she handled parts of independent
counsel Kenneth Starr's investigation of President Clinton—Johnson has
a well-earned reputation for sympathy with prosecutors and hands down
stiff sentences to guilty defendants. Before President Carter nominated
her as a federal judge in 1980, she had been a government attorney for
seven years and had served a decade as a judge in D.C. local courts. Outside the courtroom, Rostenkowski complained bitterly that Johnson was
biased. But there was little he could do about it.

Not until ten days after the indictment did Rostenkowski vigorously assert his innocence. "I will wash away the mud that has been splattered upon my reputation," he told reporters at the courthouse on June 10, after pleading not guilty to Judge Johnson. "Some ask, 'How could you have done these things?' The answer is simple: I didn't do them." He firmly disavowed trading stamps for cash. "It never happened," he insisted, claiming ignorance of specifics of how his office and committee staffs handled mailings. Rostenkowski's comments on other charges were more ambiguous. In effect he did not contest some factual allegations, but he insisted that House rules gave him wide discretion—for example, on staff hirings and gift purchases. "I don't think I'm isolated as the only one who did it," he said following his imprisonment. "Did I put a kid on my payroll because he was my buddy's son? Did I expect him to do some work? Yes, but not a lot. . . . But the result was that it was inspiring to these kids to spend three months in Washington seeing how the government works." As for purchases of the chairs—which he said he ordered from the stationery shop in 1990–1991 because he was planning to retire in 1992—he asked, "Why are the chairs there if not for us to purchase?"

Press coverage of the indictment and his subsequent court dealings was mostly hostile to Rostenkowski. News stories barely focused on the merits of the prosecution's case, beyond provocative details of alleged misdeeds. "The press, especially the *Sun-Times,* wanted to sell papers," he said later. "There were a lot of suppositions and uninformed stories." Few reporters explored the twists and turns of the two-year inquiry. Nor, in ensuing months, did the press examine either the constitutional basis for Congress's authority to write and enforce its own rules or House members' historical immunity from court review for their official actions. Instead most reporters depicted the criminal charges as a dramatic fall from grace. "As chairman, he did what he pleased," according to a profile in the *Sun-Times.* "And that, in the end, may have been his downfall."[20] The *Sun-Times* ran photographs taken four months earlier of chairs with the House seal and other items from the Capitol that Rostenkowski was storing in the basement of the four-story apartment building next to his home.

Another press theme was the beleaguered Congress. "Although the number of scandalized lawmakers is relatively small and the controversies surrounding them vary in severity, each new episode adds a layer to the public's deep suspicions about their politicians," suggested the *Washington Post.*[21] On the day of the indictment, each of the three major television network news programs devoted several minutes to Holder's presentation; CBS and NBC also analyzed the implications for Clinton's health-care reform plan. In one of the few reports that showed his practices were hardly unique, the *Post* reported that members and their aides purchased $180,000 of fine china during the three-month period when Rostenkowski was accused of purchasing 250 pieces; and in June 1991 the stationery store sold nearly $10,000 worth of the armchairs similar to those purchased by Rostenkowski. As the article noted, each House member had separate allowances totaling as much as $1 million to pay for staff, travel, mail, and office expenses, "with the Member having the right to dip into one pot if another is used up."[22] With those other purchases, however, it was not clear that members were making gifts to friends. Chuck Neubauer of the *Sun-Times,* a Chicago journalist since the 1970s who did the most extensive reporting on Rostenkowski's problems and kept boxes stuffed with files at his desk, rejected claims of media bias. Because Rostenkowski was "very stubborn," he was reluctant to concede he had done anything wrong, Neubauer said. "Danny likes reporters to a point," he added, "but he's been burned too many times."

A few veteran political reporters—perhaps hardened by *realpolitik*—wrote sympathetically in the days following the indictment. "Nothing has been proven, then, except that federal indictments are written with all the intellectual honesty of toothpaste advertisements," wrote *Chicago Tribune* columnist Jon Margolis. "In vain, one searches the transcript of U.S. Atty. Eric Holder's announcement for the hint that Rostenkowski put this money in his pocket." He criticized "zealous prosecutors . . . determined to protect the republic from the clutches of a politician who would spend 1,500 taxpayer dollars on a teenager."[23] Some emphasized the high quality of Rostenkowski's legislative work. "What his colleagues know and affirm is that in the part of his public life they observed, Rostenkowski lived by a code as strict as any you could wish," wrote veteran columnist David Broder of the *Washington Post.* "He told you what he was going to do; he did not dissemble. He kept his word; if he promised something, he delivered. He was always up front, even when he knew you would disagree with him. . . . Seeing him brought down—even by what are alleged to be his own weaknesses—is a citywide sorrow."[24]

Two days after the case was filed, Rostenkowski announced that he and Robert Bennett had "decided to go our separate ways." In the first place, Rostenkowski had hired him to avoid a trial. In addition, Bennett's simultaneous representation of Clinton raised Rostenkowski's fears that his lawyer faced a conflict of interest in fighting federal prosecutors while also representing the chief executive. (As it turned out, Clinton stayed on the sidelines during the Rostenkowski proceedings, an illustration of the world's most powerful leader's limited influence. Following the indictment, Clinton issued a brief statement that Rostenkowski was entitled "to have his day in court.") Aside from those problems, Bennett's alleged mishandling of the plea-bargaining with Holder caused his client to lose confidence. Rostenkowski wanted to distance himself from the dealing, even though he had been regularly informed. After he told an interviewer in June 1994, "I don't know whether or not my lawyer was negotiating," a lengthy news report concluded that his comments were "false," according to four sources knowledgeable about the discussions. "They say that Rostenkowski met regularly during May and fully discussed the plea negotiations with Bennett" and two other attorneys. But the same report took Bennett to task for having "badly failed his client Rostenkowski in the basic human—and, we believe, professional—obligation to consult him fully, to outline any foreseeable problems, and to explore any concerns that Rostenkowski might have had before Bennett took on President Clinton as a client."[25]

Rostenkowski's complaints indicated that their relationship deteriorated after Bennett urged him to admit responsibility for a crime when the client did not believe he was guilty. "Bennett was talking to Holder on the phone," said Rostenkowski, who wanted his counsel to talk face-to-face with his accuser. "I said to Bob that you are not negotiating and checking his body language. I told him that he was playing with my life. . . . Bennett says that this is the best way to handle it." But Bennett met face-to-face many times with Holder, sometimes without the prosecutor's assistants who vigorously opposed what they privately criticized as the proposed settlement's lenient terms. During and following his representation of Rostenkowski, Bennett was reluctant to discuss the case publicly or to respond to criticism from his client and Rostenkowski's friends. But he briefly described some of his frustrations during a 1994 interview with a reporter. "I am very disappointed in the second-guessers and the cheap-shot artists who are tigers in their criticisms but are lambs in terms of being identified. These cases are replete with complexities, nuances, and subtleties, and unless one is on the inside in all aspects of these cases, they really should not second-guess, particularly in an anonymous fashion. I gave my client everything I had and fully complied with all of my professional and ethical obligations. I am constrained by the attorney-client relationship not to deal in specifics."[26]

Rostenkowski turned next to Dan Webb, who had handled major corruption cases as a U.S. attorney from Chicago and was widely regarded as one of the nation's top litigators. Webb was a partner in the Chicago firm of Winston and Strawn, where another attorney was former Illinois governor Jim Thompson, a Republican who was also a pal of Rostenkowski. A month later Webb added to his team Kenneth Mundy, a prominent black attorney in Washington who was a skillful courtroom tactician and had represented local mayor Marion Barry in his trial on drug-possession charges. But Mundy never took a serious role in Rostenkowski's defense, and he died suddenly in April 1995. "When you were in my kind of a problem, you listen to everyone," said Rostenkowski, defending the turnover of lawyers. But the repeated shifts made him appear uncertain, even panic-stricken, over the downward spiral. "He would have been better served with consistent and unaltered representation," said Rob Leonard, his former Ways and Means staff director, on whom Rostenkowski relied for informal legal advice. "With the benefit of hindsight, he should have done like Jim Wright and played, 'Let's Make a Deal' and called off the federal hounds," said veteran Chicago alderman Edward Burke. "But no one told him that." Or perhaps Rostenkowski wasn't listening to the advice he was getting.

With the hiring of Webb, the case now bogged down in procedural struggles. Judge Johnson set a hearing on whether Rostenkowski was immune from prosecution because constitutional separation of powers protected members of Congress from being questioned for office practices they deemed essential to their "speech or debate." Sen. Dave Durenberger, a Minnesota Republican, had used a similar defense earlier in 1994 to win dismissal of an indictment that he had falsified his Senate expense account. "The interpretation of House rules and the decision whether to discipline a member for a violation of them is a matter constitutionally committed exclusively to the House," Webb wrote. The defense also argued that the five-year statute of limitations for most federal offenses barred many of the allegations. A week after the case was argued, Johnson ruled for the government on all constitutional challenges. But Webb filed an appeal with the federal appeals court in the District of Columbia. This time Rostenkowski's side fared better. On July 18, 1995, the three-judge panel ruled unanimously that as many as eight of the seventeen counts in the original indictment were potentially flawed because courts cannot interfere with congressional rules for the use of federal funds for "official" business. Two months earlier the Supreme Court had restricted the prosecution of legislative branch officials under the law that permits criminal actions against government employees who make false statements. In March 1996 Johnson dismissed four of the seventeen counts.

Amidst the maneuvering, Johnson set May 15, 1996, as the trial date. Rostenkowski and his attorneys insisted they were fully prepared. But two years of legal wrangling—on top of two previous years of investigation—had taken their toll financially. By mid-1995 Rostenkowski's campaign fund had spent more than $1.4 million on legal fees; its balance had dipped to $50,000. And he had depleted at least $1.4 million more from the legal defense fund that political allies and lobbyists had created for him in 1993 when he still had the clout of Ways and Means chairman.[27] Now that he was no longer a member of Congress, he was severely limited in raising funds from outsiders. And he owed Webb's legal team $1 million, with the prospect of incurring at least that much more in a full trial. Even though his financial disclosure reports when he was a member of Congress showed that his net worth probably exceeded $1 million, much of it was tied up in local real estate.

Rostenkowski's growing pessimism and fatigue added to his desire to call it quits. Although he welcomed the partial victories on procedural challenges, he increasingly acknowledged Bennett's earlier warning that some charges, especially payroll and stationery-store violations, would be difficult to rebut. In November 1995 came another despiriting event: Robert Russo, one of the alleged "ghost" employees who lived next door to Rostenkowski and who claimed to have cleaned his Chicago congressional office for many years, was found guilty of lying to the grand jury and obstruction of justice. With the prospect that he too faced conviction on some counts, Rostenkowski was staring at the inevitability of imprisonment. Quite simply, he was losing the means and the will to keep fighting. "I'm two years older into this thing," he said after his guilty plea. "You become apprehensive even picking up the phone. Every phone call is a bad phone call. You are laughing on the outside and dying on the inside."[28]

Weary of the fight, Rostenkowski told Webb in early 1996 that it was time to cut the best deal to end the case. Although he refused to confess to the stamps-for-cash allegations, he was prepared to admit that he had violated House rules on his payroll arrangements and stationery-store purchases. Too many events had transpired for Rostenkowski to revive the precise deal with Holder that he had turned down in May 1994; not least was that he no longer could leverage his House seat as a bargaining chip. Still, Holder was open to a deal. A months-long trial against Webb would consume the attention of several top Holder aides. And with Rostenkowski no longer in Congress, public interest in the case had waned. So the lawyers bargained on terms that were similar to what Rostenkowski had earlier rejected, except that he was forced to accept a longer prison term. In exchange for Rostenkowski pleading guilty on two counts, Holder and Webb agreed to dismiss the others. When Holder informally discussed the deal with Judge Johnson, she insisted that federal sentencing guidelines required at least a seventeen-month sentence. Rostenkowski also agreed to pay a fine of $100,000, but he received credit for the $82,095 that he had returned to the Treasury in 1994. All that remained was the formal presentation of the agreement to the judge and her ratification.

A poignant interlude took place hours before Rostenkowski's guilty plea. Meeting at his lawyers' office in Washington, he received a telephone call from Clinton. "I've been thinking of you," the president began. With Rostenkowski telling his lawyers to remain in the room, the two of them chatted amiably about such current topics as Clinton's improving re-election prospects, Bob Dole's shortcomings in campaign debates, and the Republicans' boycotting of the recent funeral of Commerce Secretary Ron Brown, who had died in an airplane crash. Even though Clinton did not discuss the criminal case, "I could almost sense the pain with him," Rostenkowski recounted. Clinton ended the conversation, "I wish you well, pal."

The final scene played out on April 9, 1996, a cold and rainy Tuesday. The scene inside the federal courthouse was equally grim. A few minutes before 5 p.m., Rostenkowski arrived with his lawyers at Courtroom Four; he was accompanied by neither family nor friends. Gone too were the aides and lobbyists who surrounded him when he was the boss on Capitol Hill, a few blocks away. He walked straight ahead, not acknowledging the two dozen reporters who were already seated. Wearing a grey tweed sport jacket, he sat at the defendant's table between two of his attorneys. After he impatiently checked the clock on the back wall and his own watch, he scrunched his face, then he shrugged. Holder and several prosecution attorneys sat in the first row on the left side of the courtroom. When Judge Johnson entered at 5:01 and sat at the wide bench in the front of the courtroom, most of the events were scripted. As Rostenkowski cupped his chin in one hand, Webb and Assistant U.S. Attorney Thomas Motley stepped toward Johnson. "I am informed that you are both here today in connection with a plea agreement that the United States and the defendant have agreed to," she said. Motley announced the outlines of the agreement, and Webb stated that Rostenkowski consented to the terms. Then Rostenkowski stepped forward with Webb, reviewed the six-page agreement he had already signed, and quietly responded, "Yes, ma'am," when Johnson asked if he was prepared to enter his guilty plea. Johnson asked Rostenkowski several more questions to assure that he was knowingly and voluntarily agreeing to the two charges. His responses were brief and soft-spoken. More than a dozen times he answered, "Yes, ma'am," "No, your honor," and the like. It was a stark change from his customary role when he gruffly asked the questions.

Following these preliminary steps, Motley summarized the case against Rostenkowski, not only on the two counts to which he pleaded guilty but also on the post office and car-leasing arrangements. "The government would have proved a broader scheme at trial, one involving all four areas," he said. "With his plea of guilty, Mr. Rostenkowski admits his responsibility for this fundamental fraud." Johnson asked for a response. Reading from a statement, and with the requisite contrition, Rostenkowski said, "While I served in Congress, I knew that some employees I caused to be placed on my congressional payroll, on occasion, did perform personal and political services for me during times they were compensated for performing congressional duties in violation of House rules." As to the purchased items, he added, "Over the years, while I served in Congress, I occasionally obtained merchandise from the House stationery store that I knowingly caused to be charged to Congress. I knowingly gave some of this merchandise as gifts to constituents and political supporters in violation of House rules." He then pleaded guilty to two counts, including the seventeen-month sentence.

The hearing took several unusual twists. First, both attorneys waived the customary presentencing report, which is designed to assist the judge in determining the length of imprisonment. Such a review can take several weeks, but Webb requested that Johnson impose the "immediate sentence," as had been informally agreed. Rostenkowski was eager to begin—and complete—his prison time. After Webb cited Rostenkowski's thirty-six years of congressional service "that has truly had a profound impact on the nation," he added that the defendant recognized and was "willing to accept the consequences for those mistakes." But Johnson broke the quiet, almost reverential, tone with a blistering attack on Rostenkowski's conduct. "When I think of these proceedings," she said, "the one phrase that comes to my mind is betrayal of trust," both with his constituents and the nation. "In your important position in Congress, you have consistently and egregiously pursued a course of personal gain for yourself and those whom you favored, including family and friends. You have stained them as well as yourself and the high position you held by your crimes and misdeeds. You have brought a measure of disgrace upon the institution of which you had the privilege of serving for an extraordinary number of years. Rather than advance its noble purposes and lawmaking with the great experience and power you acquired, you shamelessly abused your position." Finally, before announcing the sanctions, Johnson sternly and contemptuously jammed the knife into Rostenkowski for one final twist: "The burden you and your family will be serving beyond your period of confinement will be the burden of conscience and the burden of public disgrace that will always be associated with your tenure in the Congress of this nation." Johnson's lecture left him "aghast," Rostenkowski later said. "This ding-a-ling judge wants me on my knees," he said. "Dan Webb told me to keep quiet."

The next surprise came when Johnson required that Rostenkowski pay a $1,800 monthly "cost of incarceration" to the Bureau of Prisons, which judges waive in most federal cases. Citing debts, including family responsibilities and legal fees, that had "exhausted his financial resources," Webb asked Johnson to reconsider. As Rostenkowski stood silently with his arms folded, Johnson said she needed information about his finances from the Bureau of Prisons or the court's probation department. "If he can't afford it, then I will gladly withdraw it," she said. Later Rostenkowski agreed to pay the monthly fee rather than submit an accounting of his assets. Finally Webb asked Johnson to recommend that Rostenkowski be sent to the federal penitentiary in Oxford, Wisconsin, which he termed the closest "suitable" facility where he could receive visitors. After she agreed, Webb asked that Rostenkowski have forty-five days to "get his affairs in order." Without giving a reason, Johnson reduced to thirty days the period for his voluntary surrender.

After the fifty-minute hearing concluded and the judge departed through a side door, attorneys for both sides gave printed statements to reporters. Rostenkowski stood with both hands in his pockets as Webb briefly spoke with him. Then he walked quickly from the courtroom and headed one flight down an escalator and exited into the steady rain. Without an umbrella, he stared into a bank of ten television cameras and read a two-page statement. The time for contrition was over. Emphasizing that he had confessed to the least serious charges and that he was not guilty of the post-office and obstruction-of-justice claims in the indictment, he took the offensive. "I do not believe that I am any different than the vast majority of the Members of Congress, and their staffs, who have experienced enormous difficulty in determining whether particular services by congressional employees should be classified as congressional, political or personal." Adding that he had been asked whether he was bitter, Rostenkowski continued, "While I deeply regret the trauma that this intense scrutiny has bestowed upon my family, friends and supporters, I personally have come to accept the fact that sometimes one person gets singled out, to be held up by law enforcement as an example. I simply have to accept that and move forward with my life." Finally he told reporters that he thanked his friends and supporters, and he said, "I intend to be actively involved in public life" following imprisonment. Rostenkowski then stepped aside. Webb told reporters that "life isn't fair" and that Rostenkowski had been "singled out." Without responding to questions, Rostenkowski then slipped into the front seat of a waiting Pontiac, which quickly pulled away. For the remaining reporters, Holder had tough comments about Rostenkowski's betrayal of the public trust. Pointing to the Capitol, he added, "People are not sent to that institution up there to line their pockets."

With Rostenkowski no longer a public figure, his guilty plea received less news coverage than had his indictment. The *New York Times* ran a one-column news story on page 20.[29] In an editorial the *Times* called the result "an appropriately stern punishment that carries a loud warning against official corruption." And, partly because the public statements came after 6 p.m., the three network news programs that evening only briefly summarized the story. But it was page-one news in Chicago and

Washington. Probably the most sympathetic press reaction came from *Chicago Tribune* columnist Mike Royko, who gave a local rejoinder to Judge Johnson's harsh criticism. "Being a public figure, [Rostenkowski] is held to a higher standard," Royko wrote. "And sometimes, it isn't exactly fair. Only a few decades ago, none of this would have been happening. That's because the rules changed. Most of the things he was nailed for would have been legal and common or, at worst, nickel-dime offenses when he began his career in Congress. That's the way it is in our society. The rules keep changing. Things we could once say or think are now taboo."[30]

On Capitol Hill, where Congress was shut down for the spring recess, there was a conspicuous silence, as though Rostenkowski were part of a discredited old guard that voters had swept away in November 1994. Perhaps Democrats' second thoughts had been fueled by the seventy-three first-term House Republicans who "ran against not just Rostenkowski but against precisely those qualities he undeniably represented," wrote political scientist Norman Ornstein.[31] Among the diminishing ranks of senior members who had dealt most closely with him, Rostenkowski's courtroom saga was a sad moment that mirrored the passing of an era. His offenses "seem like small potatoes that came out of politics of a different time," said Rep. Anthony Beilenson, a California Democrat. "I can't believe he's venal or corrupt. He was inattentive and he continued the old ways." Bill Frenzel, the Minnesota Republican who worked closely with Rostenkowski at Ways and Means, called the offenses less a case of greed than "a case of everybody did it. . . . He took the hit for the whole House for practices that were there since time immemorial." Still, Frenzel did not seek to justify Rostenkowski's actions. "He broke the law and he should pay the penalty. . . . There is still too much money and personal adulation in the system, especially for a Ways and Means chairman."

Months later, Rostenkowski was anything but repentant. "I'm here [in prison] for what I admitted tongue in cheek," he said. "I don't think I'm isolated as the only one who did it. . . . I'm not completely convinced that what I did was wrong." Dispensing gifts to some friends and hiring the children of others was "my way of life," he added. He worked hard at his job, he said, and he didn't have time to pay attention to all the rules changes. He remained emphatic that he did not participate in stamps-for-cash practices.

After Joe Kolter of Pennsylvania, the Democrat who was identified as

"Congressman B" in the Rota indictment, pleaded guilty in May 1996 to receiving $9,300 from such transactions, Rostenkowski denied any connection between the two cases. But prosecutors seized on Kolter's admission to assert that they could have shown similar violations by Rostenkowski. "This proves that Robert Rota was giving cash to Congressmen," said John M. Campbell, the head of the public corruption team in the U.S. attorney's office.[32] As far as much of the press was concerned, the alleged stamp transactions were obvious. When Rota received a four-month prison term, the *Washington Post* reported as a matter of fact that Rota was sentenced "for supplying former representatives Dan Rostenkowski and Joseph P. Kolter with cash in exchange for stamps." Without mentioning that prosecutors had dropped the charges against him, the *Post* added that Rostenkowski "continues to deny" that he received $20,000 in cash for stamps.[33] Likewise Judge Johnson showed her continuing hostility when she said at Rota's hearing, "I know these powerful men perhaps had such an influence on you that it was difficult to overcome, and it took a long time for you to stand up and say what was really happening."[34] She neglected to mention that, on the prosecution's recommendation, she had dismissed the post office charges against Rostenkowski.

Rostenkowski's imprisonment, set for May 9, was delayed by the Bureau of Prisons' indecision as to where he should report, and unexpected surgery at Walter Reed Army Medical Center in Washington on May 17 to remove a cancerous prostate. The operation normally requires a two-month recovery period. Following guidelines of the Bureau of Prisons, which lacks facilities for postoperative cancer treatment, Judge Johnson agreed to postpone his reporting date. On June 3, however, she ordered him to report two weeks later to the Bureau of Prisons' Federal Medical Center in Rochester, Minnesota. But his attorneys asked to delay the date of his surrender until July 22, and they requested that he report directly to Oxford, Wisconsin, as she had tentatively agreed. In part, they wrote, they wanted to spare him a move between the two prison facilities in an "unnecessary, uncomfortable and embarrassing transfer by bus in shackles." His attorneys noted his physician's estimate that Rostenkowski would not regain full control of his urinary system until late July and that "the cost of maintaining a patient at the Rochester medical center is far greater than that of housing an inmate" at Oxford. Rostenkowski, who made clear that he did not want to delay his prison term, also wanted to continue his treatment from the Washington doctor who had performed the surgery.

In what became a test of wills, Rostenkowski—before his imprisonment—was ordered to undergo a physical examination in late June at the Mayo Clinic in Minnesota; that hospital performs most procedures for the nearby Federal Medical Center. Johnson ruled on July 3 that his confinement would begin on July 22, as he requested. Even though he had received a clean bill of health, however, she insisted that he surrender at the prison hospital in Rochester, which has higher security than the Oxford facility. On that day he reported to a small office behind the prison in Rochester, beyond the range of news reporters and photographers who hoped to detail his humiliation. That began Rostenkowski's nearly five-month period as a medical patient, even though he had fully recovered from his surgery. Why? Every two or three weeks he went to Mayo for various examinations. "They didn't know what to do with me," he said. "They wanted to be thorough." In all likelihood the judge's stubborn decision forced the Rochester officials to be more meticulous than medical circumstance warranted. The delay offered an insight into the bureaucracy-ridden Bureau of Prisons, where many decisions are made with no apparent rhyme or reason. Not until December 11 was Rostenkowski moved to Oxford, about two hundred miles from Chicago and fifty miles from Peter Rostenkowski's birthplace in Stevens Point.

At Oxford for the next eight months, Rostenkowski lived with about 150 inmates who were minimal security risks. The prison camp, located in a rural area in central Wisconsin about eight miles from a state highway, has no fence between the nearby parking lot and the inmate facility, nor any bars on the inside. Inmates had an obvious incentive not to wander far if they wished to keep their incarceration as brief as possible. Rostenkowski took a four-mile walk on the prison grounds nearly every day. In the relatively hospitable environment, he shared a room with two other men. Adjacent to the prison camp is a sprawling federal correctional institute that houses more than 1,000 men; it is a more conventional prison with prisoners kept behind bars, two guard towers, high barbed-wire fences surrounding the grounds, and rolled wire at the base of the fence. Prison-camp inmates perform menial tasks at the adjacent facility. Rostenkowski, for example, was assigned to read meters on the boiler—a task that permitted him plenty of time for books, exercise, and sending occasional complaints to the Justice Department about what he viewed as unfair treatment by Judge Johnson and prison officials. It was apparent that he received no preferential treatment from the criminal justice system.

Rostenkowski was stoic about his imprisonment. "It's like the army, but we don't march," he told friends. He expressed little concern for his well-being. If he was ashamed, he voiced it chiefly in terms of failure to care for his family. In prison he made the striking decision to refuse visitors from the outside world. Presumably because of his humiliation, he turned down all requests from acquaintances in Chicago and Washington. Although prison-camp inmates were entitled to visitors on alternate weekends, he said he wanted no friends or family members—"especially my family," he said—to see him under those conditions. As a result, even though his attorneys had requested assignment to Oxford because it would be more convenient for his family, he did not see his wife and four daughters for more than a year; he did speak regularly with them and others on the prison telephone.

Even when he agreed to permit me to visit him, he demanded that I not discuss or write about his conditions before his release. He did not wish to jeopardize his early release, he said. During eight hours of conversations over a two-day period, he was eerily like the Rostenkowski of Capitol Hill. He was remarkably well informed about current events. He was animated, feisty, and hopeful about his future, including the prospect of private-sector work. In dealing with other prisoners, he said, "I'm very quiet and introverted. I don't try to solve anybody's problems and I don't assume anything. . . . Some inmates come to me. But I don't want to build up hopes that I can solve their problems." He complained about the camp's lack of services and the political pressure to deprive prisoners of customary privileges, including exercise equipment and programming on two television sets, such as the HBO cable network. "They don't want to educate us or to occupy our time," he said. "What do they want an inmate to do?" For the most part he focused on avoiding further trouble and ending his imprisonment as quickly as possible. One positive effect was that his improved diet—no steak or booze, obviously—plus regular exercise resulted in a substantial weight loss. During his first eight months at Rochester and Oxford, he shrunk from a beefy 279 pounds to a svelte 211.

With his experience and skill in the exercise of power, Rostenkowski understood the need for prison discipline. The regimentation was reminiscent of operating as a cog in an old-fashioned precinct organization. "I'm just a number here," he said. "I don't mind that at all. I don't give anyone the impression that I'm a know-it-all." Wearing an olive-green polyester uniform, he did not look so different from many other inmates who also were meeting with visitors around card tables in a small cafeteria.[35] Following his prison release, he said, he wanted to resume a normal life "so that people won't see me as a novelty. . . . It will take four or five times before people no longer say, 'There's Dan Rostenkowski, the felon.' Then I'll again be the average citizen." Did he miss the fancy dinners and high life to which he had become accustomed? "I adjust to the situation," he responded. "When I get out of here, I'll be Danny Rostenkowski again. I have enjoyed my life."

Chapter Eleven

THE DEMOCRATS' LEGACY

AS ROSTENKOWSKI WARNED, his departure brought *le déluge* to the House. But the 1994 election changes extended far beyond the chairmanship of the Ways and Means Committee or a new representative from Chicago. With the Republican takeover, the House moved boldly into a new era. The radical upheaval was spearheaded by Newt Gingrich, who vaulted from the House's backbench to command the legislative agenda as speaker. At times the new overseers went out of their way to contrast how Rostenkowski and his brethren had run the House. Gone were the independent chairmen, the back-room deal-making, and the yearning to work with the president. In their places were a new team of leaders and chairmen emphasizing cooperation with one another, an aggressive salesmanship of their program, and a strutting independence from the White House. That was the theory, at least. In reality the Republicans' game plan to downsize the federal government suffered an unexpected comeuppance in 1995 and electoral setbacks in 1996 and 1998. But Democrats failed to regain control, evidence that the 1994 results were not a fluke. With Gingrich resigning under pressure after his poor 1998 election results and his flock retaining a razor-thin majority, it will take years to gauge the House Republican's ultimate impact. In any case, their control provided a useful prism to examine the forty-year Democratic era in the House and especially at the Ways and Means Committee.

Bill Archer of Texas, the new Ways and Means chairman, stressed the need for teamwork. He moved deliberately to demystify the aura of his rank. "I would rather work with colleagues and tell them on a collegial basis where we intend to go," Archer said after he took over. He drew a contrast with Rostenkowski who, he said, "came out of the Daley school of politics. . . . He made his own decisions and kept his own counsel." But the committee that had savored its autonomy took a back seat during the 1995 session, when Gingrich set an aggressively partisan tone in seeking to reshape the federal budget. Reminiscent of Al Ullman, who headed Ways and Means in the late 1970s, Archer also pursued a futile quest to junk the federal income tax code and replace it with a nationwide consumption tax; in contrast to Ullman, however, Archer's safe Republican district in Houston's suburbs meant that he had no fear of losing reelection. There were other major changes. Many Republicans joined Ways and Means after serving only a brief House apprenticeship. Party leaders assigned members to the committee who had neither electoral security nor the legislative cachet that once were prerequisites; these newcomers won their slots in part as an opportunity to bolster their campaign fundraising.

Rostenkowski and Archer had had a chilly relationship when the strongly conservative Texan was the committee's ranking Republican and Rostenkowski typically sought out other Republicans to cut deals. Archer—who in 1970 won the House seat previously held by George Bush—was frustrated that Rostenkowski refused to confide in him. The two "wanted to get along but they never did," said former Ways and Means Democrat Mike Andrews, whose Houston-based district was adjacent to Archer's. "Each talked to me ruefully about the problem." At the root of the conflict were Rostenkowski's view that Archer was unwilling to compromise, and Archer's objections to making a deal on terms that forced him to support an entire bill. "Dan Rostenkowski didn't like Bill Archer because Archer would complain and moan about a provision," said Ray McGrath, the New York Republican who often sided with Rostenkowski. "Then Rostenkowski would give in and Archer would still vote against the bill."

Most Republicans preferred Archer's gentler approach as chairman. "He has this ability to control with a smile on his face," said Jennifer Dunn, who joined Ways and Means in 1995. "He doesn't overpower people the way that Rostenkowski might have. In debate he serves as a moderator, but he doesn't hesitate to let us know his position." In 1993 she had joined other Republicans marching to Ways and Means to object to its plan to raise taxes, but, she said, "They slammed the door in our face."

Archer also abandoned Rostenkowski's practice of dispensing special-interest tax breaks to lawmakers who supported his bills. From the start of his chairmanship, he pointedly disdained "deal-cutting" or "heavy-handed" efforts to win support. "This chairman prefers to do what is right," said a spokesman.

Although few Republicans during the 1994 national campaign singled out Rostenkowski's strong-armed control or his indictment, they offered pointed contrasts between the two parties. "The Democrats' iron-handed, one-party rule of the House of Representatives over the last four decades led to arcane, arbitrary and often secretive procedures that disenfran-chised millions of Americans from representation in Congress," accord-ing to the Contract with America, their successful campaign tract.[1] One of the new majority's first steps was to impose a six-year term limit on their committee chairmen; designed to prevent a reprise of Rostenkowski's un-fettered thirteen-year reign as chairman, that restriction led Archer to plan his retirement in 2000. Republicans made additional changes to reduce the clout of chairmen. They eliminated "proxy voting," which gave chair-men the power to dictate the outcome of a vote with the support of mem-bers who were absent from a committee debate. Another controversial reform required a three-fifths vote in the House to increase income tax rates. Sponsors said the reform was designed to weaken the ability of Ways and Means leaders to raise taxes. More broadly, Gingrich in 1995 sent a direct message to the new chairmen—and those interested in suc-ceeding them—when he bypassed several senior Republicans, whom he viewed as too passive, in appointing committee chairmen. At that point, no one was in a position to challenge Gingrich's choices or his authority. "Like Eisenhower in World War II, [Gingrich] is the Supreme Comman-der," said Rep. Bill Paxon of New York, then a leading Gingrich ally.

Gingrich's power shift was evident on issues facing Ways and Means. Probably the two most controversial bills the House passed during the hundred-day blizzard of proposals from the Contract with America were welfare reform and tax cuts. In each case, party leaders prepared the broad outlines and left Archer to do little more than fix some details. Many major decisions, Archer said at the time, were resolved at a "higher pay grade"—that is, by Gingrich and Majority Leader Richard Armey of Texas. It would be hard to imagine such deference from chairmen Ros-tenkowski or Wilbur Mills, who flaunted their independence from the House speaker. In mostly private comments, Rostenkowski was contemptuous of Archer's acquiescence in the face of attacks on his influence. "What is the sense in being chairman if you can't stamp out the legislation?" he asked. "I was sick enough to throw up when Bill Archer gave up control to the House Budget Committee" during the 1995 budget debate on tax and Medicare changes, he said, with a pound of the table. When Gingrich conducted high-stakes budget negotiations with President Clinton in late 1995, which ultimately ended in deadlock and a federal shutdown, he relied more heavily on Budget Committee chairman John Kasich. Although Archer and other chairmen privately complained about the limitations, Gingrich displayed his control with House passage of all parts of the Contract with America except for the constitutional amendment to limit the number of terms members could serve in Congress. Each measure had nearly unanimous Republican support.

Although dismayed by his legislation, veteran Democrats were awed by Gingrich's parliamentary mastery. Tom Downey recalled that the large class of "Watergate babies" was viewed as revolutionaries because "we interviewed committee chairmen." But that was "nothing compared with some of Gingrich's revolutionary changes," he said. Over four decades the Democrats' power relationships had become deeply entrenched and difficult to alter. "It was not pleasant to see legislation move so quickly and to know that we could have done more when we were in the majority," said Barbara Kennelly of Connecticut. "Gingrich has shown that you can have strong leadership," said another Ways and Means Democrat, who said that new leaders would apply that lesson when Democrats took back the House. Former Speaker Jim Wright, who met resistance from Rostenkowski and others when he sought to centralize power, also envied the changes. "Gingrich doesn't have to contend with a matrix of habits and expectations that had built up over forty years," Wright said. "Everything was new." He would have failed if he had sought more control of chairmen when he became speaker, Wright added, because "it would have been seen as a grasp for personal power."

Rostenkowski was more direct in praising the new Republican chief. "I'm impressed with Speaker Gingrich, who understands that leadership requires both boldness and discipline," he told leaders at Abbott Laboratories, a Chicago-area pharmaceutical firm. "The Democrats should learn some lessons from him." But he worried about Gingrich's dogmatic partisanship. "By using his office as a bully pulpit, [Gingrich] undermined the freedom to negotiate that a working legislature requires," he wrote in a

1996 article that was never published. Rostenkowski worried that "By centralizing power that was once dispersed to the committees, [Gingrich] denied the committee chairmen the role in crafting compromises that has historically been theirs."

The Rostenkowski years at Ways and Means were finished, and not only in name. Gone was the era in which the bipartisan committee operated as an autonomous inner sanctum. Instead intraparty consensus was the new aim. Was this a reaction to Rostenkowski's occasional independence? In a sense, yes. Members of both parties sought to limit or discourage committee leaders acting as "Lone Rangers" to push unpopular legislation. So, for example, when vocal objections by senior citizens to Medicare cutbacks reminded some of opposition to the earlier catastrophic health-insurance law, chairman Archer was forced to respond to pressure for change. Members also wanted to ensure that their chairmen would be team players. In ways that Mills would have viewed as demeaning, the new chairmen were obliged to stand behind loyally as party leaders launched an initiative, or to stroke deep-pocket campaign contributors.

Congressional power shifts can be a mixed blessing. Party unity often is worthwhile in prompting accountability. But the new strictures limited the freedom of chairmen to respond to complex circumstances. If Rostenkowski had been forced to gain Speaker Tip O'Neill's approval at each step of the tax-reform debate—as Jim Wright demanded—that would have reduced the chairman's flexibility to resolve differences among competing interests. Too often, leaders not familiar with intricate issues are unable to bridge differences or their deals fall apart. That was the result both in 1990, when the House rejected the budget deal that Democratic leaders and top officials of the Bush White House had stitched together at Andrews Air Force Base, and in the collapse of the 1995 budget negotiations between Clinton and Gingrich. More than a century ago, Woodrow Wilson, a young Princeton University political science professor who later became president, wrote, "Congress in its committee rooms is Congress at work."[2] Wilson understood the place for expertise—and, yes, the trading of favors—in policymaking. His wisdom merits deference.

Ways and Means Democrats endured painful adjustments. On most issues the new minority was irrelevant to the outcome. Sam Gibbons displayed little influence during two years as the ranking minority member on Ways and Means, which followed his seven months in 1994 as acting chairman. His weak performance justified the earlier fears of many senior Democrats. He was independent, erratic, and not much of a leader in working with either Republicans or the White House. During the March 1995 debate on welfare reform, he repeatedly yelled, "Shut up," when Republicans moved to close House debate. In October, while Ways and Means was debating the Republicans' proposal to overhaul Medicare, Gibbons was so infuriated that he had a nasty and well-publicized exchange in which he pulled at the tie of California Republican William Thomas in a Capitol hallway. Instead many Democratic strategies were crafted by large groups in Dick Gephardt's minority leader office. "There has been much more participation in policy development than we [Democrats] have ever had," said Benjamin Cardin of Maryland, a Ways and Means member. Sometimes, however, that created bad feelings. On welfare reform, many liberals griped about the conservative Democrats' disproportionate influence in designing their alternative. Given the partisan dynamics of 1995–1996, it is perilous to speculate that Rostenkowski would have been more productive in the same position. Still, the problems confirmed Rostenkowski's doubts about his intraparty adversaries.

After the 1994 election Democrats abandoned their historic dream to provide government assurance of adequate health care for all Americans. Instead they embraced Rostenkowski's incremental approach. In 1996 they won Republican support for a limited proposal to prevent insurance companies from denying coverage to individuals switching jobs or with preexisting illnesses; Rostenkowski had advocated a similar plan five years earlier that also imposed additional obligations on insurance carriers. Then, in 1997, Democrats worked with Republicans to pass legislation assuring adequate health-care coverage for children. Democrats also dropped their second-guessing of Republican attempts to fix the crisis in Medicare finances. Initially Gingrich and the Republicans called for reducing the growth rate in spending to "preserve, strengthen and protect" Medicare; their proposal called for a net reduction of $270 billion over seven years. Clinton and congressional Democratic leaders failed to offer much support. Starting in mid-1995 the Democrats' mantra was that Republicans were "cutting Medicare to pay for tax cuts for the rich." Rostenkowski deplored the partisan gridlock. "Voters are frustrated by inaction, and they don't make subtle distinctions between Democrat and Republican," he said in early 1996. The Democrats' Medicare refrain was nevertheless a political success, and they hammered on it through the

1996 election. In 1997, however, when both Clinton and Gingrich decided to cool the rhetoric and reach a budget deal, they quietly included many of the Medicare changes that had been partisan flash points.

Although the 1996 election stemmed the Democrats' decline, the contest did little to inspire the nation or to revive the nation's oldest party. In winning only 49 percent of the vote, Clinton extended the mark to eight consecutive elections in which the Democratic presidential nominee received less than 51 percent of the popular vote. Not since Lyndon Johnson in 1964 had a Democrat won a convincing national mandate. Clinton succeeded in 1996 while again keeping his distance from congressional Democrats, to their chagrin; and he offered few compelling goals to guide his second term. After they gained nine House seats that year—falling ten short of regaining control—Capitol Hill Democrats were all the more irate that the Clinton campaign gave low priority to their interests. In the 1998 elections Democrats gained five more House seats, with the help of a late-session budget showdown and the Republicans' virtually nonexistent national agenda. But their campaign message was severely blunted by the news media's relentless focus that year on Kenneth Starr's investigation of Clinton's relationship with Monica Lewinsky. Even though many of them severely condemned his behavior, Democrats were nearly unanimous in opposing the House's postelection impeachment vote. But the president, who had come to Washington with little experience in bipartisanship, found himself handcuffed for the remainder of his presidency by divided government. The contrast to Rostenkowski's successful second-term dealings with the Reagan White House could not have been more striking.

The House Democrats' minority status highlighted the changed partisan dynamics of national politics from the time when Rostenkowski had come to Washington. Then, Democrats dominated in the South, in the nation's cities, and in rural areas. Four decades later the old coalition was barely recognizable. In the 14 Southern states, their total House seats were cut in half, from 116 in 1959 to 58 in 1999, even though reapportionment gave the region 16 additional districts. Furthermore, the large increase in black House Democrats from the South—there were none before 1973—meant that the number of white Southern Democrats dropped to 37. In the nation's largest cities, Democrats still held most seats. But the black and Hispanic increase, at the same time total population was shrinking, came at the expense of more conservative white Democrats. Chicago is a typical example. When Rostenkowski joined the delegation in 1959, nine of the city's ten House Democrats were white. Four decades later they included three whites, three blacks, and one Hispanic. In both North and South, racial minorities took a more expansive view of federal spending for domestic programs. (A prime example was Charles Rangel of New York, who became the senior Ways and Means Democrat in 1997.) These shifts help to explain why the Democratic party's center of gravity moved substantially to the left. Self-styled centrist Democrats such as Rostenkowski felt isolated.

In spite of these sweeping shifts, could Democrats have avoided their 1994 downfall? Perhaps, if they had coalesced behind some version of health reform. But a variety of circumstances ambushed that scenario, not the least of which was Rostenkowski's preoccupation with his legal problems. "There was an arrogance of power," said a Clinton administration official who worked closely with House Democrats. "Democrats may have lost touch with the grass roots after forty years." Still, from a historical perspective, forty years was an exceedingly long rule. That Democrats managed to keep their House majority for as long as they did was both a political marvel and a historical misfortune. With the enterprise of savvy operators such as Democratic campaign boss Tony Coelho in the 1980s, they skillfully exploited the powers of incumbency, both within the House and from outside special-interest groups. But to what end? True enough, Democrats retained their chairmanships and their control of the power levers, which is the goal of any self-respecting political party. As Republicans knew painfully well and as Democrats learned in 1995, life as the House minority carries few benefits or motivations, other than to attain the majority. But clinging to control for forty years also forced House Democrats to make sacrifices and to forgo opportunities and the essential self-renewal that can result from a periodic cleansing of the political process. And their reign probably would have expired soon, in any case. Until a few months before the 1994 election, most Republicans expected to take over two years later. Once the Democrats imploded on health care, Gingrich accelerated his aggressive strategy to highlight Democratic shortcomings and demonstrate that Republicans offered credible policies to run the House.

As for Rostenkowski, the private citizen now spent considerable time building business relationships. Working out of the office at his Chicago home, he provided advice to local corporate executives on dealing with local and national governments. In several cases this was a payback: these same elites had sought his help when he was chairman, and he aided their contribution to the city's dynamic growth. With Virginia Fletcher, the longtime manager of his Capitol Hill office, he also maintained a modest office in an Arlington, Virginia, business suite managed by the Near North National Group, a Chicago-based insurance company; that firm was operated by several longtime friends who had been Democratic officials in Chicago. Although he released few details of his work for Near North, he advised that company both on prospects in Washington and on potential clients.

During his first year in private life, Rostenkowski boasted that he earned more income than he had ever received annually as a public official. He spent virtually no time on Capitol Hill. But his Washington visits allowed regular contact with his circle of friends and former aides, who kept him well versed on the latest political news and gossip, plus occasional chats with reporters. All of that was interrupted, of course, by his guilty plea in April 1996 and his subsequent imprisonment. Having acquired a taste for the private sector, he eagerly resumed that work after his prison release. In 1998 he also added television news analysis, including election commentary, to his portfolio. Local television executives and critics were impressed with his talent. "He gave insight into strategy and what was going on behind the scenes," said news director Debra West of WFLD-TV in Chicago. "He was very natural." *Sun-Times* TV-radio columnist Rob Feder observed that Rostenkowski had "just the right mix of inside knowledge and cynicism."

Despite his imprisonment by federal officials, Rostenkowski remained positive on Clinton. While a prison inmate he sent lengthy letters advising the president on various policy and political matters; veteran Democratic aides at the Ways and Means Committee, whom Rostenkowski continued to term "my staff," helped to prepare the correspondence. Rostenkowski said he had been told reliably that Clinton read and welcomed the advice. "I really like Bill Clinton, and I get emotional about it," he said in early 1997. After his release from Oxford, he described the national political scene to civic groups in Chicago. "The president's personal problems are much less important than the decline in the unifying power of either political party," he told the City Club in April 1998. "The leaders are there, but followers are increasingly difficult to find." As a television commentator he attacked the House Republicans' handling of impeachment, though he also criticized Clinton's behavior. Following his prison term, Rostenkowski was a guest at several political events, where he basked in the praise of fellow Democrats. At an April 1998 White House celebration of the economy, during which Clinton singled him out for praise, Rostenkowski was "welcomed by his former colleagues—with applause and hugs—like a redeemed martyr."[3] But his view of the Democrats' future was clouded by his contempt for Gephardt's undue partisanship and catering to interest groups, such as organized labor on international trade and the elderly on Medicare. In seeking to lead the Democrats back to a House majority and planning another possible presidential bid, Gephardt showed too much independence from Clinton, Rostenkowski complained. "I have told [Clinton] consistently, don't you close both eyes in the presence of Dick Gephardt," he told a handful of Washington reporters in late 1995.

Rostenkowski's district experienced major change too, but it reverted to business-as-usual more quickly than did many other remnants of the House Democrats' empire. Although his House successor took a few steps to separate himself from the lockstep conservatism of the seventy-three Republican freshmen, the pro-gun and pro-tobacco views of Michael Patrick Flanagan seemed a better fit for that class's mostly Southern and suburban outlines than for Chicago's cosmopolitan north side. The political outsider also abandoned his neighborhood-kid profile that he had used to oust his predecessor. He never developed a credible persona or plan to win reelection in the Democratic-leaning district. His 1994 victory, it became clear, had little to do with his own performance; instead it was a thumbs-down on Rostenkowski, the timeworn and criminally liable incumbent.

Whatever his own legacy for national leadership or hometown projects, after 1994 Rostenkowski retained little political influence in Chicago. His disappearance from the radar scope became apparent during the 1996 campaign for his former seat. With Flanagan's endangered status, two eager state representatives became the front-runners for the Democratic nomination to oppose him. Rod Blagojevich and Nancy Kaszak had several things in common. Both were lawyers who had begun political careers on Chicago's north side at a young age. In 1992 each had been elected to the state legislature after defeating Democratic incumbents backed by Rostenkowski's organization. Despite the yuppie enclaves in parts of the district, both the Serbian Blagojevich and the Polish Kaszak emphasized their ethnic backgrounds. And they treated Rostenkowski as a distant figure with little relevance to his former constituents. "People don't really talk much about him," Blagojevich said.

In their hard-fought primary contest, each candidate combined old and new politics in ways that Rostenkowski had resisted. Kaszak initially gained local attention leading protests against Chicago Cubs night baseball at Wrigley Field. With that base, she styled her career as a citizen activist and good-government candidate. A vital part of her 1996 campaign was support from Emily's List, a national political-action committee that endorses Democratic women who take a pro-choice position on abortion. With the group's "bundling" of small campaign contributions from its members, the backing yielded several hundred thousand dollars for Kaszak, most of it from outside her district. Blagojevich started with the strong support of his father-in-law, Alderman Richard Mell, whose effective get-out-the-vote organization had helped to salvage Rostenkowski's reelection in 1994. Mell, who had placed Blagojevich on his city payroll even before the 1990 marriage to his daughter, viewed politics as a family matter; Rod and Patti originally met at a fund-raising event for her father. While welcoming Mell's support, Blagojevich emphasized that he was not an "organization pol." During his 1996 campaign he focused on his success in building bipartisan coalitions in Springfield on property-tax relief and tougher sentencing standards for criminals. Although Kaszak criticized Blagojevich's ties to Mell, she had welcomed Mell's support for her 1992 election to the legislature.

As the primary vote approached, the war of words between the two candidates grew more nasty. Kaszak criticized Blagojevich's "old-style machine politics." In a television advertisement her campaign claimed, "Blagojevich and his alderman father-in-law have shaken down city contractors and employees for tens of thousands of dollars. That stinks." Blagojevich criticized Kaszak's ineffectiveness as a legislator and listed his endorsements from several prominent Chicago-area women legislators. He won a big boost when Mayor Daley took the unusual step of intervening in the primary, largely because of pressure from Mell. On election eve the *Chicago Tribune* reported that "the Kaszak camp has acknowledged that it has no evidence to back up the accusation of campaign shakedowns made in her TV commercial."[4] In the final vote Blagojevich defeated Kaszak 49 to 39 percent, with the remainder going to Ray Romero, a Hispanic businessman making his first bid for public office. After nearly forty years, the ethnic neighborhoods on Chicago's north side finally had a new Democratic leader. But he faced one more obstacle that Rostenkowski found unfamiliar as a young politician: a Republican incumbent.

Both national parties knew that this congressional district offered one of the Democrats' best opportunities to regain a House seat. In one of his many shortcomings, however, Flanagan seemed genuinely confident about his contest. "They want a pound of flesh," he boasted after the Democratic primary. "We beat them once. We'll beat them again. That's fine."[5] Flanagan apparently believed that—like Rostenkowski—he had two major factors going his way: his personal connection to the district and the perks of incumbency, including federal projects he directed to Chicago. And as the only House Republican in 1995 to vote against their balanced-budget plan, Flanagan thought he had sufficiently distanced himself from the unpopular Gingrich. As it turned out, his biggest problem was his own ineptitude. Unlike 1994, when he ran a shoestring candidacy against Rostenkowski, Flanagan was a poor campaigner in the public spotlight. Despite occasional independence he failed to move aggressively to separate himself from his party to survive in a district that leaned slightly Democratic. Blagojevich depicted Flanagan as the "accidental Congressman," out of touch with local values. The challenger focused on Flanagan's House votes: backing federal subsidies for tobacco production, plus his support on the House Judiciary Committee to repeal the assault-weapon ban. Rostenkowski contended that Flanagan never had a serious chance to win a second term. On one occasion he greeted Flanagan on an airplane to Washington and asked, "How do you like your job, Michael?" When Flanagan said he liked it a lot, Rostenkowski responded dismissively, "Don't get used to it." By Labor Day, national Republican strategists spread the word that Flanagan was a likely loser.

By the final weeks of the campaign, Flanagan had become such damaged goods that a *Tribune* poll showed that, by 39 to 29 percent, respondents believed they were better off with Rostenkowski as their congressman; at the time he was in federal prison. According to the *Tribune,* "There is a sense among voters that Flanagan never quite caught on, that his 1994 election was more the result of the failures of Rostenkowski, who sought re-election under the cloud of a federal corruption indictment."[6] On election day Blagojevich won 64 percent of the vote; he had more than doubled Flanagan's fund-raising. With his victory, Blagojevich expected to regain the hammerlock that Rostenkowski had wielded locally for nearly four decades. At age forty when he took office, Blagojevich was a decade older, more articulate on the issues, and far more media-savvy than Rostenkowski had been when he first was elected to Congress. But the newcomer took a different approach. Once in office, Blagojevich worked aggressively to connect with local neighborhoods and to promote his work in Washington. "I want to be a leader in the fight against gun violence and for sane gun laws," he said. Proof of his success came when he drew token opposition to reelection in 1998. In May 1999 he gained his first national spotlight when he flew to Serbia with the Reverend Jesse Jackson and won the release of three U.S. soldiers who had been held as prisoners-of-war in the Kosovo conflict.

If Rostenkowski's 1994 defeat proved only a temporary setback for his party in Chicago, the loss of his clout was a sharper blow for the city. Neither Flanagan nor Blagojevich was in a position to flex influence comparable to that of the former Ways and Means chairman. The city's influence in Congress was further weakened by declining seniority. In 1999 only one member of Congress from Chicago had served in the House more than six years; and Illinois was represented by two freshman senators, neither of them from the city—Democrat Richard Durbin and Republican Peter Fitzgerald, who defeated first-term Democrat Carol Moseley-Braun in 1998. "As a delegation, we are in the throes of growing pains," Blagojevich said. "We have to find a way of delivering for the city what Rostenkowski could do individually because of his seniority and chairmanship."

In other ways, however, the city was on a roll. As Democratic National Convention host in August 1996, Chicago showed the nation it had recovered fully from the 1968 convention horrors. During the interval, the *Wall Street Journal* reported, "Chicago not only survived but blossomed into an economic, cultural and lifestyle marvel."[7] But Rostenkowski's contributions received scant attention during the convention. Democratic leaders, starting with President Clinton, obviously had more upbeat topics to discuss than the legacy of a federal inmate. And the average citizen probably agreed with the young waitress at Gibson's, a favorite Rostenkowski steak house, who said that patrons mostly "laugh" about one of his ancient political posters that hangs in the bar.

For better and worse, those who observed Rostenkowski in public life will not remember him as just another politician. Notwithstanding the adversities at the close of his career, his legislative record and his personality left indelible marks. On Capitol Hill and in Chicago he deserves a place as a towering figure in the last half of the twentieth century. But his self-portrayal as "an average citizen" should not be automatically dismissed as false modesty. Although he made no secret that he enjoyed the accoutrements of the good life when it came to travel and hospitality, there is something about an individual who lives seven decades in his family home across the street from the family church that conveys a strong sense of place and personal roots. Rostenkowski's passion for order and familiarity were trademarks throughout his career, from his attachment to the Ways and Means Committee to his dinners with friends. No doubt that desire to avoid change occasionally got him into trouble. "The road curved, but he kept driving straight," said Rep. Dennis Eckart. That was the case not only with his legal problems but also with his approach to public policy. Above all he was a centrist, in both philosophical terms and his personal dealings. Amidst all the twists and turns in the debates over federal taxes, health care, or economic policy, Rostenkowski's views remained consistent. He defined his goals in incremental terms, both for himself and for government. He paid a price within his own party. Legislators like David Obey grew enraged that the Ways and Means chairman sold out Democratic principles of protecting the middle class. And Democratic campaign impresarios like Tony Coelho grumbled that he was not sufficiently attuned to electoral imperatives. Still other Democrats disliked him as arrogant or condescending. But Rostenkowski usually brushed off his critics and concentrated on showing that he was a strong chairman who made things happen.

Contributing to the fall of Rostenkowski and House Democrats was their failure to resolve legitimate demands from competing factions. Over the long term the public is well served by officials who prevent wild pendulum swings from one end of the spectrum to the other. The challenge, however, is to avoid the hardening of views when the same individuals remain on top for a long time. "At one point, the stability offered by seniority was workable," Rep. Tim Penny, a Minnesota Democrat, said in 1994. "But today we have seen a rigidity set in because of seniority. People here for thirty years view the institution as it was when they entered. . . . The insidious changes have been so gradual and members have been so close that they don't see them." Rostenkowski's stubbornness hampered his demeanor and his work style. He could be fearsome when his demands met resistance. "In his culture, solidarity was more important," said Rep. Barney Frank of Massachusetts, a liberal Democrat who often disagreed with Rostenkowski. "You weren't supposed to think for yourself. . . . He expected loyalty from other people." For Rostenkowski the legislator, that

quality often produced a parochial insistence to look at issues and personalities from his narrow confines of Chicago or the Ways and Means Committee. Each of these perspectives was less sensitive to changing
attitudes, including ethical appearances. Sometimes he permitted the trap-
pings of power to get the better of his neighborhood common sense. Another downside to his sense of order was excessive deference to
presidents, regardless of party.

Yet the sweep of history provided powerful vindication for Rostenkowski and his political style. One of the least expected events was the
chaotic disarray among House Republicans that resulted in the resigna-
tions of Speaker Gingrich and his designated successor, Bob Livingston
of Louisiana, in the six weeks following the 1998 elections, and led Republicans in 1999 to turn to the previously unknown Dennis Hastert of
Illinois to lead a narrowly divided House. When he was sworn in as
speaker, Hastert—whose district in Chicago's western suburbs was a
refuge point for many upwardly mobile descendants of the city's immigrants—proudly cited his background in Illinois politics, and made a
point of inviting Gov. George Ryan and Chicago Mayor Richard M.
Daley and introducing them to the House. On the night before that ceremony, hundreds jammed a reception sponsored by the Illinois State Society, in which participants hailed Hastert as a disciple of the state's
tradition of coalition politics. "We have to join hands, Democrats and Republicans, to make sure this House works," Hastert told the group. In the
history of Illinois, said Republican Rep. Ray LaHood of Peoria, "People
such as Bob Michel and Dan Rostenkowski believed in the House and
that we can solve problems when we work together. . . . That's what
Denny Hastert believes, too." Veteran Washington lobbyists cited Rostenkowski as a model in praising Hastert's ability to put together legislation. Whatever Hastert's future, it was apparent that old-style politics had
unexpectedly preempted the Gingrich-era posture of confrontation.

Even the woes of Bill Clinton gave Rostenkowski a sort of redemption. Although the investigation by independent counsel Kenneth Starr
and the eventual House impeachment of the president, followed by the
Senate trial, were played for higher political stakes than was Rostenkowski's case, the targets of the two inquiries voiced similar defenses:
(1) with enough time and money, a prosecutor can snare nearly any target,
especially someone in public life; (2) Starr's tactics paralleled those of
Jay Stephens and Eric Holder, who pursued far-flung allegations against
Rostenkowski before finally settling on relatively mundane charges; and

(3) a criminal target often gets into trouble because of mistakes by defense lawyers or an unwise legal strategy. If there was one significant difference in the two investigations, it was that Rostenkowski was more willing to concede his wrongdoing in the face of shifting public standards than was the younger president. But some Republicans drew a different lesson from the quick exits by Gingrich and Livingston plus Clinton's stubborn defense. "In contrast to Democrats, whose sole desire is to gain and hold power, Republicans believe that power is not important and that we need to do the right thing," said a senior House Republican amid the political turmoil. Still, Clinton's survival hinted a return to public acceptance of politicians' fallibility and a rejection of prosecutorial excess.

Even with these passing events, the greater lesson may be that operating the engines of government is an inherently difficult challenge for both local and national officials. Even though Rostenkowski, too, occasionally made mistakes, the fact that he far more often succeeded is a tribute to his political training—from mentors like his father, Richard Daley, Wilbur Mills, and Lyndon Johnson—as well as to his own instincts and common sense. Such skills cannot be taught in books or academic courses. They are the product of a diverse culture and experiences, combined with a measure of public-spiritedness. That few other members of Congress, Democratic or Republican, have come close to Rostenkowski in their legislative achievements has not been a coincidence. Although his successes do not excuse his personal excesses, which sometimes included violations of rules and canons, they may account for the requisite stubbornness.

Overcoming doubts—including his own—that he could perform on the political stage, Rostenkowski showed an intuitive sense of how to get the job done. "He had a unique ability to gather information and to understand the needs of members," said Bob Matsui, a Ways and Means Democrat who was a Rostenkowski admirer. "He had an uncanny knack for understanding people and how a scenario can play out." Part of that was apparent in his system of rewards and punishments. The same chairman who removed the wheels from a mutinous Democrat's chair also provided blandishments to a colleague whose support he required. "I never had anyone treat me more fairly," said Bill Brewster, the Oklahoma Democrat. Although his demands could be blunt, his sense of timing also had an astute negotiator's well-developed guile. That was especially true in the parliamentary marathons that have become a recurring part of modern legislative life, whether in more conventional committee debates such as tax reform in 1985 or in ad hoc negotiations that led to the 1990 budget deal. His longevity, accomplishments, and symbolism in the nation's shifting political landscape were unparalleled. Unlike other Democratic lawmakers in influential positions, Rostenkowski was willing to take his swings and make his deals. That helps to explain why he had a longer list of legislation to his credit than did other Democratic power brokers of his time, such as Rep. John Dingell or Sen. Edward Kennedy. His abundant pens from presidential bill-signings were totems of his proud legacy. He was part of the action, often as an indispensable player. His consensus-building skills, which have become rare, deserve respect and encouragement in a society that has become so factionalized. At a June 1994 Washington dinner with academics a week after he was indicted, he may have written his epitaph: "I want you people to be able to say, that son of a bitch, he had some guts, he had some fortitude, he realized what you had to be in order to be a national legislator."

To much of the public, Rostenkowski was more sinner than saint—even before his criminal downfall. Sometimes his actions fostered the perception of his heavy-handed style, as in his showdown with senior citizens at the Copernicus Center and during his brusque answers to reporters' questions. But another source of his public relations problems was that the news media, both in Chicago and Washington, stereotyped him as a bully and were more inclined to focus on his peccadillos than on serious issues. It should be no surprise that public officials, when they are accustomed to rebukes, become defensive with their critics. For skeptical bystanders, the consequence can be an unfairly hostile view of the political players. Because Rostenkowski so often compartmentalized his public and private audiences, he helped to create an unfair caricature. He received too little public credit for his considerable accomplishments, and he became the target of excessive criticism for his misdeeds.

In his life's autumn, Rostenkowski encountered tribulations, though not the trial he had promised to win. Before those disorders, however, the many events he had witnessed and experienced, plus his wide range of acquaintances, made him larger than life. Like other Democrats who ran the House for forty years, he could take pride in both his accomplishments and his longevity in power. Inevitably they all suffered failures and excesses. Rostenkowski certainly had his share of each, but he also retained plenty of proud legacies. In a democracy, his fellow citizens need not bestow further rewards. But his work entitles him to the public's appreciation for his service. We won't see many more like him.

Notes

Chapter 1. The Bungalow Belt and the Machine

1. *Chicago Sun-Times,* February 16, 1947.
2. Peter D'A. Jones and Melvin G. Holli, "The Ethnic in Chicago," in Holli and Jones, eds., *Ethnic Chicago* (Grand Rapids, Mich., 1984), p. 5.
3. Polish Day Association, *Poles in America, 1933* (Chicago, 1933), p. 65.
4. Edward R. Kantowicz, *Polish-American Politics in Chicago, 1888–1940* (Chicago, 1975), p. 28.
5. Ibid., p. 8.
6. Sister M. Inviolata, "Noble Street in Chicago," in *Polish American Studies,* January–June 1952, p. 3.
7. Joseph John Parot, *Polish Catholics in Chicago, 1850–1920* (DeKalb, Ill., 1981), p. 74.
8. Parot, *Polish Catholics,* p. 65.
9. Father Joe Glab, who was its pastor from 1983 to 1996, provided many details of the church's early history.
10. Andrew M. Greeley, *Neighborhood* (New York, 1977), p. 53.
11. Ibid., p. 92.
12. Kantowicz, *Politics,* p. 26.
13. Arthur W. Thurner, "Polish Americans in Chicago Politics," in *Polish American Studies,* Spring 1971, p. 28.
14. Holli and Jones, *Ethnic,* p. 10.
15. Kantowicz, *Politics,* p. 41.
16. Kantowicz, "Polish Chicago: Survival Through Solidarity," in Holli and Jones, *Ethnic,* p. 235.
17. Kantowicz, *Politics,* p. 66.
18. Ibid., p. 178.
19. Ibid., p. 208.
20. *Chicago Daily News,* March 16, 1931.
21. Polish Pageant Inc., *Poles of Chicago, 1837–1937* (Chicago, 1937), p. 213.
22. Kantowicz, *Politics,* p. 210.
23. *Chicago Sun-Times,* December 27, 1945; *Chicago Daily News,* December 31, 1946; *Chicago Sun-Times,* December 13, 1953.
24. Kantowicz, *Politics,* p. 211.
25. *Chicago Tribune,* February 20, 1939.

26. *Chicago Daily Times,* August 7, 1938.

27. *Chicago American,* August 12, 1938.

28. Len O'Connor, *Clout: Mayor Daley and His City* (Chicago, 1975), p. 88.

29. February 22, 1955, letter, in files of the Polish-American Democratic Organization (PADO), Chicago Historical Society.

30. January 25, 1955, minutes of PADO.

31. "An open letter to the Poles of Chicago," February 22, 1955, in PADO files.

32. *Chicago American,* February 23, 1955.

33. *Chicago Daily News,* April 7, 1955.

34. April 3, 1956, minutes of PADO.

35. *Chicago Tribune,* March 29, 1956.

36. *Chicago Sun-Times,* May 15, 1956.

37. *Chicago Daily News,* October 28, 1958.

38. Willard Edwards, "Rostenkowski New 'Mayor's Man' in House," *Chicago Tribune,* May 24, 1964.

39. Iris Krasnow, "Power Drive," *Chicago,* November 1991, p. 122.

40. Melvin A. Kahn and Frances J. Majors, *The Winning Ticket: Daley, the Chicago Machine and Illinois Politics* (New York, 1984), p. 107.

41. Roger Biles, *Richard J. Daley: Politics, Race and the Governing of Chicago* (DeKalb, Ill., 1995), p. 56.

42. Thomas B. Littlewood, "Bipartisan Coalition in Illinois," in William K. Hall, ed., *Illinois Government and Politics* (Dubuque, Iowa, 1975), p. 44.

43. *Chicago Tribune,* March 15, 1987.

44. Mike Royko, *Boss: Richard J. Daley of Chicago* (New York, 1971), pp. 46–47.

45. Paul Simon, "The Illinois Legislature, A Study in Corruption," in Hall, *Government,* p. 73.

46. Ibid., p. 74.

47. *Chicago Daily News,* October 1, 1971.

48. *Chicago Today,* October 1, 1971.

49. *Chicago Daily News,* April 15, 1963.

50. *Chicago Daily News,* March 22, 1965.

Chapter 2. Democrats and a Government on the Move

1. William Safire, *Safire's Political Dictionary* (New York, 1978), p. 142.

2. Oliver E. Allen, *The Tiger: The Rise and Fall of Tammany Hall* (Reading, Mass., 1993), p. 274.

3. John W. McCormack, Oral History at the Lyndon B. Johnson (LBJ) Library, p. 10.

4. John F. Manley, *The Politics of Finance: The House Committee on Ways and Means* (Boston, 1970), p. 205.

5. *Chicago Daily News,* October 19, 1960.

6. John Brademas, *The Politics of Education: Conflict and Consensus on Capitol Hill* (Norman, Okla., 1987), pp. 8–9.

7. Richard Bolling, *House Out of Order* (New York, 1965), p. 54.

8. Frank Thompson, Jr., "The Congress and You," p. 8.

9. Robert L. Hardesty, *The Johnson Years: The Difference He Made.* Austin, 1990, p. 73.

10. Bolling, *House,* p. 220.

11. Arthur M. Schlesinger, Jr. *A Thousand Days* (New York, 1965), p. 651.

12. Doris Kearns Goodwin, *The Fitzgeralds and the Kennedys* (New York, 1987), p. 704.

13. Richard J. Whalen, *The Founding Father: The Story of Joseph P. Kennedy* (New York, 1964), pp. 379–380.

14. O'Connor, *Clout,* p. 152.

15. Royko, *Boss,* p. 120.

16. Richard Reeves, *President Kennedy* (New York, 1993), p. 110.

17. Tom Wicker, *JFK & LBJ: The Influence of Personality Upon Politics* (New York, 1968), p. 124.

18. Richard Bolling, *Power in the House* (New York, 1968), p. 215.

19. Thomas P. O'Neill, Jr., Oral History at the LBJ Library, p. 29.

20. Hale Boggs, Oral History at the LBJ Library, I, p. 17.

21. Bolling, *Power,* p. 215.

22. *Newsweek,* November 28, 1983, p. 64.

23. Wilbur D. Mills, Oral History at the LBJ Library, II, p. 20.

24. Wicker, *JFK & LBJ,* p. 87.

25. Bolling, *Power,* p. 223.

26. *Chicago Daily News,* April 13, 1968.

27. Carl Albert, Oral History at the LBJ Library, III, p. 11.

28. Harry P. Haveles Jr., "The Power to Persuade: Presidential Leadership in Congress, Lyndon Johnson and the 89th and 90th Congresses," honors thesis in government, Harvard University, 1976.

29. Boggs, Oral History, p. 8.

30. D. B. Hardeman, Oral History at the LBJ Library, III, p. 43.

31. Manley, *Finance,* pp. 32–33.

32. Richard F. Fenno, Jr., *Congressmen in Committees* (Boston, 1973), p. 3.

33. Charles B. Seib, "Steering Wheel of the House," *New York Times Magazine,* March 18, 1962, p. 30.

34. Julius Duscha, "The Most Important Man on Capitol Hill Today," *New York Times Magazine,* February 25, 1968, p. 30.

35. Manley, *Finance,* p. 106.

36. Barber B. Conable, Jr., *Congress and the Income Tax* (Norman, Okla., 1989), p. 18.

37. Seib, "Steering Wheel," p. 141.

38. Mills, Oral History, II, p. 23.

39. *Congressional Record,* June 30, 1973, H5770.

40. Bolling, *Power,* p. 268.

41. Mills, Oral History, pp. I-10, II-1.

42. Ibid., p. II-2.

43. Letter from Cohen to LBJ, March 2, 1965, as quoted in Eric R. Kingson, and Edward D. Berkowitz, *Social Security and Medicare: A Policy Primer* (Westport, Conn., 1993), p. 46.

44. Mills, Oral History, p. II-7, 9.

45. Robert Dallek, *Flawed Giant: Lyndon Johnson and His Times, 1961–73* (New York, 1998), p. 329.

Chapter 3. First Bloody Signs of Trouble

1. National Committee for an Effective Congress, "The Democrats Under McCormack— A House Divided," *Congressional Report,* April 30, 1962.

2. Mills, Oral History, I, p. 31, 38.

3. Joseph A. Califano, Jr., "Balancing the Budget, L.B.J. Style," *New York Times,* December 31, 1995, p. IV-9.

4. Duscha, "Most Important Man on Capitol Hill Today," p. 64.

5. The citations in the following two paragraphs are from the White House Central File, LBJ Library.

6. Biles, *Daley,* p. 113.

7. Lawrence O'Brien, Memo to the President, August 11, 1965, White House Central File, LBJ Library.

8. Jake Jacobsen, Memo to the President, August 10, 1966, White House Central File, LBJ Library.

9. Jack Valenti, Memo to the President, August 4, 1964, White House Central File, LBJ Library.

10. "Republicans Likely to Gain 10 Midwest House Seats," *Congressional Quarterly Weekly Report,* October 21, 1966, p. 2508.

11. O'Connor, *Clout,* p. 196.

12. Royko, *Boss,* p. 169.

13. Theodore H. White, *The Making of the President 1968* (New York, 1969), p. 4. As an adolescent reporter, I struck a similar tone in an essay, "1968: A Political Year," for my undergraduate yearbook at Brown University: "A year like none other we have ever known, or perhaps endured. A tragic, disappointing, violent, interminable year. A year with some brief hopeful minutes and days. But then always the disillusion and despair."

14. Norman Mailer, *Miami and the Siege of Chicago* (New York, 1968), pp. 116, 131.

15. Royko, *Boss,* p. 182.

16. Biles, *Daley,* p. 156.

17. Royko, *Boss,* p. 184.

18. Carla Marinucci, "Chicago's Daley Wrestles with the Spirit of '68," *San Francisco Examiner,* April 18, 1996, A-18.

19. Biles, *Daley,* p. 158.

20. Carl Albert, with Danney Goble, *Little Giant* (Norman, Okla., 1990), p. 304.

21. Ibid., p. 326.

22. Ibid.

23. Roger Davidson, "Subcommittee Government," in Thomas E. Mann and Norman J. Ornstein, eds., *The New Congress* (Washington, D.C., 1981), p. 102.

24. *Chicago Daily News,* November 16, 1970.

25. Robert J. Peabody, *Leadership in Congress: Stability, Succession and Change* (Boston, 1976), pp. 173–174.

26. Tom Littlewood, "Rostenkowski Bolsters Bid in House Leadership Contest," *Chicago Sun-Times,* June 7, 1970.

27. Michael Coakley, "Rostenkowski Gaining for House Post," *Chicago Today,* July 9, 1970.

28. William J. Eaton, "Rostenkowski Drops Bid for Floor Leader," *Chicago Daily News,* December 24, 1970.

29. Joel Weisman, "Capital Hill Rebuke for Daley," *Chicago Today,* January 24, 1971, p. 66.

30. Albert, *Little Giant,* p. 327.

31. Peabody, *Leadership,* p. 206.

32. Ibid., p. 217.

33. Albert R. Hunt, "Waning Institution? Even If Mills Stays On, Ways and Means Panel Faces a Loss of Power," *Wall Street Journal,* July 10, 1973.

34. Conable, *Tax,* p. 20.

35. Myra MacPherson, "Looking Back: Wilbur Mills Recalls His Bout with Alcohol," *Washington Post,* January 4, 1978.

36. Rowland Evans and Robert Novak, "Mills for President Astounds Hill," *Washington Post,* March 9, 1972.

37. Randall Strahan, *New Ways and Means: Reform and Change in a Congressional Committee* (Chapel Hill, N.C., 1990), p. 38.

Chapter 4. The New Breed and the Limits of Reform

1. Ralph Whitehead, "Rusty Counts the House," *Chicago,* April 1978, p. 114.

2. Morton Kondracke, "Ford Would OK Nixon Immunity," *Chicago Sun-Times,* August 8, 1974.

3. John Jacobs, *A Rage for Justice* (Berkeley Calif., 1995), p. 274.

4. Ibid., p. 309.

5. John M. Barry, *The Ambition and the Power* (New York, 1989), p. 28.

6. Kahn and Majors, *The Winning Ticket* p. 1.

7. Ibid., p. 107.

8. Strahan, *New Ways and Means,* p. 60.

9. Whitehead, "Rusty," p. 114.

10. Richard E. Cohen, "Al Ullman—The Complex, Contradictory Chairman of Ways and Means," *National Journal,* March 4, 1978, p. 345.

11. Jimmy Carter, *Keeping Faith* (New York, 1982), p. 84.

12. John K. Iglehart, "Like It or Not, Congress Must Grapple with Hospital Cost Controls," *National Journal,* May 21, 1977, p. 790.

13. Califano, "Balancing the Budget," p. 150.

14. Ibid., p. 148.

Chapter 5. Mr. Chairman Confronts Mr. President

1. Dom Bonafede, "For the Democratic Party, It's a Time for Rebuilding and Seeking New Ideas," *National Journal,* February 21, 1981, p. 320.

2. Steven Rattner, "Ullman Scrambling After a 13th Term," *New York Times,* August 17, 1980.

3. Dan Rostenkowski, speech to the Economic Club of Chicago, February 17, 1981.

4. Daniel Patrick Moynihan, *Miles to Go* (Cambridge, Mass., 1996), p. 111.

5. Edward Cowan, "Congress Narrows Gap on a Tax Bill," *New York Times,* May 28, 1981.

6. Conable, *Tax,* p. 59.

7. William Greider, *The Education of David Stockman and Other Americans* (New York, 1982), pp. 33, 44.

8. Conable, *Tax,* p. 63.

9. Jonathan Fuerbringer, "The Tax Titans: A Dynamic Duo," *New York Times,* June 12, 1984.

10. Greider, *Stockman,* p. 41.

11. Paul Light, *Artful Work* (New York, 1985), p. 122.

12. Ibid., p. 124.

13. Ibid., p. 129.

Chapter 6. Wheeling and Dealing to Middle Ground

1. Strahan, *New Ways and Means,* p. 108.

2. Susan C. Schwab, *Trade-Offs: Negotiating the Omnibus Trade and Competitiveness Act* (Boston, 1994), p. 69.

3. For a detailed case study of the 1986 Tax Reform Act, see Jeffrey H. Birnbaum and Alan S. Murray, *Showdown at Gucci Gulch: Lawyers, Lobbyists and the Unlikely Triumph of Tax Reform* (New York, 1987).

4. Ibid., p. 36.

5. Donald L. Barlett and James B. Steele, *America: Who Really Pays the Taxes?* (New York, 1994), p. 204.

6. Barry, *Ambition,* p. 35.

7. Ibid., p. 37.

8. Richard E. Cohen, "Iran's Long Shadow," *National Journal,* January 3, 1987, p. 7.

9. Schwab, *Trade-Offs,* p. 86.

10. Ibid., p. 109.

11. Ibid.

12. Ibid., p. 112.

13. Barry, *Ambition,* p. 276.

14. Lawrence J. Haas, *Running on Empty* (Homewood, Ill., 1990), p. 291.

15. Ibid., p. 292.

16. Clarence Page, "Rosty's Indictment Is Startling, Even by Chicago Standards," *Chicago Tribune,* June 1, 1994.

Chapter 7. Clash of Cultures

1. Krasnow, "Power Drive," p. 140.

2. Tim McNamee, "The Making of Mr. Chairman," *Chicago Sun-Times,* June 2, 1994.

3. Paul Merrion, "Rosty Tax Bill Deal Helped Lure Chrysler," *Crain's Chicago Business,* December 2, 1985.

4. Barlett and Steele, *America,* pp. 278–279.

5. Maureen O'Donnell and Tom Seibel, "Tunnel Needs Deep Pockets," *Chicago Sun-Times,* June 9, 1993.

6. David K. Fremon, *Chicago Politics: Ward by Ward* (Bloomington, Ind., 1988), p. 215.

7. Donald L. Barlett and James B. Steele, *America: What Went Wrong* (New York, 1992), p. 194.

8. Ibid., p. 192.

9. Timothy Noah, "Chicago's Good Samaritan," *Newsweek,* September 12, 1988, p. 26.

10. Jeff Bailey and Robert Johnson, "Political Clout Steers Much Government Aid to Trendy Apartments," *Wall Street Journal,* August 25, 1986.

11. Chuck Neubauer, "Rostenkowski Goes to Bat for Pal Again," *Chicago Sun-Times,* November 30, 1983.

12. Bailey and Johnson, "Clout."

13. Henry Locke, "Huff Pushes for Probe of West Side Complex," *Chicago Defender,* November 21, 1983.

14. J. Linn Allen, "Low-income Rentals in Towers Accord," *Chicago Tribune,* April 13, 1994.

15. Ibid., "Residential Complex Rebounds Strongly," *Chicago Tribune,* July 7, 1996.

16. Ibid.

17. George Hager and Eric Pianin, *Mirage* (New York, 1997), p. 76.

18. Andrew Herrmann, "What Makes Rosty Run?—Irate Seniors," *Chicago Sun-Times,* August 18, 1989.

19. Ibid.

20. Mike Royko, "Congressman Can't Drive Home Point," *Chicago Tribune,* August 18, 1989.

21. McNamee, "Mr. Chairman," p. 20.

Chapter 8. Erosion of Divided Government

1. Jaffe's comments in this chapter are from his unpublished writing on the 1990 budget deal.

2. Lawrence J. Haas, "Rostenkowski's Way," *National Journal,* July 22, 1989, p. 1858.

3. Barry, *Ambition,* p. 756.

4. Haas, *Running,* p. 206.

5. Jeffrey H. Birnbaum, "Rostenkowski, Buttered by Bush and Battered by Democrats, Erred Badly on Capital Gains," *Wall Street Journal,* September 19, 1989.

6. Douglas A. Harbrecht, "Rostenkowski: 'My Head Is Bloodied, but I'm Not Bowed,'" *Business Week,* September 18, 1989, p. 31.

7. Donald R. Kennon and Rebecca M. Rogers, *The Committee on Ways and Means: A Bicentennial History* (Washington, D.C., 1989), p. ix.

8. John C. Yang, "Companies, Unions Wish Many Happy Returns as Birthday Gifts Flood Ways and Means Panel," *Wall Street Journal,* August 18, 1989.

9. Dan Rostenkowski, "Cold Turkey: How to End the Deficit in 5 Years," *Washington Post,* March 11, 1990.

10. Richard G. Darman, *Who's in Control?* (New York, 1996), p. 243.

11. Bill McAllister and Steven Mufson, "White House Warmly Greets Rostenkowski Deficit Plan," *Washington Post,* March 13, 1990.

12. Richard E. Cohen, "Spending Control Is GOP's Summit Goal," *National Journal,* May 19, 1990, p. 1239.

Chapter 9. Trying to Take Clinton's Hand

1. Interview on ABC-TV's "Nightline," March 24, 1992.

2. Eric D. Fingerhut, "A Democrat Throws Stones," *New York Times,* December 17, 1994.

3. Richard E. Cohen, "It All Starts Here," *National Journal,* May 8, 1993, p. 1098.

4. Adam Clymer, "For Rostenkowski, Maybe Glory, Maybe Disgrace," *New York Times,* February 10, 1993.

5. David E. Rosenbaum, "On Budget's Razor Edge, Opposites March in Step," *New York Times,* July 6, 1993.

6. Haynes Johnson and David S. Broder, *The System* (Boston, 1996), p. 171.

7. Ibid., p. 183.

8. Michael Wines and Robert Pear, "President Finds He Has Gained Ground Even If He Lost on Health Care," *New York Times,* July 30, 1996.

9. Paul Starr, "What Happened to Health Care Reform?" *American Prospect,* Winter 1995, p. 20.

10. Mitchell Locin and Michael Tackett, "Clinton Defends Visit to Rostenkowski," *Chicago Tribune,* February 26, 1994.

11. Hanke Gratteau, "Rostenkowski Seeks Victory, Vindication," *Chicago Tribune,* February 27, 1994.

12. Fremon, *Chicago Politics,* p. 246.

13. Gratteau, "Victory."

14. Ibid.

15. Ibid.

16. "Remarks to Students at Wilbur Wright College in Chicago," *Weekly Compilation of Presidential Documents,* March 7, 1994, p. 388.

17. Hanke Gratteau and Mitchell Locin, "Clinton Pays Few Old Debts," *Chicago Tribune,* March 1, 1994.

18. Mike Royko, "Rostenkowski Tests Charisma of Clinton," *Chicago Tribune,* March 1, 1994.

19. Hanke Gratteau, "Chairman Has Night to Remember," *Chicago Tribune,* March 17, 1994.

20. Hanke Gratteau and Ellen Warren, "Netsch, Rostenkowski Win," *Chicago Tribune,* March 16, 1994.

21. Johnson and Broder, *System,* p. 435.

22. Ibid., p. 509.

23. Lynn Sweet, "Rosty Says He's Short of Cash," *Chicago Sun-Times,* November 21, 1994.

24. Adam Langer, "Running Against Rosty," *Chicago Reader,* October 28, 1994, p. 1.

25. Ibid.

26. Paul Merrion, "The GOP Challenger in Rosty's Backyard," *Crain's Chicago Business,* October 17, 1994, p. 1.

27. Ibid.

28. Paul Merrion, "Look Inside Rosty's Camp Shows He Could Have Won," *Crain's Chicago Business,* November 14, 1994, p. 1.

29. William F. Connelly, Jr., and John J. Pitney, Jr., *Congress' Permanent Minority?* (Lanham, Md., 1994).

30. Sweet, "Short of Cash."

Chapter 10. The System on Trial

1. Paul Merrion, "Oh, Danny Boy: Pipes Really Calling Now," *Crain's Chicago Business,* July 26, 1993, p. 1.

2. Matt O'Connor, "Hyde Blasts Federal Officials for Lawsuit," *Chicago Tribune,* March 6, 1997.

3. Michael Tackett, "Rostenkowski Cites Emotional Toll from Legal Battle," *Chicago Tribune,* April 11, 1996.

4. Paul Rodriguez, "Postmaster Accuses Mrs. Foley," *Washington Times,* February 7, 1992.

5. Beth Donovan, "Some Members Made Big Stamp Buys," *Congressional Quarterly,* May 23, 1992, p. 1416.

6. Stuart Taylor, Jr., and Daniel Klaidman, "One Client Too Many," *American Lawyer,* July 1994, p. 65.

7. Michael Tackett and Christopher Drew, "House Scandal Guilty Plea; Rostenkowski Is Linked to Fund Scheme," *Chicago Tribune,* July 20, 1993.

8. Christopher Drew and Michael Tackett, "U.S. Probes Rostenkowski Campaign Fund Use," *Chicago Tribune,* July 21, 1993.

9. Paul Merrion, "If Rosty Gets Nailed, So Does Chicago," *Crain's Chicago Business,* January 18, 1993, p. 1.

10. Ibid.

11. Merrion, "Oh, Danny Boy."

12. Michael Tackett, "Rostenkowski Probe Decision Expected Soon," *Chicago Tribune,* May 6, 1994.

13. David Johnston, "Overtures Begin for Plea Bargain on Rostenkowski," *New York Times,* May 19, 1994.

14. "The Rostenkowski Problem," *Washington Post,* May 20, 1994.

15. David Espo, "Democrats, Assuming Rostenkowski Departing, Say They'll Manage," Associated Press, May 26, 1994.

16. Ibid.

17. Michael Tackett and Christopher Drew, "U.S. v. Rostenkowski, Indictment of a Way of Life," *Chicago Tribune,* June 1, 1994.

18. Jackie Calmes, "Rostenkowski Rejects Deal to Avoid Trial," *Wall Street Journal,* May 31, 1994.

19. Charles M. Madigan and Ray Gibson, "Ghost Payrollers Cast Long Political Shadows," *Chicago Tribune,* June 5, 1994.

20. McNamee, "The Making of Mr. Chairman."

21. Kevin Merida, "America's Latest Soap: As Congress Turns," *Washington Post,* June 5, 1994.

22. Walter Pincus, "Rostenkowski Wasn't Alone in Buying China, Chairs at House Stationery Store," *Washington Post,* July 6, 1994.

23. Jon Margolis, "Rosty's Case Exposes the Cruel Ironies of Modern 'Justice,'" *Chicago Tribune,* June 6, 1994.

24. David S. Broder, "Why Washington Grieves," *Washington Post,* June 2, 1994.

25. Taylor and Klaidman, "One Client."

26. Ibid.

27. "Legal Fees Deplete Rostenkowski Funds," *Chicago Tribune,* August 4, 1995.

28. Tackett, "Rostenkowski Cites Emotional Toll."

29. David E. Rosenbaum, "Rostenkowski Pleads Guilty to Mail Fraud," *New York Times,* April 10, 1996.

30. Mike Royko, "Rostenkowski's Sin Was Not Changing with the Times," *Chicago Tribune,* April 10, 1996.

31. Norman Ornstein, "A Pol Who Made Things Happen," *Washington Post,* May 10, 1994.

32. Toni Locy, "Kolter Guilty in Post Office Scandal," *Washington Post,* May 8, 1994.

33. Toni Locy, "Former House Postmaster Receives 4-Month Sentence," *Washington Post,* February 21, 1997.

34. Ibid.

35. After I made several requests to Rostenkowski, he agreed to permit me to visit him at Oxford in March 1997. "You are my first visitor," he said, "and you will be my last visitor." Although Bureau of Prisons regulations permit journalists to meet privately with inmates at the facility, officials in Oxford and Washington refused to grant me such an opportunity. Further evidence of the arbitrary enforcement of rules came during the second day at Oxford: the conversation was delayed for thirty minutes because the guard objected to my taking a fresh writing pad into the interview, even though another guard watched as I filled a separate pad during my first conversation with Rostenkowski. The second guard, Officer "R. Cupp," finally relented, but without explanation.

Chapter 11. The Democrats' Legacy

1. Ed Gillespie and Bob Schellhas, eds., *Contract with America* (New York, 1994), p. 13.

2. Woodrow Wilson, *Congressional Government* (Cleveland, 1956), p. 69.

3. Sandra Sobieraj, "Clinton, Democrats Celebrate Budget," Associated Press, April 23, 1998.

4. Thomas Hardy and Bob Secter, "Campaign Fires All but Dying," *Chicago Tribune,* March 18, 1996.

5. "Inside Politics," Cable News Network, April 8, 1996.

6. Charles M. Madigan, "5th Congressional District Backing Blagojevich over Incumbent," *Chicago Tribune,* October 23, 1996.

7. Jeff Bailey and Calmetta Y. Coleman, "Despite Tough Years, Chicago Has Become a Nice Place to Live," *Wall Street Journal,* August 21, 1996.

A Note on Sources

THIS BOOK is based on scores of interviews with individuals who worked closely with Dan Rostenkowski, from his Damen Avenue office in Chicago's 32nd Ward to H-208, his Capitol office just off the House floor; several sources kindly consented to multiple conversations, many of which lasted for hours. In researching the book I had extensive discussions with Rostenkowski, who was patient and generous with both his time and his insights. Under often stressful personal circumstances, he spent many hours sharing his observations and giving me the benefit of his endless anecdotes. Despite his cooperation, I neither sought nor received his authorization to write this biography. Nor did we have any arrangement other than what is accepted journalistic practice. Likewise, many of his former congressional aides were extraordinarily patient with my questions and demands, and they provided invaluable assistance in helping me understand their "boss"; among them, I am especially grateful to Jim Jaffe, Virginia Fletcher, and Nancy Panzke.

In addition to the many discussions with Rostenkowski and persons surrounding him, which were conducted with the perspective that followed the Democrats' 1994 loss of their House majority, I have brought to this book my background as a congressional reporter for *National Journal*. My experience in covering Rostenkowski and the House since 1977 has provided immeasurable aid in assembling detail and perspective. Although the book's organization and analysis are almost entirely original material, I have included without specific attribution numerous quotations from sources that originally appeared in my *National Journal* writing. I appreciate the cooperation and indulgence I have received while working on this book from the magazine's publisher, John Fox Sullivan, and editors Richard Frank, Stephen Smith, and Michael Kelly. Many other *National Journal* colleagues shared their knowledge and provided assistance, notably Jill Graham, Julie Kosterlitz, John Moore, Marilyn Werber Ser-afini, Burt Solomon, and Mike Wright.

Because I have also sought to provide readers with an overview of the House of Representatives during a lengthy period of American history, occasionally I have taken my research beyond the boundaries of Rostenkowski's activities. In examining, for example, the politics of Lyndon Johnson's Great Society in 1964–1965 as well as Bill Clinton's failed health-care proposal in 1993–1994, I have tried to give the reader insight into the rise and fall of the Democratic party at key junctures. Such narratives have benefited from extensive review of origi-nal source materials and from interviews with key participants. I did not have the opportunity to talk with some figures from the early part of the Democratic era, such as Hale Boggs of Louisiana or "Sheriff Tom" O'Brien of Chicago. But I be-lieve that my research, including many interviews and lengthy hours spent with transcripts from the very thorough and accessible Oral History project at the Lyn-don B. Johnson Library in Austin, Texas, has allowed me to make their days in the House come alive. Likewise, although my dealings with such prominent House figures as Wilbur Mills and Tip O'Neill came at the end of their careers, I have sought to convey the broad sweep of their political lives and how they con-nected with Rostenkowski.

As for the many contemporary congressional figures from both parties who have shared their experiences and thoughts with me during the past two decades, I trust they will find that I have been fair to them and that I have enhanced public comprehension of the often arcane dynamics and mind-set of Capitol Hill. For, despite its many profound changes from one year to the next and even over the course of days, the House is an institution where knowledge and a feel for its his-tory and lore can contribute to a deeper understanding of its events and players. At the very least, I have usually found, the members and the politics of the House offer a superb conduit for understanding our diverse nation. My chief regret, aside from the usual limitations of time, is that several Democratic members whom I have often interviewed over the years declined multiple requests to talk specifically about Rostenkowski; although I have faithfully tried to reflect their activities and views in this book, I regret their apparent desire to erase the mem-ory of their former colleague.

I have benefited from the work of other authors, chiefly academic scholars, who have written on the House Ways and Means Committee. In particular I am indebted to three political scientists—John Manley, Richard Fenno, and Randall Strahan—who wrote detailed and masterful books about the internal dynamics within the Ways and Means Committee during various points of the Democrats' forty-year majority. Other political scientists who have written about the commit-tee and have made my work easier include Kenneth Bowler (who later was a se-nior aide to Rostenkowski) and Catherine Rudder. I also have found useful the work of several generations of journalists who have written in detail about Congress and, especially, Ways and Means. The most prolific and skillful include Neil MacNeil of *Time,* Jeffrey Birnbaum and Alan Murray, when both reported for the *Wall Street Journal,* and—from a more narrow but also valuable perspective—Paul Merrion of *Crain's Chicago Business.*

In addition I have sought to suggest the details and flavor of Rostenkowski's life and work in his hometown. Not only were Chicago's interests and needs a dominant part of his professional focus, but the brawling history of that quintessential American city also provides a useful lens for understanding the nation's politics throughout the past century. Aides to many institutions in that city generously shared their time and knowledge, including library staff of the Chicago Historical Society, the *Chicago Sun-Times,* and the Polish Museum of America. (As careful readers will note, I have not provided specific page numbers in source notes to newspaper articles; in many of those cases I was using decades-old news clips that included only the date of publication.) And I am grateful for the assistance and friendship of many past and present Chicagoans who have helped me to sink roots into that city and its diverse neighborhoods. In addition to those named in the book, others include Richard Babcock, Charlene Barshefsky, Richard Bloom, Barbara Cohen, Margaret Kriz, and Rochelle Wegner. Alan Ehrenhalt also was especially kind in providing extended access to his collection of books on Chicago. Stanley Collender, Alvin Felzenberg, George Kundanis, Lou Peck, Basil Talbott, and Stuart Taylor read parts or all of the manuscript and offered helpful suggestions. I also am thankful for the fascinating two-hour political travelogue that William Daley provided several months before he became secretary of commerce.

Lastly I acknowledge the many instructors and guideposts that have shaped my understanding of politics in America, on both the large and small scales. Although Northampton, Massachusetts, and Providence, Rhode Island, during my youth in the 1950s and '60s were very different places than the northwest side of Chicago at that time, the elements for examining how public officials and average citizens practice politics and influence policy in a democracy do not differ radically from one time or place to another. So my understanding of Dan Rostenkowski has been shaped by a diverse group of individuals. They include the Polish friends and their warm and vigorous sense of community from my boyhood days; my uncle and favorite political scientist, Bernard Cohen; past and present journalistic colleagues, from the *Brown Daily Herald* at my alma mater to the *National Journal*; my education at Georgetown Law School and as a lowly U.S. Senate aide in learning how things supposedly work in Washington; and the loyal circle of friends—especially, for more than three decades, Terry Maguire—who have continually bolstered me. I am particularly grateful to Ivan Dee, who enhanced the quality and moved with due speed in shaping and bringing this book to market. I could never adequately acknowledge the nurture and sacrifices of my parents, Milton and Charlotte Cohen, who first introduced me to the wonders of Chicago during a family vacation in 1963; their inspiration has been integral to whatever I have accomplished. Finally, no one has understood my struggles, in this book and so much more, nearly as much as has my wife, Lyn Schlitt. Her patience, counsel, and love have made this book possible. And my desire to make up for lost time with our daughter Lily has given me the incentive to finish this book. None of these persons, or any other source, is responsible for any error or misimpression that may have found its way into the text. But all of them have enhanced my understanding of the fascinating and vital public life of Dan Rostenkowski.

R. E. C.

Washington, D.C.
May 1999

Index

41–42, 48, 66, 71, 75; relationship with
Albert, 76–77, 78–79, 80, 83, 99, 155, 156;
relationship with Boggs, 37–38, 67, 77, 79,
80, 81, 117; relationship with Richard J.
Daley, 29, 33, 40, 41, 47, 48, 54, 55, 56,
66, 72–73, 74, 76, 80–81, 95–96, 98–99,
129, 136, 168, 273, 287; relationship with
Gephardt, 112–113; relationship with
Johnson, 51, 52, 53, 54, 55, 56, 66, 287;
relationship with Kennedy administration,
46, 47–49, 51; relationship with Keogh,
36, 37, 38, 64, 67; relationship with
McCormack, 66–67; relationship with
Mills, 58, 64, 83, 87, 118, 287; relationship
with Obey, 100–102, 247-248; relationship
with O'Brien, 35–36, 46, 64, 95–96;
relationship with O'Neill, 66, 81, 97,
105–106, 107, 109, 116, 118, 120;
relationship with Rayburn, 42–43;
relationship with Wright, 96–98, 116–117;
and role of federal government, 96; serves
on Health Subcommittee, 94–95, 106–110;
serves on Interstate and Foreign
Commerce Committee, 35–36, 41; serves
on Ways and Means Committee, 55–56,
58, 59–60, 66, 70–71, 77, 78, 94–95,
105–110; and taxes, 70–71; and Vietnam
War, 69, 70–71, 81–82
Rostenkowski, Dan, AS CHAIRMAN OF WAYS
AND MEANS: ambition to be mayor of
Chicago, 178; ambition to be speaker, 136,
155–157; as bipartisan, 120, 123, 125–126,
128–130, 135, 136–137, 141, 149, 150–
151, 152, 154, 159, 160, 192, 194, 201,
206, 225, 228, 231, 276, 278, 286; and
budget deficit, 124, 127, 130, 157–158,
161, 163–164, 188, 193–194, 195, 200–
208, 226, 227–228, 287–288; as centrist, 5,
121, 123, 279, 285; Chicago helped by,
171–172, 174–178, 182–183, 185–187,
214, 236–237, 252–253; Chicago
reelection campaigns, 212–216, 234–238;
Chicago ties, 6–7, 31–32, 95, 99–100, 129,
141, 143, 149, 156, 161, 166, 167–191,
219, 233, 255; compared to Wilbur Mills,
120–121, 122, 123, 129, 136, 137, 150,
233; as consensus builder, 121, 288;
constituent service neglected by, 167,
171–172, 180–181, 189–190; criteria for
committee members, 142–143; criticized,
124–125, 126–128, 147, 154–155, 158,
160, 163, 165, 167, 168–169, 170, 173,
176, 182, 183–184, 186, 187–190, 201,
207, 214, 215, 234, 237, 256–257, 285,
288; as deal-maker, 6, 59, 120, 121–122,
128, 129, 138–140, 142–143, 145–146,
151, 157, 166, 174–175, 197, 205, 222,

227, 247, 248, 272, 273, 274, 288; as
Democratic ward committeeman,
180–181, 247; ethics standards in House
ignored by, 245–246, 247–249, 255–256,
258, 264, 267; and health care, 5–6, 158–
159, 160–161, 163–165, 187–190, 198–
199, 219, 223, 229–231, 232–233, 234,
238, 239, 254, 277–278, 288; and House
Bank investigation, 210, 211; and House
Post Office investigation, 212, 219, 222,
233, 236, 246, 248, 249–256, 263, 267–
268, 286–287; indictment against, 3–5, 7,
8, 212, 233, 238, 239, 246–247, 254–258;
and liberals, 100–101, 121, 128, 132, 136,
157, 158, 201, 207, 225, 285; as machine
Democrat, 139, 140–141, 168, 211, 243,
247, 255, 267, 273; management style,
121–123, 128–130, 135–136, 137, 138–
143, 160; and NAFTA, 231, 237; and 1983
Social Security reform, 132–137, 202; and
1990 budget deficit reduction plan, 193,
200–208, 287–288; and outside income,
183–185; as out of touch with constituents,
167, 170, 189–190, 214, 215; and
patronage, 3–4, 9–10, 211, 212, 246, 255,
256, 258, 262, 264, 267; as philanthropist,
184–185; and plea bargains, 253–254, 256,
260–261; and Poland, 191–192, 206–207;
as pragmatist, 147, 157–158, 160, 166,
209, 220; presidency revered by, 129–130,
147, 220, 272, 286; and publicity, 148–
149, 169, 173, 176, 177, 184–185, 189–
190, 193, 202–203, 214–215, 236–237,
288; and Reagan tax cut, 120, 123–128,
130–131; and redistricting, 213–214;
relationship with Archer, 273–274;
relationship with Robert Bennett, 251–252,
253, 255, 259–261, 262; relationship with
Bush, 82, 125, 137, 192, 193, 194–195,
200, 201, 203, 208, 216, 219, 220;
relationship with Clinton, 162, 194, 220–
221, 222, 225, 230, 237, 238, 250–251,
254, 260; relationship with Richard M.
Daley, 215, 234, 235, 242, 252–253;
relationship with Dole, 125–126, 128, 131,
132; relationship with Foley, 223;
relationship with Gephardt, 112–113, 143–
145, 146, 161–162, 209–210; relationship
with Michel, 152–153, 216, 228;
relationship with O'Neill, 121, 124–125,
132, 136, 159; relationship with Reagan,
123, 125, 129, 137, 148, 149, 165, 166,
174, 179; relationship with Rota, 212,
249–250, 251, 256, 268; relationship with
staff, 120–121, 122, 169, 180, 211–212,
245–246, 248, 249; relationship with
Harold Washington, 174, 178–180, 181;

A NOTE ON THE AUTHOR

Richard E. Cohen has reported on Congress since 1977 for the *National Journal,* a nonpartisan magazine located in Washington, D.C. He was born in Northampton, Massachusetts, studied at Brown University (where he was publisher of the *Brown Daily Herald*), then earned a law degree at Georgetown University. While at Georgetown he served as a legislative aide to Senator Edward Brooke of Massachusetts. Mr. Cohen went to work as a correspondent for the *National Journal* in 1973; in 1990 he won the Everett McKinley Dirksen Award for distinguished reporting on Congress. His other books include *Changing Course in Washington: Clinton and the New Congress; Washington at Work: Back Rooms and Clean Air;* and *Congressional Leadership: Seeking a New Role.* He lives in McLean, Virginia, with his wife and daughter.